ABOUT THE AUTHOR

North American D. E. Pohren took up the flamenco guitar in 1951, studying with Spanish expatriates in Mexico. At their urging, he continued his flamenco studies in Spain in 1953, and has spent the following thirty-five years doing just that in his adopted country. Along the way, he formed an artistic, and matrimonial, alliance with Madrileñan flamenco dancer Luisa Maravilla, both of which unions are still going strong today. He published his first book on the subject, THE ART OF FLAMENCO, in 1962, the first edition of LIVES AND LEGENDS OF FLAMENCO in 1964, and the third of his flamenco trilogy, A WAY OF LIFE, in 1980. There have been three more editions of THE ART OF FLAMENCO in English, the latest in 1982, as well as editions in Spanish, French and Japanese. With this second English edition of LIVES AND LEGENDS, after being out-of-print for many years, the complete trilogy is available in English at the same time for the first time.

This twenty-five-year-update of LIVES AND LEGENDS was a considerable undertaking that led to an eighty-two page supplement, plus many other additions and corrections, making the Pohren trilogy today the most complete and authoritative coverage of flamenco written by any author in any language.

The books have won national prizes in Spain, and Pohren was long ago declared «Flamencologist» and admitted into the *Cátedra de Flamencología* (Professorate of Flamenco Studies), the only non-Spaniard to have been so honored.

Mr. Pohren's contact with flamenco has by no means been merely academic. He has performed extensively with his wife around the world, has conducted a private flamenco club in Madrid, has spent a ten-year period directing a flamenco center in Andalusia, has in general immersed himself completely in the world of flamenco for the past three-and-a-half decades. In a word, his commitment has been total.

D. E. Pohren

Lives and Legends of Flamenco

A Biographical History

Copyright © 2014 by: D. E. Pohren
All rights reserved.

ISBN: 1-4991-6902-7
ISBN-13: 9781499169027

CONTENTS

FOREWORD	9
FOREWORD 1988 UPDATE	12
THE SONG	13
Introduction	15
Addition 1988 Update	32
Biographies of Singers	33
THE DANCE	171
Introduction	173
Biographies of Dancers	182
Male	182
Females	210
THE GUITAR	251
Introduction	253
The Spanish Guitar	253
The Flamenco Guitar	257
Biographies of Guitarists	265
ARTS WITHIN THE ART	325
1988 UPDATE, MAIN BODY, CONTENTS	330
INDEX	410
INDEX OF SPECIAL SUBJECTS	420
GLOSSARY	421

Following page 32, a PICTORIAL HISTORY OF MODERN FLAMENCO, consisting of forty pages of chronologically-arranged photographs dating from the last century.

FOREWORD

LIVES AND LEGENDS OF FLAMENCO is a natural sequel to my first book, THE ART OF FLAMENCO. The latter dealt with flamenco in general, its philosophy, structure, general history, components, and so forth, while touching only briefly on flamenco's creators, developers, and interpreters. That lengthy subject was left to this book, the second of the three volumes that will comprise my intial contribution towards a better understanding of this great folk art.

LIVES AND LEGENDS consists of introductions to the song, dance, and guitar, and chronologically-placed biographies of the artists and aficionados who have perhaps most affected the course of flamenco's history. Interwoven into the biographies are many discussions and anecdotes which are intended to help the reader to a better understanding of both the artist in question, and flamenco in general.

The introductions to the sections also have been designed to play a double role. Read individually before each section they will aid the reader to a better understanding of the biographies. Read one after another, before going into the biographies, they will give the reader an overall idea of flamenco's origin and development. As for the theories and concepts contained in the introductions concerning distant flamenco history: admittedly, flamenco's origins and early development are arbitrary animals at best. However, I believe that the accepted "we don't know" has become too much of an easy out, a drug that deadens investigation and thought. For we do have some historical facts at hand, and we are able to observe contemporary similarities in the music and dance of various cultures. As we delve into what is available, facts, theory, and legend fall somewhat into place, and what I believe to be a reasonably accurate history of flamenco's development can be pieced together.

The difficulties in encountering accurate information for the biographies were many. The gypsy versus non-gypsy feud was a real stumbling block, a barrier similar to that existent between the "rebs" and the "yanks" in the United States. Also, in Spain, land of "amigotes", facts dim before friendship in an astounding manner. Aficionados will almost invariably be loyal to their friends or heroes, and play down all others. Truth is obscured in the shuffle.

The very trait that endears Spain to so many of us, the Spanish (particularly the Andalusian) disregard, and even disdain, for time, has frustrated my attempts at accuracy in many instances. Thus, many of the dates in this book, particularly those concerning birth and death, are approximations. Even the date of death of a member of a family is often quickly forgotten by the rest of the family. In my inquiries, close relatives of deceased flamenco artists have proven to be as far off as ten years in their estimates of the year of death of the deceased. Time is just too fleet, and death too final. Life, not death, seems to be on their minds.

The life spans of the artists of old, especially, are often merely calculated estimates, intended only to inform the reader of the epochs in which the artists lived. I have been asked: "Why not look up the exact dates in the provincial courthouses?" The answers to this very Anglo-Saxon question are: 1) neither the birth nor death of many of the artists of old were recorded; 2) the family names of many of the artists are unknown. In flamenco, nicknames and artistic names often permanently replace the family names; 3) the exact place of birth of many of the early artists is unknown; 4) exact dates are not essential in fulfilling the purpose of this book. Were I to consider them of supreme importance, this book would never be published.

A thousand pardons to the reader whose favorite artist is not included, and to all of the deserving artists whose names have been omitted. It is simply not possible to include all of the many thousands of flamenco artists of yesterday and today. Also, if the reader's current favorite has not been dealt with as glowingly as the reader thinks he deserves, before burning the book and tearing off that nasty letter I encourage him to absorb the contents of this book, and THE ART OF FLAMENCO, with a view as to perhaps discovering why.

Basically, LIVES AND LEGENDS expresses not only my views, but those also of the too few purists that remain in this foundering art and way of life. It is a book with a message, or, better stated, a warning: the handicraft flamenco of old is being steadly replaced by a type of industrial flamenco, complete with its assembly lines and unvarying, trivial, dull, dull product. Flamenco is ceasing to be a means of expressing deep, unutterable emotion, and is instead becoming a cold, technical art utterly without emotion. This book and the last, then, can be looked upon as part of a growing movement, taking place in Spain today, to preserve the soul in this, one of the great remaining folk arts.

Madrid, July 1964.

FOREWORD, 1988 UPDATE

Much of significance has happened in the flamenco world over the past twenty-five years. Antonio Mairena led flamenco through a period of purity and unprecedented popularity; with his retirement from active flamenco, and eventual death in 1983, both the purity and the popularity began falling into a slow but steady decline. Money, not afición, is today's God, overwhelming both purity of expression and the flamenco way of life.

In recent years drugs have entered the flamenco scene in a heavy-handed manner. Before it was only liquor. Now it is the combination of drugs and booze, which is pretty potent and explains the erratic performances, or the not showing up at all, of some of today's potentially fine artists, as well as some of their far-out, pseudo-flamenco flights of "creativity."

As communications makes the world smaller, sophistication also has made strong inroads in the flamenco world, causing rapid, irresponsible evolution in all of flamenco's forms, but above all in the guitar and the dance. This movement, I fear, will eventually "elevate" flamenco to a level that will no longer emotionally reach the Andalusian people, its very creators and perpetuators, and will transform flamenco into just another form of international entertainment. It will no doubt be interesting, but largely meaningless.

In this update I shall make additions to the main text, which I shall denote as "1988 Update." The main body of the update, however, will come at the original book's end in form of an 80 page supplement, beginning on page 330. I would suggest consultation of the Index of Special Subjects (p.420), which brings to light many topics of special interest discussed throughout the text.

Las Rozas de Madrid
January 1988

THE SONG

INTRODUCTION

THE CANTE: GYPSY OR ANDALUZ? Now that flamenco is surging back to life, and even becoming socially acceptable (for the first time in its history), everyone wants the credit for having created and developed it. Endless, passionate controversy rages between the gypsies and the Andalusians, both of whom claim flamenco as their original creation, and between Andalusian provinces and cities, most of which credit themselves with playing the major role in flamenco's development.

As for the riddle of who created flamenco, the gypsies or the Andalusians, no one knows with any certainty, nor is it likely that they ever will. Both sides have good, if incomplete arguments. The Andalusians say that had the gypsies brought flamenco with them, it would be practiced among the gypsies all over Europe, as they all migrated from the same region of India; the facts are that outside of Andalusia the gypsies practice nothing even vaguely similar to flamenco (1). Therefore, they conclude, the gypsies must have adopted an already existent flamenco, or reasonable facsimile, upon their arrival to Andalusia. The gypsies, on the other hand, retort that if the Andalusians already practiced flamenco before the gypsy arrival to Andalusia, why then, at the beginning of recorded flamenco history (eighteenth century) were all of the interpreters of flamenco gypsies, and why, during the nineteenth century, were ninety-five percent of the interpreters of the pure core (*cante*

---

(1) Some musicologists cast serious doubt on this supposition. See Introduction — Dance Section for a discussion of these views.

grande) gypsies? Had the Andalusians been practicing flamenco for centuries, they reason, they certainly would have produced a few more interpreters of note.

At this point we can clear up some of the mystery by explaining each side's interpretation of just what flamenco is. The illustrious flamencologists Ricardo Molina and Antonio Mairena, in their book *"Mundo y Formas del Cante Flamenco"*, consider that the truly primitive flamenco consisted of the basic *cantes, tonás, martinetes, deblas, carceleras, siguiriyas, corridas, alboreás,* and later the *soleares, tangos, bulerías*. They credit the gypsies with the development of these *cantes*. They go on to say that the Andalusians also practiced certain folkloric *cantes* that little by little gravitated towards flamenco, such as the *fandangos* and their numerous offspring, and the country *cantes: trilleras, temporeras, caleseras, palmeras, nanas,* etc. They point out that the gypsy *cantes,* far more difficult to interpret properly than the Andalusian, were always limited to a few knowledgeable gypsy interpreters, whereas the Andalusian *cantes* were sung much more popularly, in a similar vein as the *jota* of northern Spain and other popular Spanish folk songs.

This signifies, then, that the Andalusian *cantes* would not necessarily have produced "name" *cantaores,* as they were so popularly sung and taken for granted, whereas the gypsy interpreters were highly-regarded specialists, often professionals (in the sense of living from their art), whose names have come down to us.

Let us explore the possible beginnings of these musical forms, as we know them today (flamenco's more ancient origin and development is considered in the Dance and Guitar introductions). First, the gypsy-inspired *cante*. As I wrote in "The Art of Flamenco", it is probable that the sixteenth century blending of Spain's outcasts of that period — the gypsies, Jews, Arabs, and some Christian dissenters and fugitives, all of whom banded together in isolated regions to escape persecution — produced the beginning of the hard core of *cante grande,* as we know it today. Since that time, until the ninteenth century *café cantante* period, flamenco more or less continued as an outcast manifestation, practiced by gypsies, bandits, smugglers, and other people on the rim of the law, largely behind closed doors, for even after all persecution stopped the *cante gitano* was jealously guarded from outsiders.

Andalusian folksinging, on the other hand, was a perfectly respectable art. In the beginning it certainly absorbed Arabic influences, considering that the Arabs ruled in Andalusia from the eighth through the fifteenth centuries. In fact, the *fandangos*, the grandfather of the Andalusian *cante,* has been traced to Arabic origins beyond all reasonable doubt. As the Andalusian *cantes* developed, they slowly united with the gypsy-inspired *cantes* into what we know as flamenco. This coupling did not take place, however, until the nineteenth century *café cantante* period, when gypsy and Andalusian performers were first thrown together.

This line of reasoning clears up several widely contested points: it explains the indisputable influences made upon flamenco by several cultures; it partially explains why gypsies in other parts of the world do not practice flamenco as it has developed in Spain (this point is further discussed in the Dance Introduction), and why few Andalusians were involved with the *cante gitano;* it points out that the Andalusians contributed greatly to the overall scope of flamenco; and it signifies that no one cultural group created flamenco, but that the gypsies had by far the largest influence on the *cantes grandes* and the festive *cantes,* while the Andalusians largely developed the *cantes intermedios,* the country cantes, the *cantes* still considered as folklore, and the *cantes* with strong Latin-American influences. (See *cante* chart, this section.)

So we have seen the main difference between the gypsy and the Andalusian *cante*. The Andalusian *cantes* were, at the beginning, simple country songs popularly sung, to which little importance was attached. The gypsy *cantes,* on the other hand, were highly specialized *cantes* that demanded great physical faculties and a deep knowledge of their intricacies. Many of the outstanding interpreters of these gypsy *cantes* naturally became professionals, and traveled from ranch to *venta* to village singing for food, drink, presents, and lodging. In that way, the fame of these early gypsy *cantaores* spread (exclusively by word of mouth — no printed word of them has reached us, to my knowledge), and the fame of their type of *cante* — if called "flamenco" at that time we do not know — spread with them. If this gypsy *cante* was profitable, why did it not attract Andalusian singers? Surely they could have enticed the gypsies to teach them their strange *cante*, and then have likewise exploited this pleasant, if errant, way of making a living? I have often heard the following statement, made by Andalusian flamencologists in an attempt to explain the mentioned absence of professional Andalusian artists in the early flamenco scene: "Flamenco (referring to the primitive gypsy flamenco) was so badly considered throughout its history that Andalusian families strongly discouraged any participation in it by members of their families. To become a flamenco in those days meant ostracism from the Andalusian family and society." We can, in fact, pinpoint the first reluctant crumbling of this strong stand: the beginning of the *café cantante* period (1842). It was then that flamenco first offered a more or less decent living, both monetarily and in terms of respectability, and it was then that professional Andalusian non-gypsy artists began appearing in numbers.

It was also during this early *café cantante* period that the Andalusian and gypsy *cantes* began intermingling to any extent, a natural consequence of the intermixing of the *andaluces* and the gypsies themselves. It was a rich mixture, resulting in the fascinating diversity within flamenco that we know today. However, the gypsy and Andalusian contributions to flamenco have not entirely integrated, even after 125 years. To this day the gypsies prefer their primitive *cantes*, the Andalusians theirs. This is made obvious in various ways: both groups perform better their traditional *cante*; only a small minority of Andalusians like, or understand, the *cante grande*, the original flamenco expression, which they dismiss as old-fashioned and morbid. Their idea of profound *cantes* are the pretty, more melodious *malagueñas* and *fandangos grandes*, and they are the principal backers of the singers of these *cantes*; the gypsies, on the other hand, consider the Andalusian *cantes* as pretty playthings, but insist that for true flamenco expression one must turn to the *cante gitano*.

BREAKDOWN OF THE CANTE. At this point it is convenient to clarify this discussion somewhat by the following breakdown of the *cante*, which includes an indication as to whether the *cantes* are believed to be originally and basically gypsy (G) or Anlusian-developed (A).

CANTE GRANDE

with guitar accompaniment (danceable):

Cañas (G)	Playeras (G)	Siguiriyas (G)
Livianas (G)	Polos (G)	Soleares (G)
Medio Polo (G)	Serranas (G)	Soleariyas (G)

without guitar accompaniment (all *cantes* of the forges, except the *saetas*):

Carceleras (G)	Martinetes (G)	Saetas (A)
Deblas (G)	Tonás (G)	

CANTE INTERMEDIO (all with guitar accompaniment):
    not danced:

Cartageneras (A)	Jaberas (A)	Mineras (A)
Fandangos Grandes (A)	Malagueñas (A)	Murcianas (A)
Granaínas (A)	Media Granaína (A)	Tarantas (A)

    danceable:

Peteneras (A)	Taranto (A)	Tientos Antiguos (G)

CANTE CHICO

with guitar accompaniment (danceable):

Alboreás (G)	Fandanguillos (A)	Rosas (G)
Alegrías (G)	Guajiras (A)	Rumba Gitana (G)
Bulerías (G)	Jaleos (G)	Tangos (G)
Cantiñas (G)	Mirabrás (G)	Verdiales (A)
Caracoles (G)	Romeras (G)	Zambra (G)
Chuflas (A)	Rondeñas (A)	Zorongo Gitano (A)
Colombianas (A)		

with or without guitar accompaniment, not danced (called "*cantes camperos*", or "country *cantes*"):

Bamberas (A)	Marianas (A)	Palmares (A)	Trilleras (A)
Caleseras (A)	Nanas (A)	Temporeras (A)

ANDALUSIAN FOLKLORE (not considered, as yet, part of flamenco): with guitar accompaniment (danceable):

Garrotín (A)   Roás (G)   Sevillanas (A)   Tanguillos (A)
Vito (A)

with or without guitar accompaniment (not danced):

Campanilleros (A)   Milongas (A)

Many flamencologists prefer other breakdowns of the *cante*. Some label all of the *cantes "cantes flamencos"*. Another popular breakdown is *"cantes gitanos" and "cantes flamencos"*. However, I believe the above breakdown, by no means infallible, to be the most comprehensive, once the characteristics of the categories are understood.

The *cante grande* is the serious, gypsy-inspired *cante*. It is the most difficult *cante* to perform properly, believed to have been derived largely from religious music. This category includes flamenco's most primitive *cantes*.

The *cante intermedio*, more ornamental, melodic and flowing, is somewhat easier to sing than the *cante grande*. Basically *andaluz*-inspired, these *cantes* were largely derived from the folklore of the various cultures that have mingled in Spain.

The *cantes chicos,* generally lighter, gayer, easier to interpret, have been derived from both religious and folk music.

Two factors tend to complicate this breakdown, and should be explained: 1) the subject matter of the verses sometimes goes awry. One can run across gay, even humorous verses in the *cantes grandes*, and serious, plaintive verses in the *chicos*. In my opinion, these occurrences are freaks, completely out of keeping with the intrinsic emotional qualities of the particular *cante* (i e. a happy *siguiriya*, a depressing *tango*); 2) the term *"grande"* as used in *"cante grande"* should not be confused with the *"grande"* (long) or *"corto"* (short) division to which many of the *cantes* of all three categories are subject. The terms *"grande"* or *"corto"* are merely used to designate the length and degree of difficulty of a particular *cante*. Thus a *soleá grande* contains a four-line verse and a difficult structure, while a *soleá corta* contains a three-line verse and a more simplified structure; a *malagueña grande* is in effect a *malagueña corta* enlarged upon and made more difficult, although on paper they appear identical (both have four-line verses); *siguiriyas cortas* exist (three-line verses), although the more difficult *siguiriyas grandes* are almost invariably sung (four-line verses); and so forth.

FLAMENCO IN PRINT. If the first seeds of flamenco were sown, as we have postulated, by the sixteenth-century outcast groups, why then, ask theoreticians, was there no printed mention of flamenco or any of flamenco's elements until the nineteenth century? First of all, this lack of printed matter is not certain. We have no idea whether or not flamenco's terminology has remained constant. For instance, what is known as the *siguiriyas* today is believed to have been previously called *playeras*. Before that: who knows? This uncertainty about flamenco's terminology makes it impossible to know if elements have been discussed or mentioned in print in the past. Also, it seems reasonable to assume that due to flamenco's development by an outcast society, living most of its existence on the fringe of the law, it went for years unknown or unnoticed by writers and historians, or was ignored as unworthy of consideration. This seems especially feasible if we consider that the writers of that period were highborn gentlemen likely to have had little contact with, and even have avoided, the disreputable flamenco activity of those times.

THE WORD "FLAMENCO". The mentioned disreputable flamenco activity has led to the word "flamenco" having a double meaning. Due to flamenco's hidden, semi-underworld existence and association with society's rebellious personalities, the word flamenco came to signify, other than a type of music, the act of blustering, boasting, of being generally obnoxious (1). Even today one often hears the expression *"no seas tan flamenco"* "don't be so flamenco" said to some offensive or rambunctious person, sometimes seriously, sometimes in jest. Some theorists, in fact, believe that the branding of the characters who surrounded the music as "flamencos" preceded the actual calling of the art form "flamenco", and point

---

(1) Early jazz had the same sort of unwholesome reputation due to its underworld surroundings, although the word «jazz» never achieved this double connation.

to the cited lack of mention of flamenco in any sense until the nineteenth century as support for their argument. I am more inclined to believe that the word "flamenco" came about much earlier, as I wrote in "The Art of Flamenco" (1), and, like the art itself, was known only within an inner circle. The possibility is strong that the word came into being, say, in the sixteenth century, but was not used in reference to the music and dance until much later.

WHERE THE "CANTE" WAS DEVELOPED. Let us now discuss, without getting too involved, the basic contributions made to flamenco by the various provinces and cities of Andalusia. As we shall see, the Andalusian *cante* was developed in all parts of Andalusia, while the gypsy *cante* was developed only in the provinces of Sevilla and Cádiz, extending over to include Ronda.

a) Province of Sevilla, including the flamenco centers Sevilla, Triana, Morón de la Frontera, Utrera, Alcalá de Guadaira, Dos Hermanas, Lebrija, etc.: principally the serious gypsy *cantes* of the smithies (*tonás, martinetes, deblas, carceleras*), the *cañas, polos,* and various forms of the *siguiriyas* and *soleares*.

b) Province of Cádiz (2), including Jerez de la Frontera, Arcos de la Frontera, Cádiz, Puerto Santa María, Puerto Real, Sanlúcar, Chiclana, Medina Sidonia, Isla de San Fernando, etc.: strong influence in the gypsy *cantes siguiriyas* and *soleares,* as well as in such diverse *festive cantes* as the *tangos, bulerías, alegrías, cantiñas, mirabrás, romeras, caracoles,* etc.

c) Region of Ronda, including the city of Ronda: *serranas* and *rondeñas*. Although in the province of Málaga, this area favoured the *cantes* of the provinces of Sevilla and Cádiz.

---

(1) «Another more feasible theory states that the word «flamenco» is a mispronunciation of the Arabic words «*felag*» and «*mengu*» (*felagmengu*), which means «fugitive peasant». It is likely that this term was borrowed from the Arabs (Arabic was a common language in Andalusia at that time) and applied to all of the persecuted people who fled to the mountains. Through usage in Spanish «*felagmengu*» was transformed into «flamenco», until eventually the term flamenco was adopted by the fugitives themselves and in turn applied to their music.» («The Art of Flamenco», p. 40).

(2) Within the province of Cádiz, the towns Jerez de la Frontera, to the north, and Cádiz, to the south, including their immediate surrounding areas, cultivate basically distinct *cantes*. Jerez: the *siguiriyas, soleares,* and *bulerías de Jerez*. Cádiz: quite distinct *soleares, siguiriyas,* and *bulerías* from those of Jerez, as well as the above-mentioned festive *cantes*. The towns between these two spheres of influence, such as Puerto Santa María and Puerto Real, gravitate towards both spheres, and in the confusion have come up with some of their own slightly different styles of the mentioned *cantes*.

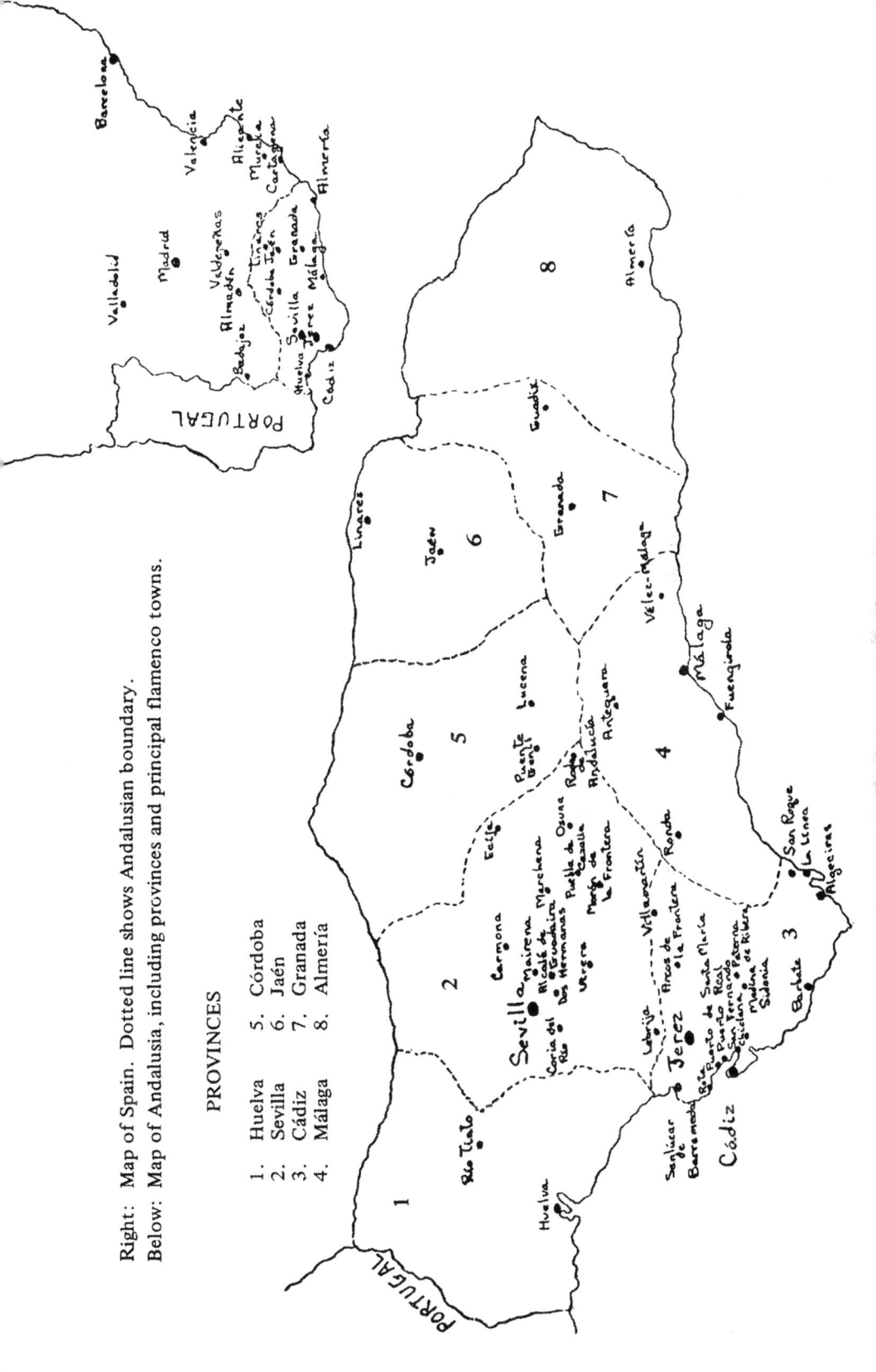

Right: Map of Spain. Dotted line shows Andalusian boundary.
Below: Map of Andalusia, including provinces and principal flamenco towns.

PROVINCES

1. Huelva
2. Sevilla
3. Cádiz
4. Málaga
5. Córdoba
6. Jaén
7. Granada
8. Almería

d) Province of Huelva: *fandangos grandes* and *fandanguillos*.

e) Province of Málaga: the *cantes* of Málaga, including the *malagueñas, jaberas, verdiales, rondeñas, tiranas* (all offspring of the *fandangos*).

f) Province of Granada: principally the *granaína* and *media granaína* (both offspring of the *fandangos*) (1).

g) Province of Murcia: *murcianas* and *mineras* (both offspring of the *fandangos*) (1).

h) Province of Almería: *tarantas, taranto,* and *cartageneras* (all offspring of the *fandangos*) (1).

i) Province of Córdoba: principally their interpretations of various existing *cantes* (*soleá de Córdoba, alegrías de Córdoba, fandangos de Lucena,* etc.), as well as a hand in developing, together with all of Andalusia, the Andalusian country *cantes* (*trilleras, temporeras, palmares, caleseras, bamberas, nanas,* etc.).

This list is not complete by any means, and is only meant to give the reader an idea of the type of *cante* typical of each province. Although regionalism is fast disappearing, even to this day the casual *aficionado* of any of the mentioned regions is likely to sing only the *cantes* of his province, or at least specialize in and prefer them.

SUPERIOR "CANTE": PAST OR PRESENT? Another interminable source of discussion among *cantaores* is whether flamenco is sung better today than it was in the past. While this is another argument that can never be decisively answered, a few interesting observations can be made. Today there are undoubtedly more complete *cantaores* than ever before. This is simply due to the radio and phonograph. Any young fellow with a reasonable amount of talent can listen to a phonograph record a number of times, be it ten or one hundred, and memorize that particular *cante*. If he dedicated years to doing this, he would have to envy no one in superficial knowledge of the *cante*. In days past it was a thousand times more difficult. If a singer wanted to properly learn the *cantes* of Enrique el Mellizo, for instance, he had to

---

(1) The *cantes* of these categories are also more broadly referred to as the *cantes de Levante* (*cantes* of eastern Spain). The *cantes de Málaga* (group e) are also sometimes included among the *cantes de Levante*.

travel to Cádiz and hope to ingratiate himself with Enrique. As secrecy was generally the practice, the chances are that Enrique would send him to the devil. As a result of this, most singers sang only the established *cantes* of their regions, plus whatever they were sharp enough to pick up from singers outside of their locales. To supplement this knowledge, these *cantaores* had nowhere to turn but to their own imagination and creativeness.

Here lies the crux of the difference. Today, singers command a wide repertoire of *cantes,* but are inclined to be the parrots of phonograph records. They have only a superficial knowledge of the *cantes,* not the deep-rooted knowledge born of intimacy which eventually may lead to complete sense of union with the *cante,* and which in turn can lead to fruitful and knowledgeable creation within its structure and feeling. How can the phonograph record imitators hope to feel emotion and intimacy with a *cante,* or a *toque,* that they have not lived? Simply stated: they cannot.

CREATION. The reader might be curious as to the form that creation within the *cante* may take (in this book we shall consider "creation" as "innovation" or, a dictionary definition, "make by giving a new character, function, or status"). It could be a completely new *cante* or style within an existing *cante,* the prolongation or shortening of a *tercio* within an existing *cante,* or any addition or change that improves a singer's expression of a *cante.* The flamenco world will judge. If the creation is truly worthy, it will stick, and probably be remembered by the creator's name. If not, it will be forgotten. Creation can also take the form of new verses to the *cantes,* perhaps spontaneously composed by the *cantaor.* This rarely takes place today. Nearly all present-day *cantaores* merely repeat the timeworn, traditional verses that have been passed down. Beautiful as they may be, this is like repeating the Lord's Prayer over and over again as a child until its meaning is lost in over-familiarity. In fact, constructive creation in the *cante* has become badly bogged down in this century. There is little attempted creation now among the purists, and what is created is mostly frowned upon. This is due, basically, to the extreme degree of decadence to which flamenco has been driven by commercialism, causing the purists to doggedly embrace tradition in an effort to stem the trend. Today faithfulness to the old masters is considered more worthy than attempts to improve upon their *cantes*, or alter them in any way. The singer who improvises upon a traditional version of a *cante* is more apt to be thought of as ignorant of the traditional version than as creative, no matter how meritorious his innovation. This has not been true thoughout flamenco's history, but is a condition, as we have seen, brought on by the desperate attempt to defend the remaining purity of flamenco's *cantes* from mediocrity and possible extinction through commercialism. Viewed in that light, creative caution has some small justification, especially considering the above-mentioned lack of intimacy and deep-rooted knowledge of many of today's *cantaores* in their *cante*.

HARDSHIPS. We have seen the difficulties that old-time singers had in learning the *cante*. That was not their only hardship. Much has been written about the miserable conditions of the lower classes in Andalusia during past centuries. Malnutrition was common, and as a result a shocking number of *cantaores* contracted tuberculosis through exerting constant pressure on their lungs while in a weakened state. A contributing factor was that the *siguiriyas, soleares,* and *cantes* of the smithies, the most physically difficult of flamenco's *cantes*, were then the most widely sung. In addition, the old saying "flamencos don't eat" enters into play. It perhaps seems a silly saying, but it is accurate. Flamencos readily pass up eating for *cante*, wine, movement. They claim they sing better without food, and purposely eat the minimum during moments of *juerga* ("moments of *juerga*" signifying three hours, three days, a week, or, for some, a lifetime).

There were, and are, also mental hazards. Núñez de Prado points out that many great *cante grande* singers, particularly **siguiriyeros,** have been adversely affected by their *cante*. By "great" he means those who have truly felt the deep, black currents of emotion that characterize the *siguiriyas;* who become so entangled in their lament of death and disenchantment that reality escapes them (or perhaps they discover it. Who are we to judge?). It is true that many of the greatest *siguiriyeros* have been dark, moody men. Whether the *siguiriyas* made them that way, or whether they were attracted to the *siguiriyas* precisely because they were that way, is difficult to say.

More concretely, a great menace, both mental and physical, to the old-time flamencos, due to their lively way of life, was venereal disease. Before the great discovery of Dr. Alexander Fleming (1), a man held in reverence in flamenco circles, venereal disease ran rampant, and can be cited as the direct cause of a good deal of the blindness, lameness, deformation, and mental instability found among flamenco artists of old, and among all of Spain's noticeable number of blind and maimed.

As if their life was not complicated enough, flamenco singers of days past had another cross to bear. According to Fernando de Triana (who in turn quotes his great-grandfather, a *cantaor* called Fernando Gómez "el Cachivero"), in the years before the *cafés cantantes* the capo (*cejilla*) for the guitar did not exist, and singers had to sing in the natural tones of *mi* or *la,* adapting their voices to the guitar. He goes on to say that the strain was what made the singers' voices so hoarse, ultimately shortening their careers as singers. Fernando, I believe, was exaggerating a little. Even without the capo a guitarist can bridge to a singer's tone or, if he is not so talented, tighten or loosen the strings of the guitar until achieving the desired pitch. Besides, as guitarists were extremely scarce in those days, singers sang mostly without guitar accompaniment; if their voices were (are) hoarse, it is simply because gypsies more often than not seem to acquire this trait, although no one has ever conclusively explained why.

VOCAL TYPES. While on the subject of voices, it is interesting to note (my interpretation of) Ricardo Molina and Antonio Mairena's outline of the different types of voices possessed by flamenco singers ("*Mundo y Formas del Cante Flamenco*", p. 82). This will clear up an important but little-discussed topic, and will

---

(1) The discoverer of penicillin, the first effective cure for venereal disease. Discovered in 1928, penicillin was proved effective against disease in 1940, marketed shortly after. Many Spanish brothels prominently display portraits of Dr. Fleming, a true hero-figure.

serve as a reference for the biographies. They list five vocal types, all of which pertain to both men and women:

1) *Voz Afillá.* This was the preferred type of voice up to and including the nineteenth century, being regarded as particularly effective in interpreting the gypsy *cantes* (*cantes* of the smithies, *siguiriyas, soleares, bulerías, tangos*, etc.). Named after one of the early singers of the last century, Diego el Fillo, this type of voice — rough, raucous, a little foggy — was actually considered essential for the *cante grande;* so much so that clear-voiced *cantaores* often took great quantities of *aguardiente* and other liquids, as well as other steps, to achieve the proper hoarseness. The emission of the *voz afillá* is controlled to a certain extent by the throat. Today Manolo Caracol, among others, possesses this type of voice.

2) *Voz Redonda o Flamenca* (full or flamenco voice). This type of voice, sweet, mellow, manly, is emitted from the lungs without throaty interruptions. A relatively modern denomination, its prototype was the late Tomás Pavón.

3) *Voz Natural.* This type of voice is very similar to the *voz redonda,* except that it contains moments of raucousness (*afillá, con rajo*), and is consequently more moving and gypsy. The *voz natural,* or natural voice, comes from the lungs, the moments of *rajo* being produced by throaty interventions. Its prototype was Manuel Torre. Presently Antonio Mairena possesses this type of voice, or, as can also be said, utilizes this style of delivery.

4) *Voz Fácil* (easy or relaxed voice). This type of voice is fresh, flexible, and without strain, excellent for the festive *cantes.* Presently La Perla de Cádiz and Mariquita Vargas, among others, possess this type of voice.

5) *Voz de Falsete* (falsetto voice). The word "falsetto" is derived from "false". Its dictionary definition is "an unnatural, high-pitched voice". This type of voice, the easiest of all to produce, is completely out of place in the *cante grande* and the *cante gitano* in general. It does, however, go well with the Andalusian *cantes.* It most famous exponent has been Antonio Chacón . Today it is the most widely heard vocal type in commercial

flamenco, being possessed by Pepe Marchena, Juanito Valderrama, and many other *cante bonito* singers.

BORN TO BE SUNG. When listening to discussions of the *cante* one often hears the phrases "born to be sung", or "born to be danced". The purists maintain that certain *cantes* were born strictly to be sung, and it is in unspeakably bad taste to misuse them to accompany the dance. Included in this category are all of the *cantes grandes* except the original *soleares para bailar* (a type of *soleares* traditionally sung for the dance). They say that these *cantes* are entities in themselves, and cannot be fully appreciated amidst other distractions. If they *must* be sung during a number which includes a dance, let them be sung in their entirety first (say the purists), and then let the dancer have his opportunity.

Of course, they are right. One cannot fully appreciate a *siguiriyas*, for instance, while watching a dancer; the attention of the spectator sways in one direction, and he loses the full impact of both the *cante* and the *baile*. However, there are rare exceptions to this; the exceptional dancer can occasionally blend into the mood of a *cante* so well as to give the *cante* even further meaning and impact. In all of the hundreds of times I have seen the *siguiriyas* sung and danced together, I have rarely seen this oneness come about. It takes a very special type of dancing; to be avoided are all attention-getting devices, such as footwork, great flouncing about, all showmanship and falsity; even the dancer capable of this type of dance will only rarely be able to accomplish it, when the mood and *duende* actually take possession of him.

With rare exceptions, then, it can be agreed that some *cantes* were born to be sung. This is largely overlooked today, much to the dismay of singing greats and knowledgeable *aficionados*. Such sacred *cantes* as the *siguiriyas* and the *soleares* are badly mutilated in commercial *tablaos*. Purists are still dubious about Antonio's dancing *por martinetes*. But today such malpractice is so common that the purists will eventually give in, and such phrases as "born to be sung" will most likely cease to be heard.

BORN TO BE DANCED. Other *cantes*, less sacred in nature, were "born to be danced", such as the *bulerías, tangos, alegrías, rumba,* certain danceable *soleares,* etc. In addition, as previously stated, it is considered acceptable today (by the purists) to dance to any of the *cantes* "born to be sung" as long as it is not simultaneously with the singer.

VERSES. It is curious to note, as the reader reads through the verses attributed to the various *cantaores* in the biographies, that those of the men are often deep and philosophical, while those created by women tend to be more simple, direct accounts of their everyday feelings, nine times out of ten dealing with love. Also, verses created by gypsies are usually more primitive and less philosophically sophisticated than those of the *andaluces.*

Students of Spanish will discern that many of the verses are printed with the same incorrect grammar in which they are sung. This is intended to give the reader an idea of the flavour of the flamenco language and *cante.*

FADS. One important factor that has had to be taken into consideration in the biographies is the fact that, like all musical forms, the *cante flamenco* is prone to fads. A particular *cante* blossoms into popularity, and carries many performers to fame who are not necessarily good flamenco singers in the traditional sense. Many of these are one-*cante* specialists who achieve popularity and money all out of proportion to their talent and contribution to flamenco. On the other hand, well-grounded singers may ride the fad to fame, and become falsely known as one-*cante* specialists. Only tedious investigation, especially concerning singers of the past, can unravel the truth.

The *cante andaluz,* particularly, is prone to fads, while the *cante gitano grande* remains always in the background, sublime to the purists, unpopular among the general public. The most spectacular crazes within flamenco have been; *malagueñas,* c. 1870-1905; *tientos,* c. 1905-1920; *fandanguillos* and *fandangos,* c. 1920-1940; Latin-American-inspired *cantes (guajiras, colombianas, milongas),* c. 1930-1950; *rumbas* and *bulerías,* c. 1950 to the present.

JUDGING A SINGER. Before going into the biographies it might be advisable to summarize the factors by which a singer is judged. In order of importance they may well be: 1) depth of knowledge in his specialities; 2) *duende;* 3) creativity; 4) delivery; 5) voice; 6) quality of verses; 7) quantity of repertoire.

Theatrical singing, on the other hand, is quite distinct from *juerga* singing. Outstanding *juerga* singers do not usually serve for the theater, and vice versa. In a theater the singer is judged more, even by the flamencos themselves, by: 1) voice (it must be loud and penetrating — the use of an amplifying system automatically annuls the singer's effort) 2) stage presence; 3) adequate delivery; 4) verses; 5) basic knowledge of the *cantes* sung.

The only singing considered significant by purists, of course, and thus even worthy of judgment, is that done within an intimate group of knowledgeable *aficionados*. It is only then that all of the above-mentioned *juerga* points of judgment have an opportunity to come into play.

Without further preamble, let us launch into the biographies.

1988 UPDATE

<u>CREATION</u> (continuation of "Creation," pps.25-26). In recent years there have been various attempts at creativity within the Cante. One has been the movement to take flamenco back to its Arabic roots, the result being called *Andalusí*. Lole and Manuel started the movement when she began singing Moorish-sounding love songs to a bulerías beat. The result was interesting, but not considered flamenco by the serious aficionado. Along the same lines Juan el Lebrijano and his guitar accompanist get together with a group of Moorish musicians, including an excellent Moorish singer, Mohamed Chkara, and alternate coplas. The effect is far more Moorish than flamenco, exotic and catchy and a good seller of records. El Lebrijano gets pretty far out in his traditional flamenco as well, toying with the forms in a far too abstract manner for my taste; flamenco's earthiness and rhythm get lost in the process. But el Lebrijano is tame compared to Enrique Morente, many of whose innovations are so unusual as to be nearly unrecognizable as flamenco. Some of Camarón de la Isla's innovations carry more flamenco punch - others are based on crowd-pleasing pop songs - and could take root.

Only time will tell which, if any, of these innovations will be incorporated into the main body of flamenco. But regardless of their merit, it is reassuring that creativity is again alive in the Cante.

<u>FADS</u> (continuation of "Fads," P.30). The rumba and bulerías fad has died down considerably lately, to be replaced by the present craze, sevillanas. Establishments are opening all over Spain that feature only sevillanas, replete with recorded music and a dance floor for the public. The formula is commercially perfect. People take a few lessons in the sevillanas dance (in the best of cases; others merely bluff their way through), then dance the night away in the new establishments. Finally, they acclaim, there is a participatory flamenco! Fun they have, and I am all for it, but calling it flamenco is stretching it a bit.

Gypsy singer ENRIQUE ORTEGA «The Obese» was a key member of the fabulous flamenco-bullfight Ortega family of Cádiz port.

SILVERIO FRANCONETTI (1831-1899) reigns supreme among the very few non-gypsy singers who have excelled in the profound gypsy song forms.

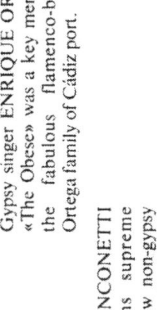
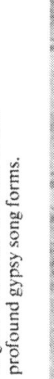

A famous group around 1880. L. to R.: Gypsy singers EL LOCO MATEO and LA LOCA MATEO: non-gypsy PACO DE LUCENA followed in the footsteps of another barber, Cádiz Paco el Barbero, to become flamenco's second serious developer of the modern style of flamenco guitar playing: gypsy dancer JOSEFITA LA PITRACA.

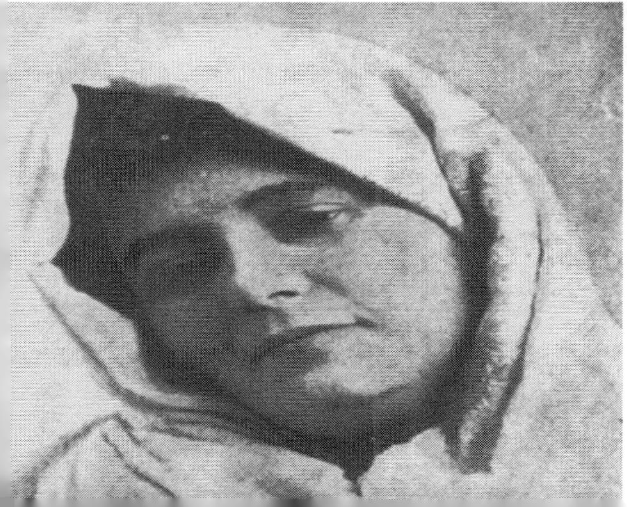

Gypsy singer TOMAS EL NITRI holds flamenco's first Golden Key of the Song, awarded to him in 1862.

MERCEDES LA SARNETA'S (c. 1837-1912) gypsy singing incarnated the tenderness and turbulence of love.

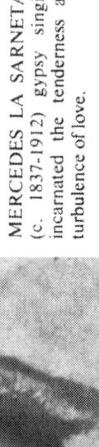
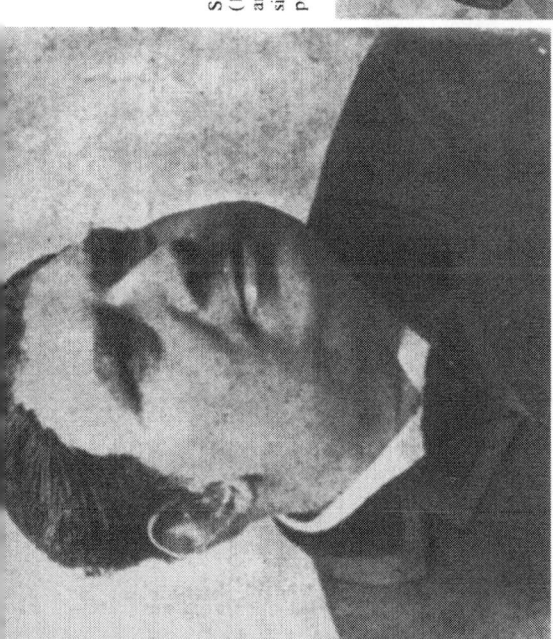

Three of the very top dancers of flamenco's known history, all gypsies from Jerez de la Frontera. L. to R.: MARIA LA CHORRUA, aunt and maestra of la Malena; JUANA LA MACARRONA, considered by many to have been the outstanding female dancer of her time; LA SORDITA, an excellent representative of the flamenco clan of Paco la Luz.

This grouping of photos well depicts the change in the flamenco dance over the last century, from the gypsy-primitive (upper row - all gypsies) to the modern stylized (lower row - all non-gypsies).

L. to R.: LA CUENCA, among the first bailaoras to don male clothing; ANTONIO DE BILBAO, the first marvel of footwork; ANTONIA MERCE «LA ARGENTINA» was one of the first to combine Spanish ballet with flamenco, thus creating a hybrid known as «Ballet Flamenco».

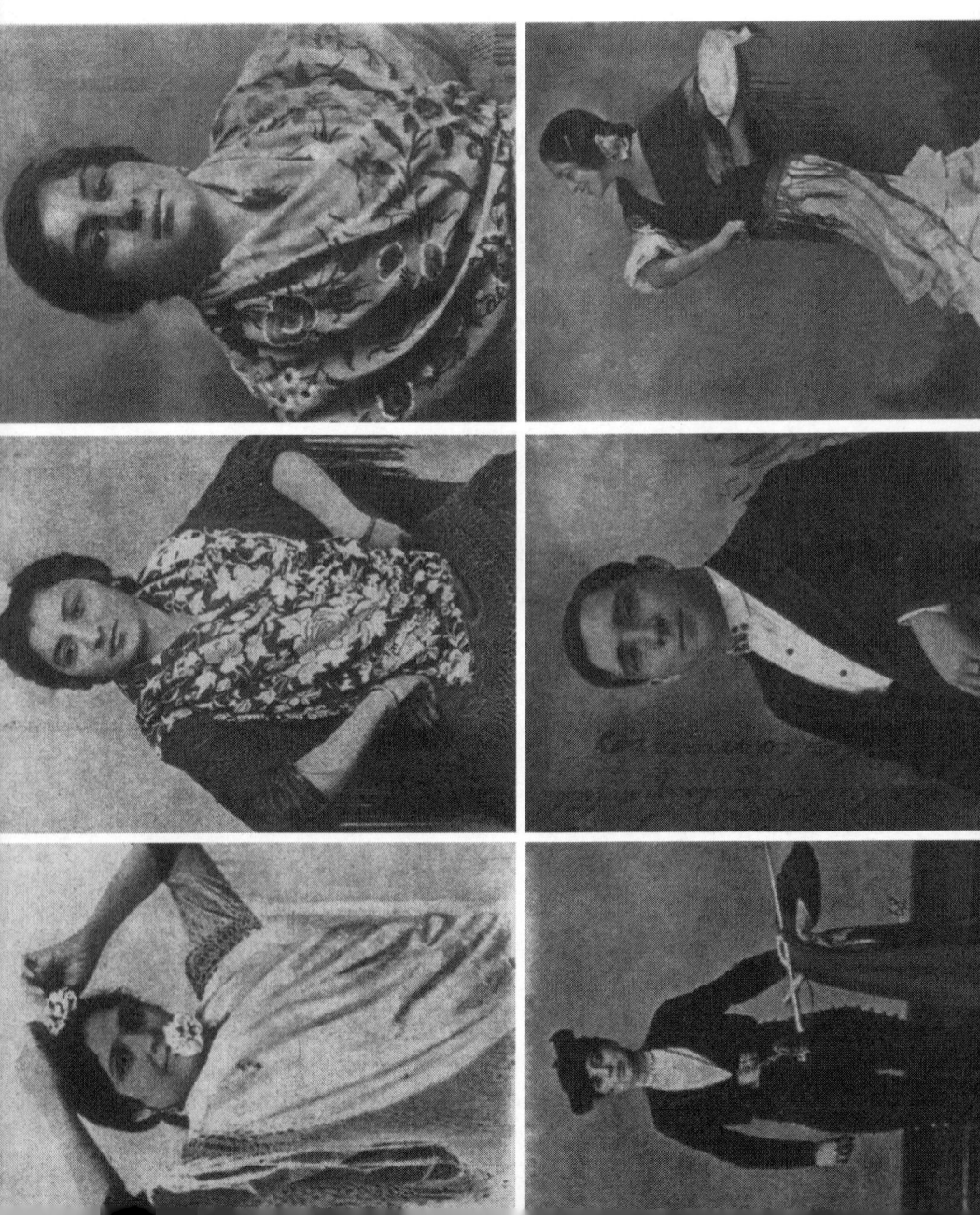

Upper photos:

These two gypsy guitarists were contemporaries, but had thoroughly distinct styles of playing. JUAN GANDULLA «HABICHUELA» (left-c. 1860-1935), born in Cádiz port, loved the traditional thumb-driven school of playing, relatively simply but imbued with feeling, while the younger RAMON MONTOYA (1880-1949), city-born in Madrid, expanded upon the playing techniques introduced by Paco el Barbero, Paco de Lucena and Javier Molina, as well as adding new techniques of his own. Considered «Father of the Modern Flamenco Guitar», Ramón also holds the dubious distinction of introducing virtuosity for virtuosity's sake.

Lower photos:

Non-gypsy JUAN BREVA (1844-1918) often accompanied himself on the guitar, but singing was definitely his forte. He popularized his *fandangos abandolaos* to such an extent that they became the most popular song form of the *café cantante* period and he the highest paid performer.

Non-gypsy JAVIER MOLINA (c. 1868-1956) excelled both as accompanist and soloist, had a profound influence in the development of the modern flamenco guitar. Javier stopped short of Ramón's guitar intricacies, as he wanted his playing always to be meaningful.

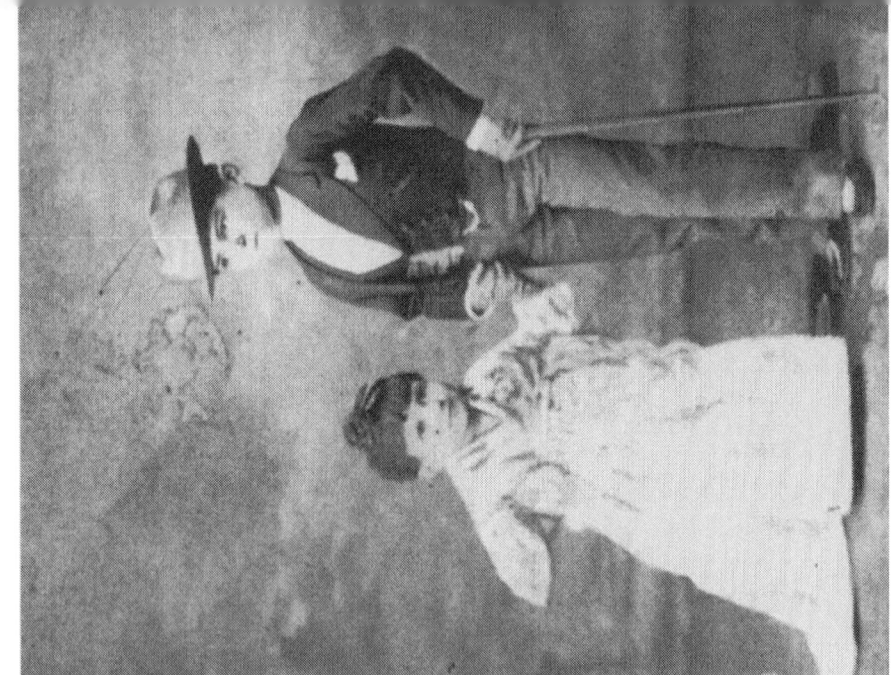

With an admirer (Conchita la Roteña, again shown in the photo of the Kursaal *cuadro* at a somewhat riper age).

With guitarist Antonio Pérez around 1875.

LAMPARILLA

Although precocious children in flamenco are not uncommon, the arrogance and self-esteem possessed by Lamparilla (c. 1860-1883) was extraordinary. A child dancing wonder, Lamparilla died young due, the legend claims, to the «fury of his fabulous dance».

Non-gypsy ANTONIO CHACON (1869-1929) is considered flamenco's all-time King of the *Cante Andaluz*. Although his appreciation for, and knowledge of, the gypsy song forms were also profound, they were suited neither to his singing voice nor his temperament.

Gypsy ENRIQUE JIMENEZ «EL MELLIZO» (1848-1906) was one of flamenco's sublime creators and certainly the greatest singer ever produced in his very flamenco hometown, the port of Cádiz.

DIEGO BERMUDEZ «EL TENAZAS» gained fame by winning first prize in the 1922 Granada flamenco contest.

THE TORRE FAMILY

JUAN SOTO MONTERO «TORRE», gypsy field worker and flamenco singer, father of Pepe and the legendary Manuel.

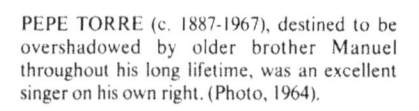

PEPE TORRE (c. 1887-1967), destined to be overshadowed by older brother Manuel throughout his long lifetime, was an excellent singer on his own right. (Photo, 1964).

MANUEL TORRE (c. 1878-1933) is remembered with awe as being the most *duende*-drenched emitter of gypsy dark sounds in flamenco's known history.

Tena el Camarero	Juan Torre	Tomás Torre	Joselito el Gallo	Manuel Torre	Enrique el Cuco	Blanqué (banderillero
	(sons of Manuel)					of Joselito).

In Sevilla's Alameda de Hércules around 1918.

(Joselito, the greatest bullfighter of his day, was killed in the bullring two years after this was taken).

Malena Seda Loreto «La Malena».

Like nearly all the best female dancers ot the *café cantante* period, gypsy MALENA SEDA LORETO «LA MALENA» (c. 1870-1953) hailed from Jerez de la Frontera. Right: age thirteen... Left: in her prime. Below: Embracing Antonio after her last performance, when over eighty years old.

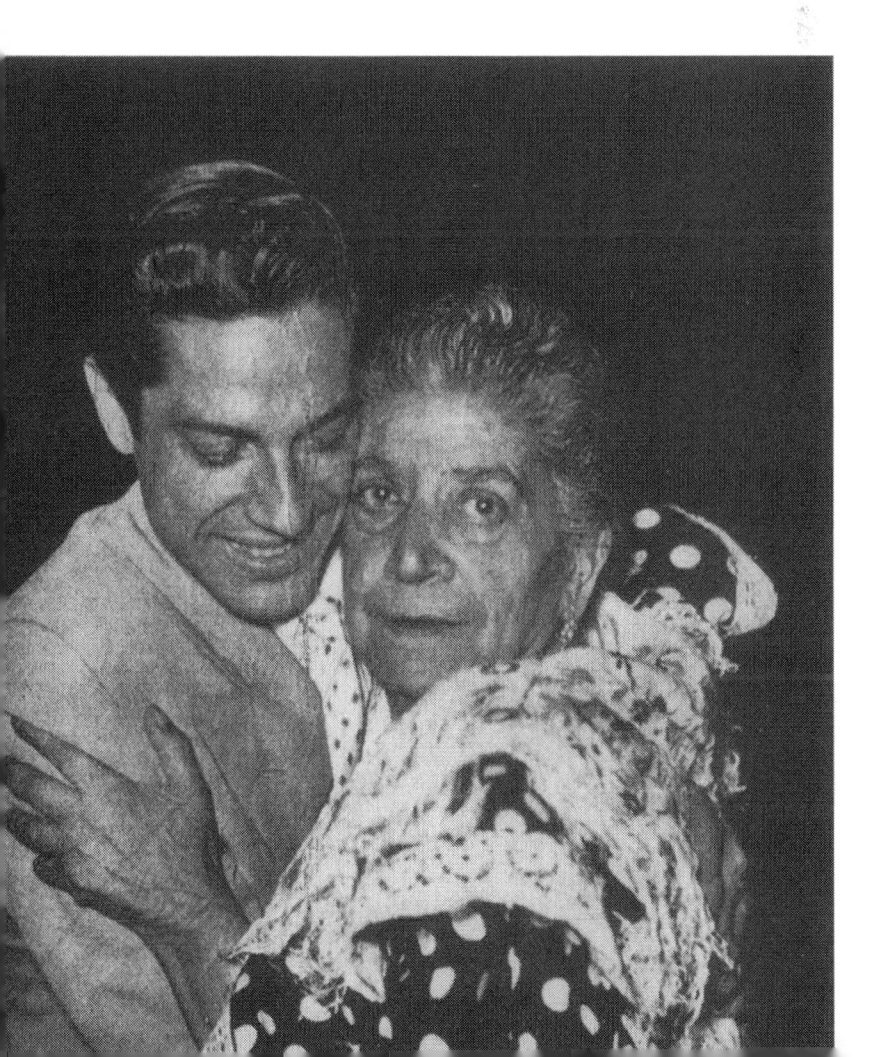

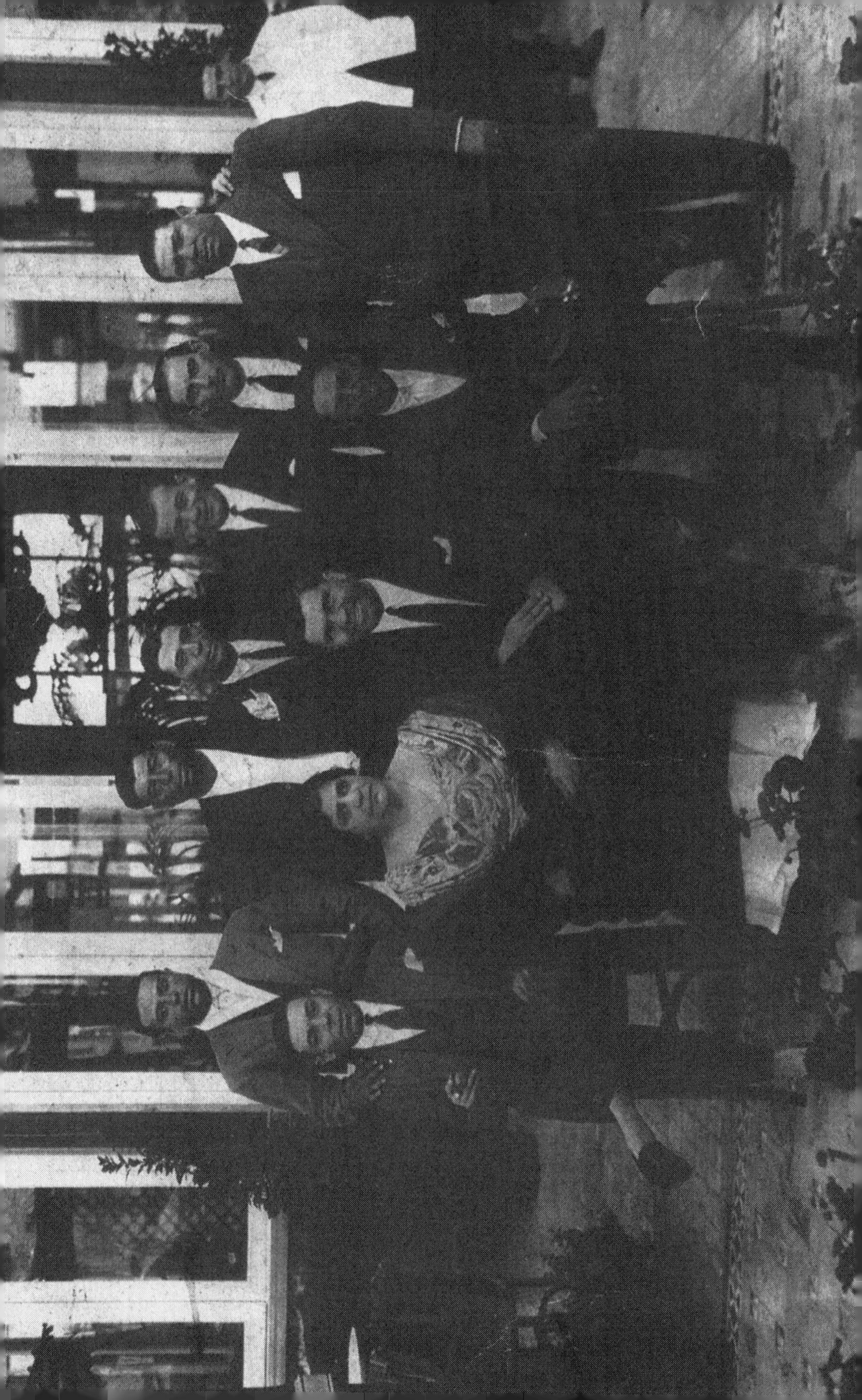

These two photos include many of the principal figures who made Sevilla's Alameda de Hércules the mecca of flamenco during the first half of this century. When the cry would go up: «¡Manuel (Torre) is singing in La Europa!», and crowds of aficionados would cluster beneath the open windows, or «Huelva is playing in the Siete Puertas...».

Standing above, L. to R.: TOMAS TORRE (G), dancing and singing son of Manuel; the legendary MANUEL TORRE (G); MANOLO DE HUELVA, nearly as legendary in guitar circles as Manuel Torre in the *Cante*; CAYETANO ORDOÑEZ «NIÑO DE LA PALMA», father of Antonio Ordoñez and in his day one of Spain's great bullfighters; guitarist ANTONIO PEREZ (son); EL NIÑO GLORIA (G), another phenomenal singer from Jerez de la Frontera.

Seated above, L. to R.: LABIOBURRA (Donkey-Lip); LA MALENA (G); MAZACO, singer; CURRITO DE LA GEROMA (G), a *fenómeno* capable of singing, dancing and playing with equal brilliance, died young, so they say, «due to over-indulgence in the fields of women and drink» (not unusual in the flamenco world of those days).

↑

Taken around 1920 in the Pasaje del Duque, Sevilla.

L. to R.:

TOMAS PAVON (G), younger brother of the Niña de los Peines, was an excellent singer of the *cante grande* who resusitated various nearly forgotten song styles; PASTORA PAVON «LA NIÑA DE LOS PEINES» (G) is considered the outstanding female singer of this century; PEPE PINTO, talented singer husband of the Niña de los Peines, sacrificed his great ability in, and knowledge of, the pure *Cante* to wealth through commercialism.

(G) = Gypsy.

Cuadro en Sevilla's Kursaal around 1918

L. to R.: Antonio Ramírez «Ramirito», Rita Ortega, Carmen de José María, Concha la Roteña, Juana Junquera, Pepe el Ecijano, María la Roteña, María Heredia, Juana Vargas la Macarrona, Rosarito Ortega, La Coriana, La Quica.

This group includes some eminent flamenco personalities, such as: RAMIREZ, considered the finest male dancer of his day; RITA ORTEGA (G), an excellent representative of the famous flamenco-bullfight Ortega family; JUANA LA MACARRONA (G), who shared honors with La Malena as the finest female dancers of their time; and LA QUICA, balancing out the *cuadro* in male garb.

(G) = Gypsy

La Quica became one of the great dancers of her epoch, then went on to teach flamenco's secrets to a goodly share of the top dancers of the next two generations. Here she is shown at ages seven and thirty.

Manuel Torre presents contest winner Manuel Vallejo with the Golden Key of the Cante, in Madrid in 1926. Other singers who have received this award are Tomás el Nitri, in 1862, and Antonio Mairena, in 1962.

1. Emilio el Faro, singer. 2. Luisito Maravilla, guitarist, at age twelve. 3. Francisco Rondan, singer. 4. La Trianita, singer. 5. Villarrubia, singer. 6. El Niño de Valdepeñas, singer. 7. Manuel Torre, singer(G). 8. El Niño de las Marianas, singer (father of Luis Maravilla). 9. Victor Rojas, guitarist (brother of Pastora Imperio). 10. Manolo Vico, master-of-ceremonies and actor. 11. Antonio el Mellizo, singer (son of Enrique)(G). 12. Manuel Vallejo, singer. 13. José Ortega, singer (G). 14. José Cepero, singer. 15. Pepe de Badajoz, guitarist. 16. Martell, guitarist. 17. Tomás Torre, singer-dancer (son of Manuel)(G). 18. Enrique Mariscal, guitarist.

This fiesta flamenca in Madrid around the year 1925 attracted many famous flamencos, including several brought up from Andalusia for the occasion. It must have been a lively fiesta, with twelve dancers, seven singers and three guitarists! 1. El Cojo de Málaga. 2. La Pompi (G). 3. La Pompi's daughter, Dolores (G). 4. La Alastra. 5. Manuela Moreno Vargas. 6. María la Morena (G). 7. Rosalía de Triana (G). 8. Aurora. 9. Antonio Moreno. 10. Enrique Mariscal. 11. La Rubia de Jerez (G). 12. Pastora la Posaera. 13. La Malena (G). 14. Loli Sánchez la Nona. 15. Matilde Sánchez. 16. La Camisona. 17. La Joselito. 18. El Niño Gloria (G). 19. Ramón Montoya (G). 20. Diego Antúnez (G). 21. Juan Mojama (G). 22. El Estampío.

(G) = Gypsy.

Jerez-born *Juan Sánchez «el Estampío»* (c. 1880-1957), one of the great dancers of this century, was not lacking in humor. After viewing a particularly bad picador's performance at a bullfight, El Estampío (The Blast) created the comic dance «del picaor», different attitudes of which are depicted here.

ANTONIO DE TRIANA (below), FAICO and LA MORITA (right) dressed as mountain bandits.

FLAMENCO THEATRICALITY

Below: PEPE MARCHENA and guitarist PEPE DE BADAJOZ in typical Andalusian ranch wear. Marchena went on to lead flamenco into a period of decadence, at first proudly, later disparagingly dubbed *Opera Flamenca,* which featured high-pitched male singers crooning flamenco's crowd-pleasing fringe song styles, or flamencoized versions of popular Andalusian songs. *Opera Flamenca* petered out with the reappearance of pure flamenco, in the 1950's.

FLAMENCO IN THE THEATRE

Flamenco play-acting for theater audiences came into vogue in the late 1920's and remained so until the cost of large companies became prohibitive in recent years. ENCARNACION LOPEZ «LA ARGENTINITA» (left) had one of the most successful of the early troupes. Upon her death in 1945 her sister, PILAR LOPEZ (shown above with ALEJANDRO VEGA), formed her own troupe and dominated theatrical flamenco for another quarter of a century.

VICENTE ESCUDERO (1895-1980) has been flamenco's most controversial dancer. For many he was a dancing god who fought a lifelong battle to keep the male dance masculine, for others an imposter who ignored too many of flamenco's basic precepts.

The wondrous CARMEN AMAYA (1913-1963), gypsy tornado, roared out of Cataluña to revolutionize the female flamenco dance. To the right: the upper portion of the powerful statue erected to Carmen in her Barcelona neighborhood of birth, the Barrio de Somorrostro. Below: Carmen at her most feminine, and Carmen with Antonio de Triana at Carnegie Hall.

Photo of statue by Elke Stolzenberg.

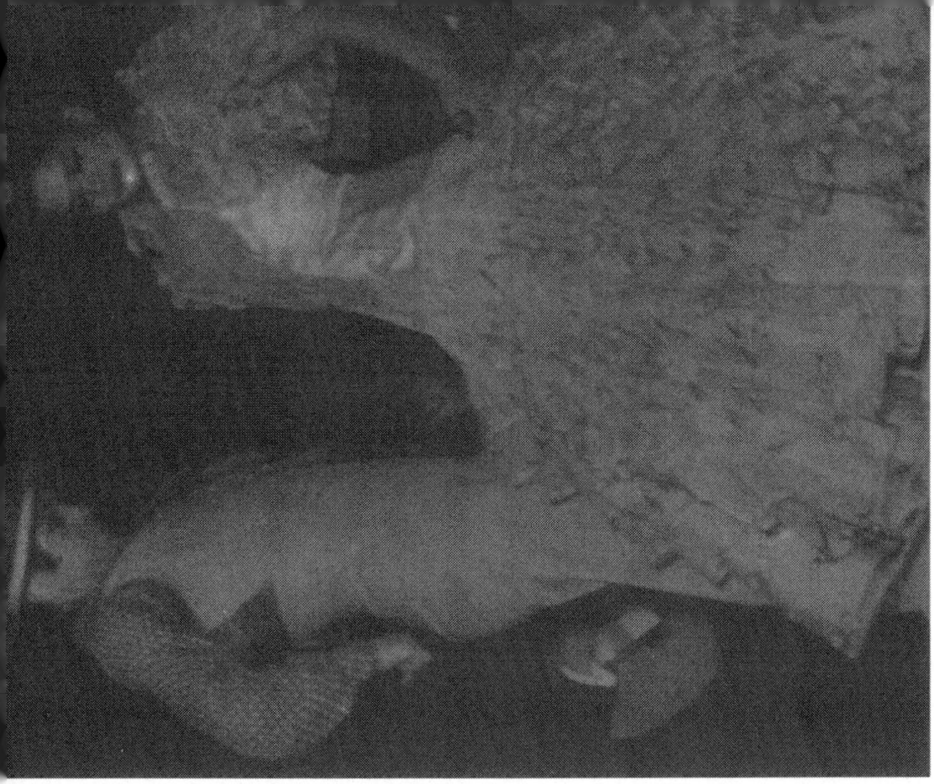

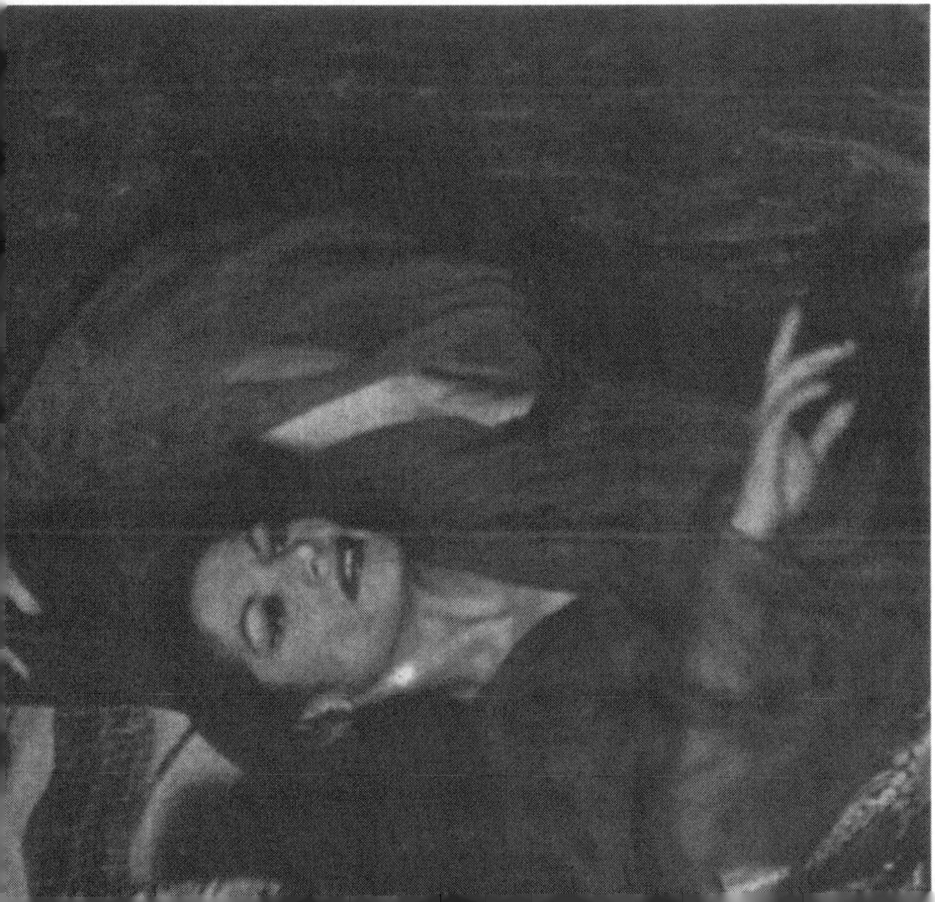

MANOLO CARACOL (Manuel Ortega: 1909-1973) has been unique in flamenco history, blatantly commercial when he wanted money, tempestuously gypsy when he wanted to be pure, one of the last of the breed whose singing could raise gooseflesh on aficionado's hides, or cause them to rip the shirt off their backs in a frenzy of abandon.

Left: Caracol as a boy of seventeen, with Pepe de Badajoz. Above left: singing to his daughter, LUISA ORTEGA, 37 years later. Above right: GABRIELA ORTEGA, another distinguised member of the Ortega clan, has long been flamenco's most excellent and moving reciter.

Photo of Gabriela by Elke Stolzenberg.

Above. *Three gypsy purists of the old school.* ANTONIO MAIRENA (left) (1909-1983), Spain's most complete singer of recent times, was holder of the Golden Key of the *Cante*. He was a tireless fighter for purity of expression, befriending many unknown purists and helping them gain recognition in the flamenco world. Such was the case of the wonderful old singer, JUAN TALEGAS (middle) (1887-1971), who taught the flamenco world many forgotten song styles. Guitarist DIEGO DEL GASTOR (1908-1973), exemplary accompanist with his own unique style of playing, was a living legend on his own right.

Below. The *Homage for Juan Talegas*, upon his death in 1971, attracted many of flamenco's top personalities. **Back row**, L. to R.: Singers JOSE MENESE, JUAN EL LEBRIJANO (singing)(G), CAMARON DE LA ISLA (G), FRANCISCO MAIRENA (G), ENRIQUE MORENTE and MANUEL MAIRENA (G).**Front row**, L. to R.: singers-dancers TOMAS TORRE (G), MIGUEL EL FUNI (G), ANTONIO MAIRENA (G), and PACO DE VALDEPEÑAS (G), and singer FERNANDA DE UTRERA (G). **Guitarists:** MANUEL SANLUCAR (left) and SAMI MARTIN.

(G) = gypsy

Photo: Elke Stolzenberg.

THE GUITAR

As we have seen near the beginning of the photo section, Ramón Montoya (1880-1949) was known as the «Father of Modern Flamenco Guitar Playing». In the following four pages we shall study what happened after Ramón.

NIÑO RICARDO'S (1904-1972) incredibly fertile mind carried the flamenco guitar to new heights of creativity, strongly influencing an entire generation of flamenco guitarists.

SABICAS (1913-   ), shown here when still a gypsy teenage prodigy in 1930, has been flamenco's greatest concertist ever until being challenged in recent times. His knowledge of the flamenco guitar is extremely profound, as is his creativity. Due to his long exile from Spain, his influence within Spain was limited until the introduction of his records, at which time his playing style and material were embraced en masse.

PERICO EL DEL LUNAR (1894-1964) was responsible for putting together, and accompanying, flamenco's first anthology, in 1952, when flamenco was at low ebb, from which an entire generation of singers learned how to sing nearly forgotten *cantes*, and guitarists to accompany them. In the photo Perico accompanies PERICON DE CADIZ, while JARRITO MONTOYA (G) plays *palmas*.

MELCHOR DE MARCHENA'S (1913-1980)(G) accompanying was unforgettably profound and beautiful. Singers used to say «If a singer is capable of singing well, he must do so with Melchor». In the photo Melchor accompanies LA PAQUERA DE JEREZ (G).

(G) = Gypsy

THE GUITAR
JUERGA PLAYING

Until recently many flamenco guitarists dedicated their artistic lives to playing for private gatherings, called *juergas* if of the earthy variety (special rooms in bars, country inns, red light houses, etc.), *fiestas* when the occasion was more refined and respect was in order (a home, mansion, palace, high-class establishment, etc.). Such artists are almost underground figures, generally know only within their immediate flamenco world. Two exceptions to this, *juerga* guitarists who became lengendary during this century, are pictured below.

MANOLO DE HUELVA (1892-1976) was long considered the best accompanist of the *Cante* flamenco has know. His technique was phenomenal for his time, but he is most revered for his extensive knowledge of the *Cante* and his inspired flights of fancy when the wine hit home at the height of a juerga. Here Manolo accompanies PERICON DE CADIZ.

DIEGO DEL GASTOR (1908-1973), although he rarely left his adopted town, Morón de la Frontera, gained international acclaim in flamenco circles due to his unique playing and his enormous depth of feeling (*duende*), as well as his expertise in accompanying the *Cante*. In the photo Diego (G) accompanies LA FERNANDA DE UTRERA (G), long recognized as flamenco's most intensively emotive *cantaora*.
(G) = gypsy
Photo: Bill Davidson

THE GUITAR
THE MODERNS
The undisputed King of today's flamenco guitar is PACO DE LUCIA (1947-   ). Unlike most of today's young virtuosos, Paco was well grounded in the basics, is an expert accompanist and supreme technician, is in general profoundly flamenco even in his most far-out playing. In the photo Paco is shown en concert with older broher, RAMON DE ALGECIRAS (left).
Photo: Elke Stolzenberg

SINGING WITHOUT GUITAR

Much singing takes place without guitar accompaniment in flamenco circles. Besides the fact that a few of flamenco's *cantes* traditionally do not admit musical accompaniment, often an adequate accompanist is simply not available at the moment of inspiration. In the photo, JOSELERO DE MORÓN (G) seems to be lost in time as he sings to LA FERNANDA DE UTRERA (G) and to FRANCISCO MAIRENA (G). (G) = gypsy.
Photo: Bill Davidson

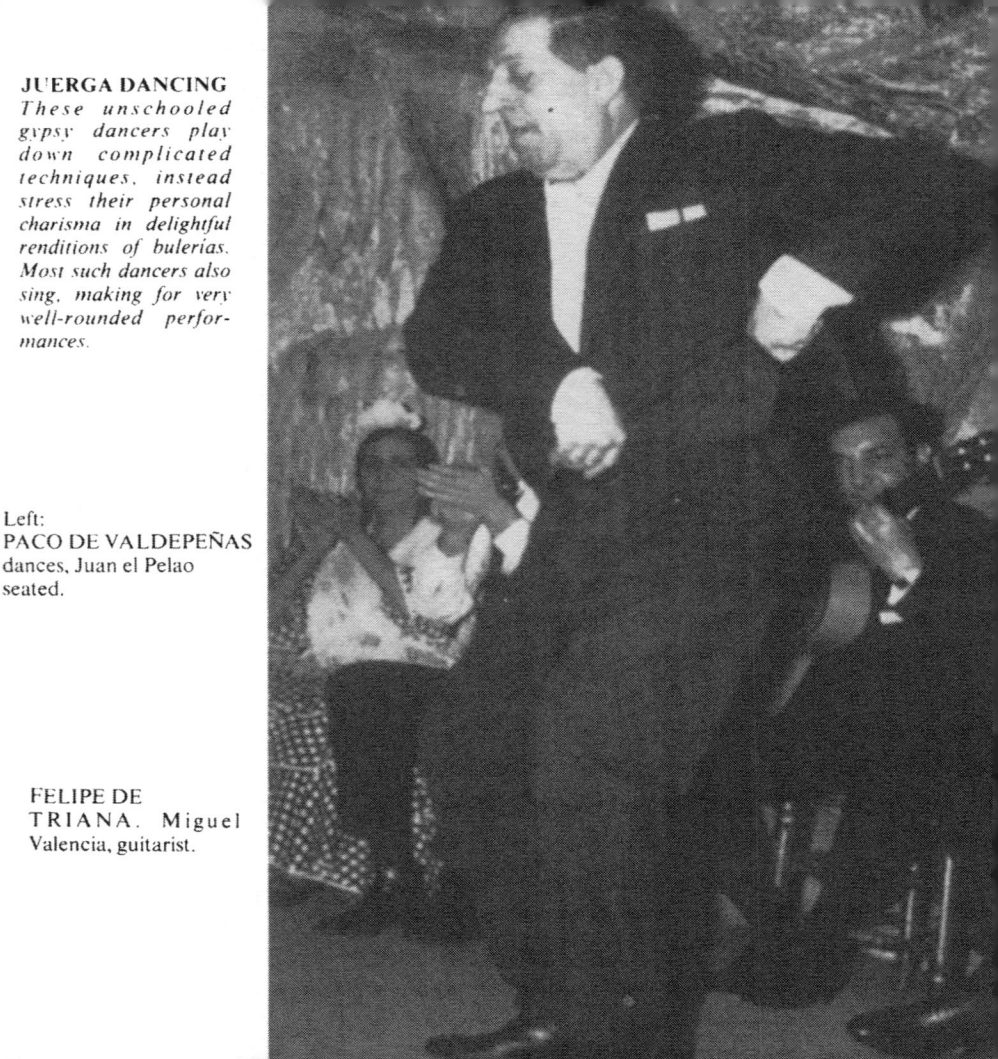

JUERGA DANCING
These unschooled gypsy dancers play down complicated techniques, instead stress their personal charisma in delightful renditions of bulerías. Most such dancers also sing, making for very well-rounded performances.

Left:
PACO DE VALDEPEÑAS dances, Juan el Pelao seated.

FELIPE DE TRIANA. Miguel Valencia, guitarist.

MIGUEL EL FUNI.
Pedro Peña, guitarist.

PEPA CAMPOS.

BALLET FLAMENCO

ROSARIO and ANTONIO, LOS CHAVALILLOS DE ESPAÑA, have been without a doubt Spain's most popular dance duo. After years together they separated, each forming his/her own troupe, and remained in the limelight. ANTONIO, above all, spread the gospel of Ballet Español, a mixture of Spanish classical, folklore and stylized ballet flamenco, to all parts of the world.

Photo, L. to R.: MARISOL; REALITO, their first instructor (general Spanish dance); ROSARIO; ANTONIO. Far right: LA QUICA who, together with her boyfriend, FRASQUILLO, gave Los Chavalillos their first flamenco instruction.

ANTONIO

Photo: Pepe Lamarca.

After Manolo Caracol (G), what singer was left who could set your spine tingling and cause you to leap from you seat shouting ¡olé!? The overwhelming first choice was TERREMOTO DE JEREZ (1934-1981) (G), who could also set the crowd roaring with laughter with his dancing antics, as shown in the photo.
(G) = gypsy

In his younger days, gypsy ANTONIO EL FARRUCO, long recognized authentic flamenco's number one dancer, could cause with his dance the same sensations as Fernando el Terremoto (page above) with his singing. El Farruco is still dancing, still possesses some of the old magic, but is now grossly overweight and with problems of health. At present, no dancer, including El Farruco, can generate the intense, tumultuous emotion he once did.

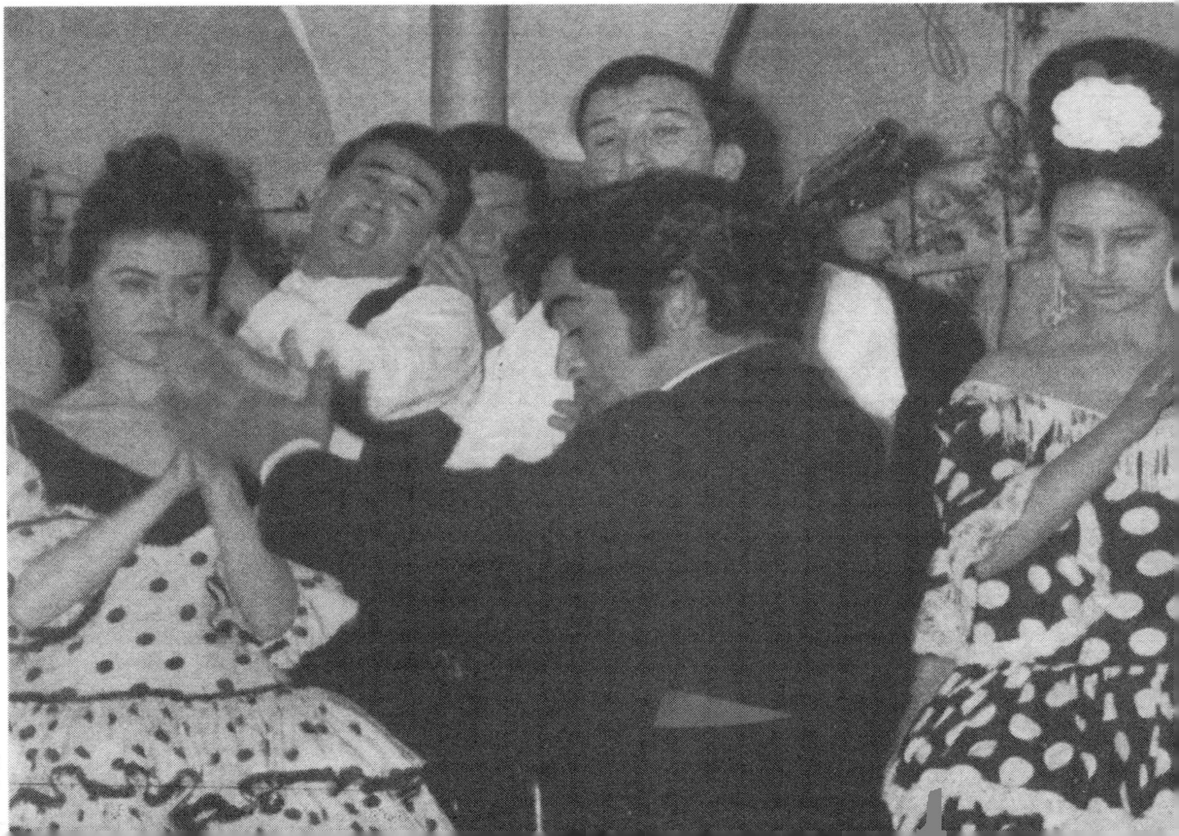

As a boy.

EL FARRUCO

Warming up.

Four of today's finest dancers. CIRO (above) (photo: Elke Stolzenberg), and CHUNI AMAYA (right) (G) working out in Madrid. Page to right: EL GÜITO (G) and MERCHE ESMERALDA.

(G) = gypsy.

Photo by Elke Stolzenberg.

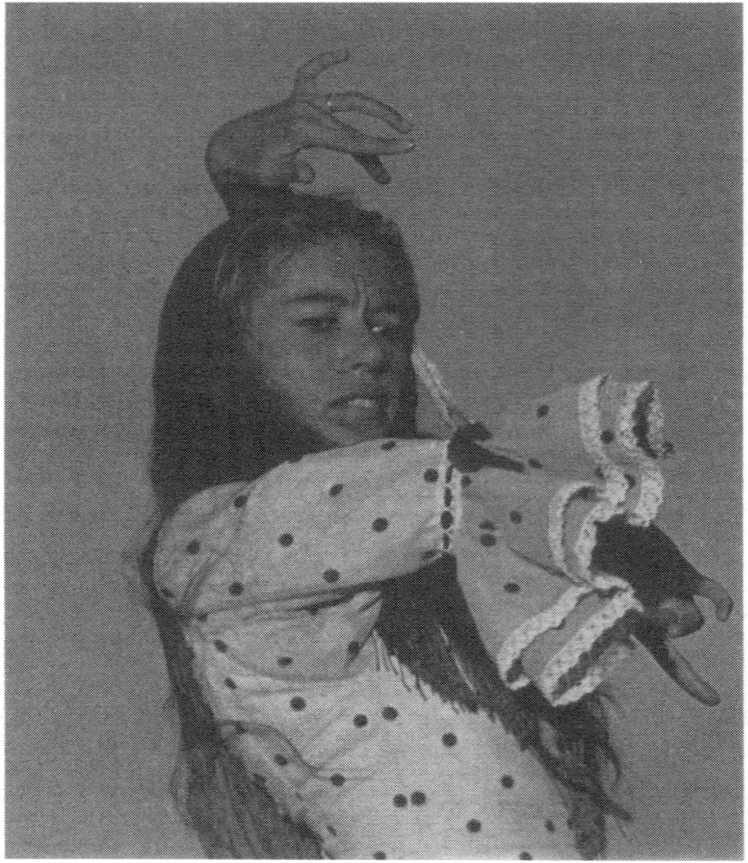

LUISA MARAVILLA Two of today's outstanding bailaoras. BLANCA DEL REY at Madrid's Corral de la Morería.

BIOGRAPHIES OF SINGERS

TIO LUIS EL DE LA JULIANA

(c. 1760 - 1830)

Tío Luis el de la Juliana (Uncle Louis, he of the Juliana, or "son of Juliana") marks the beginning of flamenco's poorly documented history. He also represents the leading figure of the *cante* for an entire epoch, the second half of the eighteenth century.

Tío Luis is said to have sung everything well, from the most profound of the *cantes grandes* to the most insignificant *cante chico* (this can only be deduced, as nothing identifiable remains of his *cante*). From Jerez de la Frontera, he was reputedly the *maestro* of, or at least strongly influenced, such legendary *cantaores* as tío Luis el Cautivo (Uncle Louis the Captive), Vicente and Juan Macarrón, tío Corro, José and Juan Cantarol, Luis Jesús, Juan de Vargas, and his son "hijo de la Juliana", all gypsy *cantaores* with supposedly complete repertoires; and also such specialists in *siguiriyas* as Juan Bernal, Curro Casado, Luis de Rueda and Cuadrillero. He is also said to have strongly influenced the *cante* of one of the great and creative *cantaores* of all times, Diego el Fillo, the first figure in the second epoch of flamenco history (first half of the nineteenth century).

EL PLANETA

(c. 1785-1860)

EL PLANETA, Cádiz-born gypsy; great-grandfather of the grandmother of Manolo Caracol, was a *cantaor* of the primitive *cantes tonás, martinetes, carceleras, siguiriyas, soleares,* etc. He was called by Esteban Calderón, a writer of that period, the "king of the *polos*". EL PLANETA worked for years in the smithies of Triana, and is thought to have been one of the principal contributors to the Triana school of *cante*. He was also the principal *maestro* of the famous Diego el Fillo. One of EL PLANETA's *siguiriyas* is still remembered, sung today by a few of the most illustrious of the *cante grande* singers, including Antonio Mairena, Juan Talegas, and Pepe Torre (1).

A la luna le pido, I ask the moon
la del alto cielo, of the high heavens
como le pido que saque a mi to help my father escape
　　　　　　　　　　[padre from his place of imprisonment.
de onde está preso.

It is thought that EL PLANETA derived his name from his many verses, like the one above, that expressed the primitive gypsy faith in the magic powers of the stars and planets.

DIEGO EL FILLO

(c. 1800-1860)

Francisco Ortega Vargas, better known as DIEGO EL FILLO, was born in Puerto Real (Cádiz) into the same family that produced the *cantaores* and *toreros* Cagancho.

A gypsy wanderer, EL FILLO's trade was blacksmithing, which he practiced in various towns of Andalusia, including Puerto Real, Triana, and Morón de la Frontera. He was therefore reared on the *cantes* of Los Puertos (tío Luis el de la Juliana and others),

---

(1) Pepe Torre recently cut the first recorded version of this unusual *cante*, sung in a major rather than the usual minor key of the *siguiriyas*, on London's «An Anthology of Cante Flamenco», thus conserving the *cante* for posterity. Pepe is accompanied beautifully on the record by Melchor de Marchena.

absorbed the *cante de Triana* at the side of El Planeta, and went on from there to become one of the truly great creators and interpreters of the *cante*.

EL FILLO is said to have sung all of the *cantes gitanos*, improving on the existing *cantes* (the *cañas*, among others), creating new styles, spontaneously creating verses: a true flamenco's flamenco. He possessed an ideal voice for the *cante jondo*, which might be described as foggily rough and raucous. This type of voice, relatively common among gypsies (Manolo Caracol, Terremoto de Jerez, to cite two), is still termed a *"voz afillá"*, after EL FILLO, and even today is considered a desirable element for the *cante gitano*.

EL FILLO lived most of his life before the coming of the *cafés cantantes*, when flamenco was still more a way of life than a way of making a living. He usually sang for pleasure, although he was a very exacting professional when the occasion arose, as can be observed by the following story:

EL FILLO once sang for a bullfighter who paid him with a gold coin, which EL FILLO found to have been filed down. He went directly in search of the bullfighter, and asked him:

"Was there anything lacking in my singing?"

The surprised bullfighter answered: "No, it was excellent, all a man could ask for."

To which EL FILLO replied: "Well, there certainly was in the payment", whereupon he demanded a fully-weighted gold coin.

Aurelio Sellé tells another pet story of EL FILLO:

One night EL FILLO was returning home from the Zafra fair with his wife, la Andonda, a tempestuous *cantaora* thirty years his minor. It had been a good fair — wine had flowed, EL FILLO's artistic talents had been greatly appreciated, money had been earned — but EL FILLO was feeling ill, suffering, in all likelihood, from a colossal hangover. In the course of their journey, afoot, they arrived at a particularly bad river-crossing where the bridge had been washed away. EL FILLO could go no further. He sat down in the rain on the river bank and conjured up his best gypsy curses against the disgusting elements, such as defecating in the milk and on a few friend's mothers, as well. La Andonda, more energetic, sized up the situation and came up with an immediate solution — she hoisted EL FILLO on her back, hauled him piggy-back through the raging water and up the opposite bank. There, drenched and exhausted, they encountered a little inn which happened to be heavy with *juerga*. EL FILLO, in true gypsy fashion, rallied immediately, ordered a bottle of *aguardiente*, downed half of it, and took his rightful place as ranking *cantaor*, singing his appreciation to his wife in the following *soleá*:

Yo me creía, serrana,	*I had thought,* serrana,
que tú a mí no me quería;	*that you didn't truly love me;*
y ahora veo claramente	*now I see clearly*
que por mí pierde la vía.	*that for me you would give your [life.*

Other excellent *cantaores* who sang during this period, and were strongly influenced by EL FILLO, were his brothers Curro Pabla and Juan Encueros (Naked John), Juan de Dios (God's John), Perico Piña (Pineapple Pete), Juana la Sandita, Pepa la Cochoca, La Lola, and many others, some of whom we shall discuss in the course of the book. The last *cantaora* mentioned, La Lola, has gained lasting fame through the following verse, from a poem by Manuel Machado, which is still recited and sung:

La Lola se va a Los Puertos,	*La Lola is going to Los Puertos,*
la Isla se queda sola.	*the Island (San Fernando) is left [alone.*

But the greatest of EL FILLO's many disciples were his cousin, Tomás el Nitri, and Silverio Franconetti, both of whom continued in his tradition and became, as well, prolific innovators in their own right.

DIEGO EL FILLO died, his voice spent in *aguardiente* and *juerga*, in poverty. His most famous *cante* remembered is the following *siguiriyas cabales*:

Desde la Polverita	*From the Polverita*
hasta Santiago,	*to Santiago,*
las fatigas de la muerte	*the anguish of death*
me arrodearon.	*surrounded me.*

MARIA BORRICO

(c. 1810-1880)

María Borrico (Little Donkey Mary) was a celebrated specialist in the *playeras* and *siguiriyas*. From Jerez de la Frontera, she was a rival, and friend, of Diego el Fillo.

TIA SARVAORA

(c. 1810-1880)

Tía Sarvaora, from Jerez de la Frontera, was a *cantaora* remembered principally for her interpretations of the *tonás*. Manuel Machado mentions her in his poem "*La Lola*".

MANUEL MOLINA

(c. 1820-1880)

Manuel (Curro) Molina was a gypsy *cantaor* who became the idol of the *aficionados* of Jerez de la Frontera around the period 1840-1865. He was an extremely grave man, dignified, unsmiling, and his *cante* was equally as grave. His *siguiriyas* differed from the wild, tremendous style of his famous contemporary, Tomás el Nitri, in that they were "vague and spiritual like a ghostly dream", to quote Núñez de Prado.

Molina was basically a *siguiriyero*, but also sang excellent *martinetes* and other *cantes*. One of his *siguiriyas* still sung today:

Me asomé a la muralla,	I climbed to the top of the wall,
me respondió el viento:	and the wind said to me:
¿para qué das esos suspiritos	what is the use of sighing
si ya no hay remedio?	if there is no remedy?

This verse well reflected Molina's later days, as at the height of his career he was forced into retirement due to sickness and consequent total deafness. He was soon forgotten, and lived the remainder of his life without his beloved *cante*, in poverty. His *cante,* however, was not forgotten, and has had a profound effect on the development of modern flamenco. Creations of his *siguiriyas* are still remembered and sung today.

When Diego el Fillo began faltering, around the years 1850 to 1855, two young men, both his disciples, were there to carry on for him. One, Tomás el Nitri, a cousin of El Fillo, was an introvert who never sang commercially, not even during the height of the *café cantante* period. He believed the *cante grande,* his specialty, too sacred for such places. The other, Silverio Franconetti, spread his *cante* to all corners, with a genuine interest in leaving disciples to carry on after his death, and a naïve desire to popularize the pure *cante* without its losing in purity. Both of these desires, together, of course, with that of monetary gain, motivated Silverio to open his Café Silverio, the most famous of the *cafés cantantes,* considered at the time a veritable university of pure *cante.*

SILVERIO FRANCONETTI

1988 Update: (1831-1899)

SILVERIO FRANCONETTI AGUILAR is a legendary figure universally regarded as one of the four or five greatest all-round *cantaores* of flamenco's documented history.

Born in Sevilla of an Italian father and Spanish mother, Silverio was reared in Morón de la Frontera, and it was there that he spent many invaluable hours listening to Diego el Fillo sing while at work in his smithy, or in the nightly *juergas* that raged in Morón during that epoch. Thus enlightened, SILVERIO went on to develop his own style of *cante.* He had a great gift of creativity, and soon the *cantes* that he had learned from El Fillo and others were stamped with SILVERIO's personality. Like el Fillo, SILVERIO was a complete singer, preferring the *cante grande.* To quote Núñez de Prado: "He dominated the *siguiriyas* to perfection, so you can imagine what he could do with the *polos*, the *martinetes*, and all of the other *cantes* that he sang." He was the favorite *cantaor* of Fernando de Triana, who said that "Silverio sang all of the *cantes*, absolutely all of them, extraordinarily well." Fernando goes on to describe SILVERIO's voice: *afillá* (hoarse and raucous), tempered, charged with *duende* and, when he wished, sweet as honey.

After SILVERIO had established a firm reputation as a *cantaor*, he spent a period of over ten years in America before returning to resume his reign and open his Café Silverio. This period is best described by the late poet Manuel Machado in the following anecdote, translated by the author:

"Back around the year 1864 it was more than ten years that SILVERIO FRANCONETTI — señor Silverio, as people had begun to call him through respect to his art and his person — had been away from Sevilla. Loves or ambitions (1) enticed him to America, our America (Spanish America), and there he existed as a peacetime *picador de toros* and a wartime officer in the Uruguayan army. In Sevilla people throught him dead and forgot about him, but not about his marvelous *cante*, which the *cantaores* of the period tried in vain to imitate.

"One good night, in a famous *café cantante*, a still young gentleman showed up sporting a well-cared-for, thick black beard, his hair graying a bit around the temples, well-dressed and bejeweled with a gold watch-chain wrapped twice around his chest and shining rings on his fingers. He ordered a bottle of good Jerez wine, and invited the flamenco artists of the *café* to drink with him. They complied with his wishes, and remained after their performances to sing and dance exclusively for this obviously rich South American Indian. They were a little regretful of the rest they were losing, but assured of being well-remunerated — at least, judging by the way the stranger spent his double doubloons, without so much as counting them.

---

(1) Another version goes that Silverio left Spain due to the death of another artist, Juan Encueros, and only dared return after he and the event were forgotten.

"The night turned to wine and the flamenco flowed, and after awhile there came to pass what the artists feared would happen, but for gold were ready to tolerate — around dawn it entered the head of the rich *payo* to try his hand at the *cante,* and he told the guitarist to accompany him in nothing less than the *siguiriyas.* The flamencos looked at each other and, amid much nudging of elbows and hidden grimaces, made the audacious but well-heeled *payo* the butt of much buffoonery.

"As the visitor began his *siguiriyas* the scene totally changed. The drowsiness, the boredom, the horseplay disappeared like magic, to be replaced by the most humble admiration and the most enthusiastic devotion. Transported to a superior world by the lips of the stranger, the men followed the modulations of that voice in a stunned silence. The women wept...

"And when that young gentleman finished the verse, the classical *siguiriyas* of the *maestro* SILVERIO, wild and tremendous, that goes:

La malita lengua	*The bad tongue*
que de mí murmura,	*that murmurs of me,*
yo lo cogiera por en medio en	*I would grasp it*
[medio,	*and leave it dumb...*
la dejara muda...	

"Stop!', exclaimed the old *bailaora* (1) who had least wanted to hear the intruder. 'There is only one person in the world who can sing that *cante,* and that person...

"'What?', the stranger asked smiling.

"'That person is you, *señor* SILVERIO!...'

"The notice spread like wildfire, and that same night SILVERIO sang all of his immense repertoire of *siguiriyas, tonás* and *serranas* likes perhaps he never sang them again in his life."

Shortly after his return from America SILVERIO opened his *café cantante,* which became *the* center of the *cante grande.* But after a number of years, the trend of *café cantante* flamenco began

---

(1) The old *bailaora* Machado refers to is said to have actually been the famous *cantaora,* María Borrico.

turning away from SILVERIO. Other *cafés* began over-commercializing their art. The *malagueñas*, which began sweeping the country in the 1870's, and similar *cantes* began replacing the *cante grande gitano*. For a while SILVERIO held firm, desperately attempting to stem the tide, not wishing to join the movement (1). But it was hopeless; within a period of a few years commercial flamenco had left SILVERIO antiquated and all but forgotten. This demonstrated one point once and for all — the *cante grande* is simply not suited for the masses, simply cannot be commercialized. It must exist among a small group of sensitive souls, as it always has, be they gypsies, bandits, beggars, noblemen, or foreigners.

SILVERIO was always very discriminating in his choice of artists to perform in his *café*. He demanded, and got, top quality. One story is told about SILVERIO's audition of a popular newcomer. Time and again SILVERIO had to tell the newcomer to slow down in his *cante* (today the management urges exactly the opposite). The boy pigheadedly ignored the *maestro's* advice, and was finally told by SILVERIO:

"OK, enough. Now you go on home, and when you learn to

---

(1) Some flamencologists maintain that Silverio played an opposite role to that which I have given him. Instead of a strong stabilizing force in the primitive *cante gitano*, they claim that he was actually the initiator of the «andalucization» of the *cante gitano* (i. e. watering it down with virtuosity, ornamentation, flourishes, and in general attempting to make the *cante* pleasing to the popuar public). Their argument is based on three points: the writings of Antonio Machado Alvarez who stated more or less what is written about the andalucization of the *cante;* that Silverio played a leading role in the commercial *café cantante* movement; and that Silverio was a non-gypsy. Theirs is a good argument. However, I maintain my stand that Silverio's *café cantante*, el Café Silverio, was his naïve attempt to present the pure *cante gitano* to a popular public. True, the *cafés cantantes* were the main cause of the andalucization of the *cante gitano*, and the gypsyization of the *cante andaluz*. But it is also almost universally agreed that Silverio's *café* was an exception to the rule, much as La Zambra today is much less contaminated than Spain's other *tablaos*. Of course, placing the responsibility on Silverio's shoulders is the obvious reaction, considering that he was the first non-gypsy to reach such great fame. People wonder: if he was not a gypsy, how could he have sung the *cante gitano* properly? Simply because he lived among the gypsies, and learned his *cante* from the greatest gypsy *cantaor* of the period, Diego el Fillo. In these modern times we must admit that environment is a much stronger tie than blood.

Two illustrious flamencologists who agree, in general, with Antonio Machado Alvarez recognize, nonetheless, that Silverio's *cante* remained strongly gypsy, and they cite him as one of the greatest *siguiriyeros*, that most gypsy of *cantes*, that flamenco has known (R. Molina - A. Mairena: «*Mundo y Formas del Cante Flamenco*», pp. 58 & 184). This seems contradictory. If Silverio was initiating the andalucization of the *cante gitano*, how can he have been one of the *cante gitano's* greatest interpreters?

Thus, in view of the majority of material written about Silverio, and his reputation and legend among most of today's old-timers, I shall give him the benefit of the doubt and pinpoint the strongest influences in the andalucization of the *cante* with Juan Breva, Antonio Chacon, and the *café cantante* movement in general.

sing as I told you, come back and try again; it's one thing to sing, another to sell the lottery."

SILVERIO was a kindly, generous man, and had the rare trait of giving every man his due without any of the usual artistic rancor. It is said that he would often sit in the audience in the rival Café Burrero, listening to Chacón's *malagueñas*, and utter *"qué bárbaro, qué bárbaro* (how fantastic), and sometimes weep with emotion. His great passion seemed to be, more than himself, the *cante flamenco*. A strange kind of man to brave, and conquer, this jungle of inflated artistic egos!

However, he was certainly no pushover. SILVERIO knew his worth, and would not bow to a lesser man. Fernando de Triana tells of the time, probably in the 1880's, when SILVERIO was headlined in a Madrid *café cantante* which also featured Juan Breva and Carito. SILVERIO, as befits the greatest singer, sang last, which is where the problem lay. For at that time Juan Breva was the rage of Spain, known as the "king of the *malagueñas*", and Carito had a honeyed, high voice very pleasing to the uninitiated public. On the other hand, SILVERIO's *cante grande*, sung in all of its raucousness and purity, held little appeal for the popular public, which resulted in a half-empty salon when it came time for SILVERIO to sing — the public would simply leave after hearing Breva and Carito. The manager, attempting to remedy the situation, innocently asked SILVERIO if he would mind singing first. That, on top of the new and humiliating experience, for SILVERIO, of having the public walk out on him, was too much. SILVERIO haughtily replied:

"Here, take the money you advanced me — he who can sing after me is yet to be born!"

As the *cante grande* slipped, so did SILVERIO. From a man comfortably wealthy, both spiritually and economically, SILVERIO finally died, of a heart attack, destitute and forgotten, a living legend who had outlived his period.

As it turns out, SILVERIO's death was timely. Had he lived a few more years, he would have seen his beloved flamenco attacked from all quarters in a phenomenon known as the *"antiflamenquismo del '98"*. Nearly all of the prominent writers of the period, newspapers, the public in general, everybody save a few dyed-in-the-wool *aficionados,* turned vehemently against flamenco, and equally as vehemently against the bullfight and anything else considered typically Spanish. This general condemnation persisted well into the twentieth century. From 1900-1950 the flamencos were scorned; flamenco was reviled and laughed at. The only flamencos who truly fared well during this half-century, with rare exceptions, were those who gave the public what it wanted, and those who joined flamenco ballets working principally out of Spain. The others, the purists who could not stomach either leaving Spain or sacrificing their integrity, returned to their towns and villages, and flamenco again became an art of the minority, an art of and for the *aficionado* who needs flamenco much as he needs the oxygen he breathes. This condition only began changing, to any extent, with the arrival of tourism in the late 1940's. Spain had seemingly become putrefied in its introverted life, had lost its sense of values to some degree, and it took outsiders to give flamenco, and the bullfight, the much-needed impetus to stage a revival — the very revival that is in full swing today.

Let us leave SILVERIO with a poem by Federico García Lorca:

PORTRAIT OF SILVERIO FRANCONETTI

A mixture of Italian
and flamenco,
how did
Silverio sing?
The dense honey of Italy
with our lemon
went into the profound lament
of the siguiriyero.
His cry was terrible.
Old-timers say
that one's hair
stood on end
and the quicksilver of mirrors
opened.

*He moved through the tones
without shattering them.
And he was a creator
and a gardener.
A creator of flowery plazas
to adorn the silence.
Now his melody
sleeps amid the echos.
Definitive and pure.
Amid the last echos!*

TOMAS EL NITRI
(c. 1830-1890)

During the same period that Silverio was attempting to retain the purity in Sevilla's *café cantante* life, another of el Fillo's disciples was the reigning figure in the then artistically rich flamenco life of Jerez de la Frontera. This man was TOMÁS EL NITRI, an eccentric gypsy, subject to frequent black moods and excesses. By nature he was perfectly suited for the *cante grande*, and through his fabulous *siguiriyas* he became known, in wide circles, as the "king of the *cante jondo*".

This, of course, invited comparison with Silverio, for the *siguiriyas* was also Silverio's preferred *cante*. Each singer had ardent, unyielding fans, but as one of EL NITRI's eccentricities was his refusal to sing before Silverio (or to sing on any occasion when circumstances were not absolutely natural), no actual comparison of this sort was ever made. It is known only that Silverio possessed a wider repertoire of *cantes*.

EL NITRI, thought to have been born in Arcos de la Frontera, a picturesque village near Jerez, was a bohemian, and felt strongly the gypsy instinct for the open road. He therefore did a great deal of wandering, which is reflected in one of his lonely *siguiriyas*:

La Pastora Divina	May the Divine Shepherdess
venga en mi compaña,	keep me company
que me veo sin calor de nadie	for I am without warmth of
y en tierra mu extraña.	[anyone
	in strange country.

EL NITRI was a lifelong foe of the commercial flamenco movement. To him flamenco was simply a daily part of his life — when he felt black, he sang *siguiriyas;* when gay, *bulerías.* 'As these moods have no timetable, how can one sing on schedule?' An excellent question, the answer to which is the same today as it was then: one cannot.

EL NITRI was the first holder of the Golden Key of the *Cante,* awarded to him in 1862. This seems a bit too ostentatious for NITRI, out of keeping with his character. I imagine he was pressured into it by well-meaning admirers. It was actually a meaningless gesture, as no contest or competition of any sort was connected with its presentation. Silverio was in America, the other greats of the period ignored.

There are contradictory legends about EL NITRI's love life: one says that he was not interested in women, the other that he became the lover of la Andonda, el Fillo's wife, after el Fillo left the scene.

Possibly the most popular verse still sung of those remembered of TOMÁS EL NITRI is this *siguiriyas:*

Por aquella ventana	*Through that window*
que al campo salía,	*that overlooked the countryside*
llamaba a la mare de mi arma	*I cried out to the mother of my*
y no me respondía.	*[soul*
	and received no answer.

Legend has it that EL NITRI died of tuberculosis, choking on blood during the most difficult part of a *siguiriyas.* Like Silverio, he left behind a legion of admirers and disciples, which has resulted in a great deal of his *cante* being remembered today (1).

---

(1) This version of El Nitri's life I have gleaned from whatever has been written about him, as well as from stories told about him by old-time flamencos. It conflicts sharply with a new version, which claims that Nitri was not born until 1863, and died in the early 1900's. Were this true, Nitri would not have learned his *cante* from Diego el Fillo, and would not have been a serious competitor of Silverio, who died in 1893. It would also disprove the oral tradition within Juan Talegas' family to the effect that El Nitri was a revered figure in Triana and Alcalá when Juan's father was a boy, and make doubtful that Nitri took up with La Andonda after El Fillo's death, as is believed (there would be too wide a difference in ages). Also, it must be taken into consideration that Núñez de Prado wrote, in 1895, of El Nitri already being dead.

The new way of thinking was brought about by the claimed discovery of El Nitri's birth and baptism certificates, in Arcos de la Frontera. But as to date no one knows El Nitri's real name, are these certificates really his? I am inclined to doubt it in view of his legend, and also of the fact that all of the old-timers with whom I have talked agree that El Nitri was no longer alive during their childhood (around the period 1890-1900).

1988 Update: The latest theories claim El Nitri was born in Puerto de Santa María, and was nephew of Diego el Fillo.

CURRO PABLAS

(c. 1830-1870)

CURRO PABLAS, the considerably younger brother of Diego el Fillo, also born in Puerto Real (Cádiz), is remembered as an outstanding *cantaor*, particularly of the *siguiriyas*, although not of the caliber of his brother.

Núñez de Prado, in his book published in 1895, tells the brief history of CURRO PABLAS (I shall have to add that Núñez de Prado was a bit of a sensationalist; it is difficult to say how much of his writing was based on fact). It seems that CURRO was a rising figure in the early *café cantante* world, competing not unfavorably with such as Silverio, etc., when he met a woman named Dolores la Bravía (Dolores the Untamed). Dolores was married, but her husband was in prison and she was a little unhinged at the time. After a few weeks of her best resisting, she left off visiting her husband, and ran off with CURRO PABLAS on an artistic tour of Spain. Word somehow sifted through to her husband, and he swore death to the man who had stolen his woman. The day of his release from jail he went searching for them, finally locating them in northern Spain where CURRO was having one artistic success after another. Dolores' husband promptly sent CURRO to the hospital with a slit stomach, and took his wife away. CURRO died a few days later, reputedly singing this final *siguiriyas* to his lost love:

Al cementerio me voy,	*To the graveyard I am destined.*
¡por Dios!, compañera,	*For God's sake, companion,*
no me dejes morir tan solito;	*don't let me die so alone;*
quiero morí a tu vera!	*I wish to die by your side.*

El Fillo sang quite a different version of the tragedy:

Mataste a mi hermano,	*You killed my brother,*
no te he perdoná.	*I cannot pardon you.*
Tú l'has matao liao en su capa,	*You killed him without provoca-*
sin jaserte na.	[tion
	while wrapped in his cape.

The confusion of the contents of these verses comes about because apparently both of El Fillo's brothers died by the blade. Thus the first verse refers to CURRO PABLAS, the second to El Fillo's other brother, Juan Encueros, who reputedly clashed with Silverio, and whose death was the cause for Silverio leaving Spain.

LA ANDONDA
(c. 1830 - 1890)

Núñez de Prado tells us that LA ANDONDA, an outstanding *cantaora* of *soleares* from Utrera (some believe from Triana), was a woman of extreme excesses; too extravagant, too proud, too violent... he wrote that, apparently unbalanced, she was often obsessed with the desire to knife fight, and was consequently feared by men and women alike. To attempt to calm these feelings she would saturate herself with liquor, and it was then that she would wail her fabulous *soleares,* often vehicles of abuse for whoever happened to be on her bad side at that moment:

Mala puñalá le den	*May they fatally knife*
a tó el que diera motivo,	*every man who gives cause;*
que me duelen las entrañas	*my insides hurt*
de jacerlo bien contigo.	*from being too good to you.*

(What a warning!)

Para yo volverte a hablar,	*To entice me to speak to you [again*
es menester que te pongas	*you would have to be wearing*
la banda de general.	*a general's ribbons.*

LA ANDONDA even reviled such an illustrious rival as Diego el Fillo, the finest *cantaor* of that period, as can be seen by this *soleá:*

La Andonda le dijo al Fillo:	*La Andonda said to el Fillo:*
Anda vete, gallo ronco,	*go away, hoarse rooster,*
a cantarle a los chiquillos ...	*and sing to children...*

Of course, as LA ANDONDA was el Fillo's blushing bride, this verse could be taken as a bit of matrimonial horseplay.

EL LOCO MATEO

(c. 1832-1890)

To date, when talking of Jerez de la Frontera, we have talked mostly of *siguiriyeros*. The *soleares* is also a strong *cante* in Jerez, in no small part due to the influence of EL LOCO MATEO, considered the greatest *cantaor* of the *soleares de Jerez* that Jerez has known. However, he was certainly not a one-*cante* specialist. He is thought to have been *the* creator of the *cante por bulerías* (this has not been confirmed). Some of his creations *por siguiriyas* are still sung. All that he sang — the *cantes* of the smithies, *por tangos* — was said to have been superb.

EL LOCO MATEO (Crazy Mathew) underwent periods of insanity, and apparently felt his *cante* with all of the sensitivity and crushing emotion of the insane. He often broke down and wept when singing a particularly sad verse, or became enraged with a cruel verse. Regardless of this, or perhaps in part due to this (1), he was considered one of the finest singers of what has been termed the "Golden Age of Flamenco". However, he led a sad existance. He knew that he was insane, and in his *soleares* he would search for the reason. Generally he heaped the blame on a former love, and would abuse her with this famous *soleá*:

Aunque en capilla te vea,	Even if I saw you in a chapel
no he de darte una limosna;	I wouldn't give you alms;
que lo que has hecho conmigo	I hope a dog devours you
anda y que un perro te coma.	because of what you have done
	[to me!

EL LOCO MATEO was born in Ronda, and lived some years in Triana before moving permanently to Jerez. It is probable, therefore, that he also knew the *cantes de Triana*. He had a sister,

---

(1) It is curious to note that genius in flamenco often goes hand in hand with eccentricity and even insanity. A few of the eccentric: Tomás el Nitri, Manuel Torre, Manolo de Huelva... of the insane: el Loco Mateo, Macandé, Rafael el Aguila...

called LA LOCA MATEO (although she was mentally healthy), who was also an excellent singer. Upon dying, EL LOCO MATEO left three excellent disciples: el Chato de Jerez, el Carito, and his sister.

ENRIQUE EL MELLIZO

1988 Update: (1848-1906)

During this same period still another ancient city contributed an historic figure to the already impressive list of *cantaores*, highlighted by Silverio, from Sevilla, and Tomás el Nitri and el Loco Mateo, from Jerez. This city was Cádiz, and the *cantaor* the fabulous gypsy, ENRIQUE JIMÉNEZ "EL MELLIZO", one of the most prolific creators in flamenco's history.

ENRIQUE took the rich *cantes* of Cádiz and improved upon them, added new ones of his own, and molded and developed the mass to such a point that the town of Cádiz and its immediate surrounding area has a complete school of *cante* within itself. His *siguiriyas, soleares* (1), *alegrías, bulerías, mirabrás, tangos* (2), etc., became accepted and widely sung throughout Andalusia, as is still the case today. His *malagueñas,* in my opinion, carry a far greater impact, in an earthy, flamenco way, than any other style of that *cante*. (The story is still told, in fact, of the time that Manuel Torre became so carried away with ENRIQUE's rendition of a *malagueñas* that he took an enthusiastic bite from a glass from which he was sipping, cutting his lips and mouth badly).

EL MELLIZO drew upon multiple sources for his inspirations. Touches of the Gregorian Chant can be found in his *soleares* and *malagueñas;* verses were spontaneously created over the loss of a loved one, or marking the end of a love affair; anything might have drawn from him some unforgettable creation. This creative

---

(1) According to A. Mairena - R Molina, previous to Enrique el Mellizo and another *cantaor*, Paquirri el Guanté ,there were no typical *soleares de Cádiz*. They claim that these *cantaores* created their own styles of this *cante*, based on the *soleares de Alcalá* and those of Mercedes la Sarneta.

(2) A. Mairena and R. Molina credit Enrique el Mellizo with ennobling and sublimating the more ancient *tangos* into the *cante por tientos*. They go on to say that Manuel Torre learned the *tientos* from Enrique, and in turn passed them on to the Niña de los Peines, who still sings them today in their original manner.

ability, based on an unfailing musical instinct, *duende* and *compás*, combined with an outstanding voice and singing style, has made EL MELLIZO a revered name in the world of flamenco. So much so, in fact, that in the opinion of Aurelio Sellé and other *aficionados*, ENRIQUE EL MELLIZO has been the greatest all-round *cantaor* of the last one hundred years. I would qualify this to say the greatest *cantaor* of the *cantes* of Cádiz: to this everyone will agree.

Manuel Torre and his younger brother Pepe (now seventy-seven) both turned to ENRIQUE for the source of much of their *cante* (as did Antonio Chacón and many others). Pepe tells of visiting EL MELLIZO in Cádiz just after the turn of the century, shortly before ENRIQUE's death. Pepe was just a boy, and was along with Manuel for the adventure. They sang and drank, enchanged *cantes* and styles, drank and sang. Soon the word got around, and friends packed into ENRIQUE's small house. "Then the *señoritos* arrived with juicy offers of *juergas,* and were flatly refused. The gypsies were too busy enjoying themselves to be bothered with money and such. If a *señorito* was particularly insistent, and was perhaps a good *aficionado* and provider in more needy times, ENRIQUE would suddenly feign sickness, doubling up in a corner, moaning, groaning, in a manner that would do justice to any stage. No one believed him, but they could not help but laugh at his originality."

ENRIQUE EL MELLIZO died in 1903, but his *cante* is as alive now as it was then. His two sons, Enrique Jiménez Hermosilla "Morsilla" and Antonio el Mellizo, both of whom were non-professionals but excellent *cantaores,* can be given part of the credit. Manuel Torre and Tomás Pavón were also admirers and interpreters of ENRIQUE's *cante,* and did a great deal to popularize it throughout the flamenco world. Presently Aurelio Sellé is the outstanding exponent of ENRIQUE's *cante de Cádiz.*

JUAN BREVA

1988 Update: (1844-1918)

Just about the time that the *cante gitano,* including the *cante grande,* was beginning to enjoy some popularity among the general public, a singer appeared from the province of Málaga with a *cante* he called the *malagueñas*. This singer, a non-gypsy named ANTONIO ORTEGA "JUAN BREVA", was destined to carry his *malagueñas* to unheard-of heights of popularity and, in the process, revolutionize to the core the popular concept of flamenco. Finally a non-gypsy had come forth singing a worthy non-gypsy *cante*, and the *andaluces*, and non-gypsies in general, rallied round their first hero (Silverio did not fit the role as well, for his *cante* was basically gypsy). JUAN BREVA, partially blind much of his life, was put upon a pedestal and acclaimed with such enthusiastic devotion that he must have been left bewildered and breathless.

Born in Vélez-Málaga of humble parentage, JUAN came to be known as the "king of the *malagueñas*", and had the honor of being the *cantaor* most in demand during the height of the *café cantante* period (1870-1895) which, incidentally, was also the height of the *malagueñas* period. At one time BREVA performed in Madrid in three places simultaneously (1884); the *Teatro Príncipe Alfonso*, and the *cafés cantantes* Barquillo and Imparcial, earning twenty-five pesetas in gold at each place, plus his lodging, a fortune at that time. But his greatest honor was in being the only flamenco singer in history to sing before the King and Queen in the Palacio Real (Royal Palace), in Madrid.

Initiated by JUAN, the *malagueñas* swept the country, and soon there were more specialists in *malagueñas* than in any other *cante*, or group of *cantes*. The singers of *cante grande*, and *cante gitano* in general, were shouldered into the background and, eventually, out of jobs, and the *malagueñas* became the popular conception of *cante grande* (at one time there were over thirty distinct styles of *malagueñas*, and even today there remain twenty-some).

It is now clear that the over-popularization of the *malagueñas* was a big step toward the decline of the *cante grande*, regardless of the fact that the *malagueñas* in itself is a beautiful *cante*. The old-time *cantaores* saw the *malagueñeros* getting the preferred jobs and earning far more money, and many of them did the obvious: they began singing *malagueñas* or, far worse, altering the *cante grande* so that it would appeal more to the popular public. As is understandable, once they had been exposed to popular acclaim and good wages, many of the traditional *cante grande* singers were no longer satisfied to return to the old life, to sing merely for pleasure and recognition within a limited, closed group. They saw the *cafés cantantes,* and later the theaters, as an escape from poverty, and purity of expression and integrity did not stand a chance (luckily, there were exceptions).

Thus, the degeneration of flamenco began with its popularization, as has been true of all folk arts. The *cafés cantantes* were the initiating culprits, the *malagueñas* and afterwards the *fandangos* and all the rest, up to and including today's *rumba,* inevitable contributing factors.

The reader might ask: "What of today's *cafés cantantes?* Won't the same thing happen?" In a way, it *is* happening, but today the circumstances are quite different from what they were one hundred years ago. The fight today is to keep flamenco from complete extinction, for all of the factors that generate a need for folk expression — the poverty, caste system, oppression (1) — are rapidly disappearing in Spain, and with them much of the folk medium of expression. Were it not for the tourists who are flocking to Spain from their sterile countries desperately in need of a good chunk of earthy tradition, flamenco would most certainly be gone in a matter of four or five decades. But that will not happen now, because where there is tourist money there will be flamenco. The quality is questionable, but even the worst of the *tablaos* springing up around the world indirectly furthers the cause by generating interest in the potential purist, who will eventually encourage and support the remaining pure artists.

But back to Juan Breva. Juan sang a form of *malagueñas* extremely similar to today's *verdiales.* He also created a *fandango,* still remembered by his name, sang well the *soleares para bailar,* and played a fine accompanying guitar. He is remembered as a good, simple man and, judging by his verses, mostly his own creations, quite a philosopher. Two of his *malagueñas:*

---

(1) «The cruel fact is, had there been no Negro slavery, there would have been no jazz.» («A Pictorical History of Jazz», by Orrin Keepnews and Bill Grauer, Jr.).

Ni la fuente más risueña ni el canario más sonoro, ni la tórtola en su breña, cantarán como yo lloro gotas de sangre por ella...	Neither the most bubbling [fountain nor the most harmonious canary nor the turtledove in the brush sing like I weep tears of blood for her...
Cuatro sabios se encontraban en la agonía de un rey; los cuatro se horrorizaban, porque al mandar Dios la ley dinero y ciencia se acaban.	Four wise men found them- [selves before the death-agony of a king; the four were horrified because money and science could not combat God's law.

JUAN BREVA made fortunes in his day, and spent every cent. When his voice faded in old age, he returned to Málaga and was quickly forgotten. Fernando de Triana, who considered JUAN the purest singer of *malagueñas* of all times, wrote that he died in such poverty that he had to sing up to the last hour to earn money for his funeral.

García Lorca dedicated the following verses to JUAN BREVA, a part of his *Poema del Cante Jondo:*

JUAN BREVA

Juan Breva had
the body of a giant
and the voice of a little girl.
There was no trill like his.

He was sorrow
singing
behind a smile.

He evokes the lemon groves
of slumbering Málaga,
and there is in his lament
traces of sea salt.

*Like Homer he sang
blind. His voice contained
something of the sea without light
and an orange pressed dry.*

PACO LA LUZ

(c. 1835 - 1900)

Among the group of outstanding non-professional *cantaores* of this period was PACO LA LUZ (Paco the Light), a Jerez de la Frontera field-foreman of farm laborers who left the indelible stamp of his personality and creativeness on the *cante gitano*. PACO was an outstanding gypsy singer of *siguiriyas*, creating new styles and *machos* within this preferred *cante*. He is also remembered for his *soleares*, and the *cantes chicos por alegrías, bulerías, caracoles,* and *mirabrás*.

PACO produced an artistic family of great merit: la Serrana, who faithfully maintained the *cante* of her father and went on to sing superbly all of the *cantes de Jerez;* and the famed dancer, la Sordita (see dance section).

PACO left behind an impressive group of disciples, including la Serrana, Juan el de Alonso, José de Paula, Salvaoriyo de Jerez, and Diego Antúnez, from Cádiz. Thus his *cante* has been well conserved, and is still widely sung today.

MERCEDES LA SARNETA

1988 Update: (c. 1837-1912)

MERCEDES LA SARNETA (also written "Serneta") is eloquently described by many *aficionados* and flamencologists as the greatest *cantaora* of *soleares* that flamenco has known. Fernando el de Triana reverently says: "Her voice was of an incomparable sweetness; between the chills produced by the *duende* of her *cantes*, and her lovely virgin face, nothing more was needed except perhaps a complimentary *oloroso* wine of Jerez or the classic *manzanilla* of Sanlúcar." The reference to her "virgin face" was not just by chance; Núñez de Prado also wrote of her as being an extremely spiritual woman, and in his book produced the following two verses, creations of LA SARNETA, which he claims were inspired by her one and only seduction:

Me acuerdo de cuando puse	*I remember when I placed*
sobre tu cara la mía,	*my face upon yours,*
y suspirando te dije:	*and sighing I whispered:*
serrano, ya estoy perdía...	*serrano, I am lost...*

Later, after her lover had deserted her:

Me acuesto sobre la cama;	*I lie upon my bed;*
a mi corazón, de ducas,	*laden with grief, the wings*
se le cayeron las alas.	*of my heart have fallen.*

Her deeply religious nature is also obvious in her following well-known creations, both *soleares*, as were the previous two:

Dije yo que me echaría	*I swore that I would wear*
hábito de San Antonio	*the habit of San Antonio*
si este hombre me quería.	*if this man would only love me.*
Delante del crucifijo	*I knelt down*
de rodillas me jinqué;	*before the crucifix;*
y a gusto la voy llevando	*I would gladly carry it*
por no dejá tu queré.	*if it would assure me of your [love (1).*

LA SARNETA, thought to have been born and raised in either Jerez or Cádiz, lived most of her life in that most flamenco of towns, Utrera, which is where her *cante* is best conserved through the superb *cante* of la Fernanda de Utrera. She also lived a few years in Madrid, in her later days, giving guitar lessons to the aristocracy. Her death, in Utrera in 1910, provoked deep mourn-

---

(1) These verses perhaps need a little explanation. It is common in Spain among the lower classes to commit oneself to wear the habit of one's favorite saint for a period of time, in hopes that the saint will help solve some problem. This means wearing a dress, or robe, of a particular color, usually with a cord tied around the waist, for six months, a year, or sometimes much longer. The second verse probably takes place in a church before the beginning of a Holy Week procession.

ing from the entire flamenco world, and inspired the following verses from her life-long admirer, Fernando el de Triana:

Cuando murió la Sarneta	When la Sarneta died
la escuela quedó serrá	her school was lost
porque se llevó la llave	because she took with her
del cante por soleá.	the secret of the soleá.

VARIOUS

Other outstanding singers, all gypsies, of this period, deserving of much more comment than I can give them due to lack of data and space include: DIEGO EL LEBRIJANO, from the village of Lebrija (Sevilla), is remembered for his fine creations within the *cante por deblas*, and his following statement: "The day that I sing with *duende* no one can equal me"; TOBALO, from Ronda, is remembered for his creation "*el polo de Tobalo*", one of several *polos* formerly sung; JUANELO, from Jerez, was said by Fernando el de Triana to have been flamenco's outstanding creator and interpreter of the *cantes tonás* and *livianas*. Machado Alvarez claimed that Juanelo sang twenty-six different types of *tonás* (only five or six remain today); EL VIEJO DE LA ISLA (the Old One of the Isle), from San Fernando, is remembered for his creations within the *siguiriyas*, and for his fine interpretations of the *cantes de Cádiz*; FRANCISCO LA PERLA (Frank the Pearl), from Cádiz, was creator of a style of *siguiriyas* still sung today; PAQUIRRI EL GUANTÉ, a co-molder of the *soleares de Cádiz* (together with Enrique el Mellizo), was also a fine dancer and guitarist who rarely left his native Cádiz. Unlike the *soleares* of his contemporary, Enrique el Mellizo, Paquirri's *soleares* did not attain great popularity outside of Cádiz, and have remained largely within the confines of that city; JUAN JUNQUERA and JUAN EL DE ALONSO, from Jerez, were outstanding interpreters of, and creators within, the *siguiriyas*, as were PERICO FRASCOLA, LOS MEZCLE, including FERNANDO ORTEGA "EL MEZCLE", cited by Javier Molina as one of the great singers of his day, and EL CIEGO DE LA PEÑA (the Blind One of the Boulder), from Sanlúcar de Barrameda, and DIEGO ANTÚNEZ and

Andrés el Loro (Andrew the Parrot), from Cádiz; Tío José el Granaíno (also called "el de Sanlúcar"), from Sanlúcar, by profession a *picador de toros*, is thought to have been the creator of both the *caracoles* and the *mirabrás*, or at least to have strongly influenced their development; Romero el Tito is considered by many to have been the creator of the *cante por romeras*. He sang, largely in accompaniment of the *baile*, during the *café cantante* period; María la Jaca (Mary the Pony), from Jerez, was an outstanding interpreter of the *siguiriyas*; Frasco el Colorao, a Triana-born gypsy contemporary of the Caganchos, has been one of the great creators within the *siguiriyas*. His *siguiriyas* were less primitive (more ornamental) than those of the Caganchos. Frasco is believed to have also had a hand in the development of other *cantes de Triana*; Enrique Ortega was an outstanding interpreter of the *cantes de Cádiz*, as well as those of his good friend, Silverio Franconetti. It was said to have been Enrique, in fact, who helped Silverio skip the country, from the port of Cádiz, when the police were breathing hotly down Silverio's neck. Enrique was one of a long line of famous flamenco artists and bullfighters of the Ortega family (see biography of Manolo Caracol and Ortega family chart); relatives of Manolo Caracol crop up with confusing regularity, and Curro Dulce (Sweet Frankie) is no exception — he was Caracol's great-grandfather. Curro, a gypsy from Cádiz, is remembered for his distinctive creations within the *siguiriyas*, some of which are still sung today.

ANTONIA LA LORO

(c. 1840-1900)

Antonia la Loro (Antonia the Parrot), gypsy childhood friend of Mercedes la Sarneta, sang excellent *soleares*, *siguiriyas*, and the *cantes de Cádiz*. Born in Cádiz, she left a job in the local cigarette factory to try her hand at singing, and ended up one of the finer *cantaoras* of the period. Like la Sarneta, she was a spiritual woman, and her *cante* was straightforward and sincere. The following are some of her particularly expressive verses, the first two *soleares*, the last a *siguiriyas*:

Cuando te encuentro en la calle,	When I meet you in the street
hasta el vello se me eriza,	I become all goose-flesh,
y no paro de mirarte	and I cannot stop gazing after
hasta perderte de vista.	[you
	until you disappear from view.
Cuando te encuentro en la es-	When I meet you on a corner
me miras con esos ojos [*quina,*	you look at me with those eyes
y los huesos me lastimas.	until my bones ache.
Cuando tengo yo pena	When I am sad
me voy a llorá	I go to weep
a la capilla donde esta la Virgen	at the altar of the
de la Soleá.	Virgin of Loneliness.

PACO EL GANDUL

(c. 1840-1905)

Francisco Hidalgo was an imaginative *cantaor* who, for some reason, shed names as he changed localities. Thus, he was known in Madrid as PACO EL GANDUL (Frank the Vagabond), in Málaga as Paco Botas (Paco Boots), and in Sevilla as Paco el Sevillano.

PACO EL GANDUL is remembered principally for his renditions of the *caracoles,* which he infected with a bounce and gaiety formerly lacking (the creator of the *caracoles,* tío José el Granaíno, sang them in a slower, more serious vein), which has remained their basic characteristic today.

PACO was a man of extreme outward dignity, but with an inward lightness of heart and passion for practical jokes that made him a favorite of the *café cantante* circuit. Although most renowned for his *caracoles,* PACO was a fine interpreter of a wide range of *cantes.*

LOS CAGANCHOS

(c. 1845-1915)

ANTONIO, MANUEL, and JOAQUÍN CAGANCHO, relatives of Diego el Fillo and heirs to his *cante,* were Triana-born gypsy *cantaores* of great merit. Although they lived during the height of the *café cantante* period, none of these proud gypsies ever deigned to sing commercially. Legends even during their lifetimes, all were blacksmiths brought up in the family forge; thus the *cantes* of the forges, the *siguiriyas*, and the other *cantes* of Triana were second nature to them, and it is not surprising that they ranked among that period's outstanding interpreters of these *cantes*. All of them specialized in the *siguiriyas*, MANUEL standing out in particular. His *siguiriyas*, original creations, have been described as "primitively sober, difficult, and completely without ornamentation."

ANTONIO and JOAQUÍN, both popularly known as "*tío*" (uncle), and MANUEL, spent their entire lifetimes in Sevilla; it took quite some talking, in fact, just to get them to leave Triana for a few hours. Their hoarse, rough *siguiriyas* were often the cause of fits of frenzy among their gypsy friends, during which moments they would tear at their clothing, roll back their eyes, and, shouting their approval uncontrollably, smash their wine glasses against the walls. As this demonstrates, there is no audience more approving (or, for that matter, disapproving), than gypsies. These moments of wild approval were all of the payment that LOS CAGANCHOS ever received for their art, and all, apparently, that they desired.

A favorite *siguiriya* of *tío* ANTONIO:

Como jases conmigo	If you do this
esta villanía,	villainy to me
así lo hagan contigo los moros	may the Moors of the Morería
de la Morería.	do the same to you.

The Moors are known in Spain as extremely cruel people. To call upon them is a great threat.

A favorite *siguiriya* of MANUEL:

Ar Señó de la Ensinia	I fast every Friday
le ayuno los viernes	for the Señor of the Ensinia
por que me ponga al pare e mi [*arma*	so that he permit me a glimpse of the father of my soul.
aonde yo le viere.	

Fernando de Triana writes that, after the *siguiriyas* of the
CAGANCHOS, the guitar, if any, would be silent, and a small, nearly
black gypsy named Juan Pelao would warm up for his fabulous
martinetes...

JUAN PELAO

(c. 1845-1910)

JUAN PELAO was a copper-skinned gypsy from Triana (Sevilla) who has very possibly been flamenco's greatest singer of *martinetes*. At least, such is his reputation. He lived during the golden epoch of Silverio, but with a very marked difference in nature: JUAN PELAO, together with a group of *cantaores* which included the Caganchos, refused their art to all but certain gypsy intimates. No amount of money could convince them to sing outside of their little circle, which used to congregate in the backroom of a little Triana grocery-store bar called the *Casa Rufina*.

When these gatherings took place the word spread, and many of Sevilla's *aficionados* would gather outside of the room and listen to what they could. On one such occasion, a well-known general (Sánchez Mira), a well-versed and favored *aficionado*, was among the gathering outside of the *juerga* room. When JUAN PELAO had finished singing a particularly excellent *martinete*, the general excitedly asked a member of the party who momentarily left the *juerga* room if he would ask JUAN PELAO to repeat that *martinete* as a personal favor to him.

This request invoked a discussion among the *cantaores*, who finally decided affirmatively, due to the fact that the general was a good *aficionado* and personal friend. JUAN sang the *martinete* again, which, according to Fernando el de Triana, was as follows:

Esgraciaíto aquer que come	The poor fellow
er pan por manita ajena:	who lives off others:
siempre mirando a la cara	always studying their faces
si la ponen mala o güena.	to detect the warmth of their
	[welcome.

The enthusiasm of the general and of the other listeners was over-whelming (understandably — what a wise *copla!*), and they immediately tried to present a large gift of money to JUAN PELAO. He, of course, refused. Later, the general, determined that such singing should be rewarded, sent a messenger around to JUAN's dwelling with one hundred pesetas and a note saying: "A gift from General Sánchez Mira to the proclaimed king of the *martinetes*". Again JUAN was about to refuse the gift, when a note of urgent good sense crept into the situation. JUAN's wife pleaded in a low voice:

"Take it, Juan Pelao, we don't even have food for the table."

JUAN swallowed his fierce price and accepted the present.

JUAN PELAO died as penniless as he had lived, but with the great personal satisfaction of having been "the king of the *martinetes*" during a period when that was a true accomplishment. JUAN was not limited to the *martinetes*, however ;there also existed a *"tonás de Juan Pelao"*, now forgotten, and creations within other *cantes*, including the *siguiriyas*.

EL CUERVO

(c. 1845-1910)

Although Juan Pelao never sang commercially, as we have seen, his *cante* did reach the *cafés cantantes* through his contemporary and disciple, EL CUERVO (the Raven), who had great success singing the *martinetes* of el Pelao, and the other *cantes* of Triana. At the height of his artistic success EL CUERVO's powerful voice ran dry, and he lived out the rest of his life in poverty .Judging by one of his *martinetes*, as follows, EL CUERVO had difficulties along other lines as well:

Mis ojitos te han de ver
en la Inquisición;
has de venir de rodillas
a pedirme perdón...

My eyes will see you
in the Inquisition;
you will have to come on bend-
                                              [ed knee
to ask me forgiveness.

SALVAORIYO DE JEREZ

(c. 1845-1915)

SALVAORIYO EL DE JEREZ, also written Salvaorillo, had the double distinction of being the favorite disciple of Silverio, and among the most favored of Paco la Luz. This brands him as one of the great *cantaores* of his period.

SALVAORIYO, a non-gypsy, carried on the schools of *cante* of both Silverio and Paco la Luz, being especially adept, as were they, at the *siguiriyas*. According to Núñez de Prado, SALVAORIYO was a "man with an internal tempest, who poured out his soul in song." R. Molina-A. Mairena list him as one of the greatest interpreters of *siguiriyas* remembered.

A *siguiriya* attributed to SALVAORIYO:

Abrase la tierra,	*May the earth form a grave,*
que no quiero vivir;	*as I do not desire to live;*
para vivir como yo estoy viviendo	*rather than live like I am living*
mejor quiero morir.	*I prefer to die.*

DOLORES LA PARRALA

(c. 1845-1915)

During this epoch the *cante flamenco* reaches still another landmark in the person of DOLORES LA PARRALA, said to have been one of the outstanding *cantaoras* in flamenco's history. It will immediately jump to the reader's mind: on a par with the Niña de los Peines? The only clue in answering this question was given by Fernando de Triana, who had the opportunity to perform with both of them. He claims that the Niña de los Peines was the only *cantaora* during his lifetime who could interpret the *cantes* of LA PARRALA with equal brilliance.

Fernando de Triana went on to tell us that LA PARRALA was the most complete *cantaora* that flamenco had seen up to her time. A disciple of Silverio, she was an excellent interpreter of all of the difficult *cantes grandes* in their various styles, as well as the *intermedios* and *chicos*. She was also apparently an imaginative creator, giving all of her *cantes* her distinctive touch . The base of her *cante* was that of Silverio; she interpreted well even the most difficult of the *maestro's cantes*.

Núñez de Prado tells us something of her life. She was a beautiful woman, and dominated the men in her life as she dominated her art. She was, in fact, quite playful, skipping from one love to another, running through one man's bankroll and grasping for another's. She periodically retired from her artistic career to gallop through the fortunes of the man that became her husband; he went bankrupt three times, and each time would lose her to a lover, or lovers, until he managed to recoup his wealth. Finally, it was three times and out for the poor fellow: when his resources became permanently depleted he saw no more of LA PARRALA.

Born in Moguer (Huelva), LA PARRALA returned to the city of Huelva to live after her final retirement. She was the *maestra* of another *cantaor* of admirable qualities, Antonio Silva el Portugués, who carried her *cantes*, and those of Silverio, well into the twentieth century. DOLORES also had a sister, Trinidad la Parrala, an admirable and well-known *cantaora* who performed for years in the *café cantante* circuit, often at the side of her famous sister.

The *soleares* was a preferred *cante* of DOLORES LA PARRALA, such as the following:

Como pajarillo triste	My heart
de rama en rama saltando,	is like a sad bird
así está mi corazón	jumping from branch to branch
el día en que no te hallo.	the day that I don't see you.

Fernando de Triana wrote of LA PARRALA's last *cante*, a *siguiriyas* sung on her deathbed. It was a last goodbye to Fernando, her old friend, admirer ,and companion, who sat with her during her last moments. Although gasping for breath, LA PARRALA still managed to sing this verse:

De estos malos ratitos	For these bad moments
que yo estoy pasando,	that I am passing
tiene la culpa mi compañerito,	my companion is at fault,
por quererlo tanto.	because I love him so.

LA PARRALA thought in terms of flamenco *coplas* up to her last breath; even a compliment to a friend had to be put into song.

She is very much alive, however, in the following García Lorca poem, entitled *Café Cantante,* which appears in his *Poema del Cante Jondo:*

> *Crystal lamps*
> *and green mirrors.*
> *Upon the dark platform*
> *la Parrala sustains*
> *a conversation*
> *with death.*
> *She calls,*
> *death does not come,*
> *and she calls again.*
> *The people*
> *choke back their sobs.*
> *In the green mirrors*
> *long trains of silk*
> *move.*

ANILLA LA DE RONDA

(c. 1850-1920)

ANILLA, from Ronda as her name indicates, gained fame with her *soleares* and the *cantes de Málaga.* Núñez de Prado writes that she was an unhappy woman, married to a man who did not return her love, and who spent most of his time pursuing other adventures. This, of course, was usual in Spain; the unusual was the man true to his wife. As a matter of fact, men were expected to act in this manner, following their animal instincts, and were considered "sissies" of a sort if they did not play the game. Paradoxically, the very wife who was benefiting from the good behavior of a rare husband inwardly and perhaps unknowingly condemned the poor man for his lack of Don Juan-like qualtities. To this day, although the Spanish male is losing his iron grip, it is common to hear women boast of their husbands' prowess with other women. But, emotions being what they are, these same boastful women are deeply hurt, victims of a system initiated by the Moors. (For those emancipated women who are thinking what *they* would do under these circumstances: no, retaliation was unthinkable in nearly all cases. Both moral and civil law forbade the woman to step out; if caught, she could be legally murdered by her husband, even though he was involved in the same kind of mischief. The basic philosophy in all of this, of course, is that man needs variety, while woman needs and desires only one man)

The above apparently irrelevant discussion is not merely gossip, or to fill in space (certainly not one of my problems in this book), but a key to the meaning of many of the verses in the book, especially those of the feminine artists. The following two *soleares* verses of ANILLA LA DE RONDA are good examples:

Yo no siento que te vayas;	I am not sorry that you are [leaving;
lo que siento es que te llevas	what I regret is that you are
la sangre de mis venas.	[taking with you the blood from my [veins

Estoy viviendo en el mundo	I am living in the world
con la esperanza perdía;	devoid of hope;
no es menester que me entierren,	it won't be necessary to bury me
porque estoy enterrá en vía...	for I am buried alive.

LA FANDITA
(c. 1850-1920)

Like Anilla la de Ronda, LA FANDITA was another suffering woman, the victim of a brutal husband — at least, according to Núñez de Prado. From Cádiz, LA FANDITA was famous for her *soleares*, two of which follow:

¡Por Dios! no me pegues más,	For the love of God, don't hit [me anymore!
porque yo me voy contigo	I'll go with you
donde me quieras llevar.	wherever you want to take me.

¡Por Dios! llévame a una huerta	Por Dios! take me to the country
y dame unos paseítos,	for some fresh air,
que me estoy cayendo muerta.	for I feel all washed out.

MACACA
(c. 1850 - 1915)

MIGUEL CRUZ "MACACA" is revered as one of flamenco's great all-round *cantaores*. He had extraordinary execution and control of his voice, and a profound knowledge of a wide range of *cantes*. Fernando de Triana states that in addition to his solo singing he was one of the finest *cantaores* for the dance.

From Sevilla, MACACA was largely influenced in his *cante* by Silverio, due to having performed for a number of years in the Café Silverio.

We have talked of Los Puertos (The Ports). The term refers to the port towns of Puerto Santa María and Puerto Real, which lie between Jerez de la Frontera and Cádiz, from whose colorful streets have emerged many outstanding flamencos. Let us discuss three of them now, all of whose life spans lie in the second half of the nineteenth century and spill into the beginning of the present.

MANOLILLO CARRERA

MANOLILLO CARRERA was a little-traveled *cantaor* whose fame emanated out of Puerto Santa María and brought many visitors to hear his *cante*. His best *cante* was the *soleá corta*, two of which are as follows:

Dijiste que me querías;
tú estás haciendo conmigo
un papel de burlería.

You told me that you loved me;
what you are doing
is pulling my leg!

Por coger la zarzamora
una espina me he clavao
que hasta el corazón me llora.

Because of grasping a bramble-
[berry
I was jabbed by a thorn
until even my heart cries.

The brambleberry, as the reader no doubt realizes, is a symbolic manner of speaking of MANOLILLO's love, perhaps the very one who ended up pulling his leg.

ROMERILLO

ROMERILLO created a distinctive style of *soleares* still remembered today. As he was from Puerto Santa María, his *soleares* are based on the *soleares* of *Los Puertos*. The following verses are of the *soleá grande*, as opposed to the *soleá corta* sung by Manolillo Carrera.

Aunque pescao te vuelvas
y te tires a la mar,
en la piedra más profunda
te tengo que ir a buscar.

Although you become a fish
and throw yourself into the sea,
I shall search for you
in the most profound depths.

Nadie diga que es locura
esto que yo estoy haciendo,
si es para darme a mí gusto;
y ese es el caudal que tengo.

No one can say that it is crazi-
[ness
the way I am carrying on,
if I do it for my pleasure;
it is my only wealth.

CHAQUETON

CHAQUETÓN, another *cantaor* from Puerto Santa María, is remembered for his excellent *soleares* and *siguiriyas*, both in the style of Los Puertos.

One of the adventures of his life is told in the following *soleares coplas*. CHAQUETÓN's courtship with his *novia* was frustrated by the opposition of both of their mothers, most likely because he was a gypsy, she not. First he is driven from his house, and even then has to see his *novia* secretly, her headkerchief being the OK sign. Note the use of the gypsy words *bata* (*madre*-mother) and *quer* (*casa*-house), possibly indicating that CHAQUETÓN did not know Spanish as well as the gypsy language, *caló*, in much more common usage then than now.

Por causa de tu queré
he reñío con mi bata
y no pueo entrá en mi quer.

Because of your love
I have fought with my mother
and cannot enter my own house.

De ná le sirve a tu bata
el ponerte guardia e noche;
que el pañuelo e tu cabeza
me sirve de pasaporte.

It will do your mother no good
to guard you closely at night;
the handkerchief on your head
serves as my passport.

ANTONIA LA DE SAN ROQUE

(c. 1850-1910)

I have only run across two famous flamenco artists, both singers, from the picturesque little town of San Roque, perched on a hill overlooking La Línea, Gibraltar, the Mediterranean, and Africa. One is today's Jarrito Montoya; the other is ANTONIA LA DE SAN ROQUE, a *cantaora* famous for her *soleares*. She was a tempestuous woman; Núñez de Prado hints strongly at her having been a lesbian. Love, in one form or another, did seem to take up a good deal of her time and thoughts, judging by her following *soleares* verses:

Anda diciendo tu mare	Your mother goes about saying
que tú eres mejor que yo;	that you're better than I;
anda, ve y dile a tu mare	go ask your mother
que en qué sueño lo soñó.	when she dreamed that up?
Hasta el corazón me duele	I've done everything in my
de brindarte con la paz,	[power
y vienes pidiendo guerra;	to keep peace between us,
¿cuándo está la guerra armá?	and now you come looking for
	[war;
	OK, when do we start?

DIEGO EL MARRURRO

(c. 1850-1920)

DIEGO EL MARRURRO is another revered figure in Jerez de la Frontera's long, illustrious list of exceptional *cantaores*. He was an imaginative creator within the *siguiriyas*, his styles of which are still widely sung by top *cantaores*. Only by top *cantaores*, I should add, as EL MARRURRO's *cante* is tortuous; certainly one of the more difficult styles of the *siguiriyas*.

EL MARRURRO also sang well the other *cantes de Jerez*, as well as diverse *cantes* from other regions. Interpretations of his *siguiriyas* have been recorded by Antonio Mairena and Manolo Caracol, and are also sung excellently today by Juan Talegas.

EL CHATO DE JEREZ
(c. 1850-1905)

SEBASTIÁN "EL CHATO DE JEREZ", the favorite disciple of El Loco Mateo and a formidable rival of Silverio, was one of the most popular of the outstanding *cantaores* of the *café cantante* period. With a great *afillá* voice, EL CHATO dominated the Jerez *cante grande* — the *soleares* and *siguiriyas* of El Loco Mateo, the *siguiriyas* of Diego el Fillo, Manuel Molina, Tomás el Nitri — and an infinity of other *cantes*. Núñez de Prado risked the following rating: second only to Silverio, on an equal footing with Tomás el Nitri in his interpretations of the *siguiriyas*.

Núñez de Prado went on to write that EL CHATO was a simple, tender, generous man, free from all pretentiousness even at the height of his fame. Unless, of course, people tried to heel him under. This he would not tolerate, as is demonstrated by an anecdote told by Fernando el de Triana. It seems that EL CHATO, together with a number of his friends, entered a *café cantante* in which he had formerly worked, and which was now under the management of an artist, Trinidad, who had performed with him in the *cuadro* during his last stand there. Although outwardly friends, EL CHATO had always been billed over La Trini, and undoubtedly Trini's feelings of friendship were tempered by artistic envy. At any rate, when the crowd recognized EL CHATO in the audience, they clamorously called for him to sing. Trini, playing the queen, called over a waiter and haughtily told him, in a loud voice, to relay a message to EL CHATO:

"Tell EL CHATO that *doña* (1) Trini says for him to go up and sing."

EL CHATO, who had heard the message, as had everyone else in the room, waited until the waiter repeated it to him, upon which he replied in an equally loud voice:

"Tell *doña* Trini that *don* CHATO just doesn't goddamn well feel like singing!"

---

(1) Until recently «*don*» and «*doña*» were titles reserved only for the upper classes; rough equivalents in English were «sir» and «lady». Presently the terms are much more commonly used, although they still denote respect due to birth and position.

Needless to say, CHATO's answer brought the house down, and La Trini retired to her office in embarrassed confusion.

The following is a *soleá corta* made famous by EL CHATO:

Yo no quiero a nadie;	*I don't desire anyone;*
con tus ojos, serrana mía,	*just with your eyes,* serrana mía,
tengo yo bastante.	*I have enough.*

Upon losing his faculties, EL CHATO suffered the usual fate of the old-time *cantaor:* poverty. He spent his last days isolated in a sanitorium, finally dying of tuberculosis.

EL CARITO
(c. 1850-1910)

EL CARITO was another disciple of El Loco Mateo and Manuel Molina to reach great heights of fame. He was a life-long friend and competitor of El Chato, although, unlike El Chato, CARITO had a high-pitched voice that flowed like honey — certainly not too flamenco, especially for those more raucous times, but very commercial. CARITO was an immediate success in the *cafés cantantes*.

It must be said that EL CARITO apparently did not go the route of the Golden Voice. Perhaps due to his pure background, or his integrity, he remained true to the traditional *cantes* of Jerez, becoming particularly adept at the *siguiriyas* and the *cante grande* in general.

EL CARITO is considered as one of the finer singers to come out of Jerez de la Frontera.

RITA LA CANTAORA
(c. 1855-1940)

RITA was another famous daughter of Jerez de la Frontera. Described by Núñez de Prado as the "Rabelais of the *Cante*", RITA captured the imagination of the public as much with her scandalous life as with her art. She specialized in the *cantes intermedios* and *chicos*, her interpretations tending to be frivolous and impure. However, the public approved, and RITA lived a life of luxury, finding work wherever she wished in the *café cantante* circuit. But, as the *cafés cantantes* faded, so faded RITA, and she lived out the last years of her long life in the Madrid neighborhood of Carabanchel Alto, in poverty.

Núñez de Prado wrote that RITA spent her life toying with love and life itself; that she was maliciously humorous and gay, sarcastic and cruel, which was reflected in many of her *coplas*:

Una silla en el infierno	*I have arranged a chair for you*
tengo puesta para ti,	*in hell,*
pa que pagues con tu lengua	*so that you will sweat blood for*
lo que has hablao mal de mí...	[all of
	the bad things you have said
	[about me...

During the end of her career, when her beauty and voice began to fade, her verses became more mellow:

Quisiera por ocasiones	*Sometimes I would like*
estar loca y no sentir,	*to be crazy and not feel,*
que el ser loco quita penas,	*for being crazy takes away grief,*
penas que no tienen fin.	*grief that has no solution.*

DIEGO BERMUDEZ "EL TENAZAS"
1988 Update: (1850-1933)

DIEGO BERMÚDEZ "EL TENAZAS" (the Pliers) was vaulted from obscurity to fame in a 1922 flamenco contest, and then contentedly settled back to die.

Born in Morón de la Frontera in 1854, DIEGO BERMÚDEZ lived the first sixty-eight years of his life a virtual unknown in the world of flamenco. Raised on the *cante* of Silverio and Diego el Fillo, he brought with him to the 1922 Granada contest the most pure *cante* imaginable, virtually unremembered by all but the most knowledgeable *aficionados*. In this way he was able to completely overshadow the other participants, and walk off with first place honors, which included first prizes in the *siguiriyas*, *soleares*, and *cañas*. No small feat considering that the man had no advance reputation, and was no longer in the prime of his *cante*.

Eduardo Molina Fajardo, in his book *"Manuel de Falla y el Cante Jondo"*, tells how EL TENAZAS, then sixty-eight years old, walked for three days, from Puente Genil to Granada, to participate in the contest. No one there had heard him sing, and no one attached much importance to the little, impassive man under the tilted *cordobés* hat.

The day before the contest several of the judges and organizers were gathered at a Granadinan *café*, including Antonio Chacón, Manuel Torre, la Niña de los Peines, Manuel de Falla, the painter Zuloaga, etc. They were taking turns singing, with EL TENAZAS looking on stonily. Finally, after Chacón had sung a particularly fine *malagueñas*, EL TENAZAS opened up. He sang, and sang, and the expressions of the group changed from polite surprise to amazement to acceptance into their select group. Falla expressed all of their feelings by simply stating: "This man is an arsenal of pure *cante*." And this, despite the fact that EL TENAZAS had retired from singing thirty years earlier after having a lung punctured in a knife fight. His voice, high and clear, was not even particularly flamenco. But EL TENAZAS knew the old-time *cantes*, and was extremely flamenco and true in his interpretations. According to Ricardo Molina, in fact, EL TENAZAS was the last of the great singers of the *cañas*, which was one of the favorite *cantes* of Silverio (recordings exist of EL TENAZAS' *cañas*, but they are difficult to come by).

During the contest itself, EL TENAZAS captured the hearts and tears of the *aficionados*, especially of the old-timers who understood the treasures that he was unveiling. Molina Fajardo writes that EL TENAZAS began by singing the two following *siguiriyas*:

Mundito engañoso,	*Deceitful world,*
las güertas que da,	*with the turns you give,*
que los pasitos que yo doy p'a-	*each step I take forward*
[*lante*	*seems to take me backwards.*
se me van p'atrás.	
Como sé que contigo	*As I know*
no me he de lográ,	*that you'll never be mine,*
por eso mis penas nunca van a	*my sorrow never lessens*
[*menos,*	*but always grows.*
siempre van a más.	

Behind the platform an old gypsy woman was weeping. Next to her La Macarrona called out her warm approval. EL TENAZAS continued singing, and when he finished, above the ovations could be heard the shouts of the stirred *aficionados:* "*Padre del Cante Jondo*".

In addition to the amateur *aficionados* who competed for the prizes, the professionals Manuel Torre, la Niña de los Peines, la Macarrona, and others were hired to lend the contest more appeal and authenticity (the contest was much criticized because of being limited to non-professionals. The professionals said, quite rightly, that there were not enough amateurs with such a profound knowledge of the *cante* as the contest required. The organizers had the romantic notion that the pure *cante* is of the people. Sadly, it is not; generally speaking, it is of the professionals, and only a minority of them).

Three excellent professional guitarists were hired to play for the event: Manolo de Huelva, Ramón Montoya, and José Cuéllar. The judges, presided over by Antonio Chacón, included Amalio Cuenca, eminent flamenco guitarist, and Andrés Segovia, who played flamenco as well as classical at that time. The principal organizers were Manuel de Falla, Federico García Lorca, and Ignacio Zuloaga.

The prizes winners were: EL TENAZAS; Manolo Caracol, then a boy of eleven; Francisco Gálvez "Yerbagüena", a legendary gypsy from Granada; José Soler "Niño de Linares"; Carmen Salinas, of Granada; María Amaya "la Gazpacha", a relative of Carmen Amaya; and two little Granadinas, Concha Sierra and "la Goyita". The prize for the outstanding guitarist of the contest was split between Manolo de Huelva and José Cuéllar.

It was disillusioning to the organizers that the true purpose of the *concurso* failed, at least during their lifetimes. Their grand illusion, particularly that of Manuel de Falla, was to attempt to save the *cante jondo* from extinction. The Granada contest was designed as only the first step. As a followup, they intended to open flamenco schools in Andalusian cities, and hire flamenco's old-timers to instruct the youngsters in the pure *cante*. The *Centro Artístico* of Granada, which was to have played an important part in this plan, at the last minute pulled out, and the whole idea collapsed. De Falla deserted his dream in disgust, and it was not until some thirty years later that the loose ends were somewhat gathered together by the Cordovan author, Ricardo Molina, in the form of *Concursos de Cante Jondo*, three of which have been presented in Córdoba — in 1956, 1959, and 1962.

The flamenco academy idea was likewise not entirely forgotten. In 1960, the flamencologist Juan de la Plata organized a Conservatory of Flamenco in Jerez de la Frontera, and in August of 1963 Juan and the Conservatory presented a "First International Course of *Arte Flamenco*" (1). Málaga followed suit in October of the same year with a week-long program of flamenco discussions and demonstrations (1), organized by the *Peña Juan Breva*. So the movement, still in its delicate growing stages, is definitely gaining momentum. So much so, in fact, that it appears that Manuel de Falla's dream may yet come true!

JUANIQUI DE UTRERA
(c. 1860 - 1920)

JUANIQUI DE UTRERA, also called Juaniqui de Lebrija, was born in Lebrija (Sevilla), but lived most of his life in a little hut near Utrera. He is renowned for his *soleares*, which are said by Molina-Mairena to have "echos of the old *soleares de Triana*". A *cantiña* creation of his is also remembered, as are his *bulerías* and *tangos*. JUANIQUI was a simple, *simpático* gypsy, and during his lifetime his hut was open to all who desired to hear his fine *cante*.

JUANIQUI and La Sarneta were the principal molders of what today is considered the Utrera school of *cante*.

RAMON EL OLLERO
(c. 1860-1920)

A Triana-born non-gypsy, RAMÓN EL OLLERO (Raymond the Pot-maker) had a great influence on the *soleares de Triana*. Build-

---

(1) Intended to be annual events.

ing on the ancient Trianan *soleares*, RAMÓN created his own style which enjoyed great popularity, spreading across the river into Sevilla and eventually as far as Córdoba, where they were to become the basis for the *soleares de Córdoba*. R. Molina-A. Mairena write that EL OLLERO's *soleares* lost their gypsy air and authenticity, becoming transformed into an *andaluz* rather than a gypsy style of the *soleares*. Other than EL OLLERO, fine interpreters of these *soleares* included the non-gypsy singers el Cuende, la Gómez, and Fernando de Triana.

Molina-Mairena believe EL OLLERO's *soleares* were transplanted to Córdoba by a *picador* named el Mediaoreja (Half-Ear) around the beginning of this century.

VARIOUS

Around the last quarter of the past century and the first quarter of the present, several outstanding singers left their mark on flamenco, of whom I have only sparse information. They include: MARÍA LA MORENA, a Triana-born gypsy considered one of the most excellent singers of *bulerías* and *soleares* that flamenco has known; JOSÉ IYANDA, born in Linares, raised in Jerez, created his own style of *soleares* which, together with that of Frijones, has become the basis of the *soleares de Jerez;* PIPINI DE UTRERA created his own style of the *cantiñas;* IGNACIO EZPELETA, a gypsy from Cádiz, made original contributions to the *alegrías* and other *cantes de Cádiz* that are now considered classical; EL TIZNAO (the Black, or Smudgy, One), from Cádiz, was an excellent interpreter of the *cantiñas, alegrías,* and other *cantes* of Cádiz, as was EL TUERTO (One-Eye); TÍO JOSÉ DE LA PAULA was a moving interpreter of the *soleares de Jerez;* DOLORES LA DE LA HUERTA was an outstanding singer of *fandangos,* cited by Fernando el de Triana as the top *cantaora* of the *fandangos de Lucena* of her time; RAFAEL RIVAS, a *fandanguero,* rose to fame with his sarcastic and humorous *fandangos de Lucena,* his hometown; TOMÁS EL PAPELISTA (Thomas the Paper-Maker) was a Madrid-born *cantaor* said by Fernando el de Triana to have been an idol of his time; CHICLANITA, a respected *cantaor* from Cádiz, was praised for his vast knowledge of the *cante* by

Rafael Lafuente in his *"Los Gitanos, El Flamenco, y Los Flamencos"*. CHICLANITA died in Cádiz, well in his eighties, in the late 1940's; EL TRONI, from Sanlúcar, was another fine *cantaor* from the province of Cádiz, as was EL CARBONERILLO DE JEREZ.

ANTONIO CHACON
1988 Update: (1869-1929)

ANTONIO CHACÓN has very likely been the most famous singer in flamenco history. In the eyes of many he has been the greatest.

First off, let us qualify the above statement to read: "the greatest *cantaor* of the *cante andaluz*". Now we are closer to the truth, and on the verge of clarifying a muddy way of thinking that predominates in flamenco today. *Aficionados* are prone to state flatly that one or another *cantaor* is the "greatest"; but the fact is that since the entrance of the *cante andaluz* into the realm of flamenco, this distinction has had to be shared. For at least the past one hundred years there have been, simultaneously, a "greatest" singer of the *cante gitano*, and a "greatest" singer of the *cante andaluz*. CHACÓN was no exception to the rule. Although he possessed a vast knowledge of the *cante gitano*, he was far surpassed in its interpretation by not one, but many gypsy *cantaores* during his epoch (1).

ANTONIO CHACÓN was, then, the outstanding *cantaor* of his epoch, and quite possibly of all time, of the *cante andaluz*. As history so clearly shows, in this role CHACÓN unwittingly became the third significant link in flamenco's fall from purity to decadence. We have seen under the section "Juan Breva" that the first link was the very act of exploiting a pure folk art in the *cafés cantantes;* the second link was Juan Breva who, although his *cante*

---

(1) Nor can such complete *cantaores* as today's Niña de los Peines and Antonio Mairena be excepted from this rule. Although they interpret all of flamenco's *cantes* excellently, their *cantes andaluces* are certainly gypsy-oriented. They are outstanding singers of the *cante gitano*, which in their cases *expands to include their gypsy versions of the cantes andaluces*. Only if we consider that the *cante gitano* was the original manifestation of flamenco, and that the *cante andaluz* has only relatively recently become a part of flamenco, can we reason that the outstanding *cantaor* of the *cante gitano* could perhaps be considered the king of the entire realm of the *cante* — if we must concern ourselves with the selection of kings. Only with this in mind can we view Antonio Chacón in the proper perspective.

was pure in itself, first popularized a type of flamenco directed at the likes of the masses; and the third link was ANTONIO CHACÓN, like Breva a purist and great creator within his type of *cante*, but nevertheless a *cantaor* who knowingly appealed to a popular public. Do not misunderstand: CHACÓN never strayed from great purity within his type of *cante*; it is merely that due to his popularization of the *cantes intermedios* and *chicos*, most particularly his *malagueñas, granaínas, media granaína, tarantas, cartageneras, caracoles,* and *mirabrás,* with his high, honied, falsetto voice and melodious, flowing style of singing, the general public turned in disgust from the *cante gitano* and its raucousness and primitive crudity, its gypsyisms and bad grammar, its wailing lament and raw emotion. CHACÓN taught the public a drawing-room brand of flamenco which, even during his lifetime, reached its inevitable climax in the "*ópera flamenca*" period of this century. The public now knew what it wanted, and the youngsters who came up towards the end of CHACÓN's era bent over backwards to give it to them. They did not have nor understand the integrity and purity of CHACÓN within his style, and they truly went to hell. Thus the "*ópera flamenca*" period became the fourth and last link in the chain (see the section *Opera Flamenca*). As Tomás Borrás put it:

> *They don't know how to listen, nor do they understand the*
> *different styles, the secret ritual, the closed religion;*
> *they say that the agonized wails are due to tooth aches,*
> *they make timid jokes, the cold-necked idiots.*
>
> *The epoch has arrived when the* cuadro *is called*
> *"ópera flamenca", and in cement movie houses,*
> *instead of* siguiriyas *and* martinetes, *they sing*
> *la milonga and a furcio, lyrics by the Quinteros'.*
>
> *They ask Chacón: "Do you know fandanguillos?"*
> *"That* cante *is for young gentlemen"— he responds,*
> *full of bitterness. "Variety-show flamencos, the youngsters*
> *that have come up have killed the serious* cante.
> *They don't know how to listen..."*

The irony of it, CHACÓN condemning the very movement for which he laid the groundwork! A student of human nature, he should have known better; it is so obvious that anything designed to appeal to the masses cannot long retain any degree of purity.

ANTONIO CHACÓN was born of non-gypsy parents in Jerez de la Frontera in 1865. Like his father, he was slated to become a shoemaker, but around the age of ten artistic ideas began filling his head. Strictly against the will of his parents he started frequenting the *cafés cantantes* and sneaking into private *juergas*. Before long he was singing, and at the age of fourteen got his first artistic break — Enrique el Mellizo heard him sing, and convinced CHACÓN's father to let him introduce the boy into the Cádiz *café cantante* where Enrique was then featured. CHACÓN began his grand career earning seven pesetas a night.

At the beginning CHACÓN sang the only thing he knew: the *cante gitano*. His flamenco background had been strictly serious. He had learned his *cante* from the great Jerez *maestros* of the *siguiriyas, soleares*, and *cantes* of the forges, and those *cantes* were what he naturally began singing, together with the gypsy *bulerías, tangos*, and so forth. But it soon became clear that he simply was not suited for that type of *cante*, no matter how extensive his knowledge or how hard he tried. His greatest drawback was his voice. It fell flat in the *cante gitano*. However, he soon learned that it *was* ideally suited for the style of *cante* that was making Juan Breva the highest paid flamenco performer of those times. He did the obvious: he reluctantly switched from the *cante gitano* to the *cante andaluz*, and his rapid ascent began. He was soon contracted by the Café Burrero, in Sevilla, and he was on his way to great popularity, fame, and fortune (1).

Due to his upbringing in the very mecca of the *cante gitano*, his subsequent association with the great *maestro* of the *cante de Cádiz*, Enrique el Mellizo, and his lifelong curiosity and love for the *cante*, CHACÓN became one of the most well-versed *cantaores* in flamenco's history. He was a tireless student of the *cante*, and would go far out of his way to listen to, and learn, a rare *cante*,

---

(1) Javier Molina, in his book «*Javier Molina, Jerezano y Tocaor*», talks of early adventures shared with Chacón, when, in their teens, they tramped from village to village, performing in the fairs and the little *cafés cantantes* that dotted with profusion all of Andalusia. This around the years 1880-1885, when flamenco was at its fullest bloom.

many times from *aficionados* in remote villages. In this way, CHACÓN revived many nearly forgotten *cantes*. He often astounded his gypsy contemporaries by his vast knowledge of the *cante gitano* and his great talent for interpreting it to technical perfection. But his true emotion, his *duende*, found release in his adopted *cante intermedio*. He could do as he pleased with his *malagueñas* or his *granaínas*, and often made even the most hard-to-please audience weep with emotion.

CHACÓN's first love, however, always remained the *cante gitano*, and he spent literal fortunes in listening to it in private *juergas*. He would not have had to pay on such occasions, as he was a great friend of all of the flamencos, but his inbred humility and generosity made him feel that they were the truly deserving, those little-recognized *cantaores* of the *cante grande*, and that his money, earned through exploiting a style of *cante* that he did not truly respect, could end up in no better hands. Who were these greats? In CHACÓN's opinion, Manuel Torre was the greatest *cantaor* that the *cante gitano* has known. Other favorites were Tomás and Arturo Pavón, la Niña de los Peines, Enrique el Mellizo and his sons, "Morsilla" and Antonio, Joaquín el de la Paula, el Niño Gloria, Juanito Mojama, Frijones, and others.

Although largely self-educated, CHACÓN became a gentleman *cantaor*. Refined, dignified, with a passive, smiling nature, he was the first *cantaor* to use grammatically correct Spanish in his singing (rather than the low-class, gypsyfied Spanish traditionally used; naturally enough, I might add). He finally achieved such refinement in his *cante* and manner of being that, by universal agreement, he was honored with the name prefix "*don*", used exclusively in those days for the blue-blooded class. It was considered an extreme honor for a person of humble birth to be called by this prefix; his is a unique case in flamenco's history to date.

CHACÓN was a life-long opponent of phonograph recordings. However, shortly before his death he was forced by financial distress to cut several records which, I am constantly assured, have conserved for posterity a quality of *cante* far inferior to that of CHACÓN's prime. They are valuable, however, in that they do show the authentic *cante* of CHACÓN, and his purity of style within his *cante*. The guitar accompaniments, by Perico el del Lunar and

Ramón Montoya (on separate records), are also of great interest.

CHACÓN had many disciples, a few of whom remained true to his tradition. Many more, however, commercialized (commercialize) his *cante* to a much greater degree than CHACÓN had ever dreamed of doing.

ANTONIO CHACÓN died in Madrid in 1929, and was sincerely mourned throughout the entire flamenco world. He died, as the phrase goes, "without even enough money for tobacco". He had spent it all on his beloved *cante*.

1988 Update: The definitive work on Chacón was published in 1986, entitled "Vida y Cante de Don Antonio Chacón", by José Blas Vega.

LOS MALAGUEÑEROS

We have talked of the *malagueñas*, initially popularized by Juan Breva, taken up by Antonio Chacón, developed until there were over twenty-five styles of the same *cante,* and popularized until it became the revolutionary *cante* of flamenco. Hand in hand with the *malagueñas* went its offspring, the *jaberas, tiranas, verdiales, rondeñas,* and the *cantes de Levante* (see section "*Cantes de Levante*"), and specialists in these *cantes* sprang up like spring wheat. Many of these *cantaores,* although some only one-*cante* specialists, achieved great fame and fortune. Let us look in on a few of those remembered basically for their *cantes de Málaga:*[1] la Trini, el Perote, el Canario, la Rubia, and Fosforito.

LA TRINI (1868-1920), from Málaga, is regarded as possibly the greatest female singer of *malagueñas* that flamenco has known. She created her own style, similar to that of Antonio Chacón, with such success that today the *malagueña de la Trini* is one of the most popularly sung.

LA TRINI began her career as a crowd pleaser. She had all of the assets: a beautiful face, an elegant figure, a refined taste in dressing, and a beautiful, flexible, if expressionless voice. What more could be expected, or wanted, of a fifteen-year-old girl? Then LA TRINI suffered a series of misfortunes: declining health; an eye being mistakenly jabbed out by the knife of her lover, Agustín; unhappy love affairs; all of which combined to make LA TRINI a less happy woman, but a far better artist. She had suffered, her suffering shone in her singing, and she became one of the most moving singers of her time.

After one duel with death, a serious operation, LA TRINI created this famous *malagueña:*

No se borra de mi mente	The memory of the fourteenth [of April
el día catorce de abril;	refuses to leave my mind;
y siempre tendré presente	I shall always remember
que en ese día me vi	that on that day I saw myself
a las puertas de la muerte	at the doors of death.

Another famous *malagueña de la Trini,* commemorating some lost love:

Cuando me pongo a pensar	When I begin thinking
lo lejos que estoy de ti,	of how far I am from you,
no me canso de llorar:	I cannot stop weeping:
porque sé que te perdí	because I know that I have
para no verte jamás.	lost you forever.

The village of Alora, in the mountains behind Málaga, has played an important role in the development of the *cante por malagueñas.* Alora has consistently produced outstanding *malagueñeros,* even to this day, two of whom we shall discuss on these pages: JUAN TRUJILLO "EL PEROTE", and his friend and rival, EL CANARIO.

Both of these *cantaores* had high, sweet, falsetto voices, as is so often true of singers of *malagueñas.* This is due in part to the *malagueñas* being basically a non-gypsy *cante,* the non-gypsy voice being generally less coarse than that of the gypsy, and to the fact that the very structure of the *malagueñas,* both emotional and physical, attracts falsetto singers. (The outstanding exception to this is the *malagueña* of Enrique el Mellizo, created by a gypsy and obviously, if one compares, a *cante* better suited for rougher emotions and raucous voices; it is the most flamenco *malagueña* of all in that it is the *malagueña* that most maintains the *jondo,* earthy qualities of the traditional *cante grande*).

EL PEROTE (c. 1865-1910) created a style of *malagueñas* which is still one of the most widely sung today. He also sang many other *cantes* well, above all those of *Levante*, and excelled in singing for dancing.

The poet Máximo Andaluz tells of PEROTE's artistic assault on Sevilla. He arrived from his village, a cocksure young kid of twenty, ready to set the flamenco world back on its heels and outsing Breva and Chacón and La Trini and God, if necessary. Within two days he found work in a lowly *café cantante* in Triana, and immediately began his own publicity campaign. Fully realizing that in the artistic world any manner of attracting attention is valid and valuable, EL PEROTE soon had all of Sevilla talking about the impetuous little brat who sang the following *malagueña:*

Aquí están las del Perote,	And now we have those of Pe-
las que suben al tablao,	[rote,
las mejores malagueñas	those that mount the platform,
que en Sevilla se han cantao!	the best malagueñas
	that have been sung in Sevilla.

It worked. PEROTE made quite a splash in the artistic world, for besides being good Madison Avenue material, his *malagueñas* were truly worthy of consideration.

EL PEROTE married the dancing daughter of the guitarist Antonio Pérez. Both died young, at the peak of their artistic careers.

The name of EL CANARIO (c. 1870-1900), Perote's companion from the village of Alora, is invariably linked with that of LA RUBIA DE MÁLAGA, another famed singer of *malagueñas*. And for good reason, as we shall see.

EL CANARIO (the Canary) went to Sevilla around the age of fourteen to gain fame and fortune with his *malagueñas*. No success. He retired from the scene, rectified his *cante,* and when he again appeared, his success was instantaneous. So much so that EL CANARIO gained many followers and imitators, one of whom was La Rubia de Málaga.

La Rubia was so smitten with EL CANARIO's *cante,* in fact, that it was all she wanted to sing. This was all well and good until her success with EL CANARIO's creations became more than he could bear. He then set about to destroy her artistically. Night after night he turned up at her performances; when she sang something of his, he would call for the attention of the public and sing it properly for them, much to their delight, and would point out her lack of originality and creativity (how many creative artists have felt like doing the same!) He finally worked La Rubia into such a state that she called upon her father to intervene.

La Rubia's father, not being of a passive nature, intervened only once — and EL CANARIO was found dead of knife wounds near the *café* of his greatest achievements, El Burrero, in Sevilla.

Ironically, La Rubia finally did develop her own style of *cante*, but by then it was too late. As a result of her part in the murder of EL CANARIO, she was ostracized by the public, and was finally forced to leave Sevilla. She tried Madrid, but the story had spread throughout Spain, and her public was cold, often jeering and insulting. EL CANARIO had achieved his purpose: her artistic life was destroyed.

FRANCISCO LEMA "FOSFORITO" (c. 1870-1940), from Cádiz (no relation to today's Fosforito), created a difficult style of *malagueñas* that brought him considerable fame at a relatively early age. He soon became so proficient as to become the competitor, and great friend, of Antonio Chacón.

Sevilla's Café del Burrero was the scene, and the *malagueñas* the theme. Late in the evening *aficionados* would flock to El Burrero to hear Chacón and Fosforito. Silverio would finish singing in his *café* and bring his crowd over; other *cafés* would do likewise, and El Burrero would fill to overflowing. The platform would be cleared of all but one guitarist, and Chacón and Fosforito would alternately deliver their lament. Who was better? It was difficult to compare; their styles were quite different, and it is said that the one who sang last usually came out on top (this competition was only in the *malagueñas*; Chacón was far superior as an overall singer).

Fernando el de Triana wrote an anecdote telling of Fosforito's first days in the Café del Burrero, when just a boy of eighteen. Fosforito, extraordinarily tall for a Spaniard, lit a cigarette from one of the gas lights, which were placed well beyond the reach of the normal Spaniard. The *cantaor* Paco el Gandul sat observing him, and finally commented, straight-faced:

"How old are you, boy?"
"Eighteen."
"*¡Ozú!* By the time you're twenty-five you'll be lighting up from the sun!"

Sevilla was a small, provincial town at the time (even more so than now), and this joke was soon known by all, undoubtedly helping to put Fosforito in the limelight for the first time.

Two of the *malagueñas* made famous by Fosforito follow. The first he sang in a relatively simple style *(corta)*, the second as a *malagueña larga (grande)*, of much more difficult execution.

Ar campo me voy a llorá	I am going to the country to [weep
donde no me vea la gente;	where I won't be seen;
porque me hace pasá	you make me suffer
las fatigas de la muerte,	the pangs of death,
y no te pueo orviá...	and I can't get you out of my [mind.

Yo soy como el árbol solo	I am like a solitary tree
que está en medio del camino,	far down the road;
no tengo calor de naide;	I receive warmth from no one.
¡maldito sea mi sino,	Damn my destiny!,
que a sufrir no hay quien me [iguale!	in suffering I am unrivaled...

Fosforito had an inimitable style, and rode the crest of bubbling popularity until his voice began to fade. When that happened the following verse became popular, which pretty well describes Fosforito's fate:

Fosforito ya no canta;	*Fosforito no longer sings,*
Fosforito se apagó.	*he's all burned out.*
Para cantar malagueñas	*To hear* malagueñas
hay que llamar a Chacón.	*it is necessary to call Chacón.*

Fosforito lived out his last years in Madrid, near Los Gabrieles (1), scene of so many former triumphs and good times. The

---

(1) Los Gabrieles is an establishment, located on Madrid's Calle Echegaray, that was at one time the principal *juerga* center of Madrid.

poet Máximo Andaluz movingly describes FOSFORITO's last days, in his "*Romancero del Cante*":

> *Fosforito is a spectre.*
> *He lives in any manner,*
> *if it can be called living*
> *the life that he leads.*
>
> *But whoever wishes to*
> *look him up, can,*
> *in a little store*
> *near Los Gabrieles,*
> *where, his eyesight bad,*
> *he passes the hours thinking,*
> *all wrinkled up in a corner,*
> *of his former pleasures and sorrows,*
> *almost as if he were waiting*
> *to be called to a fiesta* (1).

CANTES DE LEVANTE

Specialists in the *cantes de Levante* (*tarantas, taranto, cartageneras, mineras, murcianas, granaínas, media granaína*) also came into prominence during this period. Many *cantaores* not born in the area known as Levante (provinces of Almería, Murcia, and Granada) made important contributions to these *cantes*. We might especially cite ANTONIO CHACÓN, CAYETANO MURIEL "EL NIÑO DE CABRA", MANUEL CENTENO, EL COJO DE MÁLAGA, MANUEL VALLEJO, EL NIÑO DE ESCACENA, PENA HIJO, and among those living today, LA NIÑA DE LOS PEINES. Perhaps the most deserving of mention of those *cantaores* born in Levante itself were: the singers of *granaínas*, from the province of Granada, FRASQUITO YERBAGÜENA (prize winner in the 1922 Granada contest, said by many to have been the greatest singer of the old-time *granaínas grandes* that that *cante* has known), PAQUILLO "EL DEL GAS" (Frankie, he of the Gas, or, in modern American jargon, "the Gasser"), EL CALABACINO (the

---

(1) An excerpt from «Romance de Fosforito», from the book «Romancero del Cante».

Calabash Bottle), and El Tejeringuero (the Churro-Maker); and those from the province of Almería, specialists in the *tarantas, taranto,* and the *cartageneras.* Of the last group we shall now briefly discuss three: Rojo el Alpargatero, Pepe el Marmolista, and Conchilla la Peñaranda.

Antonio Grau Mora "Rojo el Alpargatero" (Red, the Alpargata-Maker) and Pepe "el Marmolista" (Joe, the Marble-Craftsman) were two outstanding non-professional creators and interpreters of the *cantes de Almería.* They rarely left their province of birth, and it was up to one of their disciples, Conchilla la Peñaranda, to popularize and spread their *cante* into the rest of Andalusia.

Conchilla la Peñaranda "la Cartagenera" was principally a follower of Rojo el Alpargatero. She took the creations of her *maestro* throughout Spain's *cafés cantantes* with great success, and became one of the most popular figures of her epoch.

Flamenco performers, especially females, in those days were badly viewed, and La Peñaranda, being from a "nice" family, had to withstand considerable public outrage upon becoming a professional flamenco artist. In fact, female artists were considered little better than prostitutes (this still holds true to a much lesser extent today, at least in certain conservative circles), as can be seen in the following *cartagenera* that became popular around her home province:

Conchita la Peñaranda,   *Conchita la Peñaranda,*
la que canta en el café,   *she who sings in the café,*
ha perdido la vergüenza   *has lost all shame*
siendo tan mujer de bien.   *having been such a good woman.*

La Peñaranda was a very sensitive woman, and the ups and downs of her life were displayed for all to see through her verses. Such as the following *cartageneras,* created because of the constant deceptions she suffered at the hands of her chosen:

Son las tres de la mañana;   *It's three in the morning;*
¿dónde estará ese muchacho?   *where could that boy be?*
¡Estará bebiendo vino   *He'll be drinking wine*
y luego vendrá borracho!   *and later will come home drunk!*

Acaba, penita, acaba,	Finish, grief, finish,
acaba ya de una vez,	be gone once and for all,
que con el morir acaba	for death defeats
la pena y el padecer.	grief and suffering.

The following is a particularly beautiful *cartagenera* of Rojo el Alpargatero, made famous by LA PEÑARANDA:

Cómo quieres que en las olas	How could you think that in the [waves
no haya perlas a millares,	there are not thousands of pearls,
si en la orilla del mar	when I saw you crying one after- [noon
te vi llorando una tarde.	by the side of the sea?

LA LOBATA AND EL LOLI

LA LOBATA was a famed *cantaora* accomplished in the *cantes soleares, martinetes,* and *siguiriyas,* no less. Her voice was extremely coarse and flamenco.

Her nephew, MANUEL LOBATO "EL LOLI", also concentrated on the *cantes grandes,* especially those of Paco la Luz. In addition, he created a singular *malagueña,* solemn and *jondo,* which is still remembered today as the *malagueña del Loli.*

LA LOBATA and EL LOLI were gypsies of Jerez de la Frontera.

EL PULI

(c. 1867-1930)

EL PULI, a gypsy *cantaor* from Jerez de la Frontera, is remembered more for an incident in his life than his interpretations of the *cantes de Jerez.*

It seems that EL PULI had a sister, who in turn had a lover, who in turn committed a crime. The law moved in. But the sister, calculating that her lover would be fairly useless to her tucked away in prison, and that brothers are expendable, had the last word; she swore witness against her brother, who went to prison.

While in prison EL PULI became attached to the *cante* of the prisoners, the *carceleras* (from *cárcel* — jail), and made the following verse famous:

Me llevaron a la Sala,	They took me to court
me tomaron declaración;	and made me declare;
la pícara de mi hermana	my bitch of a sister
con su lengua me perdió.	with her tongue did me in.

Everyone knew the truth, and before his full sentence was completed EL PULI was set free. His only vengeance was to sing his famous *carcelera* here, there, and everywhere, making his sister's life (we hope) miserable.

EL PULI is listed by R. Molina - A. Mairena as one of the great interpreters of the *siguiriyas*.

FRIJONES
(c. 1870-1930)

ANTONIO VARGAS "FRIJONES", a gypsy *cantaor* from Jerez de la Frontera, was the creator of a grand style of *soleares* which has become the base of the *soleares de Jerez*. Another of his strong *cantes*, the *tangos*, are now known as the *tangos de Jerez*. The name of FRIJONES is one of the more revered in the history of Jerez flamenco.

SOLEA LA DE JUANELO

True to her name, this gypsy *cantaora*, daughter of the great Juanelo de Jerez, was outstanding in her interpretations of the *soleá*. According to Fernando, she was also a great beauty. One of her well-known *soleares* verses is:

Yo se lo pedí a Jesús,	I asked a favor of Jesús,
el que está en Santa María,	he that is in Santa María
que me quite de limosna	that he alleviate the love
el querer que te tenía.	that I felt for you.

LA BILBA

LA BILBÁ was an exceptional *cantaora* of the *cantes de Triana*, specializing in the *soleares*. From Triana, she sang in various *cafés cantantes* during her artistic career.

FERNANDO EL DE TRIANA

(c. 1870-1940)

FERNANDO EL DE TRIANA was a popular *cantaor* during the *café cantante* period, with a pure style of *cante* and a wide repertoire, although his style and voice were better suited for the *cantes intermedios* and *chicos*. He was an ingenious and often spontaneous creator of verses for the *cantes*.

FERNANDO is mostly remembered for his famous book "*Arte y Artistas Flamencos*", an invaluable work without which we would be largely in the dark about many of flamenco's past performers. It is definitely recommended reading for all Spanish-reading flamenco lovers.

Besides his other numerous talents, FERNANDO played a respectable guitar. He died, pretty well fed up with the modern trend of flamenco, in Camas (Sevilla).

MERCEDES LA CHATA DE MADRID

"And here we have a rare case", wrote Fernando el de Triana in 1935, "a family of flamencos from as far off as Madrid." (If Fernando had lived to see today's influx of non-Spaniards into flamenco, he would have had a stroke). This famous family, of which there were five, produced two artists of renown: MERCEDES, and Joaquín el Feo (see dance section).

MERCEDES "LA CHATA DE MADRID", born around the year 1870 in Madrid's neighborhood of Lavapiés, was a rarity in those times. She spoke the *chulo*-style talk of her neighborhood, but sang in perfect *andaluz*. She triumphed in all of Spain, and is remembered as an outstanding figure of that time.

EL PIYAYO

(c. 1872 - 1937)

RAFAEL FLORES NIETO "EL PIYAYO" (Little Rogue) was a *cantaor* from Málaga remembered for his unusual creation, the *tangos de Piyayo*. While serving his military stint in Cuba, around the latter part of the last century, he became strongly influenced by the Cuban *guajiras*, which came to serve as the inspiration for his *tangos*. PIYAYO's *tangos* enjoyed a period of popularity, and even now around Málaga there are singers who sing them with their original flavor — lazier, with more of a Caribbean air, than the gypsy *tangos*.

Two verses, recently repopularized by Antonio Mairena, tell of EL PIYAYO's life:

Adiós patio de la cárcel,	*Goodbye patio of the jail*
rincón de la barbería,	*with your corner barber shop*
que el que no tiene dinero	*where those who have no money*
se afeita con agua fría.	*shave with cold water.*

According to old *aficionados*, the Málaga jail was a familiar scene to EL PIYAYO. He was a wild type of gypsy, and his brushes with the law were not infrequent. Drunkenness and horse thieving seemed to be his major sins.

Estando yo de guardia un día	*While standing guard one day*
en los montes de Ginés,	*in the mountains of Ginés*
me dijo mi Coronel	*my Colonel asked me*
que adonde pertenecía;	*from where I hailed;*
yo le dije Andalucía,	*I replied from the fifth capital*
de la quinta capital,	*of Andalusia,*
donde se rama la sal	*blessed with local color*
de las mujeres bonitas	*and beautiful women*
y de los hombres valientes,	*and the valiant men*
barrio de la Trinidad.	*of the neighborhood of Trinidad*
	(Málaga).

EL PIYAYO's *cante* enjoyed more success during his lifetime than did EL PIYAYO himself. He was a one-*cante* specialist, and a thin, embittered man living in near poverty. Until death made him immortal, in fact, the spectacle of EL PIYAYO singing his *tangos* to his own guitar accompaniment, in the small taverns of Málaga, was largely taken for granted. He was considered as just another flamenco among many.

MANUEL TORRE

(c. 1878-1933)

Who is this MANUEL TORRE, of whom so much has been written? Who, thirty years after his death, crops up in every discussion of the *cante* that takes place? Who is actually still a dominating figure in the *cante grande*?

Beginning calmly and reasonably, I can state without fear of contradiction that TORRE shared with Antonio Chacón top singing honors during their epoch. I shall let the flamencos take it from there:

Fernando el de Triana, when asked who sang better, Chacón or TORRE, replied that Chacón was a better singer, but that TORRE arrived more directly and overwhelmingly to the heart;

Juan Talegas, who had the good fortune of hearing both TORRE and Chacón, preferred the "more primitive *cante* of TORRE, which was often more than one could bear";

Chacón himself, considered the most knowledgeable *cantaor* since Silverio, paid MANUEL TORRE the greatest tribute: "When at his best, MANUEL TORRE is the greatest *cantaor* of the *cante gitano* that I have heard." This from a man who had heard Enrique el Melizo, Silverio, Tomás el Nitri, all of the greats of his long lifetime, and who was himself called '*emperador del cante jondo*';

and, finally, the universal consensus of opinion of the world of flamenco: MANUEL TORRE has been the unrivaled master in the art of expressing agonizing misery and desolation, and likewise in expressing exhilarating, uncontainable gaiety.

The grand guitarist and purist, Diego del Gastor, often talks of the old *juergas*, and excitedly (even after so many years) describes MANUEL TORRE's transformation from a mediocre *cantaor* to the greatest of them all:

"Of course, it was necessary to humour all of Manuel's eccentricities, such as his habit of taking two or three hunting dogs to a *juerga*, and of wiling away the *juerga* hours in idle talk, mostly about his dogs and fighting cocks, while impatient *aficionados* sat squirming in their seats. Or his wandering in the garden observing nature until the wee hours of the morning, and then his possible refusal to sing at all, or to sing badly. And MANUEL could not be pushed. Many were the impatient marquises and counts that MANUEL sent to the devil before storming out of a *fiesta*, enraged because they urged him to sing before he felt ready. Everyone would keep looking for the tell-tale sign of MANUEL's inspiration: his loosening of his collar button — during the elegant times when he wore one, that is. Then he would throw down several water glasses of wine, or a large glass of *cazalla* (strong *aguardiente*), clear his throat, and everyone knew that great things were in store."

Diego himself threw down a water glass of wine, his eyes glowing, and then continued:

"I have seen MANUEL transformed three times, when the veins stood out on his face and he tore at his clothing as if that helped him release his torrent of passion. His face and eyes would become wild and crazy, and his *cante* absolutely unbearable, until one also found himself ripping off his shirt and shouting or weeping uncontrollably...

"As great as some singers are today, no one has been capable of evoking such emotion since MANUEL, and I'm sure not before either."

MANUEL TORRE was born Manuel de Soto Loreto in Jerez de la Frontera in 1878. The name *Torre* (Tower) was given him by his father, also a *cantaor*, due to his unusual height, and soon Manuel was MANUEL TORRE to everyone. Like his family, MANUEL early began working as a field laborer in the sweeping cattle ranches and vineyards of Jerez, and it was in the fields, and after work back in the humble houses of the *barrio* Santiago, where MANUEL began to sing. He drew his *cante* from many sources, but principally from his uncle, Joaquín la Cherna (or Serna), also a field worker and sometimes vendor of a type of fish called "*la cherna*" (jewfish). According to MANUEL's brother, Pepe, Joaquín passed on to MANUEL *cantes* of many of the former greats of Jerez, but primarily of the two *cantaores* he most admired: Diego el Marrurro and Juanelo, as well as Joaquín's own creations, principally within the *siguiriyas*.

MANUEL was very moody as a boy, and early developed a preference for the *cante* that was to make him famous: the *siguiriyas*. However, he was by no means a one-*cante* specialist; he sang beautifully, and always with his special talent for originality, such diverse *cantes* as the *soleares, tonás, martinetes, tangos, tarantas, bulerías, saetas, campanilleros,* and so forth. But it was with the *siguiriyas* that MANUEL was to achieve his greatest moments.

It was early demonstrated that MANUEL had great talent for the *cante*, and the *cante* became his and his family's escape from the low-paid drudgery of the fields. When still in his teens, just about the time that Silverio Franconetti was dying in Sevilla (1893), MANUEL TORRE moved there, with his family, almost as if to take over Silverio's reign.

MANUEL began singing in Sevilla's Novedades, and went on to sing in various *cafés cantantes,* although they did not offer precisely his atmosphere. It was in private *juergas* where MANUEL gained most of his fame and money, both of which were considerable, although he could hang on only to his fame. MANUEL's brother Pepe reminisces that the only period during which MANUEL was truly prosperous was during three years spent in Málaga, when he was kept so busy that he could not spend his money as rapidly as he earned it.

Ricardo Molina and Antonio Mairena state that MANUEL was the first *cantaor* to sing directly from the lungs with what is termed a "*voz natural*". He caused a sensation with his new way of singing, and the *voz natural* and its counterpart, the *voz redonda* (see breakdown in the *cante* introduction), have displaced, to a large extent, the formerly predominant style of *cante gitano* voice, the "*voz afillá*".

Perhaps the greatest thing about MANUEL's *cante* was that it was simply a means of expressing his emotions, nothing more and nothing less. He was not concerned with style, and did not attempt to make his *cante* pretty or more acceptable to more people. I have on record one of his *bulerías* in which a wildness emerges, a devil-may-care disregard for tonal perfection and operatic silliness that makes the gaiety and humor of life come bubbling up from within — such a relief from the over-striving for technical perfection found in so many *cantaores* of past and present. MANUEL seemed to say: 'This is me and this is my *cante*. I'm rough and my *cante* is rough; if you don't like it, go elsewhere'. Then he might add: 'But remember one thing —if you will lower your defenses, rub away a little of your pseudo-civilization, I'll give you a thousand times more emotion, more *duende*, than all of the pretty boys with their golden voices playing patty-cake in the drawing room'. Then, with a twinkle in his eye, he might sing some silly verse which would make you laugh with joy:

Quiero que me compre, por Dios,	*I want you to buy me,*
cómprame, por Dios,	*buy me, for goodness sake,*
una camiseta que, siquiera	*an undershirt that at least*
me tape la barriguita.	*covers my tummy.*

And if you waited around long enough, were patient enough, he would eventually dredge up the dark, weird, uncomfortable emotions with a black *siguiriya*, and then you would know just exactly what he had been talking about.

MANUEL's favorite *cante*, as we have said, was the *siguiriyas*, and among his interminable repertoire of *siguiriyas* was a creation of his that begins with "*Era un día señalaíto de Santiago y Santa Ana*". This verse, that MANUEL sang to an extremely difficult style of *siguiriyas*, has become the most famous *siguiriyas* verse sung today among those who are able to manipulate this difficult style. I bring it up because it has an interesting history.

MANUEL's brother Pepe, now seventy-seven and an excellent *cantaor* in his own right, told me the story in Sevilla the other day over a few *copitas de tinto*. Pepe started out by saying that besides being interesting, the story demonstrates MANUEL's great powers of innovation and spontaneous reaction. The story takes place in Triana, in 1930, at a benefit gathering for the ailing Currito de la Geroma, a guitarist, singer, and dancer of great fame, son of the famous *bailaora*, la Geroma. It is important to remember that it was the eve of the saints' days of *Santiago y Santa Ana.*

"All of Sevilla's flamenco artists and *aficionados* were there, and many had come from neighboring towns, some from as far away as Jerez, Córdoba, Cádiz, even Málaga. MANUEL was there because of his great friendship with Currito, but was not expecting to sing. But as the night wore on, the audience became more and more impatient to hear MANUEL, and finally began stamping their feet and clapping, and would not stop until MANUEL gave his consent. MANUEL hesitated, then, seizing a half bottle of *manzanilla* and downing it in one long gulp, he rose to the challenge (MANUEL rarely sang well when called upon to do so, and always tried to avoid such situations).

"However, this time the wine, atmosphere, and adoring public had its hoped-for-effect, and MANUEL had one of his seizures when he became the world's greatest *cantaor*. He began singing his favorite style of *siguiriyas*, a style that had been traditional in our family, but had been enlarged upon and in the process made much more powerful and difficult by MANUEL. He created the following verse as he sang:

Era un día señalaíto	It was the day of
de Santiago y Santa Ana	Santiago *and* Santa Ana
ay, ay, ayyy…	*ay, ay, ayyy…*
de Santiago y Santa Ana,	of Santiago *and* Santa Ana,
ayyy, ayyy…	*ayyy, ayyy…*
le rogué yo a Dios	I begged God
que aliviara las ducas	that he alleviate the suffering
a la mare mía de mi corazón.	of the mother of my heart.

MANUEL's *cante* caused turmoil. The crowd arose as one person to pay him tribute, and quieted down only after many minutes of standing ovation."

As Pepe told me the story his eyes were aglow, he was reliving the scene, singing bits of MANUEL's *cante,* and he finished by feeling MANUEL's triumph, their triumph, that there would never be another to approach MANUEL!

After MANUEL's initial training in the *cantes de Jerez*, under his uncle Joaquín la Cherna, he went on to sing a wide variety of *cantes*. Besides the *cantes de Jerez*, which always remained his favorites, MANUEL developed a particular predilection for the *cantes de Alcalá* and those of Cádiz. He would often get together with the masters of those schools, Joaquín el de la Paula and Enrique el Mellizo, respectively, and swap *cantes* during long, lively days of *juerga*.

Pepe Torre insistently points out that MANUEL was always original in his *cante*, a natural creator. "Take the example of the *siguiriya* that I learned from an old gypsy in Cádiz", commented Pepe. "When I sang it for MANUEL he fell in love with it, and insisted that I repeat it until he had it absorbed. Then we forgot about it until one night, in Carmona, at the peak of a *juerga*, MANUEL sang this same *siguiriya*, but in an astounding manner, *redoblao* (longer and more difficult), much more beautiful and moving. It was more than one could bear! *¡Que no se podía aguantá!*" (1).

MANUEL was inwardly quite religious, and two of his favorite *cantes* were the *campanilleros* and the *saetas*, flamenco's *cantes* for the devout. Pepe claims that MANUEL first became interested in the *campanilleros* through his friend, Dr. Jesús Centeno de Villaverde, who was the creator of many of the *campanilleros* verses sung by MANUEL. Two of these verses, based on religious history, are as follows:

A la puerta de un rico avariento
llegó Jesucristo y limosna pidió,
al igual que darle la limosna
los perros que había se los achu-
                                      [*chó*
y Dios permitió...
que al momento los perros mu-
                                       [*rieron*
y el rico avariento pobre se
                                       [*queó...*
	At the door of a rich miser
	Jesus Christ asked for charity;
	instead of charity
	the dogs were loosed upon him,
	but God permitted —
	that the dogs drop dead
	and the miser be left poor.

---

(1) In Sevilla this expression, invariably used when talking of Manuel Torre, signifies unqualified approval. In Castilian Spanish it means exactly the opposite.

*Si supieras la entrada que tuvo
el Rey de los Cielos en Jerusalén,
que no quiso coches ni calesas
sino un jumentito que alquilao
[fue.
Y se demostró
que las puertas del cielo divinas
las abre tan sólo la santa hu-
[mildad.*

*If you only knew the entrance
[that the
King of the Heavens made into
[Jerusalem;
he didn't want buggies nor carts
but a little rented donkey.
And he demonstrated
that the divine doors of Heaven
open only for saintly humility.*

The story is still told in Sevilla of the particular Holy Week procession, back in the late 1920's, when MANUEL sang for two hours straight to the *Virgen de la Macarena*, hopelessly snarling up the processions and other traffic to no one's apparent concern. How much more authentic Holy Week must have been then! (Laws have since been passed that the processions must not be held up for more than a few minutes at a time. Certainly a sensible ruling, but truly a shame).

After a long love-affair with La Niña de los Peines, during which MANUEL instructed La Niña in much of her early *cante*, MANUEL married the celebrated *bailaora*, La Gamba (see dance section). They lived in Sevilla, near *La Alameda de Hércules*, and had two children, Juan and Tomás, neither of whom possesses his father's artistic genius for the *cante*, although Tomás is a fine country-style *bailaor*.

During MANUEL's last years his eccentricities, and poverty, grew more pronounced. When he died, at the age of fifty-four, surrounded by his dogs and English cocks, deep mourning swept the flamenco world, and it is poetically said that the following *soleá* hung over Sevilla like a black cloud:

*Cuatro soleares de luto,
cuatro jipíos agoreros...
cuatro siguiriyas negras,
iban formando el cortejo...*

*Four soleares of mourning,
four prophetic cries,
four black siguiriyas
formed the last procession...*

NIÑO DE CABRA

1988 Update: (1860-1948)

CAYETANO MURIEL "EL NIÑO DE CABRA" was the most famous, and preferred, disciple of Antonio Chacón. His voice was very similar to that of Chacón, and he interpreted Chacón's *cantes* beautifully; he considered them too perfectly conceived to be altered in any way. However, outside of Chacón's school, CAYETANO proved to be a creator in his own right. Particularly remembered are his *fandangos de Lucena;* he is considered the greatest *maestro* that that *cante* has had. He also ennobled such *cantes* as the *verdiales* and *jaberas* and, in general, sang excellently all of the various *cantes intermedios.*

From Cabra, a village near Córdoba, CAYETANO greatly disliked commercial singing, and did not, therefore, achieve much popular success.

One of Chacón's *malagueñas* that EL NIÑO DE CABRA interpreted excellently was:

En un hospital la vi,	In a hospital I saw her,
y allí fueron mis quebrantos:	and there was the scene of my
¡quién había de decir	[grief:
que mujer que quise tanto	who could have said
iba a tener tan mal fin!	that the woman I loved so much
	would end up so badly!

EL HERRERO

(c. 1880 - 1945)

FERNANDO SÁNCHEZ "EL HERRERO" (the Blacksmith) was one of the great complete singers of his day. A disciple of Antonio Silva "El Portugués", EL HERRERO was an heir to the *cantes* of Silverio (Silverio - La Parrala - El Portugués - El Herrero). A serious man who preferred the *cante grande*, EL HERRERO did not enjoy commercial success.

NIÑO DE LAS MORAS
1988 Update: (1889-1970)

Eighty-four-year-old Niño de las Moras is, to my knowledge, flamenco's oldest active *cantaor*. When Málaga and Fuengirola began having flamenco contests two years ago El Niño de las Moras, bent with age and toothless, appeared out of the mountains of Málaga. No one took the little old man seriously until he displayed a profound knowledge of the old styles of the *cantes* of Málaga and Levante, to walk effortlessly off with first prizes in all four contests (those of 1962 and 1963 in both Fuengirola and Málaga).

Although El Niño de las Moras' faculties are waning, and he has trouble executing difficult passages, his *cante*, straightforward and unassuming, is still moving and true.

ARTURO PAVON
(c. 1880-1959)

Arturo Pavón, gypsy brother of the Niña de los Peines and Tomás Pavón, was a never-recorded, non-commercial, almost unknown *cantaor*, thought by many intimates to have possessed a knowledge of the *cante* as broad, or broader than that of Tomás and Pastora. However, he was not blessed with the faculties for the outstanding interpretations that he knew how to deliver, and was therefore overshadowed by his sister and brother.

Arturo, a quiet, shy, dignified man, sang only for pleasure. Like his brother, his specialties were the *soleares* and *siguiriyas*.

Arturo was born in Sevilla, and lived his entire life there, just off La Alameda de Hércules. Surviving him are his wife, Eloísa Albéniz, a dancer of past fame and presently a leading dance instructor in Sevilla, and his son, Arturo (see section "Arturo Pavón, hijo").

JOAQUIN EL DE LA PAULA
1988 Update: (1875-1933)

Joaquín el de la Paula (Jonathan, he of the Paula) was the cave-dwelling gypsy largely responsible for the development of the

Alcalá school of *cante,* to the point that today the *soleares de Alcalá* are the most widely-varied and widely-sung *soleares* remaining.

JOAQUÍN cannot be said to have been the sole creator of the *cantes de Alcalá,* consisting basically of very distinctive styles of *soleares* and *bulerías.* These *cantes* have been handed down for generations, JOAQUÍN having inherited them directly from his father, his father from his father, and so forth. JOAQUÍN did, however, make many innovations, mold and solidify the *cantes,* stamping them with a greatness formerly lacking. His creation of verses, many poetic and beautiful, often spontaneous, was never-ending.

JOAQUÍN lived in a cave below the hilltop castle of Alcalá de Guadaira, in the same area where much of his family still lives, including his son, and his cousin, Manolito el de la María, who is presently considered among the greatest remaining interpreters of the *cantes* of JOAQUÍN. Like Manolito, JOAQUÍN sang for pleasure (rarely for money), loved his wine, women, and lazy life. His *cante* was the dominating force in his life; he would burst into song at any time, any occasion could provoke spontaneous, witty verses and a quick little dance.

JOAQUÍN's brother, Agustín Talegas, was also an excellent singer, remembered more for his outstanding *siguiriyas* than his *soleares.* Agustín was the father of today's famous Juan Talegas.

Today Manolito el de la María, Juan Talegas, and Antonio Mairena comprise the nucleus of an abundance of interpreters of the *cante de Alcalá.*

JOAQUÍN died quietly, at the age of sixty-five, in his cave in Alcalá. His death, virtually unnoticed among the general public, for JOAQUÍN never exploited his art, was widely mourned in the flamenco world.

EL NIÑO GLORIA AND LA POMPI

Family groups of artists are common in the flamenco world. Within the family all of the advantages exist: the proper atmosphere, 24-hour-a-day instruction, contacts, and bread (someone is always working). A few such family groups of renown have been:

Diego el Fillo and his two brothers, Curro Pablas and Juan Encueros; Paco la Luz and his daughters, la Serrana and la Sordita; the fabulous Ortega family (see biography of Manolo Caracol), always with at least two or three artists in the limelight; Manuel, Antonio, and Joaquín Cagancho; Manuel, Pepe, and Tomás Torre; la Mejorana and children Pastora Imperio and Víctor Rojas; the Pavón family, which has produced three of the great singers of this century, Arturo, Pastora "la Niña de los Peines", and Tomás; Carmen Amaya and her numerous clan; the family of dancers known as Los Pelaos; and many more. One of the more illustrious of the family groups has been Frijones de Jerez and his niece and nephew, LA POMPI and EL NIÑO GLORIA, respectively, whom we shall now discuss.

It is quite an accomplishment in this competitive flamenco world to be considered the greatest in anything. RAFAEL RAMOS ANTÚNEZ "EL NIÑO GLORIA" (the Glory Child) is one of the chosen few: he is considered as having been the greatest *cantaor* of both the *bulerías* and the *saetas* of this century, if not of all time.

EL NIÑO GLORIA (c. 1887-1937) represented a different concept from the commercialism that surrounds us today, which is creating an atmosphere in which it is difficult to hear *cante* unless the green is produced (city, provincial, and national laws, prohibiting the *cante* almost everywhere, do not help). A flamenco's flamenco, he sang for pleasure, and was, at the drop of a hat, spontaneous, gay, sad, original. His favorite *cantes* were the *bulerías, saetas, martinetes, soleares, siguiriyas, tangos,* and *fandangos,* and his flamenco versions of the Christmas-time *villancicos* are still reverently talked of. He sang with a *voz natural*, relatively highpitched but very masculine, with touches of *rajo*, cutting, exciting, and was particularly gifted with the necessary faculties for the *cante*.

They still tell of EL GLORIA's *Semana Santa* singing, when he would be seized by true fervor and sing to the Virgin with such honesty and intensity, combined with his great talent, that even the milling, skeptical crowds felt their religious fires rekindled. And they tell of his fabulous singing in the Christmas Eve *fiestas,* when his *villancicos* would reverberate from the walls and give the people great warmth inside and make them want to dance and sing. And they tell of his *bulerías,* sung anywhere and at any time, that brought laughter and tears to the eyes, and made the gypsies shout and dance and carry on.

EL GLORIA had a few flings at organized flamenco, one of which was his memorable stint with La Argentinita's *Calles de Cádiz".* He also cut several records, which well demonstrate his electrifying *cante* but which, I am assured, were inferior to his true moments of inspiration.

Born a gypsy in Jerez de la Frontera, EL NIÑO GLORIA has left a profound influence in the flamenco world which can be seen reflected in the *cante* of such singers as Antonio Mairena and Manolo Caracol, two of his most ardent admirers.

EL GLORIA, a longtime sufferer from asthma, died in the Spanish Civil War.

LUISA RAMOS ANTUNEZ "LA POMPI" (the Behind) (c. 1885-1950), gypsy sister of El Niño Gloria, was an oustanding *cantaora* of the *soleares, siguiriyas,* and *bulerías de Jerez,* being particularly famous for her *bulerías* and her *saetas por siguiriyas,* which came to be one of the highlights of the Jerez Holy Week.

LA POMPI worked in various *cafés cantantes,* and spent one period in a touring troupe headed by Caracol I, the father of Manolo Caracol. She is thought to have died in Sevilla around the year 1950.

PEPE TORRE

1988 Update: (1887-1967)

PEPE TORRE, the younger brother of the famous Manuel Torre, is a nearly forgotten remainder of the great days of Sevilla's *Alameda de Hércules,* the liveliest mecca of flamenco during the first fifty years of this century.

Now in his seventy-seventh year, PEPE has a vast knowledge of the *cante* such as is possessed by few living *cantaores.* He has lived with, knows, and sings the *cante* of such singers as Enrique el Mellizo, Diego el Marrurro, Paco la Luz, his brother Manuel, Joaquín el de la Paula, Tomás Pavón, Pastora Pavón, and many more. Yet PEPE is not in fashion. He lives in near poverty just off La Alameda de Hércules, is rarely called for private engagements and, for some reason, is never called upon to judge today's numerous contests of the *cante* (actually, the reason is really no mystery — it is due to PEPE's overly turbulent and forthright character. He recently told me that he would love to go to some of these modern contests and shout to the ignorant young whippersnappers that they have no shame!).

PEPE was born in Jerez de la Frontera in 1887. As a youth he was spared the field work traditional in the family due to accompanying Manuel, nine years his elder, to Sevilla in search of artistic work . Manuel's art was readily accepted, and in Sevilla they stayed. PEPE also was soon singing in various *cafés* and, around the year 1913, began a twenty year association with the company of the *bailaora* Pastora Imperio.

PEPE has always had a lively curiosity about his art. At various times during his youth he made artistic sojourns into the realms of famous *cantaores* in order to hear and study their styles of *cante*. Thus he remembers fondly nearly a month spent with Enrique el Mellizo, in Cádiz, around the turn of the century, and two weeks with Joaquín de la Paula, in Alcalá de Guadaira. But most particularly he cherishes the forty-five-odd years spent in close companionship with his brother Manuel.

Although PEPE would never say nor recognize such a thing, being the younger brother of Manuel certainly had its drawbacks. Instead of being generally accepted on his own merits, PEPE was always referred to as "Manuel's kid brother". Whereas he could have been highly regarded for his own *cante*, he chose to go everywhere with Manuel, and was constantly overshadowed by Manuel's genius (as were all *cantaores*). But PEPE worshipped his older brother, and still, over thirty years after his death, continues to worship him.

One has only to sit down with PEPE and listen to him sing a few *cantes* to realize that he is one of the few left who sings the true *cante antiguo*. Aurelio Sellé states flatly that PEPE is one of the remaining greats, as do many other knowledgeable artists. Of course, PEPE's singing faculties are waning, and his voice often clouds up with wintertime cold and rain. He is at his best in mid-summer, when he loves to talk of the *Cante,* and feel the power of a clear voice at his command. "Singers tend to shout too much these days," he will say. "The best *cante* is sung *a media voz* (with a half voice), but singers avoid this because it is more difficult than shouting. For instance..." And PEPE shouts a *cante,* and then sings it again properly, and if his voice remains clear and he is in command of his *cante,* his eyes glow with triumph and pleasure.

Like his brother Manuel, PEPE has had a life-long *afición* for fighting cocks, and even today makes the principal part of his living from entering them in competitions.

Another member of the family, TOMÁS TORRE, has also been a respected *cantaor* during this century. A nephew of Manuel and Pepe, Tomás rarely performed professionally, although it is said that his *cante* could have earned him a name as one of the greats of this century. Tomás rarely left his place of birth, Jerez de la Frontera, dying there in 1955.

JUAN TALEGAS

1988 Update: (1887-1971)

JUAN TALEGAS is one of the most pure and profound singers living today. His *cante* is classical, steeped in gypsy tradition. When JUAN begins singing the air becomes electrified, and all frivolity ceases as when a preacher begins his sermon. His style is simple and unadorned, his voice natural, coarse, straightforward, powerful, and *jondo.*

JUAN concentrates on a few *cantes,* within each of which he commands an infinity of styles. The *soleares, siguiriyas, tonás* and *martinetes* are his favorites, and he enjoys the *bulerías* as a change-of-pace. JUAN has the knack of interpreting the *cantes* of others in his own style, such as the *soleares* of his uncle, Joaquín el de la Paula, in such a way as to achieve originality while still retaining the traditional content of the *cante.* This lends added excitement and merit to JUAN's *cantes.*

JUAN, son of the non-professional gypsy *cantaor* Agustín Fernández "Talegas", was born in Alcalá de Guadaira, but has lived many years in the neighboring town of Dos Hermanas. He has never sung professionally, and has a mixture of scorn and pity for those who mold their *cante* to the taste of the general public. Instead of turning professional, JUAN has been engaged during most of his life in the honorable gypsy trade of horse and cattle dealing, being what is called a *corredor* (middle man between seller and buyer). When this business declined some years ago with the introduction of tractors on the large estates in Andalusia, JUAN found it necessary to earn more and more of his livelihood from the *cante*. He began to sing in *juergas* and *fiestas*, his fame spread, and commercial offers began coming in. JUAN, however, was too concerned with the traditional and pure in the *cante* to accept these offers, and he has limited himself to *juergas* and a few recordings.

Diego del Gastor tells of the time, some forty years ago, when he first heard JUAN sing. It was at a gathering on the estate of an important bull-breeder, near Morón de la Frontera. Many of the most illustrious artists of the period were there, incuding Manuel Torre, La Niña de los Peines, and Pepe Torre among the *cantaores*, and Diego, and Pepe Naranjo, on the guitars. JUAN was there not as an artist, but as a *corredor de ganado*; although he had a certain fame as a singer at that time, not many of the gathering had heard him sing. At the height of the *fiesta* someone suggested that JUAN sing, and sing he did. JUAN was then in his prime, in full possesion of his faculties, and Diego still marvels at the fabulous *siguiriyas, soleares,* and *martinetes* that left the gathering breathless.

Another anecdote is told of JUAN by the grand old *aficionado*, *don* Antonio de la Puerta Tamayo. It seems that JUAN was once taking a taxi to a flamenco gathering when the taxi was involved in an accident. Outwardly JUAN was nearly as good as new, but as he began carrying on so, moaning in gypsy fashion that his time had come, it was feared that he had suffered serious internal injuries. JUAN was put in bed and a doctor called, which only served to work JUAN up further. Finally a priest was called.

The priest came, and, frightened by JUAN's moans and grave appearance, suggested that JUAN repent before taking the last rites. Misunderstanding beautifully, JUAN bolted upright in bed and exclaimed indignantly:

"I'll repent all right. For the glory of my mother, I'll repent. I repent ever having taken that goddamned taxi, and I swear I'll never set foot in one again!"

Needless to say, JUAN pulled through.

JUAN first gained national fame in the 1959 Córdoba contest of *cante jondo*, in which he won first prizes in the *siguiriyas*, *martinetes* (including the *tonás*), and the *soleares*. Since then he has been called upon to judge various other *concursos de cante*, such as the 1962 Córdoba contest for the Golden Key, won by Antonio Mairena.

JUAN's fame continues to spread as the few bands that he has cut for recording companies are released, and as books are published. Today his singing has been cut back a bit by a recent heart attack, from which he is recovering well. Always optimistic, JUAN figures that he will be around with his invaluable art and colorful personality for some time to come.

Ricardo Molina and Antonio Mairena calculate that JUAN sings styles of *siguiriyas* dating back to Diego el Fillo, which have been passed down to JUAN through Tomás el Nitri and his father, Agustín Talegas. JUAN also interprets the *siguiriyas* styles of such past greats as El Planeta, Diego el Marrurro, Curro Dulce, Paco la Luz, Enrique el Mellizo, Manuel Torre, Francisco la Perla, Manuel Cagancho, Frasco el Colorao, El Loco Mateo, and others, and *soleares* of Joaquín el de la Paula, Frijones, Enrique el Mellizo, La Sarneta, and others. He is also credited with knowing more styles of *tonás* than any other living *cantaor*. Clearly JUAN should be contracted to make an anthology before it is too late!

AURELIO SELLE

1988 Update: (1887-1974)

We have talked of the creative genius of Enrique el Mellizo, and of the *gaditano* school of *cante* ("*gaditano*" meaning "of

Cádiz"), of which Enrique was the principal developer and contributor. Who today is left to carry on this school, consisting of a rich mixture of *siguiriyas, soleares, tangos, tientos, bulerías, alegrías, mirabrás, romeras, cantiñas, and malagueñas?* There are the excellent *cantaores* Pericón de Cádiz, Manolo Vargas, and a few others, but today's recognized *maestro* of the *cantes de Cádiz* is Aurelio Sellé.

Aurelio's life has been *andaluza* to the core. His first love was bullfighting; he was a *novillero* during the early Joselito-Belmonte era when his career was interrupted by a stint in the military service. While in the service Aurelio found himself singing more and more, and showed such promise by the time he was discharged that he decided to dedicate himself to the *cante* rather than return to the bull ring. During his subsequent rise to his present position as one of today's great *cantaores* Aurelio often regretted leaving his first love, for which his *afición* has never dimmed. Even today, at the age of seventy-seven, he is one of the presiding officials of the Cádiz bull ring.

Flamenco *aficionados* have ample cause to celebrate his decision, however, as Aurelio's knowledge of the *cante*, and his manner of interpreting it, is a treasure to be closely guarded. His style of singing emphasizes calm emotion, but with an underlying turbulence that might at any moment surge to the surface. His cardinal quality is, perhaps, subtlety. His quiet suggestiveness makes us understand more clearly that which many other *cantaores* wish to force upon us. His voice, classifiable as *redonda*, suggests antiquity and authority, which adds to the spell.

Aurelio, born of non-gypsy parents in Cádiz, was a personal disciple of Enrique el Mellizo, whom he considers the greatest *cantaor* of the past one-hundred years. Aurelio interprets a multitude of Enrique's *cantes* faithfully as to what he considers the emotional and aesthetic content, although he has made many innovations, adapting the *cantes* to his personality and physical faculties. This is not only forgivable but encouraged, for each human being must manifest his individuality in his art, within the limitations, in the case of flamenco, of a certain structure.

Aurelio has always maintained a non-professional status in his chosen art, limiting his activity almost entirely to *juergas* and *fiestas*. Netiher his *cante* nor his personality could tolerate commercialism.

Today, with age creeping upon him, his voice and faculties waning, AURELIO has settled back to nearly full retirement in his native Cádiz. He has just completed collaboration on a book dealing with his life, and the flamenco and flamencos of Cádiz (see book section). He also acts once or twice a year as a judge at contests of the *cante*. Presently freshly recorded records of AURELIO are being released, as well as some bands on certain anthologies. These are excellent, although his old records, cut during his prime, are a far better indication of his great *cante*.

The following verses are my translations of excerpts from a poem dedicated to AURELIO by the *andaluz* poet, José María Pemán:

> *The voice of Aurelio blossoms forth*
> *when a guitar cites him*
> por soleares.
> *Without silk*
> *or ornamentation,*
> *clean, serene, his mouth imbued*
> *with honey and sea salt,*
> *he fights* por naturales
> *the bull of suffering.*
> ... ...
> *And he sings in jest*
> *how Cádiz makes sport of authority,*
> *and even mocks, singing,*
> *the sadness that he feels:*
> *with a* tris, *and a* tris, *and a* tras,
> *you are the foolish innocent* (1),
> *and you, gentleman, know the rest!*
> ... ...
> *And this is Aurelio's* cante... *everything is there!*
> *Feeling and dreaming, thinking and laughing.*
> *The entire* cante... *And what a way*
> *of saying that there is nothing more to be said!*

---

(1) From a famous *tango* verse, which can also be sung *por tientos*.

PEPE NUÑEZ DE LA MATRONA
1988 Update: (1887-1980)

The year 1887 seems a banner year for flamenco. We have discussed three great artists who were born that year, Juan Talegas, Aurelio Sellé, and Pepe Torre, all dedicated to the maintenance and furtherance of the pure *cante*. To that illustrious threesome can be added another seventy-seven-year-old who has also dedicated his life to the *cante puro*, PEPE NÚÑEZ DE LA MATRONA (Pepe Núñez "he of the midwife", so called because his mother was a midwife).

PEPE, a Sevilla-born non-gypsy, began singing at the age of twelve, "if you can call that singing", to quote PEPE. He continued: "At that age one can know a few *cantes*, but to actually know how to sing them, to understand what one is singing, only comes with maturity."

Precisely because PEPE was not a gypsy, he had to overcome obstacles in his early artistic career unknown to gypsy aspirants. As was true of nearly all Andalusian families at that time, PEPE's family was strongly opposed to his becoming a flamenco artist, and PEPE had to sneak about to *juergas*, gatherings, wherever he could hear the *cante*. At the age of fourteen he got his first opportunity in a small *café cantante* in Villamartín, a little village on the Sevilla-Ronda road, and was exhilarated at his first earnings: four and one-half pesetas a night. With that as a start, PEPE spent several years working the small *cafés* and *juergas* in Sevilla, Córdoba, and Madrid, until finally, in 1908, he moved permanently to Madrid.

PEPE's long residence in Madrid has caused him much unjust criticism, much as Carmen Amaya's long stays in America were widely criticized. Unknowing or biased critics, always on the lookout for something, anything, to criticize, say that PEPE sings "*a la madrileña*", that he has "lost contact with Andalusia, which is reflected in his *cante*", and other such vague barbs (1). These

---
(1) Many critics err in considering a general truth to be all-inclusive. If many of the flamenco artists who spend long periods outside of Andalusia become lost in foreign influences and commercialism, they reason that this is the case with all of them. Carmen Amaya has proven the fallibility of this line of reasoning. She spent most of her artistic life outside of Spain, and critics, hurt because she had deserted her *Patria*, wrote wildly that her dancing had become contaminated, that she danced «*a la americana*», and so forth (as is to be expected, her worst critics did not see her dance outside of Spain). How they had to eat their words when she returned, in 1962, to film «*La Historia de los Tarantos*» in which she danced magnificently, perhaps better than ever.

statements have no basis in truth. PEPE is a professional *cantaor* and goes where his *cante* takes him. He has been all over the world, spending periods in Paris, London, New York. Regardless of where he went, however, PEPE retained his pure core of *cante*. As a matter of fact, he has sat back and watched many lesser *cantaores* bastardize their art and rise to fame and fortune, while his great worth was known only among the initiated. He refused to go the route.

PEPE is a complete *cantaor*, specializing in the *cantes grandes*. He greatly prefers the *cante antiguo*, and he seems antiquity personified when he sings. His manner of delivery is unique in flamenco; he flamenco-izes his pronunciation to the point of exaggeration which, instead of detracting, adds a certain favorable quality to his *cante*. His vocal inflections are slow, deliberate, pronounced, his *redonda* voice powerful and penetrating. Certainly there is no doubt as to the identity of the singer when PEPE sings.

PEPE prefers such *cantes* as the *siguiriyas, tonás* and *martinetes, serranas, livianas* and other *cantes grandes,* and also sings well such *cantes* as the *tientos, peteneras,* and so forth. R. Molina - A. Mairena point out his particular brilliance in the *serranas,* of which he is probably today's outstanding interpreter.

As was true of all pure *cante grande* singers, life for PEPE was difficult until flamenco's resurrection in the early 1950's, when he was "discovered" and recorded in the famous anthology organized by Perico el del Lunar. Since that time his fame has spread both in and out of Spain, and PEPE at last finds his stubborn insistence upon the *cante puro* somewhat rewarded — more so spiritually than economically, however, for *cantaores puros* never get rich, and usually have difficulty just making ends meet.

PEPE presently resides in the *barrio de Lavapiés,* in Madrid. Ever energetic, and with a true missionary's dedication, PEPE is awaiting the possible materialization of a tour of the world's cultural centers as a member of a lecture-demonstration team. Subject? The *cante puro,* of course.

JOSE CEPERO
(c. 1888-1960)

José Cepero was one of the finer *cantaores* of this century. From Jerez de la Frontera, Cepero composed all of the verses that he sang, earning himself a reputation as the "Poet of the *Cante*". Like most *cantaores* from Jerez, Cepero concentrated on the *siguiriyas*, *soleares*, and *bulerías*, although he is also remembered for his excellent *fandangos viejos* and other *cantes*. His voice was classifiable as *redonda*.

Cepero moved into the Madrid professional flamenco world in 1921, and remained there most of his life. In 1928 he won the gold cup in a flamenco contest in the *Teatro de la Zarzuela*.

One of Cepero's original *soleares* verses:

A Dios le pío salú	*I ask God for health,*
y la poquita que tengo	*but the little I have*
me la estás quitando tú.	*you are driving from me.*

NIÑO DE LAS MARIANAS
(c. 1889-1963)

Luis López Benítez "Niño de las Marianas", born in Sevilla of non-gyspy parents, is called by some the creator, by others the resuscitator, of the *cante por marianas*. In the opinion of most, however, including that of his son, El Niño de las Marianas revived a more ancient, nearly forgotten Andalusian country *cante*, and remodeled it in the structure of the *tientos* (the *marianas* is also called *"los tientos de las marianas"*). At any rate, he enjoyed a period of great popularity with his *marianas*, and is considered the finest interpreter of that *cante* to date.

Other than the *cante* that made him famous and from which he derived his nickname, El Niño de las Marianas specialized in the *cantes* of Antonio Chacón, for which his voice and singing style were ideally suited.

El Niño de las Marianas last sang in public in 1954 although he had faded from the limelight long before, when the *marianas* lost popularity. He was the father of the guitarist Luis Maravilla, and cousin of the famed Niño de Cabra. He lived the latter part of his life in Madrid.

The *cante por marianas* has again become a rarity, although it can still be coaxed from a few old-timers. Bernardo el de los Lobitos has recorded an excellent *marianas* in the Hispavox anthologies which, according to Luis Maravilla, is faithful to that of his father.

PASTORA PAVON "LA NIÑA DE LOS PEINES"

1988 Update: (1890-1969)

Do words exist to describe the superlative cante of PASTORA PAVÓN "LA NIÑA DE LOS PEINES"? I am afraid not. However much is said will be understatement. With that clear, let us give it a try.

PASTORA PAVÓN has reigned supreme in the world of feminine *cante* for over half a century. That is certain. And it is highly probable that she would have been the supreme figure in any epoch, regardless of the competition .

PASTORA has an exhaustive knowledge of the *cante*, all, absolutely all of which she sings beautifully. Pick out any *cante*, from the most difficult *cante grande* to the most frivolous *cante chico*, and she will weave a web of *cante* that cannot fail to move and astound. Her talent for originality is unsurpassed today, resulting in her versions of the *cantes* being widely imitated by *cantaores* and *cantaoras* alike, but never successfully; like Carmen Amaya in the dance, or Manuel Torre in the masculine *cante*, the art of PASTORA is inimitable. Nevertheless, a reasonable facsimile of PASTORA's *cante* will be projected with reverence into many succeeding generations by her host of disciples and admirers.

In view of the above, the reader will naturally think that the NIÑA DE LOS PEINES has been a much-lauded personality in Spain, particularly among the general flamenco public. Negative. Like so many geniuses of the arts, PASTORA has been generally ignored and neglected outside of the relatively small circle of truly knowledgeable *juerga aficionados*. She has never approached the general popularity of Pepe Marchena or Juanito Valderrama, for instance, which is understandable enough — PASTORA has simply refused, probably would not even know how, to prostitute her art.

PASTORA PAVÓN was born of gypsy parents in Sevilla, and has there maintained her residence throughout her lifetime. She made her artistic debut shortly after the turn of the century, causing an immediate sensation with her *"tientos de los peines"*, from which *cante* it is said she derived her nickname, "Niña de los Peines". (These *tientos*, as well as much of the rest of PASTORA's early *cante*, she reputedly learned from her youthful lover, Manuel Torre).

As at that time flamenco had not yet gone completely under, PASTORA enjoyed some years of success with her gypsy *siguiriyas, bulerías, tangos,* etc., until the *"ópera flamenca"* movement became firmly entrenched. Then life became more difficult, and PASTORA's *cante* became largely relegated to its traditional habitat of *fiestas* and small gatherings.

García Lorca told an anecdote of PASTORA which took place when she was still playing the *café cantante* circuit. One night, at a *café* in Cádiz, PASTORA did not particularly feel like singing. She felt, like all flamenco artists do at times, that no one out there would understand; why invest the effort if it is to go unappreciated? She was consequently toying with her *cantes* in a cold, flashy display of technique and knowledge, feeling quite smug and apart from it all, when a low voice cut in at the end of one of her *cantes:*

"*Viva París...*" (Long live Paris).

The effect was instantaneous. PASTORA snapped out of her reverie, her eyes flashed fire. What a challenge! She stormily threw down an impressive portion of a bottle of *aguardiente,* and her voice, overflowing with *rajo* and *duende,* enveloped the audience in a gypsy sermon that only the highpriestess of the *cante* was capable of delivering. (It is said that afterwards the author of the remark and PASTORA got quite high together celebrating the event).

Which are PASTORA's outstanding *cantes?* All of them. It is difficult to single out particular ones, although I can cite those that have perhaps brought her the most fame. Her *siguiriyas* and *saetas* are greatly renowned, as are her *bulerías, tangos, tientos,* and *peteneras.* Within the *cantes intermedios,* perhaps her most famous *cantes* are her interpretations of the *tarantas* and *malagueñas*. Particularly lauded are her interpretations, all fixed with her stamp of originality, of the *siguiriyas, bulerías, tangos* and *peteneras,* of which she is the undisputed queen. Complete in the ultimate sense of the word, PASTORA's genius extends even to the least sung and least known of the *cantes,* which is demonstrated by her superb interpretations of the *bamberas, marianas* and *farrucas,* among others.

PASTORA has been compared to Dolores la Parrala, which is not unreasonable. Both were the outstanding and most complete *cantaoras* of their time, and both led lively love-lives. Fernando el de Triana claims in his book that only the NIÑA DE LOS PEINES, of all of the *cantaoras* that he had listened to during his long lifetime, was capable of properly interpreting the difficult *cantes* of La Parrala. It is supposed that La Parrala, having been a non-gypsy, and having been the disciple of another non-gypsy, Silverio Franconetti, sang with a less gypsy style than PASTORA. We do not know.

PASTORA's voice, during her youth clear, mellow, and manly (*voz redonda*), turned more harsh as she grew older, until in her last records it is almost raspy, disagreeable to the general public but with a certain added charm for *aficionados.* Jazz fans will note a remarkable similarity between PASTORA and such early blues singers as Ma Rainey or Bessie Smith, particularly in their earthy approach, rough, untrained voices, and profound, primitive emotion.

PASTORA is by no means the only famous artist of the Pavón family. Her brother Tomás is considered one of the all-time greats of the *cante.* Another brother ,Arturo, was also excellent; his son Arturo Jr., is also vitally involved in flamenco. Another artist was added to the family with PASTORA's marriage to Pepe Pinto, a knowledgeable although extremely commercial *cantaor.*

PASTORA came briefly out of retirement at an homage given her in Córdoba in 1961. All of flamenco's hierarchy were present, and PASTORA disappointed no one as she again demonstrated that she is flamenco's number one *cantaora.*

TOMAS PAVON
(c. 1893-1952)

TOMÁS PAVÓN, the dry, introverted gypsy brother of the Niña de los Peines, hated, and usually refused, to sing outside of his inner circle of friends and admirers. Nevertheless, his talent was such that he came to be recognized as the dominating figure of the 1930-1950 period, and one of the great *cantaores* of all times.

Like his sister, TOMÁS had a lively curiosity in the lesser sung *cantes*, and revived and renovated such *cantes* as the *deblas* and ancient styles of the *tonás*. These accomplishments must be considered particularly brilliant in view of the fact that there was absolutely no interest in those *cantes* during his lifetime. It was strictly art for art's sake.

Probably the greatest early influence in TOMÁS formation as a *cantaor* was the *cante* of Enrique el Mellizo (*cantes de Cádiz*). Although TOMÁS never knew Enrique personally (Enrique died when TOMÁS was a young boy), Enrique's influence was widely spread at that time, his living disciples were many, and TOMÁS gravitated towards that source. His brother Arturo, and Manuel Torre, were also bottomless sources from which TOMÁS drew.

TOMÁS went on to become an extremely complete singer. He interpreted many styles of the *siguiriyas de Jerez* and the *soleares de Alcalá*, among others. Another specialty was his *bulerías de golpe*, which he sang, in the old style, much like a fast *soleares* (slower and more somber than today's *bulerías*). The *martinetes, tientos, tangos,* and many others, were also favorites.

TOMÁS had what has been termed a "full or flamenco voice". This type of voice, mellow and manly, emitted from the lungs, is very effective although unfortunately lacking in gypsy *rajo*, such an important element of the traditional *cante*. I find it difficult to become as involved with this type of voice as with the voice *afillá* of Caracol, or a natural voice (with *rajo*) like that presently possessed by Juan Talegas, Antonio Mairena, etc. Of course, this vocal quality has nothing to do with the merit of the *cantaor*, being largely beyond his control.

Anselmo González Climent writes of TOMÁS ("*Bulerías*", p. 116):

"Tomás Pavón was one of the most *jondo* and formal *cantaores* of this century. And so extensive has been his influence — despite his circumspect character and professional career — that an entire school of *cante* can be credited to his Trianan genius. Far from public adoration, he cultivated a type of *cante* for the minority. And his case is even more notable if we consider that his importance as a *cantaor* was not in the least diminished by the brilliant personality of his sister, Pastora.

"Within his vital sphere the *bulerías* became dignified to the level of the *soleares*. Tomás Pavón, due to his manner of being, had no other possibility than to interpret them thus. Solemn and direct as few are, he could not let himself go in aesthetic or modern styles. His entire being was a poignant testimony of simplicity, a lesson of authentic sobriety of style. Because of this his memory and influence do not fade: on the contrary, they grow in importance."

TOMÁS PAVÓN died quietly, as he had lived, in Sevilla in 1952.

BERNARDO EL DE LOS LOBITOS
1988 Update: (1887-1969)

BERNARDO ALVAREZ PÉREZ "EL DE LOS LOBITOS" is one of today's most knowledgeable and respected singers. Born in Alcalá de Guadaira of non-gypsy parents, BERNARDO received his nickname from a *bulerías* verse that he popularized, which went *"anoche soñaba que los lobos me comían"* (last night I dreamed that the wolves were eating me).

BERNARDO has an easy, calm style of singing, and a *voz redonda*. He sings a wide range of *cantes,* personally prefers the *cante grande,* but is far better known for his *cante intermedio* and *cante chico.* He is one of the few singers who still sings such ancient *andaluz cantes* as the *trilleras, nanas, marianas, caleseras, bamberas,* and *temporeras, cantes* beautiful in their simplicity. Some of these *cantes* he recorded on the Westminster and Hispavox anthologies, and are well worth having.

BERNARDO has sung in the company of Antonio, as well as in various others, although he has been basically a *juerga* singer. He is presently semi-retired, spending about half of the year in his home in Alcalá de Guadaira, the other half singing for *juergas* in Madrid.

LA ANTEQUERANA
1988 Update: (c. 1896-1969)

Fernando de Triana wrote of JOSEFA MORENO "LA ANTEQUERANA" (*Arte y Artistas Flamencos*, p. 243), in 1935: "There was an epoch when we expected La Antequerana to become one of the top *cante de Levante* singers. Then, for unknown reasons, she dropped from the artistic scene. She was also a fine guitarist."

The other day, much to my surprise, LA ANTEQUERANA was presented to me in Madrid. In view of Fernando's comments of thirty years ago, I was fascinated by her story, and we sat down to rehash her eventful life.

LA ANTEQUERANA was from, as her name implies, Antequera, a mountain town in the province of Málaga. As a child she stole moments from her daily chores to listen to the playing and singing of the owner of a nearby grocery store. Her interest grew, and she early expressed the desire to become an artist, a desire that her non-gypsy family firmly squelched. Undaunted, at the age of ten LA ANTEQUERANA ran away from home clutching her cheap guitar, and her lifetime of adventure began in earnest. With only her then limited knowledge of the *cante* and guitar as a means of support, she managed to reach Madrid. There she played and sang for her room and board for a period of time, in the meantime enlarging upon and perfecting her art. Her voice was powerful and clear and pleasing to the public, and she found help and encouragement. The year 1909 found LA ANTEQUERANA in the Jerez *café cantante La Primera*. From there she journeyed on to Tangier, Melilla, and, finally, America.

LA ANTEQUERANA, at the age of sixteen, was singing to the Spanish population in New York City. Of those days she remembers: "I made them cry, and I also cried while I sang. Those huge buildings generated sadness. The noise and the *'chow chow'* of the Americans made me dizzy. The only refuge for me and the rest of the Spaniards was to sing our *cantes* until my throat filled with tears. There I passed months as if in a hospital, wishing to escape..."

Finally the opportunity arose for LA ANTEQUERANA to perform in Cuba and Mexico, where she stayed from 1913-1917. She returned to Spain, made a name for herself, then again journeyed to America. By now LA ANTEQUERANA was a relatively renowned and wealthy artist, but as she earned, she threw. She found that she loved to gamble, and over the years lost her money, jewels, everything but her José Ramírez guitar to the roulette wheel.

Today LA ANTEQUERANA lives a precarious existence in the streets of Madrid. Forbidden to sing due to a lung illness, with death a possible consequence, she must still sing for her bed and bread, going with her guitar from bar to bar in Madrid's old section. Many are the dismal, *juerga*-less nights that she has to slump in a dark doorway, guitar at her side, awaiting dawn and the opening of the *cafés*, with their promise of warmth and a possible invitation to a hot coffee.

LA ANTEQUERANA has truly lived *"a la flamenca"*, and is paying the inevitable consequences, as did nearly all of her contemporaries.

Where was she in 1935, when Fernando and the flamenco world had lost track of her?

"*Hijo*, I was performing in America. A group of bullfighters hired me for a *juerga* in Madrid one night, just before their departure for Mexico. We were having such a good time that at the last minute they invited me to come along, so that we could continue the *juerga*. So, of course, I did. I didn't have time to say goodbye to anyone, but simply disappeared for some years.

"*Ay, qué vida aquélla. Qué loca estaba.* How crazy I was. But what fun we had..."

ISABELITA DE JEREZ

(c. 1898-1955)

In Jerez they say that ISABELITA is the finest *cantaora* that they have produced in this century, certainly no small statement considering the quantity and quality of Jerez' *cante*.

Isabelita was born of the gypsies El Chalao (Mixed-up Kid) and La Morena (the Dark One), and was brought up on the *cante* of her father. According to Juan de la Plata, she soon graduated to the *maestros* Diego el Marrurro, Frijones, and José de la Paula, subsequently becoming an extremely complete and moving *cantaora*. She married another Jerez *cantaor*, José Durán, who, after Isabelita's death, remarried to the dancer Rosita Durán.

Isabelita began acting when relatively young, earning, at her first job, seven and one-half pesetas a night. She went on to nation-wide fame. She made twelve 78 rpm records during the prime of her *cante*, which today are extremely difficult to come by.

JUANITO MOJAMA
(c. 1898-1958)

Juanito Mojama, a little-recognized *cantaor* from Jerez de la Frontera, is considered by purists as one of this century's great interpreters of the *siguiriyas* and the *bulerías*.

Juanito had neither the personality nor the inclination for commercial singing, and spent nearly his entire career performing in private *juergas* and *fiestas*. He spent long periods in Madrid, frequenting Pastora Imperio's Venta La Capitana, which no longer exists, and other flamenco taverns.

Anselmo González Climent ("*Bulerías*") writes of Juanito: "The *cante* of Juanito Mojama, primitive and modern at the same time, brilliant and severe, has not known how to capture great popularity. Truthfully he presents a strong plate of flamenco, reserved for only the most profoundly indoctrinated."

Fernando el de Triana believed Juanito's *cante* to be extremely personal and pure within the old school of Manuel Molina. What is little remembered is that Juanito was also an impressive and colorful dancer por *bulerías* and *tangos*.

CABEZA
(c. 1900-1955)

Francisco Fernández "Cabeza" was another member of the Frijones-Niño Gloria-Pompi family who was blessed, or damned, depending of one's outlook, with many gypsy points of honor. For instance, he refused to sing *por fandangos*, considering it an inferior *cante*. His loyalty to this concept was such that instances are known when he was thrown out of *juergas* by *fandango*-loving *aficionados*. Considering that the prime of his artistic life fell precisely in the midst of the *fandango* epoch, CABEZA's integrity must have caused him some hardship. Also, CABEZA disliked leaving the Jerez area, and thus lost many lucrative artistic offers.

CABEZA was strong in the *siguiriyas* and the other *cantes grandes de Jerez*.

MANUEL VALLEJO

1988 Update: (1891-1960)

MANUEL VALLEJO was one of this century's finest singers, although not to the extent that his reputation might lead one to believe; his fame was blown all out of proportion to the caliber of his *cante* by his winning, as a youth in his twenties, the second Golden Key of the *Cante*, in Madrid in 1926. This phenomenon occurred only because flamenco's great *cantaores* of the period (Manuel Torre, Tomás Pavón, La Niña de los Peines, Aurelio Sellé, Antonio Chacón, Juan Talegas, El Niño Gloria, Juanito Mojama, and so forth) did not enter the contest. Like so many contests, it was considered a farce within the flamenco world, but accepted at face value by the general public.

VALLEJO is remembered principally as a *fandanguero*, although in truth he possessed a wide knowledge of the *cante*. He is considered one of the great singers of *bulerías*, and his *siguiriyas* were also highly respected. His voice, which he generally utilized at maximum strength, was high-pitched and unpleasantly shrill. This gave the impression, all too frequently, that he was shouting at the top of his lungs.

VALLEJO maintained a balance between modern and traditional flamenco, and a relative purity of style, although he did mold his *cantes*, to a certain extent, to the likes of the public.

MANUEL CENTENO

1988 Update: (1885-1961)

Manuel Centeno was one of the last great interpreters of the old school of the *cantes de Levante,* and is considered one of the outstanding *saeteros* of this century. Other than these preferred *cantes* he had a wide knowledge of the *cante* in general. He had a relatively high-pitched *voz redonda,* and a particularly moving style of singing. He died while on tour in 1960.

1988 Update: It is said that Manuel Centeno was the first, in 1919, to sing the saetas as they are sung today, to the *compás* of the siguiriyas.

PEPE PEREZ DE GUZMAN

(c. 1900-1950)

Pepe Pérez de Guzmán, a member of an aristocratic family of Huelva, shares honors with Antonio Rengel in being the greatest remembered *cantaores* of *fandangos* and *fandanguillos.* Guzmán was not only an outstanding interpreter, but created his own style of *fandanguillos* still sung today.

ANTONIO RENGEL

(c. 1900-1961)

Ricardo Molina and Antonio Mairena write, in *"Mundo y Formas del Cante Flamenco",* words to the effect that Antonio Rengel and Pepe Pérez de Guzmán were head and shoulders above all other singers of *fandangos.*

Rengel, they go on to say, was encyclopedic in his knowledge of all of the countless styles of *fandangos* and *fandanguillos,* and interpreted them with the utmost nobility and purity. In addition, they state that Rengel was "the indisputable *maestro* of the *serranas* during the last thirty years (of his life)". Rengel apparently interpreted Silverio's style of *serranas,* which reached him through Antonio Silva "el Portugués" and Dolores la Parrala.

VARIOUS

Artists whose careers fell largely in the second quarter of this century, to whom little space can be dedicated, include: JOAQUÍN VARGAS "EL COJO DE MÁLAGA", an excellent gypsy *cantaor* of the *tarantas* and other *cantes mineros;* EL COJO DE HUELVA (the Lame One, from Huelva) gained fame with his *fandangos, chuflas, tanguillos,* and *alegrías;* ANICA LA PRIÑACA, a veteran *cantaora* from Jerez now around seventy years old, is extremly respected in flamenco circles for her classical *cantes de Jerez* and *cantes* of the smithies; EL NIÑO MEDINA gained fame due to his creations within the *cante por peteneras,* which are reputedly the versions sung by La Niña de los Peines today. Others say, however, that these innovations within the *peteneras* must be credited, wholly or in part, to La Niña de los Peines. The consensus of opinion seems to favor Niño Medina; EL NIÑO DE ESCACENA gained fame through his excellent interpretations of the *fandangos* and its derivatives, the *cantes de Málaga* and *Levante,* as well as the American-influenced *cantes;* PENA HIJO, possessed with a magnificent voice and excellent knowledge of the classical *cante,* largely wasted his potential through commercialism; JESÚS PEROSANZ, born in Madrid in 1907, interpreted well, if commercially, the *cantes de Levante y Málaga;* ALMENDRO gained fame basically through his interpretations of the *fandangos* and their derivatives; ANTONIO EL SEVILLANO was considered a great hope for flamenco due to his wide knowledge of the classical *cante.* His influence, however, did not spread beyond the *fandangos, sevillanas,* and *bulerías.* In his fifties, he is presently living semi-retired in his native Sevilla; PEPE PALANCA is a *fandanguero* who innovated his own style of *fandangos cortos* still widely sung today. In his fifties, the height of his popularity was in the 1930's and 1940's. PALANCA presently lives semi-retired in his native Arahal (Sevilla); EL NIÑO DE AZNALCÓLLAR is a *fandanguero* of some former fame. In his fifties, he still pursues *juergas* in the Sevilla area He is from the village of Aznalcóllar (Sevilla); JUAN ACOSTA is a specialist in the festive *cantes de Cádiz.* He won several contests and achieved some fame during his active career. In his fifties, he presently is employed by one of the wine companies in his native Jerez; EL NIÑO DE BARBATE is a fine non-professional interpreter of the *cante grande*. In his fifties, he presently resides in the costal town of Barbate (Cádiz); JUAN CAMACHO is another non-professional interpreter of the *cante grande*. In his fifties, he resides in the port town of Rota (Cádiz); ROSALÍA DE TRIANA and PERLA DE TRIANA are two little-known gypsy *cantaoras*, from Triana (Sevilla), who have just recently come to the attention of the flamenco world due to their participation in London Record's "An Anthology of *Cante Flamenco*". Both *cantaoras* interpret the *cantes de Triana*, ROSALÍA with particular brilliance; MANOLO MANZANILLA is a *cantaor* of fame who retired from professional life some years ago to open commercial flamenco establishments, which include the Venta Manzanilla, a center of Madrid's flamenco activity for years, and a *tablao* in Almería. MANZANILLA specializes, in his singing, in the *cante grande;* ENRIQUE OROZCO is one of today's top interpreters of the *cantes* of the mines, within which category of *cantes* he has won various contest prizes in La Unión and Cartagena, mining centers of Spain. In his early fifties, he has resided for many years in Madrid.

PERICON DE CADIZ

1988 Update: (1902-1980)

JUAN MARTÍNEZ VILCHES "PERICÓN DE CÁDIZ" has risen from a boyhood street vendor in Cádiz, when he sang the glories of his wares, to one of flamenco's finest singers.

PERICÓN was early influenced by the extraordinary *cante* of the Mellizo family, of Tío José el Granaíno, of Ignacio Ezpeleta, of Aurelio Sellé, and of a host of other fine old-time *cantaores* from the Cádiz region, and consequently interprets excellently the *alegrías, bulerías, tangos, cantiñas, malagueñas del Mellizo, soleares, siguiriyas, mirabrás, caracoles* and other *cantes de Cádiz*, as well as many *cantes* from outside the Cádiz sphere of influence. He definitely seems the first in line to inherit the throne of Aurelio Sellé, the aging *maestro* of the Cádiz school of *cante*.

PERICÓN is truly in love with his art, even after more than fifty years as a professional. Each time I go by his Madrileñan residence he has new tapes for me to listen to that were always made a few nights earlier during some spontaneous session...

He explained to me why he is called PERICÓN. It seems that when he was a tyke of four years he wanted to be a *"picador de toros"*, but each time he expressed his desire his baby tongue turned the word into *"pericaón"*. This was ultimately shortened to PERICÓN, and thus remains. Over the years PERICÓN's interest in the *toros* has not diminished. One of his sons was a bullfighter and now manages other bullfighters, and PERICÓN is an ardent fan, *"como debe ser un buen gaditano"*.

PERICÓN's beginning as a professional singer is characteristic of the flamenco way of life of those times. At the age of ten his family and friends convinced him to sing in a Cádiz carnival. In PERICÓN's words:

"It seems that I had success, because I was offered the circulating candy concession, which consisted of wandering around Cádiz with my pockets full of *caramelos* and advertising my wares through my *cante*. It went well for me but not so well for my boss, as few people wanted the *caramelos*, but they all gave me coins for my *cante*."

Not long after, PERICÓN's professional life began in earnest. He began singing in *cafés cantantes* throughout the province of Cádiz, of which PERICÓN has many stories to tell.

PERICÓN recalls that many of the small country *cafés cantantes* in those days used the barter system to pay off the artists. He particularly remembers one time when he and a friend were paid in *alfajores*, which is a type of candy. They quickly realized that protesting was useless, and so they carted their wares up the road to the next *venta* and traded them in for whatever item of use was available — which happened to be an old horse, obviously on its last legs, and, what seemed to be more important at the time, all they could drink.

As they sipped their first drinks they discussed the fate of their old horse — he obviously could not make it back to Cádiz, and selling it was out of the ... but wait a minute ... if wine could make *them* feel so much better, just maybe...

So the horse began hitting the bottle with them. Sure enough, he began getting friskier and friskier, as, of course, did PERICÓN and human friend. About when they figured that the horse had reached his peak they hopped on and cantered down to the next *venta*, making quite an impression as they galloped up in a final burst of speed. They quickly sold the horse for a tidy profit, and just as quickly headed down the road before the horse sobered up.

Part of PERICÓN's repertoire in those days was a number of sleight-of-hand tricks. He says the audiences in the small country *cafés cantantes* were the simplest of folk, very easy to fool, "but", he added, "it wasn't advisable to get caught. They took it all very seriously!"

"One night he decided to do his rising-table act in a *café cantante* that had an open patio surrounded by second-story balconies. Located in opposite balconies, of course, were four helpers, each with a wire attached to a corner of the table. Everything went along fine for a time, the table rising and careening about, PERICÓN gesturing commandingly at it and uttering mysterious words.

Suddenly one of the wires broke. The jerk tore the wires from the hands of the others, and the table came crashing down into the middle of the stage, narrowly missing PERICÓN, its wires falling only too obviously into the crowd.

An old hand, PERICÓN darted out the back way and mysteriously vanished.

Needless to say, the old flamenco *cafés* offered the artists a precarious, if colorful, existence.

PERICÓN's first fling at big-time theatrical flamenco was a five-year stint with the company of Conchita Piquer, starting in 1940, in which they carried on the tradition of La Argentinita's "*Las Calles de Cádiz*" (1). La Argentinita granted Conchita Piquer permission to restage the show, which La Piquer did with good taste and great success. Many of the same artists were hired that had performed with La Argentinita, such as La Malena, La Macarrona, La Sordita, as well as such newcomers as the guitarists Melchor de Marchena, Esteban Sanlúcar, and others. PERICÓN's

---

(1) Consult section «La Argentinita» for further particulars on «*Las Calles de Cádiz*».

performances in this show earned him a fine reputation, and he was on his way. He has risen steadily since, although, like nearly all artists, he has his detractors, who claim that he was a borderline "*ópera flamenca*" singer in the past. Were this true, PERICÓN would have been a part of the commercial movement generated by Pepe Marchena. I can detect no trace of this. I cannot vouch for each remote moment of his artistic career, of course, but I can state that the great deal of his *cante* that I have heard does credit to the Cádiz tradition.

PERICÓN, a non-gypsy, has a husky, clear voice, classifiable as *redonda*. He is included in many anthologies, including the Hispavox, Westminster, and "*La Voz de su Amo*" (*Cantaores Famosos*). His contest prizes include: first prize for the *soleares* (Madrid 1936); first prize for the *siguiriyas* (Madrid 1948); and second prize for the *alegrías* (Cádiz 1952). He has spent the past twelve years as a member of the featured *cuadro* in Madrid's La Zambra.

PERICÓN has some unusual observations to make in connection with the *cante*, such as:

"The *cante* has no borders. Non-Spaniards are capable of feeling its *duende* just as deeply as the Spaniards. Take the example of Ava Gardner, for instance. She often stays after hours at La Zambra and asks me to sing for her. Many times when I finish I notice that she is weeping with emotion. She has a boundless love for flamenco that has nothing to do with blood."

An entertaining storyteller, PERICÓN tells limitless anecdotes about his beloved flamenco, a few of which I shall print here, for they describe beautifully the way of life of the people who made flamenco what it is. The first concerns PERICÓN, the second the old-time *cantaor*, Tío José el Granaíno, the others simply the flamenco life of those times.

"When I went to Paris to record the anthology I of course didn't know my may around, nor did I talk the '*frachute*'. I got hopelessly lost once or twice, and finally bought a box of chalk. Then each time I left my hotel I made chalk marks along my route, and simply followed them back. Everything went fine until some wise guy erased them one day. ¡Ojú, me hice un taco! I was hours in finding my way back."

"Remember the old-time juke boxes that one had to listen to through rubber tubes. No, of course you wouldn't remember, that was way before your time. At any rate, the contraption was in the form of a big box with all kinds of red tubes sticking out of it, so that various people could listen to the recording at once. Well, one day the owner of one of these wanted to record *tío* José el Granaíno, who wasn't a *granaíno* at all but a *gaditano*, so that we could all enjoy the old fellow's wonderful *cante*. We ran over to the *barrio de* Santa María to fetch him, and he came along not having any idea what we were talking about. You should have seen his reaction. He took one look at the machine and exclaimed: 'Coño, I haven't shown my *cante* to anyone, and you expect me to teach it to this octopus?!'"

"The flamenco life of those times (it began changing about forty years ago) was really something. What atmosphere and hell-raising! The gypsy neighborhoods, the *barrios de* Santa María, in Cádiz, Santiago, in Jerez, Triana, in Sevilla, and all the rest, were free-for-alls at any hour of the day or night. The *'tiendas de montañés'* (grocery store-bar combinations) were open all night long, and a person in search of a good time had only to enter one of the gypsy neighborhoods.

"The custom then was for the *señoritos* to hire a *cantaor* and a *tocaor* and ride through the streets of *el barrio de* Santa María in a horse and buggy during the wee hours of the morning, singing and playing and having a ball. Now, of course, such a thing would not be permitted, but then the *serenos* and police in the streets would shout *olés* and get invited to drinks for their understanding. Some nights thirty or forty buggies would roll through the streets, and the people would flock to their balconies to encourage the artists and implore the buggy-drivers to stop under their balconies. ¡Qué cachondeo! One favorite *sereno* (sort of nighttime cop) invariably was invited to a drink by each buggy that passed. He would shout over to a nearby *café* that he would have a coffee presently, and to charge the inviting *señoritos* for it. Of course he did not drink anywhere near the thirty drinks he may have been invited to, and come morning he and the waiter would add up the extra invites. Then, instead of drinks, the *sereno* would gather up a whole armful of *tortas de aceite* (a type of pastry) and take them home to his family for breakfast.

"I remember one time when a tipsy old *cantaor* with a huge voice was being driven through the *barrio de* Santa María singing a *tango* that starts out 'Dolores' (name of a girl). When sung, of course, it goes 'Do-loooooooo-res', and is sung three times in a row with a little guitar music to break it up.

"This particular night the horse and buggy happened to stop under the balcony of the famous *cantaor*, El Morsilla (son of Enrique el Mellizo), who was also in his cups after a hard day of *juergas*. El Morsilla, the ugliest gypsy ever born, was sleeping out on his balcony when the first huge 'Do-looooooo-res' issued forth. Morsilla snapped awake, quickly sized up the situation, and, unseen from below, seized his opportunity. He wrapped his white sheet around his head and body like a girl in her shawl, leaned over the balcony and, after the second 'Do-looooooo-res', answered with an immense 'Whaaaaaaaaaaaa-aaat'.

"I don't know if anyone in the buggy understood that ugly black face sticking out of a white sheet was supposed to represent Dolores, but the driver of the buggy certainly didn't catch the joke. All he saw was a sudden apparition shouting at them in a rage. Man, his whip came down on that horse with all of his strength, and they went racing away through the narrow streets of Santa María at a full gallop. To this day he talks of the ghost he saw in the *barrio de* Santa María. No one can convince him differently.

"What days those were, ¡*vaya!* Now you walk through the old gypsy neighborhoods after midnight and it's like the morgue. The art of flamenco has somehow remained, but what made it great, the atmosphere that made it possible, has all but disappeared."

PERICÓN lapsed into silence, staring helplessly into his wine glass. One last phrase escaped him before he recaptured his customary gaiety:

"¡*Qué pena...!*"

PEPE PINTO

1988 Update: (c.1903-1971)

PEPE PINTO is reputedly one of flamenco's finer, and most knowledgeable, singers. I say "reputedly", for I have never heard him in this role other than for an occasional old record. Since his early days of great promise, PEPE chose to turn commercial — very commercial — and has reserved his pure *cante* exclusively for a group of intimates.

Born in Sevilla, PINTO presently owns a bar, the "Bar Pinto", located on Sevilla's Plaza la Campana, which is a meeting place for many of Sevilla's flamencos. He is the husband of La Niña de los Peines.

PINTO is most widely renowned for his *fandangos* and his *bulerías*.

MANOLITO EL DE LA MARIA

1988 Update: (1904-1966)

MANOLITO EL DE LA MARÍA (little Emmanuel, he of the Mary) ranks alongside of Juan Talegas and Antonio Mairena in being the outstanding guardians of the pure core of the *cante de Alcalá* (consisting of various styles of *soleares* and *bulerías*). Each of the three gives these *cantes* a little different emphasis, personality, and feeling, as is fitting. The interpretations of all three are superb.

MANOLITO's *cante* varies with his mood. Sometimes he injects a quality of bubbling life, other times an indescribable sadness, other times a profundity that reaches into the obscure and unknown. MANOLITO becomes transformed through his *cante;* he completely sheds his personality, he is no longer MANOLITO, but becomes raw emotion causing gooseflesh to rise on the listener's skin and tears to jump to his eyes. His voice, hoarse, foggy, tending towards a *voz afillá*, enhances his *duende*.

Except for a small but devout following in the immediate Sevilla-Alcalá region, MANOLITO is relatively unknown even in the flamenco world. He has never sung commercially, nor cut records, and is even a rare guest at paid *juergas*. This is due entirely to MANOLITO's bohemian don't-give-a-damn attitude. Although penniless, he is happily situated in his little world of family and flamenco friends, where he finds all of the recognition that he apparently needs.

But when a *juerga* does crop up, MANOLITO is sure to make it a memorable one. He is a natural comedian, blessed with a quick, spontaneous wit. When properly fueled up, and in surroundings of his liking, there is no holding him. The *bulerías, tangos, rumba* come bubbling out, he dances, gets others to dance, carries off the wildest of antics without appearing ridiculous, as only a true comedian can. (The times, out in MANOLITO's cave neighborhood among intimates, when all vestiges of formality are put aside and the gypsies set about comparing the sizes of the holes in their socks and of their big toes that emerge triumphantly from the holes, and they drink wine from MANOLITO's dusty old shoe). Yet it is when the hours have passed and spirits begin to flag that MANOLITO's *cante* becames raw and unique. He sings on and on *por soleares*, sometimes becoming so emotionally involved with his *cante* that tears stream down his face as he sings. There is no escape for the listener; he must follow MANOLITO in his melancholy. The experience is unforgettable!

MANOLITO learned his *cante* from his uncle, the great Joaquín el de la Paula. Apart from the *cante*, the two gypsies' courses have been similar. MANOLITO lives in a cave at the foot of a hillside castle, as did Joaquín. A great love for wine, women, and adventure characterizes MANOLITO's life, as it did Joaquín's. And MANOLITO is artistically pure, as was Joaquín.

MANOLITO has added innovations of his own to his inherited *cante*. He has demonstrated for me three ways of singing a particular *soleá*: the first as was traditional in the family; the second as it was sung by Joaquín; and the third as it is sung by MANOLITO. MANOLITO has added a distinctive, particularly beautiful touch, and in so doing gives the *cante* a little more life, makes it, as is said in Spanish, *más valiente*.

MANOLITO has had one colorful episode in the jungles of organized flamenco, so foreign to him and all unsophisticated flamencos.

It was in the 1962 Jerez flamenco contest. The author entered MANOLITO's name on the list of contestants. He was accepted, and we faced our first problem: what could he wear? This was rapidly solved by MANOLITO's appeal to the widow of a late friend of his, and MANOLITO soon appeared elegantly replete in his late friend's only suit, white shirt, tie, the whole shebang. We motored down to Jerez and installed ourselves for the three-day affair.

MANOLITO was to sing early the second evening of the contest. He prepared for the ordeal in the corner bar. But somehow his turn was postponed over and over again, until finally, well after midnight, after five hours of joyful preparation and *juerga* with local *aficionados*, MANOLITO was called.

Glassy-eyed, concentrating on each step, MANOLITO staggered on stage. He had been blowing his nose when called, and still had the handkerchief in his hand. What to do with it? Somehow it would not fit into his breast pocket (from where it had been removed). He tried stuffing it in his cuff. No good. Puzzled, he studied the handkerchief closely, as if expecting it to offer a solution. The solution came; with a grand gesture of finality, he stuffed that problem away in his lower coat-pocket. The audience tittered, someone shouted "*¡Viva el vino de Jerez!*" "Long live the wine of Jerez!"

MANOLITO warmed up for his *cante*. Feeling the crowd's sympathy, he decided to give them a good show. He swung into one of his famous dances, and caught himself, by a miracle, from falling flat on his face in the middle of the stage. He smiled happily. What good fun! The audience roared. MANOLITO raised a commanding hand, they quieted down, he began singing a *soleá de Alcalá*. Just warming up, still good fun. At the end of a *copla* he thought of dancing again. A little steadier this time, and — oops — one hand on the floor stopped his fall. The audience roared again.

But now, after regaining his equilibrium, MANOLITO became very serious. Enough horseplay, we came here to sing! And sing he did, a whole series of *soleares de Alcalá* as only MANOLITO can. An old gypsy couple seated next to us muttered, for the first and only time in the contest, "*¡Esto es er cante!*" "This is the *cante!"* MANOLITO sang on and on, much longer than his allotted time, lost in his *cante,* as was the entire audience. When he finished, the audience again roared, but this time in earnest admiration. Truly, that was the *cante!*

I shall relate another episode, brought about by MANOLITO, which will give the reader a little insight into gypsy mental processes. One night in Sevilla a happy rapping sounded on our door. I opened, and there stood MANOLITO with a clan of gypsy friends ranging from a great grandmother to her three-week-old great grandchild.

Shaking of hands, introductions, wine-drinking, chatter... at MANOLITO's request I broke out the guitar, and to MANOLITO's singing everyone danced, including the great grandmother. Amidst the din and gaiety it occurred to me that we were somehow being tested, but for the life of me I could not figure out why. It soon became clear when the tiny gypsy baby was unveiled for our admiration and thrust into my wife's eager arms, and roundabout probes made us understand that the baby, born out of wedlock to a coquettish fifteen-year-old gypsy girl, one of those present, was ours but for the accepting. MANOLITO took me aside and hinted that it would be a great hardship for the unwed little girl to keep her baby, and that they were looking for a suitable home for it. Ours was considered more than suitable, for the baby would grow up amidst what they considered luxury and, more important, he would be surrounded by a flamenco atmosphere. Of course, flamenco was the principal consideration!

We gently and somewhat reluctantly refused their indirect offer, and off they went, smiling and understanding, into the night.

MANOLITO presently lives with his family of five on the upper edge of Alcalá de Guadaira. A sheep-shearer by trade, MANOLITO labors at his seasonal profession during the months of July and August (that is, unless his employers naïvely pay him on a weekly or bi-weekly basis — the chances are that they won't see him again until his paycheck runs out). He also occasionally works during the height of the olive harvest. The rest of the time? The life of the untamed gypsy, to a background music of *palmas* and *cante puro!*

CANALEJAS DE PUERTO REAL
1988 Update: (c.1904-197?)

The artistic career of CANALEJAS DE PUERTO REAL has been divided, roughly, into three epochs: 1) the *cante* of his youth, pure, traditional, outstanding; 2) his deviation into commercialism (late twenties and thirties), when he became an idol of the people through his *fandangos* and popular *bulerías;* 3) his return to the classical *cante*, with occasional commercial sidetrips.

Because of his association with commercial flamenco, CANALEJAS is considered by some as outside the realm of the pure classical *cante*. True, his *cante* on occasion is watered down to appeal to a popular public even today. Nevertheless, CANALEJAS conserves a pure core of *cante* that, when he wishes (unlike Pepe Pinto, CANALEJAS often does wish), is classical and emotional like the *cante* of few.

CANALEJAS commands a wide knowledge of the *cante*, and has a voice, feeling, and style of delivery fitting for all of flamenco's *cantes*. He sing with a calm, effortless style, his fairly high-pitched, yet husky voice weaving in and around the *compás*. His vocal faculties are considerable, but he rarely abuses his latent virtuosity. While not of a turbulent, gypsy nature, his *siguiriyas, soleares, bulerías, alegrías, fandangos, malagueñas, verdiales,* and other *cantes* carry an extraordinary impact, when he is singing seriously, not at all commercial in nature.

Born a non-gypsy in Puerto Real, CANALEJAS presently lives in semi-retirement in the town of Jaén.

JACINTO ALMADEN
1988 Update: (c.1905-1968)

FRANCISCO ANTOLÍN GALLEGO "EL NIÑO DE ALMADÉN", or "JACINTO ALMADÉN", born the son of a miner in the mining country of Almadén, was early liberated from the drudgery of the mines by his promising *cante*. He was first introduced to the public by another *cantaor*, El Niño del Genil, as a possible heir to the Antonio Chacón school of *cante*.

ALMADÉN has followed closely in the footsteps of Antonio Chacón. Like Chacón, ALMADÉN has a wide knowledge of the *cante*, but sings truly well only the *andaluz*-inspired *cantes*, with an exception or two. He particularly excels in the *cantes* that carried Chacón to such great fame, the *cantes* of the mines, and the *cantes* of Málaga and Granada. He also interprets beautifully the *tientos antiguos*. Generally speaking, however ,the drive and primitive emotion of the *cante gitano* escape him, as they did Chacón.

Another similarity between ALMADÉN and Chacón is their style of voice, although ALMADÉN's contains more *rajo*, and has a haunting quality that was not found in Chacón's voice, at least not on his records. ALMADÉN's voice, then, is classifiable as *redonda*, tending on some *cantes* towards *falsete*.

Like so many artists, ALMADÉN not infrequently makes silly statements that he must surely later regret. Such as a recent interview in a Málaga newspaper, in which he stated that he is presently the only *cantaor* who is capable of giving a two and one-half hours recital of the *Cante*. In stating this, he is almost insultingly underestimating his reading public. I would not want to go on record as saying just how many *cantaores* could accomplish this feat. I shall state, however, that Antonio Mairena could very likely triple that time limit.

ALMADÉN has spent long periods of his artistic career touring outside of Spain. He is presently back in Spain, seemingly to take life a little easier. His permanent residence is in Madrid.

E L   P I L I

(c. 1907 —

PEDRO JIMÉNEZ "EL PILI", a gypsy born in the poor Madrid neighborhood of Embajadores, has risen from a street vendor of men's clothing to one of today's more respected *cantaores*. His temperament and excellent *rajo* voice are best suited to his preferred *cante grande*.

EL PILI gained his nickname as a result of his youthful clumsiness; each time he toppled over his mother cheerfully said *"arriba pilili"*, a neighborhood term meaning "up and at'em, little one." He has been known since as EL PILI, as well as by another nickname, "*cara negra*" (black face).

As a youth, EL PILI was just another *aficionado* of the *cante*, without the vaguest notion of becoming a professional. Then, in 1933, he was persuaded to enter an amateur flamenco contest, which he won with his interpretations of the *siguiriyas, soleares,* and *martinetes.* Encouraged, he turned professional, and in 1947 finally began hitting the big time with the ballet of Pilar López. Since that time he has been with Antonio and Rosario, Vicente Escudero, and has spent a number of years performing in Madrid's Corral de la Morería.

Opera Flamenca

We have seen, in the biography of Antonio Chacón, four basic links (1) in the chain of events that carried flamenco from relative purity (previous to 1860) to utter commercial decadence, and a consequent withdrawal of most of the professional purists back into an exclusive ingroup to wait out the fad (during the approximate period 1910-1950). As time wore on, however, there was less and less of a demand for the purists, and many of the hungrier and less determined deflected to the opposition. The up-and-coming youngsters were also largely drawn to the commercial movement, for obvious reasons, with the resultant dilemma that for a considerable period the pure *cante* was not far from extinction.

Thus, in a period of half a century, flamenco had completed its cycle: traditionally outcast, it had come out in the open, been badly stung, and, bitter and disillusioned, had hurriedly retreated back to cover, leaving behind an active phenomenon, also called flamenco, which in truth had little relationship with true flamenco. This remaining commercial manifestation was known, at first proudly, and later disparagingly, as "*ópera flamenca*", and, in truth, had

---

(1) 1) *Cafés Cantantes.* 2) Juan Breva. 3) Antonio Chacón. 4) *Opera Flamenca.*

operatic overtones. Characteristic of this movement were: clear, beautiful, often trained voices, nearly always falsetto; the use and abuse of operatic and *zarzuela* arias; verses of the *cantes* relating directly to a central plot, often acted as well as sung, danced, and played; orchestral as often as guitar accompaniment (sometimes played simultaneously, or interchangeably in the same number); and, in general, a complete watering-down of flamenco in all ways in order to appeal to both a *zarzuela* and popularly-oriented public.

This flamenco-inspired theater decayed to such an extent that even Antonio Chacón, the champion of the popular public just the generation before, was condemned as an old-fashioned purist and rejected from it. Predominently girlish-voiced men sang almost nothing but *milongas, tanguillos, guajiras, colombianas, zambras, el garrotín,* badly-contaminated *fandanguillos* (1), and popular ditties and songs in a more-or-less flamenco style, raising the fad to such drunken heights that its colossal hangover is still distressing us today. Even in our increasingly enlightened flamenco age, "*ópera flamenca*" vocal stylings still plague us, and many of their masters are still firmly entrenched, with more arriving on the scene each day (2). Angelillo, Pepe Marchena, and Juanito Valderrama, whom we shall discuss now, have perhaps been the most famous proponents of this movement. Others are mentioned in the biography of Pepe Marchena.

ANGELILLO

Madrid-born ANGEL SAMPEDRO MONTERO "ANGELILLO" (Little Angel) was at one time the rage of the "*ópera flamenca*" movement.

---

(1) The *fandangos*, both the *grandes* and the *fandanguillos*, became the popular rage, and countless *fandangueros* sprang up as did *malagueñeros* in the last half of the past century. Many of the *fandangueros* took their *cante* seriously, and were not necessarily connected with the «*ópera flamenca*» movement. Nevertheless, they also played an important role in keeping the *cante grande*, and *cante gitano* in general, under wraps.

(2) R. Molina - A. Mairena date the «*ópera flamenca*» period from 1910-1936. That period was perhaps the height of the fervor, and 1936 serves as a double date: the beginning of the Spanish civil war, when all theater stopped in Spain; and the approximate date when Spanish theatrical ballet companies, more pure offspring of the «*ópera flamenca*», began including elements of traditional flamenco, giving work to a few of the purists (Ballet of La Argentinita, etc.). But the «*ópera flamenca*» movement by no means stopped in 1936. It easily bridged the gap of the war, and even today the majority of theatrical flamenco has to be classified as «*ópera flamenca*», or its very close descendant.

His high, fluty, falsetto voice was brilliantly clear and flexible, and with it he played an important role in popularizing his preferred *cantes:* the *milongas, colombianas, guajiras* and *fandanguillos.* During his reign he cut a grand total of over five hundred records. He is presently in his middle fifties.

PEPE MARCHENA

PEPE TEJADA "NIÑO DE MARCHENA", more often called PEPE MARCHENA, is without a doubt the most controversial flamenco figure of the twentieth century. The self-proclaimed *"maestro de maestros"*, MARCHENA has a host of admirers in whose eyes he can do no wrong; these are *aficionados* whose knowledge of the *cante* does not quite reach beyond the *fandangos.* On the other hand, the initiated condemn his *cante* almost unconditionally. The truth leans heavily towards the latter judgement.

PEPE MARCHENA entered the flamenco world as an unusually gifted and creative young *cantaor*, and was proclaimed by Chacón himself as his most likely successor for the title "king of the *cante andaluz*". For a time MARCHENA toed the mark, and was indeed a promising young *cantaor*. But gradually his creations became wilder and further out, until he finally created himself right out of the limits of good flamenco. He irresponsibly mixed *cantes* and styles of *cantes*, added popular elements, and in general adapted his *cantes* to popular tastes. The public responded, and MARCHENA attained a popularity among the masses unequalled by any other flamenco artist of this century. His influence became widespread, and he attracted armies of imitators. The result: MARCHENA and his followers have done more to tear down the structure of traditional flamenco than any other artist, or group, in the known history of flamenco.

Marchenistas offer a common defense for the *cante* of MARCHENA and his school, stating that he has returned the *cante* to the masses. They proudly admit that he has dolled it up, attired it in frills and ribbons, so to speak, and thus made it more readily acceptable to the people from whence it came, and where it belongs.

This argument can only pertain to the *andaluz*-inspired *cante*, for we have seen that the *cante gitano*, the true gypsy-inspired *cante*, was never part of the masses; has, in fact, been rejected by the masses since its inception. The *andaluz*-inspired *cante*, on the other hand, can be said to have once belonged to the masses in an extremely simplified form. This form has evolved over the years into the *cante andaluz* as we know it today, having been developed, largely by professionals, into an intricate art form, a form that has *not* outgrown, as many *marchenistas* claim, the simple tastes of the masses. They must keep in mind that Antonio Chacón before MARCHENA was extremely popular with the public, and he never swayed from a pure *cante* far superior to that of MARCHENA. It was not necessary to offer the masses an inferior product — once it was offered, however, it was gleefully accepted.

Thus it cannot be denied that MARCHENA has given the masses a type of music that is much to their liking. Segments of these *cantes andaluces* are his original creations, some of which are worthy and will be remembered as the *cantes* of PEPE MARCHENA. His *malagueña* is included among these, as is, perhaps, his *fandango*. Most of his so-called creations, however, are not creations at all, but merely traditional *cantes*, popular songs, or combinations of *cantes* made over in a cheap, obvious fashion to appeal to the most base tastes.

MARCHENA has, then, endeared the *cante andaluz* to perhaps a larger segment of the Spanish people, but most of it in such a form that it can no longer be classed as flamenco.

Other *marchenistas* readily admit MARCHENA's flagrant commercialism, but claim that in private he can sing outstanding flamenco. Apparently MARCHENA does possess a vast knowledge of the *cante*, but I have been assured by well-informed sources that he cannot, or chooses not to, interpret it properly, other than *por malagueñas, fandangos,* and one or two of the *cantes chicos*. The proper interpretations of, and feeling for, the *cantes gitanos* especially evade him, regardless of the fact that he has spent a great deal of time with gypsy singing greats, and knows a great deal of their *cante*.

The dubious merit of the majority of his *cante* aside, PEPE

MARCHENA has proven a fine friend to more than one down-and-out flamenco. He has performed free in many benefit festivals, raising money for one or another artist, has provided the money for several decent burials of flamenco artists, including that of Manuel Torre, and so forth.

MARCHENA, in his late fifties, is still active today, and with Spain's new medium, television, is unfortunately more widely viewed than ever before. I emphasize "unfortunately", for MARCHENA's TV singing is of rock-bottom quality, far inferior to the quality of which he is capable. He also takes his company on tour each year, and cuts, and has cut, numberless records.

From MARCHENA's point of view, he is a success. He is undoubtedly the flamenco artist with the highest income, at least of those who have remained in Spain, and certainly its most well-known *cantaor*. This has been true, amazingly enough, for the past forty years.

A non-gypsy, MARCHENA derived his name from the village of his birth, Marchena (Sevilla).

Who, other than MARCHENA, comprises the group that has done so much to create and popularize flamenco's impurities? The list is unending, so I shall just mention those who are perhaps the most significant, roughly in chronological order: PEPE PINTO, JUANITO VALDERRAMA, ANGELILLO, LA NIÑA DE ANTEQUERA, LA NIÑA DE LA PUEBLA, TOMÁS DE ANTEQUERA, RAFAEL FARINA and his brother, CANDELAS, MIGUEL DE LOS REYES, ENRIQUE MONTOYA, ANTONIO MOLINA, MANOLO ESCOBAR, and so on and so forth. Many others have played a dual role, having presented to the public at times commercial, at times extremely pure *cante*. The most renowned of this group are perhaps MANOLO CARACOL and JUANITO VAREA.

JUANITO VALDERRAMA

JUANITO VALDERRAMA deserves special mention because of the unbelievably low quality of what he commercially passes off as flamenco. He is, without a doubt, one of the most irresponsible *cantaores* to have represented flamenco in its history.

VALDERRAMA is, however, easier to laugh off than Pepe Marchena, for most of his commercial offerings are so extremely exaggerated that no one can possibly take them seriously. Examples: JUANITO and Dolores Abril's TV renditions of the "flamenco twist" and the "flamenco cha-cha-cha", his singing of popular songs, the cornier the better, to flamenco rhythms, and such.

JUANITO, in his late fifties, certainly cannot plead ignorance. He knows good flamenco, and a great deal of it, as can be observed by his two-record anthology recently released. His voice, high-pitched, classifiable as falsetto, is little suited for the *cante gitano;* however, he shows himself capable, in these records, of singing everything from the difficult *martinetes* and *siguiriyas* to the *cantes intermedios,* more suitable for his voice, and the *cantes chicos.* Even more surprising, he accomplishes his anthology with something of a purity of style and spirit.

VALDERRAMA represents just another example of integrity bowing to the System, spelled M-O-N-E-Y.

MANUEL VARGAS

1988 Update: (1907-1968)

The gypsy MANUEL VARGAS, renowned for his flashing smile and personality that have lit up Madrid's La Zambra for the past eight years, must be singled out as one of the top interpreters and maintainers of the Cádiz school of *cante*

Born in Cádiz, MANUEL early absorbed the *cante* of such singers as Enrique Morsilla and Antonio el Mellizo, both sons of the great Enrique el Mellizo; of Aurelio Sellé, the present *maestro* of the Cádiz school; and of various other lesser known singers. But MANUEL did not turn professionally to flamenco for many years; like his father before him, he made a lucrative living in the fish business. He was often urged to turn to the *cante* for a living, but, in his words: "I did not relish the idea of mingling with boisterous drunks at nightly *juergas,* which too often led to the artist drinking heavily in self-defense. And as I had a sufficient income from my business..."

Finally, in 1955, when MANUEL was forty-six years old, he was made an offer that was to his liking, and spent one year touring with the troupe of Mariemma. In 1956 he was contracted for La Zambra, where he is still a featured performer.

MANUEL has an easy, pleasing style of singing, and a great purity of expression. His voice, at times soft, at times shrill and harsh, is capable of communicating an infectious gaiety or profound seriousness. This can be verified by MANUEL's several excellent records now on the Spanish market.

Other than the *cante*, MANUEL's great passion is the bulls. One of his cherished memories and adventures was a season spent as a member of a bullfighter's *cuadrilla*, traveling throughout Central and South America.

The whole thing started over a few drinks in a Cádiz *venta*. A *matador* friend of MANUEL was about to embark for America, and with each glass of wine it seemed more feasible that MANUEL should go too. Think of the bulls and flamenco they could share, and the hell they could raise! Another drink settled it — MANUEL turned over his business temporarily to a friend, the bullfighter got him included in the official *cuadrilla* list as a sword carrier, and they were off. MANUEL got an all-expenses-paid trip, a good dose of his beloved bullfighting, and the opportunity of introducing his *cante* to the New World. And a whopping good time!

MANUEL has entered only one flamenco contest in his life, in which he won first prize for the *alegrías* (Cádiz - 1952) in stiff competition. As of this writing he has just embarked for a six-month stint at the New York World Fair, together with various other members of La Zambra's *cuadro*.

ANTONIO MAIRENA

1988 Update: (1909-1983)

Various epochs in the history of flamenco have come to be remembered by their outstanding *cantaor* or *cantaores*, such as the epochs of Tío Luis de la Juliana, Diego el Fillo, Silverio Franconetti and Tomás el Nitri, Manuel Torre, Tomás Pavón... The present era may well be referred to, in the future, as the epoch of ANTONIO MAIRENA.

There is little question in the minds of *aficionados* that MAIrena is presently flamenco's greatest living *cantaor*. There is no doubt that he is the most complete. Mairena is capable, as are few *cantaores*, of singing exceptionally well the most difficult *cantes grandes*, in all of their many styles, as well as the *cantes intermedios* and *cantes chicos*. He truly excels in the *cante gitano*, but is also perfectly at ease in the *andaluz*-inspired *cantes*. He draws the line, of course, at *cantes* that he considers non-flamenco in nature, such as the *milongas*, *garrotín*, and other *cantes* connected with the *ópera flamenca* movement. His voice is huge, flexible, filled with *rajo* when he wishes, and under his complete command.

Mairena has gone well out of his way to preserve and defend the pure *cante*, and in so doing has perhaps played the most important role of any flamenco artist in bringing about its resurgence. While most other pure *cantaores* merely retired from professional life when the decadent period set in, Mairena took upon himself a missionary role and actively set about preaching the gospel. As he remained active in the professional flamenco world within Spain — not in night clubs and theaters, where his *cante* was unwanted, but behind the scenes in *juergas* and *fiestas* — his example gained many *aficionados* to the cause. On a larger scale, he has been the guiding light in the organization of various remembrance festivals and other manifestations honoring such artists as Juan Talegas, La Niña de los Peines, Pastora Imperio, and others, which have caused talk, acclaim, recording opportunities, and have served to remind *aficionados* of the pure *cante*, and pure flamenco in general. His outspoken stand has of course made him many enemies and deprived him of many pesetas. For years it was a discouraging and losing battle, but he stood his ground uncompromisingly until, finally, after a lifetime of public incomprehension and rejection, Mairena and the purists appear to be coming out on top.

Antonio Mairena, born Antonio Cruz García, of gypsy parents, began singing as a boy in his family's blacksmith shop in the village of Mairena del Alcor, near Sevilla. He drew much of his early inspiration from the *maestros* Manuel Torre, Joaquín de la Paula, La Aguarocha, El Niño Gloria, and, much later, Juan Talegas. He early gained fame as a *saetero*, but his professional life did not begin until 1929, when he shared a theater stage in Sevilla with such greats as La Macarrona, La Malena, La Sordita, and Javier Molina. He then teamed up for a period with the outstanding guitarist, Javier Molina, and became a well-known figure around the center of flamenco activity at that time, Sevilla's Alameda de Hércules ,in the company of such artists as Tomás Pavón, Pastora Pavón, El Niño Gloria, Manuel Centeno, and Manuel Torre, to name only a few of the singers. Since that time Sevilla has remained MAIRENA's home base of operations, although he has spent several extended periods in Madrid, especially during the period 1942-1954, when he frequented Pastora Imperio's *venta* "La Capitana". During his career he has appeared as a headliner in an occasional company, notably that of ANTONIO, and has performed in old friend Pastora Imperio's *tablaos*, "El Duende", in Madrid, and "La Venta Real", in Sevilla. He has also embarked on various tours with his own company. As we have seen, however, until recently the unpopularity of the pure *cante gitano* caused him to direct most of his artistic efforts towards small, private gatherings.

The year 1962 was a banner year in MAIRENA's artistic life, and an important step forward for the cause. He not only was the deserving winner of the Golden Key of the Cante, in Córdoba, but was the chief guest at the Granada Summer Festival, among other activities. All of this has brought him fame and some fortune, but most important, has placed him in just the position of which he has always dreamed. He now has the opportunity of re-educating the wayward *aficionados*, and of tackling the problem of educating the popular public. He has launched into this enthusiastically, using diverse methods: his extraordinary *cante*, which is available to the public through his personal appearances and his many records; his organization of anthologies of flamenco, featuring various artists singing their specialties in their purest form (i. e. "*An Anthology of Cante Flamenco*", on the London label); and the book "*Mundo y Formas del Cante Flamenco*", written in collaboration with Ricardo Molina, which contains the deepest discussion of the *cante* to date. Because of his position as today's number one *cantaor*, people now listen to, and respect, his *cante* and his opinions, and great headway is being made. MAIRENA is thankful that his life's work has culminated while he is still in the prime of his *cante*, and he is fully prepared and eager to accomplish as much as possible.

We have seen that the *cante* of ANTONIO MAIRENA is pure and complete. His lively curiosity and desire to resuscitate the *cante* has caused him to investigate all possible sources, and he has amassed a vast knowledge of the worthy *cantes*. He is capable of singing all of the many styles of *siguiriyas* and *soleares* remembered. He has gleaned, from Tomás Pavón, Manuel Torre, Juan Talegas, and others, an impressive erudition in the *cantes* of the smithies; his range within these *cantes* (*tonás* of various types, including the *martinetes, carceleras, deblas*) is possibly equalled today only by Juan Talegas — in execution of them MAIRENA is presently far out in front, for only he combines such knowledge *and* the physical faculties to interpret these arduous *cantes* to their fullest. Two *cantes* often lightly passed over, the *tangos* and the *bulerías*, are also taken very seriously by MAIRENA. He commands an infinity of styles within each. One of his records is dedicated solely to various styles of *tangos*, which vary in pace and content from serious and slow to fast and frivolous. He is one of the few living *cantaores* who can unravel the obscure differences between the various styles of *bulerías* from Jerez, los Puertos, Cádiz, Alcalá, Utrera, Sevilla, Triana... He is a most excellent interpreter, also, of *cantes* that he does not particularly admire, such as the *polos*; his interpretation of this *cante* is the best that I have heard. But to avoid going on for pages, we can sum up this part of the discussion by stating: his knowledge is vast and profound, and in his mouth the *cantes*, even those he considers mediocre or uninteresting, turn to gold.

In spite of all of this, or possibly because of it, MAIRENA has his detractors. The reader might ask: what can they possibly say? Amidst the usual foolishness caused by ignorance or envy, we can single out two points worthy of discussion: the existence, or lack of, creativity and emotion in his *cante*. Is MAIRENA's *cante* creative? There is no doubt that he has had to partially create segments of nearly forgotten *cantes* that he has revived. No one today actually knows exactly how the *siguiriyas* of El Planeta were sung, for instance; only a vague outline has come down to us, the rest was added by MAIRENA in the musically logical manner in which El Planeta probably sang them. This is a form of creation. Besides this, every *cantaor* of greatness innovates and adapts *cantes* to his personality, style, and physical capabilities. In this sense MAIRENA is again a creator. However, he has too much integrity and *vergüenza* to do what so many so-called creators have done, which is to tag their slightly-changed adaptations of existing *cantes* with their names, in order to be remembered as creators. MAIRENA feels that a true creation, deserving to be remembered by the name of its creator, must be widely different and original. To date MAIRENA has dedicated himself, as we have seen, to resuscitate and maintain the already existent *cantes,* and has not attempted to create his own school. Notwithstanding, the creative potential is there. It is very possible that before his career ends there will exist *siguiriyas, soleares,* and perhaps other original sytles of *cantes* referred to as the *cantes* of ANTONIO MAIRENA.

The second point: does MAIRENA's *cante* transmit great *duende?* Not, I would say, in the open, earthy, uninhibited way of a Caracol, Manolito de María, or Fernanda de Utrera. MAIRENA's *duende* is more contained. He possesses a more complex, less primitive type of personality, and he has certain barriers to overcome before his *duende* breaks completely through. This sometimes causes the impression on casual or impatient *aficionados* that his *cante* is cold and impersonal, especially when he is singing publicly (in cold and impersonal surroundings). Like all flamencos, possibly more than most, MAIRENA needs atmosphere before his animal feelings begin churning about. His truly memorable *cante* emerges when all of his vast resources coordinate at the height of *juergas.* It is then, with the warm glow of wine inside and inhibitions flown, after he has danced and sung *por bulerías* and *tangos* for an hour or two and his voice has taken on added *rajo,* that his *duende* emerges in quantity and his *cante* attains true greatness.

ANTONIO is not the only Mairena who sings. His three brothers, Francisco, Juan, and Manuel, also sing excellent flamenco. Francisco and Juan, non-professionals, live in Mairena, and still maintain the family forge. Francisco also manages the local *casino.* Manuel, the youngest of the brothers, has recently turned professional (see section "Manuel Mairena").

Francisco is the finer *cantaor* of Antonio's two older brothers. He sings, when the spirit moves him, excellent *soleares* and *siguiriyas*. But just to observe him listening to Antonio is a pleasure in itself; Francisco silently sings along with him, making all of the facial movements and reflecting each emotional tug, a beautiful, unconscious pantomime that is a reminder of just how involved one can become in this absorbing art.

Juan Segovia, the well-versed Jerez *aficionado*, tells of the first time that he heard Francisco sing. Several of flamenco's top artists were gathered at a private *juerga* in Jerez, including Antonio Mairena, Juan Talegas, Terremoto, María Vargas, the guitarist Moraíto, and others of similar stature. Francisco was along more or less to keep Antonio company. No one at the *fiesta* had ever heard Francisco sing well, other than Antonio, and his first two or three *cantes* early in the evening gave the gathering little reason to be impressed. The *juerga* rolled along, and nothing more was heard from Francisco — the gathering calculated that he had had his mediocre fling at singing, but was by now too intimidated by the excellent *cante* of the *maestros* to give it another go.

However, about four in the morning Francisco opened up. Juan Segovia claims that he has not seen such a transformation in a singer since the days of Manuel Torre. "Francisco sang *por siguiriyas* like a man possessed, his emotion and *duende* encompassed the gathering; when he sang of love, they felt this love, and when he sang of death, they felt death. It was one of the most profound experiences that I have undergone."

This transformation that raises flamenco to the ultimate expression does not come about often in Francisco, nor in any *cantaor* In most, never.

MANOLO CARACOL

1988 Update: (1909-1973)

Manuel Ortega "Caracol." has gained international fame as much for his flamboyant personality as for his extraordinary *cante*.

He is one of the few *cantaores* of the decadent age of flamenco who has been able to prostitute his art wildly, passionately, and still retain a hard, pure core of excellent, traditional, sometimes creative *cante*.

Caracol has been the F. Scott Fitzgerald of flamenco. He has played hard, spent grandly, irresponsibly added to the decadence of flamenco (he is generally credited with originating flamenco singing to orchestral accompaniment), unashamedly swallowed his integrity and played up to the popular public (and often still does so), and yet at the same time his undeniable genius has enabled him to be one of the chief contributors to the prolongation and development of pure flamenco. When the craziness of the *"ópera flamenca"* filtered away and serious flamenco began a comeback, Caracol was there to record a valuable anthology only a short time before he began losing his voice and health due to his excesses. In his anthology Caracol gives an example of his vast knowledge of the *cante*, while clearly demonstrating that the *cante gitano* is his cup of tea.

During his prime, Caracol made, and spent, fortunes. The gypsies, and Spaniards in general, feel that to invite, to pay, is to gain prestige; by this criterion Caracol had a corner on the market. He was actually willing to fight for the privilege of paying. And so he paid, often in the neighborhood of thousands of *pesetas* a throw.

His frequent *juergas* are still talked about. They were as senseless, extravagant, and resplendent, in a flamenco way, as those of the "roaring twenties" of the United States. On an impulse Caracol would notify fifteen or twenty of flamenco's top artists, plus many of the top-priced prostitutes of Madrid. Around this core he would build succulent platters of food, inconsumable quantities of wines and liquors, a guest-list ranging from the most down-trodden gypsy to the most distinguished marquis, and the drive for a three-day *juerga* that might cost him anywhere from one thousand to three thousand dollars, a fortune in Spain at that time.

An they swung into action! Caracol always reigned as the gayest, drunkest, most argumentative, wildest, most flamenco, most generous. The highlights of the *juergas* would always issue from the *aguardiente*-soaked *rajo* throat of CARACOL in his gypsy deliveries of the *siguiriyas, bulerías, soleares, tangos, martinetes,* until he and his guests would be overcome with emotion. It was during these sessions that CARACOL truly let his genius run rampant in priceless demonstrations of just what this thing called *cante gitano* really is.

CARACOL was born into the most illustrious bullfight and flamenco family of all times. His ancestors and present relatives include: the bullfighter Fernando el Gallo and his famous sons, Joselito el Gallo, generally considered the greatest bullfighter of all times, and Rafael el Gallo, the erratic gypsy bullfighting genius who died in the late 1950's; and the flamencos El Planeta, Curro Dulce, Enrique Ortega, Carlota Ortega, Ignacio Ezpeleta, Gabriela Ortega (dancing mother of the mentioned bullfighters), CARACOL's father, Manuel Sr. (Caracol I), said to have been an excellent and knowledgeable *cantaor*, Rita Ortega, and today's Gabriela and Regla Ortega. And this is just naming a few of the most illustrious. (See Ortega family chart).

It is not surprising, in view of this background, that CARACOL never had a doubt as to his calling. He early began singing the *cantes* of his father, and by the age of twelve he won one of the first prizes in the 1922 *Concurso de Cante* in Granada. From them on, CARACOL performed anywhere and everywhere, and soon became a famous figure. In the 1940's he "discovered" Lola Flores, and formed an extremely successful team with her that lasted for some years.

CARACOL has gone into several artistic enterprises, such as a *tablao* in Mexico City. His latest venture is a Madrid *tablao*, "Los Canasteros", managed by CARACOL himself, which could assure his future if he handles it properly. So far, during the little over a year that he has been in business, he is doing fine.

Los Canasteros, actually, is probably CARACOL's last chance to keep intact his artistic and financial legend. His voice and faculties are waning and he would undoubtedly not work too often if he sat at home waiting to be called. Nothing would please his many enemies more, for CARACOL has stepped on many toes and

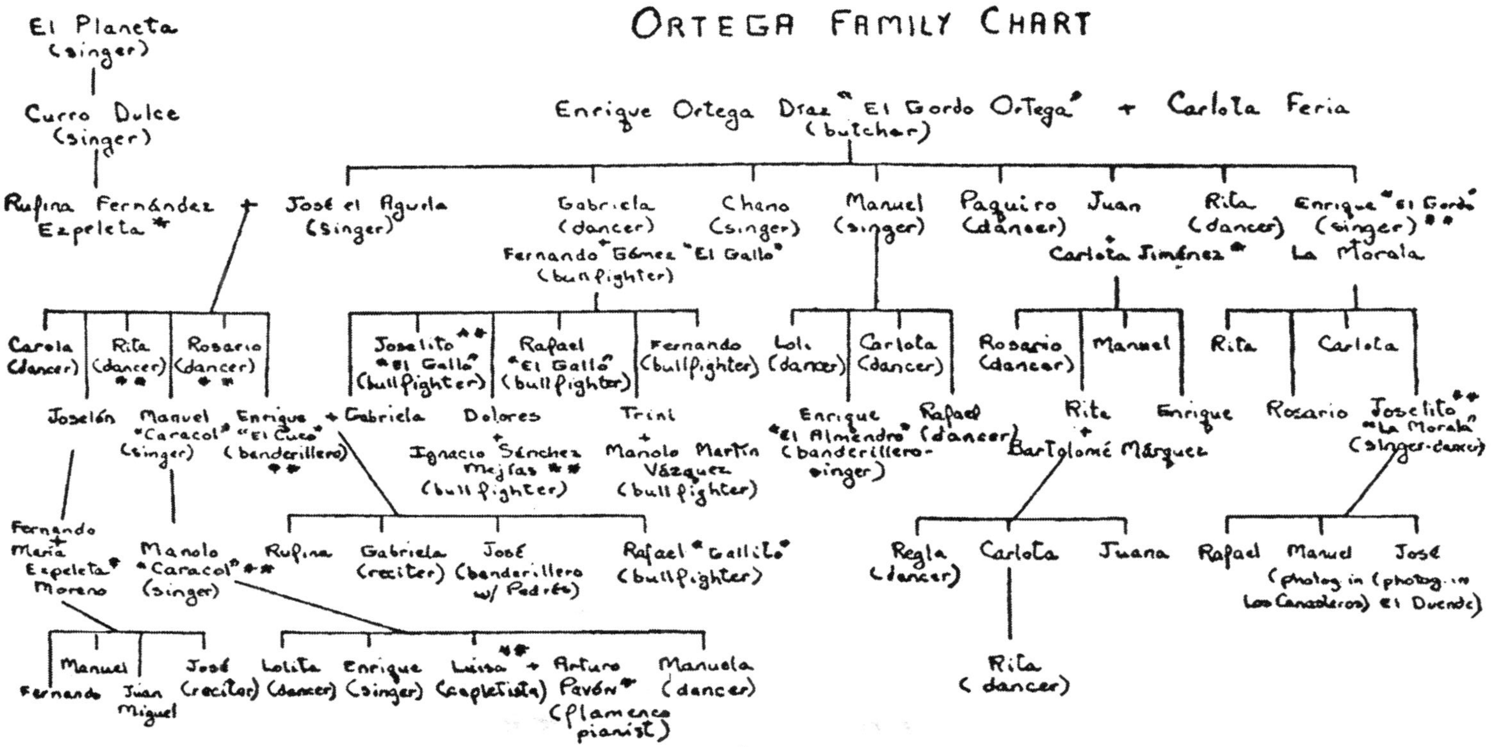

Ortega Family Chart

Enrique Ortega Díaz "El Gordo Ortega" + Carlota Feria
(butcher)

Children:
- José el Águila (singer) + Rufina Fernández Ezpeleta *
- Gabriela (dancer) + Fernando Gómez "El Gallo" (bullfighter)
- Chano (singer)
- Manuel (singer)
- Paquiro Juan (dancer) + Carlota Jiménez "La Morala"
- Rita (dancer)
- Enrique "El Gordo" (singer) **

El Planeta (singer) — Curro Dulce (singer) — Rufina Fernández Ezpeleta *

Children of José el Águila + Rufina:
- Carlota (dancer)
- Rita (dancer) **
- Rosario (dancer)

Children of Gabriela + Fernando Gómez "El Gallo":
- Joselito "El Gallo" (bullfighter) **
- Rafael "El Gallo" (bullfighter)
- Fernando (bullfighter)

Gabriela + Ignacio Sánchez Mejías (bullfighter)
- Dolores
- Trini + Manolo Martín Vázquez (bullfighter)

- José (banderillero w/ Padrés)
- Rafael "Gallito" (bullfighter)

Children of Paquiro Juan + Carlota Jiménez:
- Lola (dancer)
- Carlota (dancer) + Enrique "El Almendro" (banderillero-singer)
- Rosario (dancer) + Rafael (dancer) Bartolomé Márquez
- Manuel
- Rita
- Enrique

Children of Enrique "El Gordo":
- Rosario + Joselito "La Morala" (singer-dancer)
- Carlota
- Rita

Rosario + Joselito "La Morala":
- Juana
- Rafael
- Manuel photog. in (Los Canasteros)
- José photog. in (El Duende)

Carlota (dancer) + ?
- Regla (dancer)
- Rita (dancer)

Carlota + ? :
- Joselón Manuel Enrique "El Cuco" (singer) + Gabriela (banderillero) **
- Manolo "Caracol" (singer)
- Rufina
- Gabriela (reciter)
- Lolita (dancer)
- Enrique (singer) (cepetón)
- Luisa + Arturo Pavón * (flamenco pianist)
- Manuela (dancer)

Joselón + ?:
- Fernando María
- Ezpeleta Moreno

Manolo "Caracol" **:
- Manuel
- Fernando
- Juan
- Miguel
- José (reciter)

★ Connections, by marriage, with other famous flamenco families. Namely: los Ezpeleta (Ignacio), los Jiménez (Enrique el Mellizo), and los Pavón (Arturo, Pastora, Tomás).
★★ Artists whose photographs are included in the book.

In private gatherings all of the Ortegas perform. However, I have denoted the artistic preference of only the full or part time professionals. Only the most artistically significant branches of the family have been outlined.

hurt a multitude of feelings during his fiery career. For example, when recently asked whom he likes among present-day *cantaores*. he snapped: "No one — only myself!" He did deign to mention his past favorites, however: Manuel Torre, La Niña de los Peines, Tomás Pavón, and Antonio Chacón. Favorite guitarist? Melchor de Marchena.

But all said and done, even CARACOL's most vehement enemies cannot deny his artistic greatness. I have recently had another opportunity to listen to CARACOL in a casual atmosphere. It was in the half light of dawn in the gypsy *casetas* of the Sevilla fair. He was relaxed, drinking, at his best, and I came away again convinced that in expressing the *duende* of the true *cante gitano* there is no one that surpasses MANOLO CARACOL.

PEPE "EL CULATA"

1988 Update: (c. 1910-1975)

PEPE "EL CULATA" (the Butt-end), gypsy-born in Sevilla, is a fine present-day interpreter of the *cante grande*. He has spent several years singing in accompaniment of the *baile* in Madrid's La Zambra, and has not attracted the attention that he deserves. He has a strong *voz redonda*.

PEPE VALENCIA

(1910 —

Sevilla's PEPE VALENCIA, a non-professional, has gained great fame as a *saetero* (singer of *saetas*), so much so that during each Holy Week in Sevilla PEPE is much sought after as the emotional nucleus of Holy Week worshipers. He is ideal for such outdoor singing, as he has what is probably the most powerful voice in flamenco today (he sang in my apartment once, without really letting loose, and literally shook the walls).

PEPE, a butcher by trade, is not limited to the *saetas*, although they are definitely his strongest *cante*. He also sings well such *cantes* as the *deblas*, *carceleras*, and *soleares*.

NIÑO DE MALAGA

(c. 1910 —

EL NIÑO DE MÁLAGA, from Málaga, is one of flamenco's finer interpreters of the *cantes* of his region (*cantes de Málaga*), as well as the *cantes de Levante*. A long-time featured singer with the Ballet of Antonio and Rosario, the Niño de Málaga can be heard on the Westminster and Hispavox anthologies of flamenco. His voice is a fairly high-pitched, yet rough, *voz redonda*.

LUIS TORRE CADIZ

1988 Update: (1910-1985)

LUIS TORRE CÁDIZ, also called "JOSELERO", is an excellent non-professional *cantaor* of the traditional school of purists produced by the province of Sevilla. Born in La Puebla de Cazalla, LUIS moved to Morón de la Frontera at the age of twelve, and has lived there since. He had the good fortune of becoming the brother-in-law of the guitarist Diego del Gastor, and was thus assured of first-rate accompaniment on all singing occasions. Two of LUIS' immediate family of seven are also artists: his son Paco Torre "el Andorrano", a young singer of promise, and a daughter, La Niña Amparo, a *bailaora* now retired because of marriage.

LUIS neither acts nor looks the popular conception of a gypsy, but he is, as his name will testify. He is a pensive, retiring, good man, largely attracted to the serious *cantes* in particular, and all of the gypsy-inspired *cante* in general — although he by no means falls down in the Andalusian *cantes*. His favorite *cantes* are *por soleares, siguiriyas, martinetes, bulerías, malagueñas del Mellizo*, and *tarantas*. In effect, LUIS is a well-rounded singer, and takes his flamenco seriously; he perhaps lacks flamboyancy, which lowers his commercial acceptance, but makes his *cante* truer to the initiated.

A salesman by profession, LUIS began singing at the age of eight, and has since channeled his talents towards *juergas*. He has recently begun to gain well-deserved recognition by winning prizes in two flamenco contests: first place in both Jerez and Ecija in 1962, with his interpretations of the *siguiriyas, soleares,* and *bulerías.*

Apart from his most serious art, LUIS is, quite unintentionally an extremely funny story-teller. During one night of *juerga* in Morón, not long after LUIS had made eyes smart with an unforgettable rendition of the *malagueñas del Mellizo,* he began to talk of his first visit to Madrid.

"El Quino (a *bailaor* of fame from Morón) and I accompanted our wealthy landowner friend to Madrid as his personal entertainers and friends. He could not stand to be away from flamenco any time at all, and he always took half a troupe with him. He treated us like kings. Each of us was fitted for four new suits for the occasion, so stiff and fine that you could hear us coming half way down the block. He put us up in a fine hotel, gave us lots of spending money, and told us to look the big town over — he would only need us every other day.

"We were like two kids. Neither of us had been to a big city before. We dressed up in our crinkliest suits, bought the biggest, most expensive Havana cigars we could find, fortified ourselves with *vino tinto*, and marched straight down to Pedro Chicote's (1). On the way down we practiced looking important — you know, that casual air and squint-eyed look that important men always have —; we pulled open Chicote's door, pulled aside the thick, red velvet curtain, and whew! the stench of perfume hit us. The place reeked of beautiful women, all tightly stuffed into the most elegant dresses we'd ever seen — matter of fact, they were the most elegant women we'd ever seen —- all apparently sprayed from head to toe with perfume. We must have looked pretty bewildered. not at all important like we'd practiced, because the bouncer came over and asked us what we wanted, obviously preparing to lead us right back out. However, we dropped the name of our rich landowner friend, who was one of Chicote's best clients, and the bouncer waved us in to a choice spot at the bar."

---

(1) Chicote's, the most famous bar in Madrid, used to specialize in high-class floozies for highborn gentlemen. Chicote presently is better known for his famous bottle collection, part of which is now being displayed at the New York World's Fair.

Luis went on to tell of their elbow-rubbing with marquises, dukes, sundry millionaires, and exotic women, the likes of whom they had never imagined to exist outside of Hollywood movies. Their comments to each other, their first and subsequent reactions to this sophisticated world of sin, are hilarious, but belong in a story of another sort which I shall reserve for a more appropriate occasion. It is sufficient to say that after three weeks in Madrid "we had learned so much that we might have been born in Pedro Chicote's!"

JUANITO VAREA

1988 Update: (1913-1985)

JUANITO VAREA is a fine, present-day *cantaor*, capable of excellent *cante*, but also capable of commercializing his *cante* to an unnecessary extent. This commercial weakness is undoubtedly due to the influences of two singers in whose companies JUANITO has performed: Angelillo and Pepe Marchena. He has also performed with La Niña de los Peines and Manuel Vallejo, however, which helps account for the purity of his classical *cante*.

Born of non-artistic, non-gypsy parents in Burreana (Castellón), JUANITO began singing professionally at age fif' n in Barcelona, with the troupe of Angelillo. The *"ópera flam. ·*' movement was at its height, and Angelillo was its leader. Thus, there is little doubt as to the type of *cante* that JUANITO was required to sing at this stage of his career. JUANITO has gone on to become highly regarded by the Pepe Marchena commercialists, but also commands considerable respect among the purists, for, as has been stated, JUANITO sings excellent *cante* when he so chooses.

JUANITO has a high-pitched *voz redonda*, which is convertible into a *voz falsete* when he sings *a la Marchena*. His voice is both powerful and flexible.

JUANITO has been one of the featured singers at La Zambra during the past eight years. He is presently performing at the New York World's Fair, as a member of La Zambra troupe.

RAFAEL ROMERO

(c. 1917 —

RAFAEL ROMERO "EL GALLINA" was born of gypsy parents in Andújar (Jaén). Although Andújar is on the fringe of flamenco country, he early felt the desire to sing; he showed great promise, and, against the wishes of his parents, became an artist. It can be safely considered to have been a good move, for EL GALLINA has risen to a position today as one of flamenco's outstanding *cantaores*, as well as one of the principal guardians of the *cante puro*.

ROMERO excels in the *cante gitano*, although he is an extremely knowledgeable *cantaor*, capable of interpreting excellently many of the *cantes andaluces* (i. e. his *peteneras*). The Westminster and Hispavox anthologies illustrate a good selection of his finer *cantes: tonás chicos, martinetes, deblas, siguiriyas gitanas, la caña, peteneras, alboreás,* and *mirabrás*.

ROMERO has an ideal voice, tending strongly towards the *afillá*, and an integrity which has kept his *cante* pure in spite of his many years in the professional circuit. He has spent a number of those years with various companies, including that of José Greco, until settling down to an indefinite commitment in Madrid's La Zambra.

ROMERO is one of the few *cantaores* to have taken on students of the *cante*, including several non-Spaniards. His permanent residence is in Madrid.

PEPE VALENCIA

(c. 1917 —

PEPE VALENCIA first achieved international fame in flamenco circles through the record *"Pena y Alegría de Andalucía"*, featuring PEPE's singing, and the guitar of Luis Maravilla. This record, which won the French "record of the year" award in 1952, shows PEPE's singing to be accomplished and moving, his repertoire varied. His voice is classifiable as *redonda*.

Born in Valencia, PEPE has worked with various flamenco companies, including that of Pilar López. He presently resides in Buenos Aires.

LA FERNANDA AND LA BERNARDA, DE UTRERA

LA FERNANDA and LA BERNARDA DE UTRERA, inseparable gypsy sisters, are two of flamenco's most respected *cantaoras*. From the extremely flamenco town of Utrera, they have been raised on the superb *cante* of Mercedes la Sarneta and Juaniqui de Utrera, and today are the most gifted *maestras* of the Utrera school of *cante*.

LA FERNANDA, in her early forties, is famed for the quality rather than the quantity of her *cante*. As Manolito el de la María specializes in the *cantes de Alcalá*, so LA FERNANDA specializes in the *cantes de Utrera*, which consist basically of the *soleares* and *fandangos por soleares* of La Sarneta, and the *bulerías* and *tangos* of Juaniqui. In her interpretation of these *cantes* LA FERNANDA is queen. Her manner of delivery is warm, intimate, and so charged with *compás* and *duende* that *aficionados* invariably come away from a session of her *cante* feverishly insisting that LA FERNANDA is today's top active *cantaora*, regardless of her lack of a complete repertoire. I wholeheartedly agree! I greatly prefer a two or three-*cante* specialist, such as LA FERNANDA or Manolito el de la María, to a more complete singer of studied *cantes* lacking depth and therefore *duende*, as is the case of so many so-called "complete" singers today.

FERNANDA has a beautiful, moving voice *afillá*, soft, foggy, actually caressing, certainly not suitable for a large auditorium or noisy *tablao*, but ideal for a small, select gathering where true flamenco flows. Only in this atmosphere does FERNANDA relax and sing as only she is capable.

LA FERNANDA interprets other *cantes* as well as those mentioned, but greatly prefers, and usually will not move out of, her specialties.

LA BERNARDA, in her late thirties, is among todays' most moving interpreters of the *bulerías*, and is second only to FERNANDA in the interpretation of the other *cantes* of Utrera. BERNARDA's *bulerías* are wild, exciting — they seem to express everything gypsy: liberty, arrogance, rebellion. They are perfectly suited to her voice, which is classifiable as a *voz natural*. BERNARDA's *bulerías*, in fact, are similar in their gypsy wildness to those of Manuel Torre, the prototype of the *voz natural*.

The sisters have a curious relationship. FERNANDA, outgoing, *simpática*, is the spokesman of the two. She does most of the talking, makes the deals, and even sometimes takes the bows for BERNARDA after a BERNARDA performance, in commercial surroundings, when BERNARDA is feeling particularly withdrawn and reticent. One senses that BERNARDA is more old-school gypsy than FERNANDA, that she resents any *payo* intrusion in their affairs, and can only let loose in a *juerga* atmosphere. And yet she is the first to commercialize her *bulerías* in her *tablao* performing. At any rate, both seem to take their relationship for granted, and they (generally) get along with the utmost cordiality.

Recently the sisters have been lured into Spain's *tablao* circuit, where their non-stylized *cante* goes largely unappreciated. FERNANDA, a purist by nature, has not commercialized her *cante*, but certainly, and I might add, naturally, sings in a half-hearted manner in such surroundings. BERNARDA, on the other hand, has been easier prey for the system, and is not above introducing into her *bulerías* Mexican *rancheras* and other incongruous elements. Her argument may well be: "When in Rome ... etc ...", an argument perhaps appropriate for the mediocre, but impotent when confronted by true greatness.

The *cante* of LA FERNANDA and LA BERNARDA can be best appreciated, for those unable to hear them in intimate surroundings, through the admirable record "*Sevilla, Cuna del Cante Flamenco*", on which each sings an excellent band (this record also features such singers as Juan Talegas, Antonio Mairena, and others of stature. The Spanish record company Columbia is also presently cutting a few 45 rpm records featuring the sisters.

When not fulfilling their *tablao* commitments, LA FERNANDA and LA BERNARDA live at home in Utrera, a house almost always filled to overflowing with flamencos, liable at any moment to erupt into *juerga*. The sisters are presently performing at the New York World's Fair.

The only other artist of note in their family is a dancer-singer of some fame known as "La Feonga".

EL GORDITO DE TRIANA

1988 Update: (c. 1917-1970)

EL GORDITO DE TRIANA (Triana Fats), actually possessed of a slight build, is one of today's finer *fandangueros*. Purists have a tendency to look down on specialists in the *fandango* field — the *fandangos* are relatively easy to sing, and are often just crowd pleasers — but it must be recognized that EL GORDITO so fills his *fandangos trianeros* with *duende* and meaning that they are transformed into a true *cante jondo*.

A Triana-born gypsy, EL GORDITO is blessed with an excellent *voz afillá*. Regrettably, he is basically a one-*cante* specialist. He does dabble in Triana's other *cantes*, but none approach his *fandangos*.

GORDITO's excellent *fandangos* are included on the record "Sevilla — Cuna del Cante Flamenco". He lives in Sevilla, and earns his bread in *juerga* singing.

EL CHAQUETA

1988 Update: (c. 1925-1975)

EL CHAQUETA is one of the leading exponents of the *cantes de Cádiz*, and is, as well, extremely knowledgeable in other areas of the *cante*. Born in La Línea de la Concepción, EL CHAQUETA began singing at the age of seven. The greatest influences in his *cante* have been Aurelio Sellé and La Niña de los Peines. He has been active professionally in the *tablao* circuit for many years.

Blessed with a voice sounding somewhat like a gravel truck unloading, EL CHAQUETA takes some getting used to (it has not always been thus — rumors of a corrective operation on his throat are circulating). On top of this he enjoys imbibing, which, combined with his throat trouble, sometimes causes his voice to waver about the scale uncontrollably, with the fascinating effect of one held note resembling three or four.

EL CHAQUETA can be heard on the Westminster anthology interpreting the *romeras* and the *cabales*.

PORRINA DE BADAJOZ

1988 Update: (c. 1926-1977)

Every group has its dandy, and flamenco is no exception. This distinction is indisputably held by PORRINA DE BADAJOZ, one of flamenco's potentially fine young singers.

When truly decked out, PORRINA employs in his dress everything but neon lights. A wide, pin-stripe blue suit set off by a huge red carnation and a non-matching bright red tie, perhaps splashed with green flowers, which draws the eye to PORRINA's shirt — when tastefully selected, pale blue or green, but more often of vari-colored stripes or, his favorite, midnight black. Our gaze travels down, and we note bright red or green socks clashing colorfully with cream-colored, or black or brown and white shoes. There are also rumors of occasionally worn spats. Finishing touches include a colorful breast pocket handkerchief, a diamond stick-pin, one or two huge diamond rings, and black dark glasses, worn day and night. When PORRINA steps regally down from his chauffeur-driven American model, Salvador Dalí shrinks back into the crowd, frantically determining to extend his mustache another inch or perhaps curl his ears.

Obviously such grandeur deserves a title, and PORRINA, a former gypsy shoe-shine boy in his native Badajoz, has come up with a fine one: El Marqués de Porrinas. He insists on being announced thus, and has refused to perform if his wishes are not complied with.

PORRINA is a small man with a huge, magnificent voice, sometimes *redonda*, sometimes *falsete*, which he manipulates well in his *cante*. He has all of the potential of becoming a fine singer, for, although he has fallen into the role of a *fandanguero*, he knows considerable *cante*. It is likely that his potential will remain unfulfilled, however; he seems to lack the purist's *afición*, and he is far too commercially oriented. In his rare attempts at the *cante grande* one can perceive that he perhaps has the knowledge of the *cante*, but it does not come off well — he commercializes it, pretties it up, and it loses its strength and vital force. He is much more at home in the *cante intermedio*, whose basically melodious *cantes* suit well his notion of flamenco, and in the *cante chico*. Among the *chicos* his *bulerías* and *tangos* are outstanding, or at least can be when he wishes; in these *cantes*, strangely enough, he injects all of the drive and force lacking in his *cante grande*.

I recently had an opportunity to observe PORRINA at close quarters, in a gathering in which he and his excellent accompanist, Pepe de Badajoz, were the artists of honor. PORRINA faithfully followed the sketch of characteristics outlined above, although he generally sang better, and showed a wider knowledge of the *cante*, then he does in commercial settings. As interesting as his *cante* were some of his ideas. He recognizes that the non-Spaniard has been flamenco's salvation, that the foreign embracement of flamenco has caused Spaniards to pry open their closed minds in surprise and grudgingly recognize an art that many had come to loathe. He goes on to predict that this very foreign enthusiasm will carry flamenco to unexcelled heights of popularity and prosperity.

Regarding his own art, PORRINA declared that he is not overly-concerned with tradition in the *cante*. He believes that as long as he can sing a *cante* well, there is no reason not to sing it as he desires, which may not be as it was sung by its creator. In this he is absolutely right, for this concept was, before stagnation set in, the very basis of flamenco. However, to carry it off well both genius and taste are essential — Pepe Marchena has the same idea, and has strayed rather far off course. PORRINA's tendency, I fear, is not to create within pure flamenco, but merely to make the *cante* prettier and more acceptable to the *tablao* public to whom he most frequently sings. His attempts at *cante grande* testify to this. He adds flourishes, sings much of it in a *voz falsete*, and in the process sacrifices its character and meaning. In PORRINA's mouth the *cante grande* becomes *cante intermedio*.

PORRINA, one of flamenco's high-income artists, resides winters in Madrid, summers on the Costa del Sol. He is married and has a family, including a son who plays the guitar.

MANOLITA DE JEREZ

(c. 1927 —

MANOLITA CAUQUI BENÍTEZ "MANOLITA DE JEREZ", an excellent Jerez-born *cantaora*, has performed largely outside of Spain since 1950, and is consequently little-remembered by Spanish *aficionados*.

A complete *cantaora*, MANOLITA excels in the *cantes de Jerez*, the *fandangos*, and the *malagueñas de Chacón*. Her *voz natural* is ideal for any category of *cante*.

Juan de la Plata, in his book *"Flamencos de Jerez"*, honors MANOLITA as the "finest and most complete present-day *cantaora* from Jerez". She has been with José Greco's company for some years, and can be heard on his Decca release *"Danzas Flamencas"*.

LA PERLA DE CADIZ

1988 Update: (1925-1975)

As Manolita de Jerez is today's outstanding *cantaora* of the *cantes de Jerez*, so LA PERLA DE CÁDIZ (the Pearl of Cádiz) is presently the finest *cantaora* of the *cantes* from the nearby port of Cádiz.

LA PERLA, a *gaditana* housewife, is complete within the *cantes de Cádiz*, although she seems to prefer the less serious *cantiñas, alegrías, tientos, tangos*, and, above all, her admirable *bulerías*. Her voice is classified as a *voz fácil*, due to her easy handling of her *cantes*.

In the interpretation of the *cantes* of this important corner of flamenco, approval of the old *maestro*, Aurelio Sellé, can only be earned through true merit. He approves wholeheartedly of LA PERLA.

To my knowledge, the extent of LA PERLA's recording activity is two bands on the excellent record "*Sevilla — Cuna del Cante Flamenco*".

LA PERLA won first prize in the 1959 Córdoba contest of *cante* in the category *alegrías, mirabrás,* and *romeras,* all *cantes de Cádiz*.

ROQUE MONTOYA "JARRITO"

(c. 1928 —

ROQUE MONTOYA "JARRITO", gypsy-born in San Roque (Cádiz), caused quite a stir in the flamenco world during the first part of his career. He showed an exceptional ability and facility for the *cante,* which was encouraged by such singers as Tomás and Pastora Pavón, and JARRITO grew into one of flamenco's most knowledgeable and versatile young singers.

Today JARRITO is an old pro in the commercial circuit, and in many ways he shows it. While his *cante* itself remains relatively pure — JARRITO takes great pride in his purity of expression — his stage presence and mannerisms basely appeal to the public. Everything is worked out in much too smooth a manner; a wrist gesture here, two steps back here, raise left eyebrow now, a commanding gesture of right hand and arm there, three steps forward ... if it is not all rehearsed, it gives every appearance of being so. Needless to say, this lack of naturalness strongly detracts from his excellent *cante* and its emotional content; it is far more satisfactory to close one's eyes, or listen to his records, than to watch him perform. This same criticism pertains, to a lesser extent, to others, including Porrina de Badajoz.

JARRITO commands a wide repertoire of *cantes* and a lively *afición* that causes him to delve deeper into the *cante*. He will very likely end up with a truly profound knowledge, and become one of flamenco's valuable "encyclopedic" *cantaores*. Unless, of course, his commercial activities overshadow and discolor his *afición* and his *cante*. I can testify that as of two years ago this had not come to pass. A party of four of us sat in the Torres Bermejas, in Madrid, waiting for JARRITO to sing in the late show. By the time he came on nearly everyone had left, and his entire audience consisted of six unknown persons. Not in the least nonplussed, he asked us what we would like to hear. Considering how he probably felt at that late hour, we decided to let him off easy, and requested: *"por fandangos"*. To our great surprise and delight, however, he politely refused, and instead sang and explained a group of difficult *tonás,* beginning with the *toná chica,* and continuing into the *deblas* and *martinetes redoblaos* and *naturales.* That, to an audience whom to all appearances was uninitiated, was true *afición* and nobility.

As happens so often in Andalusia, JARRITO picked up his nickname through some childhood incident (the knocking over of a *jarro,* or earthenware jug), and it is still with him.

JARRITO has a style of voice not unlike that of his early mentor, Tomás Pavón. That is to say, a *voz redonda,* strong, flexible, and clear.

When not touring America or Europe, JARRITO can usually be found in one of Madrid's *tablaos.* His residence is in Madrid.

FOSFORITO

1988 Update: (1932 —

ANTONIO FERNÁNDEZ DÍAZ "FOSFORITO", of Puente Genil (Córdoba), is today's most talked about young *cantaor.* His entrance into prominence was sensational; he swept all prizes in the 1956 Córdoba contest of *cante* (for non-professionals), which brought him a flood of recording and performing opportunities and subsequent fame.

Fortunately, FOSFORITO is a purist and an excellent *cantaor.* I say "fortunately", for his fame has been as convenient for flamenco as it has for himself. It has helped a great deal in breaking the ground for today's classical flamenco movement, as it riveted the public's attention on a young idol who was singing a type of *cante* of which many were completely ignorant. It made little-initiated *aficionados* sit up and take notice, and they began to compare the offerings of Marchena and his group to those of FOSFORITO. For those who must worship a popularly accepted hero-figure, FOSFORITO substituted very nicely for Marchena, and flamenco took another step forward.

FOSFORITO sings a wide range of *cantes*. His depth within particular *cantes* is also good, considering his relative youth. He tends strongly towards the serious *cantes*, as his voice, temperament and demeanor are all of a solemn nature. A non-gypsy, he seems equally at home in both the gypsy and *andaluz*-inspired *cante*, although a basic influence of the Córdoba school of *cante* can be detected in many of his interpretations.

Presently a full-fledged professional on the *café cantante* circuit, FOSFORITO has to date retained his integrity. The only concessions that he grants the public are perhaps more *fandangos* than he would like, and an overly sophisticated delivery. But his *cante* itself has not become contaminated, to my knowledge. This has caused him some distress, as some of the more commercial establishments are not prepared for his type of flamenco, and often the crowds keep right on babbling.

For many years, including the period when most of his records were cut, FOSFORITO suffered from a throat ailment which reduced the resonance and strength of his voice. This has since been corrected by an operation, and today FOSFORITO feels himself capable of surpassing his past *cante*.

FOSFORITO is a dedicated young man, and his approach to the *cante* is somewhat intellectual. His activities include talks and demonstrations of the *cante* and, generally speaking, a genuine effort to spread the tidings of the *flamenco puro*.

FOSFORITO's residence, and base of operations, is Madrid. He and his family have lived there some ten years.

EL CHOCOLATE

(c. 1931 —

EL CHOCOLATE, a fine young gypsy *cantaor* from Sevilla, is a virtual unknown highly respected by other flamencos. He is a complete singer, specializing in the *cantes gitanos*, and especially those of Triana. He has not as yet had much to do with the *tablao* circuit, other than his appearances in Sevilla's Cortijo el Guajiro; he did appear in the 1962 Key of the *Cante* contest in Córdoba, and made an impressive showing.

EL CHOCOLATE, so-called because of his gypsy-chocolate coloring, has been influenced basically by three other gypsy *cantaores* from the province of Sevilla: Antonio Mairena, Juan Talegas, and Manolo Caracol. There is little doubt but that he will play a major role in the future maintenance and furtherance of flamenco.

ANTONIO RANCHEL Y ALVAREZ DE SOTOMAYOR

(c. 1931 —

ANTONIO RANCHEL Y ALVAREZ DE SOTOMAYOR, from Lucena (Córdoba), is another of flamenco's fine young singers. From an aristocratic family, SOTOMAYOR specializes in the *cantes de Córdoba* (*fandangos de Lucena, alegrías* and *soleares de Córdoba,* etc.), although he sings many of flamenco's other *cantes,* some better than others.

The main criticism that is usually made of SOTOMAYOR's singing — not actually a criticism at all — is that during his development he was too strongly influenced by the *cantaor* Fosforito. This has given them a similarity of style, but their impact on the listener is, in my opinion, quite different. Fosforito is more turbulent, more strongly emotional, while SOTOMAYOR is quieter, with a natural, less forced style. Like his favorite guitar accompanist, Pepe Martínez, SOTOMAYOR's style is at times too contained, and as such is better suited to the *andaluz* rather than the gypsy-inspired *cantes.* He is pleasing to listen to, however, and emits a definite undercurrent of *duende.*

SOTOMAYOR won first prize for his *fandangos de Lucena* in the 1959 Córdoba contest of *cante jondo.*

TERREMOTO DE JEREZ

1988 Update: (1934-1981)

FERNANDO FERNÁNDEZ "TERREMOTO DE JEREZ" is the latest artist from Jerez de la Fróntera's boiling pot of flamenco, *el barrio* Santiago, on the road to fame.

TERREMOTO has been surrounded by flamenco from birth. By his eighth year he both danced and sang well. At age twelve he was hired as a dancer in the company of Manolo Caracol, with whom he stayed until one wine-inspired episode: after a bit of grown-up tippling, young TERREMOTO went on stage to do his usual dance number, which enjoyed such success that he decided to sing a little. He signaled Melchor de Marchena to accompany him, and he sang and sang until the audience was on its feet crying out for more. This was all well and good until he finally arrived backstage. According to TERREMOTO, Caracol, fuming, promptly informed him that he had been hired as a dancer, not a singer, and that he could bloody well start on his journey back to Jerez.

TERREMOTO returned to Jerez, to be again absorbed by the *barrio Santiago*. His next opportunity came several years later, when he was contracted to cut his only record to date, a 45 rpm containing his three outstanding cantes: *bulerías, soleares,* and *siguiriyas*. At the same time, only three or four years ago, a television producer wanted to launch TERREMOTO's career on TV; the eccentric TEREMOTO refused on the grounds that he did not have the proper apparel. Again he returned to Jerez, still relatively unknown. His next opportunity arrived with the 1962 Jerez flamenco contest, in which TERREMOTO won a major prize. That, together with the minor sensation caused by his record, finally sent TERREMOTO on his way. He was snapped up by Pastora Imperio to perform in her chain of *tablaos,* and he is still with her as of this writing.

TERREMOTO now considers himself a singer. He has a great *rajo* voice (*voz afillá*), and a rough, purely gypsy style of delivery. He specializes in the *bulerías, siguiriyas,* and *soleares de Jerez,* the only *cantes* he sings truly well, to which he imparts a wild, vivid *duende*. Although presently overly stout, he still dances excellent *bulerías*, giving them an authentic gypsy flavor too rarely seen today.

Among the *cantaores* whom TERREMOTO admires are the late Niño Gloria, Antonio Mairena, and El Chocolate. Within the gypsy style of dance he claims that his brother, also called TERREMOTO, presently living in Buenos Aires, is unexcelled.

MANUEL MAIRENA

(c. 1934 —

MANOLO MAIRENA, younger brother of Antonio Mairena, is a young man who will certainly be a leading figure in the flamenco of tomorrow.

As is natural and fortunate, MANOLO's *cante* is very similar to his brother's in style, taste, voice, and even delivery. Both have a strong preference for the *cante gitano*. The main difference between them is that Antonio has some twenty years more of dedicated experience and investigation. This gap, however, can be bridged with the years.

MANOLO only embarked on his professional career about two years ago. He has since appeared as a leading singer in brother Antonio's company, in the 1962 Córdoba flamenco contest, in the Madrid *tablao* Los Canasteros, and so forth.

PEPE DE ALGECIRAS

(c. 1946 —

PEPE DE ALGECIRAS is a teenage *cantaor* with a fine talent for the *cante*. Even at his age he is a complete *cantaor*, as he demonstrated at the 1962 Jerez flamenco contest, in which he interpreted excellently such widely varying *cantes* as the *martinetes, siguiriyas, serranas, soleares, bulerías,* and *malagueñas*. A non-gypsy, his ability to interpret well both the gypsy and *andaluz cantes* is a rare and valuable talent.

Pepe could well serve as an example and hope for the younger Spanish set. He demonstrates clearly that there can be more to teenage life than the encroaching rock and roll, twist, drag-racing, marijuana ... Pepe sows his wild oats with bouncing *bulerías* and *tangos*, is delighted with flamenco and his exploits within it.

Pepe's art is proving to be not only pleasurable, but profitable. He was a sensation at the above-mentioned Jerez contest, making the big name pros scramble to hold him to a single prize (*malagueñas*). Shortly after this stirring success he was snapped up by José Greco, and is presently a featured singer in Greco's company.

Pepe comes from a family flamenco through and through. He learned most of his *cante* from his father, an *aficionado* of some renown and obviously a purist. His brother Paco, fourteen years old, will be one of flamenco's future outstanding guitarists. His other brothers and sisters are claimed by the family to be of equal quality as these two wonders. Their father has been the inspiration and *maestro* behind each of them, as much in the guitar as in the singing and dancing.

Pepe's voice, still high-pitched and boyish, is classifiable as *redonda*.

It can be safely predicted that Pepe, his guitar-playing brother Paco, and the family in general will be among flamenco's true leaders for decades to come.

OTHERS

Singers whose artistic careers are presently active, to whom the space for more complete biographies cannot be apportioned: Platerito de Alcalá, around fifty, is a gypsy from Alcalá de Guadaira just emerging as a professional. His specialty is the *cante de Alcalá;* El Niño de Montefrío (Málaga), non-gypsy, is a good interpreter of the *cantes de Málaga* and *Levante;* Juan Gambero Martín "el Niño de la Loma", non-gypsy, in his forties, from Fuengirola (Málaga), is a fine interpreter of the various styles of *malagueñas* as well as the other *cantes de Málaga* and *Levante*. He has won contest prizes in Córdoba, Málaga, and Fuengirola; Dolores de Córdoba, gypsy, from the province of Córdoba, is a moving but contaminated *cantaora* of *fandangos*. She is a longtime artist in Madrid's Corral de la Morería; MANUEL FERNÁNDEZ "SERNITA", non-gypsy, from Jerez, is a specialist in the *soleares*, *malagueñas*, and *alegrías*, as well as the other *cantes de Cádiz*. SERNITA has recently turned professional, and is playing Spain's *tablao* circuit; LA SALLAGO, gypsy, from Jerez, has a fine reputation in the flamenco world for her *cantes de Jerez* and *Cádiz*. Her husky, moving voice and style is reminiscent of a less wild but more complete Paquera; LA CHIVA, gypsy, from Jerez, is an up-and-coming specialist in the *cantes de Jerez*, which she sings in a wailing, primitive style not unlike that of Manolita de Jerez. To date LA CHIVA has not turned to commercial performing, but sings mostly in juergas, provincial fairs, and such; LA PAQUERA is one of the prides of Jerez. A *cantaora* of humble gypsy parentage, LA PAQUERA is essentially a one-*cante* specialist: *por bulerías*, which she sings in a truly moving, primitive style. LA PAQUERA is doing well with her *bulerías*, at least judging by her chauffer-driven foreign model; MARIQUITA VARGAS, gypsy, is presently the finest *cantaora* from Spain's *manzanilla* capital, Sanlúcar de Barrameda. She interprets principally the *cantes* of *Jerez* and *Cádiz*, excelling in the *bulerías*, *soleares*, and *alegrías*; ANTONIO DE CEUTA, gypsy, is a fine interpreter of the *cantes gitanos*, presently residing and performing in Málaga; ANTONIO CRUZ, non-gypsy, in his twenties, from Puerto Real (Cádiz), is a non-professional specialist in the *cantes grandes*. CRUZ was the deserving winner of first prize for *aficionados* in the 1962 Jerez flamenco contest; PEDRO LAVADO, non-gypsy, in his twenties, from Puente Genil (Córdoba), a follower of Fosforito, won first prize in the 1959 Córdoba contest for *serranas*; JESÚS HEREDIA FLORES, non-gypsy, in his twenties, of Ecija (Sevilla), was a prize winner in the 1959 Córdoba contest for his *cantes de Málaga y Levante;* JOSÉ MENESE, non-gypsy, around twenty, from the Puebla de Cazalla (Sevilla), is a young interpreter of the *cante grande* of great promise. Menese was appearing in Madrid's La Zambra before recently being called into military service. Fortunately, Menese has entered a delightfully understanding service that is permitting him to sing in the many summer flamenco festivals that are being presented throughout Andalusia. Menese has a powerful *rajo* voice and a fine command of the *cante grande*. *Aficionados* are excited, and the word is spreading: "Menese is the boy to watch". Los Hermanos Toronjo, a non-gypsy brother team from the province of Huelva, caused sensation among the popular public with their dual-voiced *fandanguillos*. Duets in the *cante* have always been darkly frowned upon by purists, and the Toronjos are not exceptions; Los Hermanos Reyes is another *fandanguillos* team that quickly jumped on the Toronjo bandwagon; Beni de Cádiz is a young singer admired more for his wit and *gracia* than for his *cante;* two *cantaores* from Utrera, Curro and Gaspar, have achieved some fame as promising young singers: Perrate de Utrera is one of the finer interpreters of the *cante de Utrera;* El Lebrijano is a young blond gypsy who shows great promise in the *cante gitano*.

THE DANCE

INTRODUCTION

Today nearly all theoreticians of the dance agree that the *baile* flamenco is directly descended from the ancient religious dances of the Indian Hindus. Even now a *jondo* dance is extremely similar in nature, movement, and emotion to a traditional Hindu classical dance (1). The arm and hand movements and the footwork, above all, have a striking affinity, although in other ways the two dance forms have grown apart; flamenco has evolved as a much more forceful and overwhelming art, more directly emotional to uninitiated audiences. In its evolution flamenco has lost, or shed, many of the traditional elements of the Indian dance; the flamenco dance is not symbolic or storytelling, for instance, nor does it employ the multitude of set eye and facial movements characteristic of much of the classical Indian dance. In effect, what

---

(1) Flamenco dancing may well have evolved from the following still-existent schools of Indian classical dance:

BHARATA NATYA, for women, consists of storytelling by means of elaborate hand and facial gestures, with short «intermissions» of abstract dance based on very intricate, shoeless footwork. The stories told are from the *Vedas* (scriptures of Hinduism, thought to date back to c. 1500 B. C.) and the *Upanishads* (dialogues on metaphysics, c. 550 B. C.). Costumes are worn. From south central India;

KATHUK, for both men and women, is the style of Indian dance with the most intricate footwork, every bit as much so as the most complicated flamenco *zapateado*. It is danced barefoot, with bell anklets. The arm and face movements are no longer symbolic. Costumes are worn. From northern India;

KATHAKALI, for men, consists of dance dramas based on the *Vedas* and the *Upanishads*, depicting demons and gods, oftentimes very fierce. Until recently both male and female parts were danced by men. Elaborate costumes are worn. Kathakali, which emphasizes virility, is probably the oldest and most primitive of the classical Indian dance schools.

Other than the prescribed storytelling, all of these dance forms permit sponteneity within the framework of the style, although not as freely as is permissible in flamenco. They are all accompanied by musical instruments and singing. In the forms *Bharata Natya* and *Kathakali* the singers relate the scriptural story that the dancers are unfolding.

in all likelihood has taken place is that the highly-civilized Brahmanic temple dances were adopted by a lesser-developed people, shorn of many subtleties, and returned to a more natural and primitive art form concerned only with the expression of oneself and one's emotions.

Let us attempt to construct a brief history of the development of these Indian dances within Spain. First of all, how did they reach Spain? Traditionally performed only in the temples during Brahmanic religious rites, these dances eventually began to be danced more popularly outside the church in India. It was then that they were first introduced into other lands by way of early Mediterranean trading vessels and overland caravans. The point of entrance into Spain was most certainly Gadir, later called Gades, today called Cádiz, the oldest city in Spain, founded by the Phoenicians around 1100 B.C. Gadir was an extremely important city, and it is likely that professional Indian dancers were brought in to entertain the city's royalty, probably during the time of the Greeks (c. 500-250 B. C.), less likely during the reign of the Romans (c. 250 B.C. - 475 A.D.) (1). These civilizations, with their emphasis on culture, undoubtedly introduced this religious dancing into their own temples, so that by the arrival of the Visigoths in Andalusia (c. 450 - 700 A.D.), this type of religious dancing had already become so traditional as to be carried over into the primitive Spanish Christian church, encouraged and even performed by early Christian priests (2).

The Visigoths accepted Catholicism and merged with the Hispano-Roman population, and religious dancing continued throughout their reign.

It is postulated that during the reign of the Moors (c. 711-1492 A.D.) these sacred dances were danced more and more popularly outside the confines of the church, possibly even by Spain's

---

(1) Hindu musicians and singers surely accompanied the dancers, and thus also introduced their art forms into Spain during this same period. This would partly explain the strong similarities that still exist between certain types of Hindu singing and music, and flamenco.

(2) «It is now known that the fathers of the primitive church openly admitted, and even fomented with their examples, the adoption by the Christian cult of certain elements of the sacred oriental dances, frequently danced by the very priests themselves.» («El Baile Andaluz», by Caballero Bonald, p. 59).

first gypsies, who were thought to have arrived as camp-followers of the Moorish armies (after having arrived in North Africa from their homeground, India, by way of Pakistan, Persia, and Arabia). As both the gypsies and the Moors already cultivated a type of dance largely derived from the Brahmanic religious dances, their arrival most certainly gave the existing Andalusian dances a shot in the arm.

Considering that the Moors ruled in Andalusia for eight centuries, it would be ridiculous to deny their influence in the development of the Andalusian dance. However, as their dance was also based on the Indian dance, it is probable that few drastic changes took place in the existent dance. The movements of the arms and hands and upper torso, especially, remained intact. The chief change was the Moorish discouragement of feminine footwork due to a ruling in the Koran to the effect that women will not utilize footwork so as not to show their legs. This ruling, and the lack of technical training among gypsy dancers, were most certainly the main reasons why feminine footwork was nearly nonexistent in flamenco until this century.

Another historical event in the development of the flamenco dance was the arrival of the second migration of gypsies to Spain around 1450, shortly before the Moors were expelled from their last footholds in Andalusia. The gypsies arrived from India by the northern route (Persia, Russia, etc.), bringing with them their interpretations of Indian dances and songs, and adding fresh fuel to the Andalusian folklore.

Here we must pause to defend our position from some Andalusian musicologists who, in the eternal struggle between *andaluces* and gypsies, insist that the gypsies played no creative role in the development of flamenco. They firmly believe that the gypsies had no dance or song of their own, but adopted the culture of each land where they came to rest; in this case, an already existent Andalusian folklore which they believe to have developed in Andalusia free from "outside" influences. The entire basis of their argument concerning the gypsies is that had the gypsies previously danced and sung anything similar to flamenco, gypsies from all countries would possess the same art and the fact is, they finish, gypsies from no part of the world other than Andalusia dance, sing, or play anything remotely similar to flamenco.

We shall answer their gypsy argument presently, but first let us investigate just what special elements have permitted Andalusian folklore to develop "free from outside influence". In their patriotic insistence on regional purity of expression I cannot help but think that these Andalusian musicologists have overlooked one thing: that Andalusia is a fabulous blend of races and cultures, and as such has only relatively recently developed a culture it can call its own. If they would only permit themselves to think of their blood mixture: Phoenician, Greek, Celtic, Roman, Vandal, Visigothic, Moorish, Negro (Negroes were first introduced into Spain as Moorish slaves and soldiers), Jewish, Syrian, Indian, and so forth. And as much as both sides might wish to deny the fact, there has certainly been a strong intermixing of gypsy and *andaluz* blood in Andalusia. There are few pure gypsies left in Andalusia, and as for pure *andaluces;* just what is a pure *andaluz?*

Now back to the Andalusian musicologists argument that had the gypsies brought with them a musical culture in any way connected with flamenco, gypsies of other countries would also practice flamenco which, they say, they do not. One of the many dissenting voices to this theory is that of Vicente Escudero. He writes in his book "*Mi Baile*" that he has spent some time and effort tracing the course of the fifteenth century gypsy migration from India, and found startling similarities between the music and dance of the Spanish gypsies, and the gypsies of other lands. He states that in Russia he saw a gypsy dance a dance very similar to the *farruca* in its *compás*, footwork, and movements of arms and upper torso, although the dance had developed there as more acrobatic. He notices that many of the *falsetas* of the Hungarian gypsy violin and the flamenco guitar are nearly identical, as much in feeling as in structure. In India he heard a gypsy woman sing a *cante* very similar to the *siguiriyas*, and goes on to say that many of the songs and dances of present-day India are closely related to those of flamenco. In stating this he is backing up the observations of several Indian and Pakistanian musicologists, all of whom describe with something of amazement the striking similarities between the two art forms. Many resemblances can also be noted between Moroccan music and flamenco; one can surmise that some centuries ago they perhaps had a common foundation, remembering that gypsy tribes are thought to have accompanied the Moors in their eighth century invasion of Andalusia.

However, there are gypsies in other countries who, truthfully, practice nothing remotely similar to flamenco. If Vicente Escudero and the many others of his school of thought are correct, and the gypsies did practice something resembling flamenco upon their arrival to Spain, why then do not the gypsies of all countries practice flamenco? An obvious answer to this could be that the music, culture, and atmosphere of the country in which particular tribes stopped tended either to encourage and further the gypsies' music and dance, or cause them to disappear altogether. Andalusia, of course, had an encouraging atmosphere, despite certain bans and restrictions (consult the *Cante* Introduction for a further development of this point); Russia and the Slavic countries possessed a folk music that was receptive to that of the gypsies. England and Germany and similar countries, on the other hand, possessed nothing in their culture or atmosphere that could even vaguely encourage the gypsies in their art, and undoubtedly it died out as new gypsy generations absorbed the customs and culture of their adopted countries.

Be that as it may, it is safe to say that the flamenco dance, and flamenco in general, has been brewing in Andalusia for many centuries. During the time of the Moors this type of dance was undoubtedly both religious and popular. After the Moors were forced out all religious connotations in the dance ceased. The dances were not only banned from the church because of their increasing sensuality and "sinful movements", but at one time persecutions were carried out against interpreters of certain dances regardless of where they were danced. It was then that the dance, together with the *cante*, went underground, becoming an art of the "lawless elements" of society. This happened more or less simultaneously with the sixteenth century edicts ordering the expulsion of the Moors, gypsies, and Jews, and can probably be cited as the beginning of the formation of flamenco as we know it today.

Our recorded history of the flamenco dance, however, does not begin until the beginning of the *café cantante* period of the last century (1842). The large majority of flamenco dancers at that time were gypsies. Their dance repertoire was sparse, and their techniques fundamental. The *jondo* dances were, for women, the *alegrías* and its derivatives (*cantiñas, rosas,* etc.), for men, the *alegrías* and the *zapateado;* the light dance, danced only by women, was the *tangos de Cádiz*. Little by little a few other dances were added: masculine *farrucas* and *bulerías,* feminine *tanguillos, bulerías, farrucas, soleares,* and, inevitably, *zapateados*. The footwork of the men was relatively primitive; the women, with very few exceptions, used almost no footwork at all, but concentrated largely on the more feminine arms, hands, and upper torso in general. This type of dance was soon to be altered by two revolutionaries of the *baile flamenco:* Antonio el de Bilbao and Carmen Amaya, both of whom came on the scene like cyclones to change the trend of the flamenco dance from non-technical to technical, from simple and direct to difficult and complex.

It was not until the formation of the large theatrical companies, in the late 1920's and early 1930's, that the flamenco dance began radically expanding in scope. It was in these companies that *cantes* formerly considered too sacred to be danced were innovated as dances. The *baile* suddenly became *the* attraction while the *cante* was relegated to a supporting role, and dancers sought diversity. Soon even the *cañas* were being danced, innovated as a dance in the early 1930's by La Argentinita; in 1940 Vicente Escudero innovated the *baile por siguiriyas* after much deliberation, for he too had grown up considering the *siguiriyas* too sacred a *cante* to be danced. With the ice broken, a profusion of other dances followed, both serious and light — *por martinetes, taranto, rumba, serranas, polos, peteneras, rondeña toque, zorongo gitano, guajiras,* and so forth —, and by the 1950's the flamenco dance had vastly expanded its repertoire.

This expansion of the dance has added a far greater diversity to flamenco. It now possesses two extremes formerly lacking: the profundity of a *siguiriya*, a *soleá* or a *taranto*, and the wild, uncontained gaiety of a *bulerías*. These dances, when interpreted by the exceptional few, are sublime.

There are other tendencies in the flamenco dance, however, that are doing a great deal to neutralize the above-mentioned progress. One has been the increasing use of castanets, formerly not used in flamenco dancing, which seriously hinder the proper movement of the arms and hands. (Purists consider that users of castanets in flamenco do so to cover up mediocre arms and hands). Another has been the tendency of *bailaoras* to go beyond their more conservative, feminine footwork, also at the expense of the upper torso, arms, and hands, into direct competition with the men, turning much of the *baile flamenco* into a non-aesthetic race towards high-speed, intricate, overly-extended footwork. This has gone hand-in-hand with another development: a confusion of the sexes in the dance. How many present-day *bailaoras* dress in male clothing and emphasize almost nothing but footwork and brusqueness in their dance; and, conversely, how many male dancers look everything but masculine when dancing. The condition that men be men and women, women, or at least appear to be, is an absolute necessity in the *baile flamenco* if it is to be effective. Otherwise it is false and even ludricrous.

The combination of advanced techniques and commercial settings has prepared the way for yet another deadly phenomenon in the dance, and in all branches of flamenco. In order to demonstrate their technical training to the utmost, commercial flamenco dancers almost universally dance set routines night after night, month after month, and, yes, year after dull year. These routines are painstakingly worked out with the guitarist, singer, and general *cuadro*, and become second nature to the performers until they can perform them effortlessly, without thought, and entirely without spontaneity. Thus, flamenco is rapidly changing from one of the most creatively spontaneous arts the world has known to an art form totally lacking in imagination and impulsive freedom, without which flamenco has left far less claim to greatness.

These routines are encouraged by commercial management and artists alike. Dance academies grind out numberless dolls moving through identical dances, with no knowledge of true flamenco dancing and no instinct for improvisation. Even when an exceptional dancer does come along who is capable of spontaneous improvisation, he quickly learns that such doings are forbidden fruit. The system simply does not permit is. Fellow members of the *cuadro* complain that they cannot follow improvisation properly, and the management therefore forbids it because the ultimate product is often-times disjointed and messy. The artist's pride in his ability to improvise, or successfully follow another's improvisation, has been nearly lost in the shuffle. What little pride remains in flamenco that it can permit itself this stupor, this lethal undoing of a great art!

In order to avoid misunderstanding, we should perhaps define more clearly just what is meant by spontaneous improvisation. I do not use the term in its strictly pure sense, which would be the rendering of a completely new version of a *baile* (*toque, cante*) each time it is performed. Perhaps it was that way at one time, but that would be asking too much today. Besides, certain elements in the dance of any and every dancer are molded by his personality and physical makeup, and must remain the same. But the dance should at least have *something* original each time it is danced, if it is only the rearrangement of the components of the routine.

As an illustration, let us discuss the long-range effects of the dance of a well-known dancer, just one of the hundreds of examples we could select to demonstrate the public disillusion generated by a routinist. This dancer has for some time been featured in one of the better Madrid *tablaos*, and thus is one of the first dancers to be seen by visiting *aficionados*. The first time they see her they are bowled over, they fall in love, and they hurry back to see her again. The second night she is equally as effective, except that they begin to notice that she does exactly the same *siguiriyas* and *guajiras* as she did the previous time. They go again and sit through two more shows, comparing ,and observe with disenchantment that each time these same two dances are danced, and each time with exactly the same movements, footwork, and expression, even to the arching of eyebrows and the animal cries of lust and suffering. The *aficionados* make one last stab, perhaps at one of her concerts outside of the *tablao*, in hopes that in a different atmosphere she will break the routine. But again the same. The ultimate reaction of these viewers? They cannot help but feel like lovers deceived; they still recognize that she is a fine dancer and actress, but the seemingly spontaneous emotion that had so captivated them: dissipated. They end up feeling that they have, literally, been taken.

Is this her fault? In a way, yes, but it is now so strongly prevalent in the System as to be tradition. Anyone who bucks the System is toying with the ostracism of fellow artists and the disapproval of the management. Instead of being admired for their imagination and creative ability, the few remaining creative artists are actually written off as this is unbelievable, but unfortunately true) proponents of an inferior "country-gypsy style"; they are actually sneered at for their creativity and spontaneity! Truly the defense mechanisms, the self-deception, the self-justification employed by the mediocre in this and all arts is appalling. The danger and stagnation comes when the mediocre not only predominate in numbers, but manage to wrestle a commanding position. This is the situation in flamenco today.

Trusting that the preceding pages will suffice to give a rough history of the evasive *baile flamenco*, and to point out the overall trends and directions that the *baile* has taken, let us now attempt to fill in the more modern gaps through the biographies of flamenco's outstanding dancers — certainly no easy task, as the lives of the early dancers are poorly documented and sketchy at best.

As the masculine and feminine styles of dance are so clearly defined, it will clarify our discussion if we consider them separately. First, then, the masculine element.

BAILAORES

MIRACIELOS
(c. 1800 - 1870)

According to Vicente Escudero, MIRACIELOS (The Sky Watcher) was the first dancer to find his way into recorded flamenco history. Sr. Escudero goes on to state that MIRACIELOS was the first *bailaor* to dance to flamenco guitar accompaniment, a statement that can be neither refuted nor confirmed.

MIRACIELOS, a gypsy thought to have been born in Cádiz, reputedly danced a primitive *zapateado* and forms of the *alegrías* (*rosas, romeras*, etc.). He was blessed with creative ability and, together with El Raspao, prepared the way for the phenomenal rise and development of the *baile flamenco*.

MIRACIELOS was at his prime during the second quarter of the past century. He achieved fame in the early *cafés cantantes*, and is cited by Sr. Escudero as the initiator of a line of *bailaores* which carries up to the present time: El Raspao, Enrique el Jorobao, Antonio de Bilbao, and Vicente Escudero.

EL RASPAO
(c. 1820 - 1880)

ANTONIO EL RASPAO (the Scratched), a gypsy reputedly from Cádiz, was the other early *maestro* of great fame. He made further innovations in the dances of Miracielos, strongly influencing the entire trend of the *baile flamenco*. He was the *maestro* of Enrique el Jorobao, Antonio el Pintor, and others.

ENRIQUE EL JOROBAO

(c. 1840 - 1910)

A tribute to old-time flamenco is that ENRIQUE EL JOROBAO (Henry the Hunchback) could become a legendary figure of the *baile flamenco* despite his deformed back. This, I am afraid, would be out of the question today; ENRIQUE would not stand a chance regardless of his talents.

ENRIQUE, a gypsy born in Cádiz, was reputedly the creator of what is known today as the *zapateado de las campanas*, which was further developed and popularized by Antonio el de Bilbao and Juan Sánchez "el Estampío", among others. A disciple of El Raspao, ENRIQUE was the *maestro* and inspiration of Antonio el de Bilbao.

ANTONIO EL PINTOR AND LAMPARILLA

ANTONIO EL PINTOR (Anthony the Painter) and LAMPARILLA (Little Lamp), although father and son, were artistically far removed, according to Fernando el de Triana.

ANTONIO EL PINTOR (c. 1835-1900) was most renowned because of his association as a student with El Raspao, and his footwork. His dance, however, was mediocre. He apparently raised his arms over his head at the beginning of a dance, assumed a fetching smile, and remained thus throughout the entire dance.

LAMPARILLA (c. 1860-1883), on the other hand, was a child *fenómeno*. His dancing was complete. His arms, hands, posture, footwork, and entire manner of dancing were well-balanced in a way that escaped his father. In his photos in this book it is evident that even as a child LAMPARILLA possessed two essentials of the male dance, arrogance and self-possession.

LAMPARILLA died at an early age, killed, so goes the legend, by the "fury of his fabulous dance".

ANTONIO EL DE BILBAO

(c. 1880 - 1945)

ANTONIO EL DE BILBAO can be cited as flamenco's first virtuoso of the feet, and as such the principal trend-setter for today's complex dance. ANTONIO's intricate footwork so confounded the public, in fact, that he was considered flamenco's number one *bailaor* despite the mediocre state of the rest of his dance (from the waist up).

It is said that when the famous *bailaor* Ramirito first saw ANTONIO EL DE BILBAO dance, in Madrid around the year 1925, he became neurotic. Ramirito had considered himself exceptional in his footwork, never dreaming it could reach the complexity so easily achieved by ANTONIO.

Born in Sevilla of non-gypsy parents, ANTONIO was taken to Bilbao at an early age, where he trained for classical Spanish dancing before turning to the more lucrative flamenco. He was a disciple of Enrique el Jorobao, and went on to become the *maestro* of a *bailaor* considered by many supreme in the present century: Vicente Escudero.

The story is told of ANTONIO DE BILBAO's first appearance as an artist in Sevilla. He was to dance in a *café cantante* there, accompanied by the guitarist Luis Molina. Posters went up announcing the event, displaying the unlikely *payos:* ANTONIO, a pudgy little man from Bilbao (it was not announced that he was born in Sevilla), and Luis, a *madrileño* sporting a wide, black mustache and a Derby hat.

"Ho, ho, what good fun!", the flamencos cried. The word spread rapidly, and opening night the place was packed with artists and *aficionados* eagerly awaiting the spectacle. There was no doubt in anyone's mind that the two *payos* from the North would make complete asses of themselves.

The show began. ANTONIO EL DE BILBAO nonchalantly mounted

a great wooden table. Luis Molina stood nearby with a foot propped comfortably on the edge of a chair. The crowd was in fine humor — witty comments circulated through the room about the appearance of the two so-called artists. The *sevillanos*, at their best when making fun of others, were having a ball, but not for long ... to the open-mouthed amazement of all, *"esos tíos"* (those uncles) launched into a *zapateado* the likes of which no one in the audience had ever seen. Superior Sevillanan airs and wiseacre smiles vanished like magic as ANTONIO's feet began spitting fire, executing impossible intricacies in perfect time to Luis' lightening *picado*, an unbelievable *picado* that followed each movement of ANTONIO's feet to perfection.

On and on, twenty full minutes of the most complicated *zapateado*, wildest *picado*, and accomplished teamwork that had ever been seen in Sevilla. Flamenco-wise, the merits of their performance may have been questionable, but one thing is certain: no one in Sevilla ever again laughed at ANTONIO DE BILBAO or Luis Molina.

F A I C O

(c. 1880 - 1938)

FRANCISCO MENDOZA RÍOS "FAICO", a Triana-born gypsy, son of the *cantaora de soleares*, La Aguarocha, is remembered as the creator of the *baile por farruca*. His dance has been described to me as majestic and profound, for the *farruca* was then considered more of a *jondo* dance than it is today.

FAICO spent World War I in Russia, and made the very best of his stay. He charmed the Russians with his dance, and when he left, around 1920, he carried away with him a beautiful Russian wife. They journeyed to Paris, where FAICO had further successes with his dance, until the great tragedy of his life befell him. An admirer of FAICO's wife drugged him and ran off with the Russian beauty.

FAICO made his way back to Spain, brokenhearted and disillusioned, and spent the remainder of his days in Sevilla. He never saw his wife again. (The present-day *bailaor,* El Faico, is not related to the subject of this biography).

ESTAMPÍO

(c. 1880 - 1957)

JUAN SÁNCHEZ VALENCIA "EL ESTAMPÍO" (the Blast), until his death among the few conservers of the old-style of dance, was one of this century's truly outstanding *bailaores.*

EL ESTAMPÍO combined excellent footwork with expressive, but masculine, arms and hands. He was equally adept and creative within both the profound and light dances, many of his innovations and interpretations being so worthy as to still be danced today, including one or two of his rare comic creations.

EL ESTAMPÍO was born in the gypsy quarter of Santiago, in Jerez de la Frontera, into a family of very humble means. During his childhood he was just another urchin tumbling about the streets of Jerez, dancing instinctively whenever the opportunity arose to earn a few coins for his family. While in his teens he decided to take lessons, and became the most promising and dedicated student of Salud Rodríguez, dancing daughter of a flamenco guitarist called El Ciego (the Blind One). (The fact of having studied with a woman very probably explains EL ESTAMPÍO's accomplished arm and hand movements). EL ESTAMPÍO developed fast and well, and in his twenties achieved considerable fame in the flamenco world, the world which ultimately recognized him, and a *bailaor* from Castilla, Vicente Escudero, as the preeminent *bailaores* of their time.

Juan de la Plata writes that EL ESTAMPÍO, before turning wholeheartedly to the dance, tried his hand at bullfighting under the name of El Feo (the Ugly One). He fought in a few amateur fights without *picadores,* but then decided to concentrate wholly on his dancing. His bullfight training was not wasted, however, inasmuch as the posturing and movements in his dance were often the very same as those he employed in his bullfighting. Entire dances, in fact, were inspired by bull ring incidents, such as his comic dance *"del picaor"*, created one night during a *juerga* after having viewed an extremely bad performance by a *picador*.

After years of performing in companies and *cafés cantantes*, EL ESTAMPÍO finally settled down to teach in a little academy in Madrid, in which he guided many of today's outstanding dancers. During his last few years, worn and tired, he had to teach from a sitting position; even this did not halt his stream of worshipful students.

EL ESTAMPÍO's death, in 1957, caused wide mourning in the flamenco world, for besides being a man loved and respected, it was recognized that another of flamenco's irreplaceable old purists had left the scene. Like most flamencos of his day, EL ESTAMPÍO died in near poverty. He outlived all of his family, and his few personal effects were sold by the government in El Rastro, in Madrid (dubbed in English "thieve's market"). Included in these effects were the photos of EL ESTAMPÍO printed in this book, which were retrieved from El Rastro by ESTAMPÍO's close friend, the *bailaora* La Quica.

JOAQUIN EL FEO

(c. 1880 - 1940)

Madrid-born JOAQUÍN EL FEO (Jonathan the Ugly One) is said, by the flamencologist Caballero Bonald, to have developed the *farruca* and the *tientos* to hitherto unknown heights of majesty. Brother of the famous *cantaora*, Mercedes, la Chata de Madrid, JOAQUÍN was also an excellent guitarist.

R A M I R E Z

(c. 1885 - 1930)

ANTONIO LÓPEZ RAMÍREZ "RAMIRITO", from the Jerez neighborhood of Santiago, was one of flamenco's most renowned *bailaores* during the first third of this century. He is said to have contributed creatively to the *baile*, and to have maintained a well-balanced, old-style dance. He is generally remembered as very elegant and colorful, both in his person and in his dance.

Augusto Butler writes of him, in note twenty-four of Javier Molina's book:

"We could see him daily, season after season, in the large *cuadro* of Sevilla's Kursaal, between the years 1920-1925, where he was the outstanding *bailaor*. (Ed. note: the photo of the Kursaal *cuadro* included in this book has been dated by La Quica at 1918). His sensational number was his *farruca*, which was even superior to that of El Faico, its creator.

"One of the principal characteristics of his art was that he was very manly in his dance, which is, and has always been, unusual among *bailaores*.

"Ramirito, according to what I have heard, died insane, in the asylum Miraflores, in Sevilla, or in the Capuchinos, in Cádiz, around the year 1930, still relatively young".

VICENTE ESCUDERO

1988 Update: (c. 1895-1980)

VICENTE ESCUDERO, the world-renowned *bailaor* from Castilla, is without a doubt the most controversial *bailaor* of this century. To many VICENTE is a God who can do no wrong. These admirers include the vast majority of the general public as well as the intellectuals, including nearly all writers on the subject. Among the majority of his artistic contemporaries, however, VICENTE ESCUDERO is by no means a revered name.

Why this difference of opinion? Who is right? Depending on their points of view, both factions have good arguments.

VICENTE used to say: *"Copiar es igual que robar."* "Copying is the same as robbing." He not only used to say it, but meant it. With this in mind, we can begin to undertand VICENTE ESCUDERO and his dance. For VICENTE's dance is truly unusual and original; he is a creator in the purest sense of the word. VICENTE could not be bothered with rules and regulations. He broke norms, shattered traditions, and was consequently called *"loco"* for many years before finally becoming generally recognized as the supreme *bailaor* of his time.

VICENTE early felt an irresistible attraction to flamenco, or rather, to certain facets of flamenco. He liked flamenco's drive and force, its subtlety, its beauty and passion, but he could not, and would not, be contained by what he considered its insignificant and unimaginative traditions. When VICENTE danced, he wanted to be completely free to dance as he pleased.

One of the revered traditions scorned by VICENTE was the *compás*. He could not stand to be confined within its well-defined structure, and he rebelled. He found accompanists who were willing to forego the *compás* and just follow his whims and fancies, thus setting the stage for the widely-varied opinions about his dance. The public in general did not know or care much about the *compás*, as long as VICENTE could produce his type of dance. To flamenco artists, however, one who cannot, or does not, keep the *compás* is not even to be seriously considered. They also point out that at times VICENTE employed many "tricks" in his dance, such as the snapping and clicking of his fingernails, one white and one black boot, and so forth.

Before going on, it might be wise to arbitrate in this dispute, at least for the purposes of this text. Flamenco artists, of course, are absolutely right in stating that traditional flamenco without *compás* is not good flamenco. Such an innovation generally accepted could lead to the complete destruction of flamenco's structure as we know it. However, in my opinion we must consider VICENTE ESCUDERO as the great exception, much as was Carmen Amaya in the feminine dance. We must judge his genius and accept, or overlook, his eccentricities in view of his great contribution to flamenco, while at the same time giving thanks that his more revolutionary ideas did not become popular in the flamenco world.

For regardless of his eccentricities, VICENTE has contributed greatly to maintaining the old-time *jondo* dance. When VICENTE settles down to dance what he considers pure flamenco, putting all tricks aside, he is traditional to the core. His movements and posturing are age-old, his *duende* is profound; his economy of movement and rock-earthed hardness gave pause to many a *bailaor* of the more frantic modern school. He was always there to condemn the statement "It is necessary to adapt art to the epoch in which we live", made by those who wanted to stylize and modernize flamenco, by retorting flatly: "Flamenco dancing admits neither evolution nor stylization, as it was born stylized." Thus VICENTE has at one and the same time been a decided revolutionary as well as a staunch defender of the ancient *baile jondo*.

VICENTE was born and raised in Valladolid, spending much of his childhood around the gypsy neighborhoods. (It is generally agreed that, contrary to his gypsy appearance, VICENTE is not a gypsy. VICENTE himself is evasive about the point). He tells in his book *"Mi Baile"* how he used to help the gypsies in their horse-trading. His job was to cling to the legs of whatever horse was being sold and cry:

"No, no, don't sell my horse, he's the most wonderful, gentle horse I've ever had. Oh, please, please!"

That nearly always clinched the deal. The hard-hearted buyer would immediately produce the money so as not to lose such a good buy, and shortly after would probably end up flying ungracefully over the horse's head. VICENTE says that "fortunately I ran faster than a train in those days".

VICENTE grew to be a problem child. He wanted to be, of all of the unheard of things in Valladolid, a flamenco dancer. His father repeatedly got him jobs in Valladolid print shops, only to have him lose them due to dancing and horsing around on the job. In the meantime, VICENTE danced at fairs and whenever else he could, but consistently ran up against flamenco's big problem of old: secrecy. No one would teach him the fundamentals of the dance, such as the *compás, palmas,* etc. (He calls this not being *"enterao"*, or "clued in"). Around the age of seventeen he began to be hired in *cafés cantantes*, but always lost the jobs as soon as it became evident that he was not *"enterao"*.

Still no one would teach him the fundamentals, until finally he met Antonio el de Bilbao, who saw the promise of the lad and taught him what he needed to know. Then VICENTE was accepted in the *cafés cantantes* and began making a name for himself, only to quickly become disenchanted. He found that he did not like the atmosphere of the *cafés cantantes*, especially the boisterous drunks that gathered night after night.

So he walked out, and began playing theatrical "*fines de fiestas*" throughout Spain (intermission and closing acts for theatrical shows). Before long he went to Portugal and commenced his off-beat flamenco, firstly because he could not find a guitarist there who knew the rhythms, later because he began to enjoy the liberty gained by dropping the *compás*.

Next stop, Paris, where VICENTE was to build such a reputation for himself that his name leapt the Pyrenees and became known throughout Spain. Shortly after VICENTE's first Paris recital, in 1922, he became strongly influenced by the Dadaistic and surrealistic schools of painting, to such an extent that he took up painting himself and, what for us is more significant, began applying these concepts to his flamenco dancing. With an entire philosophy to back up his own instinctive feelings, VICENTE really let himself go. He began giving concerts to the clashing of two orchestras going separate ways, or to the humming of dynamos set at different pitches. This, he states in his book, was the most creatively delightful period of his career. He went so far as to rent a little deserted theater in a bohemian section of Paris in which to rehearse and give exhibitions of his surrealistic flamenco dance. That almost no one came to these recitals served only to delight him further. VICENTE feels that the doings of geniuses are never appreciated by contemporary generations; the gathering of crowds at his recitals would have only denoted failure.

It was not long, however, before VICENTE was in great demand by the newly-forming Spanish ballet companies. He worked frequently and well with La Argentina and Pastora Imperio, and it is then that his dance began attracting widespread acclaim. VICENTE became a *bailarín* as well as a *bailaor*, but had the rare talent of keeping these two distinct types of dance separate; his flamenco remained primitive and free from ostentatiousness, while at the same time the possibilities inherent in Spanish ballet awakened his interest and he began choreographing and dancing, together with La Argentina, such Spanish classical numbers as *El Amor Brujo*.

Since those days of the late twenties and early thirties VICENTE has danced wherever and whenever he wished .He considers his artistic successes in various countries, particularly in the United States and France, significant parts of his career, for VICENTE is internationally oriented. He recognizes by instinct and experience that probably as large a percentage of the audience understands and feels his *baile* outside of Spain as within (in fact, nearly all well-traveled flamenco artists eventually, and often reluctantly, come to this conclusion — it is not that foreign audiences understand much of what is going on, it is simply that neither do Spanish audiences).

VICENTE's preferred dances? The mainstays of his flamenco have always been the traditional *alegrías* and *zapateado*, although the dance that most moves him is *por siguiriyas*. VICENTE himself was the first dancer in history to dance the *siguiriyas*, in 1940, which he did only after much deliberation, as the *siguiriyas* had always been respected as a *cante* too sacred to be danced. VICENTE's decision to do so was based on his belief that any of flamenco's *cantes* are danceable as long as they are danced with taste, knowledge, feeling, and responsibility. As he once rather pompously said: "I could even dance in a temple without profaning it." Many of the dances popular today are viewed by VICENTE with contempt, such as the *bulerías*, which he states are "a mixture of bad taste and confusion".

VICENTE has definite opinions about other dancers. As of 1947 he admired only three *bailaoras* — Pastora Imperio, Carmen Amaya, and Regla Ortega, and only one *bailaor* — himself. These were the flamenco dancers who properly knew how to interpret *jondo* dances, according to VICENTE. As can be imagined, these outspoken statements, combined with his artistic eccentricities and the general envy of what is considered his "undeserved fame" have made VICENTE masses of enemies in the artistic flamenco world who retaliate against him whenever the opportunity arises.

VICENTE also sings flamenco. He has a good knowledge of the *cante*, and his voice and singing style strongly suggest days past. As in the dance, he interprets the *cantes* to suit his own personality, sometimes with excellent results. He has cut at least one long-play record as well as several 45 rpm's.

The prolific VICENTE has also had two books published. The first, a fascinating book called *"Mi Baile"* (My Dance), published in 1947, talks of his life and dance. The second is devoted to his drawings and sketches of dance and flamenco topics.

Now nearly completely retired, VICENTE lives in an hotel in Barcelona, a city he finds culturally and artistically stimulating.

FRASQUILLO
(c. 1898 - 1940)

FRANCISCO LEÓN "FRASQUILLO", although cut down when at the height of his career, is remembered as one of this century's great *bailaores*. Born a non-gypsy in Utrera, FRASQUILLO was first fired with the dancing passion when he saw Antonio el de Bilbao dance in Sevilla's Café Novedades (where spectators sipped *fifty-céntimos* cups of coffee for hours). From that moment on FRASQUILLO's dream was to dance like his idol, and he used to spend all of his spare time, and odd moments he could slip away from his shoemakers's apprentice job, practicing on the top of Sevilla-moored freight cars, the only place he could find where he did not disturb the neighbors.

FRASQUILLO did not have to wait long for his first opportunity. He was hired at the age of twelve to dance in the very Café Novedades where he first became inspired by Antonio el de Bilbao, and before many years had passed he was known throughout Spain as an up-and-coming *bailaor* of the old school.

In 1920 FRASQUILLO married La Quica, a *bailaora* destined to become as renowned as her husband. They rose to fame together throughout Spain, but, strangely enough, rarely danced together as partners. Each preferred to dance with others, although they nearly always performed in the same *cuadros* and troupes.

FRASQUILLO's favorite dances were the *zapateado*, *alegrías*, and *bulerías*. Fernando de Triana states that FRASQUILLO was one of the few remaining exponents of the masculine *baile antiguo*.

FRASQUILLO and La Quica had one dancing daughter, Mercedes León, who carried on their fine school of dance. FRASQUILLO died at the age of forty-two, from wounds received in the Spanish Civil War.

PACO LABERINTO

1988 Update: (c.1910-1974)

PACO LABERINTO, a non-gypsy from Jerez, is a veteran of many years of fine flamenco dancing. Virile, elegant, proud, PACO's dancing is of the old school. That is to say, largely free of mannerisms and unnecessary movement.

PACO was raised in the gypsy *barrio de* Santiago, and his dance was learned from and among the gypsies. He did not begin to dance professionally until the age of thirty, with the company of Conquita Piquer. Since then he has acted throughout the world, having been featured with such companies as Manolo Caracol, Carmen Amaya, Lola Flores, and others.

Although PACO dances all of the traditional *bailes jondos,* he is most renowned for his fiery *bulerías.* Many *aficionados,* in fact, consider him to have been this century's finest interpreter of this dance.

Today PACO lives semi-retired in his native Jerez de la Frontera.

LOS PELAOS

Juan, El Fati, Faico, Antonio, and Ricardo Heredia, "LOS PELAOS", constitute what is today the most impressive family of *bailaores* performing. Madrid-born gypsies all, Juan, El Fati, and Faico are brothers, Antonio is the son of Juan, and Ricardo the son of El Fati. The father of the three brothers was a guitarist called Sebastián el Pelao, who toured for seventeen years with Carmen Amaya; his brother, El Gato, and another *bailaor,* Manolillo la Rosa, were praised by Carmen Amaya as the finest dancers *por farruca* that she had seen; the grandparents were Jerez-born gypsies, also *aficionados* of the *baile*.

Forty-six-year-old JUAN, a moving *bailaor* of the old school, is probably capable of the most profound dancing of the clan. He began dancing at the age of ten with the company of Conchita Piquer, and is thus already a veteran of thirty-six years of professional dancing.

Juan is a serious person, and his dance is serious. As such, he suffers the usual fate of the purist out of his setting; he does not attract enough attention to himself in the *tablaos*, and so goes largely unnoticed by the uninitiated crowds.

EL FATI's dance is serious, coarse, expressive, but largely unpretentious, and thus he suffers the same fate as brother Juan. El Fati's career has largely paralleled that of Juan. They both began dancing in the company of Conchita Piquer in 1928, and have spent much of their professional life performing together. Their latest stint was a three-year tour of America with La Chunga (1959-1962).

Since returning from America, forty-three-year-old El Fati has been performing in Madrid's Corral de la Morería, where his dance is, unfortunately, generally far removed from the pure dance of which he is capable.

The most famous *bailaor* of the group is thirty-two-year-old FAICO, a small, curly-haired fireball of a fellow. When Faico gets rolling in his favorite, and best, dance, *por bulerías*, he is truly a lesson in spontaneity and improvisation, and shows the *bulerías* at their most gypsy rambunctious. He is also extremely accomplished, in a manner much more smooth and commercial than that of his brothers, in all of flamenco's other dances.

The main drawback in Faico's dance, and it is a big one, is a bump and grind routine that he is liable to throw into any dance at any unlikely moment, regardless of the seriousness of the dance. If not the innovator of this completely incongruous movement in the flamenco dance, Faico is definitely the main cause of its catching on, and today many tasteless dancers are employing this "technique" to the applause of an equally tasteless segment of the public.

Faico began his career as a youth in the company of Pilar López. He has since been the featured dancer in many companeis and *cuadros*.

Twenty-three-year-old ANTONIO began his professional career with Pilar López at the age of four. He is an accomplished dancer, although not yet of the caliber of his father.

RICARDO, the youngest of the PELAOS, is a twenty-one-year-old youth who shows great promise in his dance. Like Faico and Antonio, Ricardo started his career with Pilar López at an early age.

Ricardo's dance is somewhat reminiscent of that of El Farruco; animal virility, cruel footwork, arrogance and profundity, although Ricardo lacks maturity in his dance. He is too easily swayed by gimmicks and commercial fads, such as his uncle Faico's bumps and grinds. At present he is in a crucial stage of his career: he could just as easily become a truly great flamenco dancer as another commercial nonentity. Only time will tell.

JIMENEZ AND VARGAS

When one thinks of MANOLO VARGAS he also thinks of ROBERTO JIMÉNEZ, and vice versa. Thus I shall discuss these two *bailaores*, whose careers have run such parallel courses, together.

Both VARGAS (c. 1914 —) and JIMÉNEZ (c. 1919 —) were born and raised in Mexico and started their dance instruction in the Mexico City studios of Oscar Tarriba. As Oscar points out, JIMÉNEZ took to the *baile* like a fish to water, from the beginning showing a great talent, particularly for the footwork. VARGAS, on the other hand, had a very difficult time of it, and can well serve as an example of accomplishment through perseverance. The most difficult part of the *baile* for VARGAS was the most basic: an understanding and feeling for the rhythms of each of the various *bailes*. He simply could not distinguish the subtle differences ,and it took him months and years of arduous concentration to finally overcome this obstacle. It was only then that VARGAS could know if he could make it as a *bailaor*. The result was resoundingly affirmative.

After some years with Tarriba in Mexico City, both boys studied with Juan Sánchez "el Estampío", absorbing something of his old style of dance and his intricate footwork. VARGAS got his first big break with the troupe of La Argentinita, and continued in the troupe when Pilar López took over after her sister's death. It was then that JIMÉNEZ joined the troupe.

VARGAS and JIMÉNEZ spent years with Pilar López before deciding to form their own company, which they have done successfully. Their company is presently one of the tops in the flamenco-classical Spanish ballet field.

About their dancing. JIMÉNEZ is a master of intricate, excellent footwork, his body posture is arrogant and ramrod stiff, his whole appearance flamenco, but ... he is cold, lacking the vital spark of *duende* that is the very basis of the more emotional dance of MANOLO VARGAS. VARTAS would make a better *juerga* dancer — he is flexible, seemingly relaxed, with a well-proportioned combination of good arms, body, feet, and inspiration.

The JIMÉNEZ-VARGAS company spends much of its time on tour in the United States, and is proving to be an excellent sounding board for non-Spanish artists. They often contract one or two American guitarists, several American dancers, oftentimes in starring roles, and even an occasional American *cantaor;* certainly a democratic policy which undoubtedly solves many of the troupe's administrative, artistic, and financial problems.

ANTONIO

1988 Update: (c. 1922 —

Ask anyone who is presently the world's greatest male Spanish dancer, and the answer is always ANTONIO RUIZ SOLER "ANTONIO". And who is the greatest flamenco dancer? That is another question, but rest assured that ANTONIO, although most renowned for his classical Spanish dancing, is definitely among the top few in flamenco.

ANTONIO has been blessed with the talent to dance both Spanish classical and flamenco exceptionally well. This requires an ambivalence rarely found in the dancer; either they dance well classical *or* flamenco. This is easily understood, as these two forms of dance are extremely dissimilar. The classical, with the exception of that classical which is flamenco-inspired, is cold and calculated, with a beauty that is little emotional. Flamenco, when danced properly, is the exact opposite. Of all of the dancers who dance both of these forms, ANTONIO is among the few capable of completely separating the distinct techniques and emotions inherent in each.

ANTONIO possesses in his flamenco dancing all of the essential aspects: virility, force, expressive footwork, good taste, a well-balanced interplay between the dances of the upper and lower torso, subtlety, and *duende*. What is more, he is one of the few flamencos who can dance spontaneously as effectively as he can dance a pre-arranged number, regardless of the fact that all of his theatrical numbers are rehearsed to perfection. This is one facet of flamenco where true greatness emerges; most modern flamenco dancers (singers, guitarists), if deprived of their arrangements, fall down on improvisation. This is due to only one thing, once a certain level of technical proficiency has been reached: they do not truly *feel* their art. (What is more embarrassing than the grimaces of a dancer who is pretending unfelt emotions, or the confusion of a professional who forgets his dance arrangement?).

ANTONIO's dancing, exceptional as it is, is not without gimmicks and commercialisms; the deft swirling of capes, the undue handling and tossing about of hats, and such. But he resorts to such doings far less than one would expect, in view of the strictly commercial nature of his artistic life. In fact, ANTONIO's great gift for flamenco is somewhat a miracle if one considers his completely un-flamenco life apart from the theater and rehearsals. He is always among the first to embrace all of the modern modes; the twist, the surf, corny movie musicals in which he dances a la Fred Astaire, social events, premières, and so forth. ANTONIO is certainly flamenco's great paradox.

ANTONIO is perhaps *the* first *bailaor* in the realm of mixed flamenco dancing, a tributary of flamenco that more often than not falls firmly on its backsides. How often it is obvious that neither partner gives a damn about the other, that they are dancing egotistically, even trying to outdo each other. In ANTONIO's hands, however, mixed dancing comes alive; now vivid desire, now love, now tragedy, now frivolity, always with a complete awareness of his partner. When ANTONIO dances with a partner one senses a male-female relationship, not a battle of over-sized egos. (It is said that ANTONIO firmly sets the tone of the relationship behind the scenes; he demands complete submissiveness. *He* leads, *she* follows. Once this is understood, there is no fighting for the prime position — ANTONIO has it, as the male must — and they are left free to dance).

ANTONIO's partner of many years was Rosario. They began together as "Los Chavalillos de España" in Sevilla, studying with the *maestro* Realito. (ANTONIO later studied a more flamenco type of dance with El Estampío and Frasquillo). After some years of preparation they ventured out to conquer the world, subsequently becoming the most famous Spanish dance team in history. After twenty-two years and countless successes they broke up, each forming his own company. ANTONIO has had many dancing partners since, but it is generally agreed that he danced with Rosario better than with the others; through long years of dancing together they had reached the desired point of being able to anticipate each other's moods and movements, lending to their dance a peculiar magic. Now, much to the delight of nostalgic *aficionados,* ANTONIO and Rosario have again joined forces, and during the last two years have performed several theatrical stands together.

Since leaving his native Sevilla, ANTONIO and his company have been all over the world, and ANTONIO has become one of Spain's most famous international figures, ranking in the company of such artists as Pablo Picasso, Andrés Segovia, Pablo Casals, Carmen Amaya, and Salvador Dalí. ANTONIO now vaguely talks of cutting down his out-of-Spain engagements, of limiting himself to a few recitals each year within Spain. As for completely retiring, I do not believe that there is cause for alarm; ANTONIO's whole life is his art, and he will carry on with it as long as he is physically able. Considering his excellent physical condition, this will undoubtedly be for some time to come.

ANTONIO is often asked which style of dance he prefers. His answer is flamenco. And what dance? His creation *por martinetes*, a dance he introduced into flamenco's repertoire some fifteen years ago in the movie "*Duende y Misterio del Flamenco*" (in English called simply "Flamenco"). The *martinetes*, a *cante* of the forge traditionally void of even a danceable *compás*, had never been danced, nor had anyone even considered dancing it. ANTONIO, therefore, was braving the considerable wrath of the purists in attempting it. Undaunted, ANTONIO got Antonio Mairena to sing it while hammering out the *compás* of the *siguiriyas* on an anvil, chose the foot of the great gorge in Ronda as the setting, and set about creating one of the great moments in the *baile flamenco*. (ANTONIO created one of flamenco's great moments, yes, but without a doubt imitators of less genius would destroy the *martinetes*, much as they do the *baile por siguiriyas* first innovated by Vicente Escudero. We may be thankful that the *baile por martinetes* has not become widespread).

Besides his *martinetes*, ANTONIO dances all of flamenco's *bailes* well. He has the valuable ability to infect his public with whatever emotion he feels. With his *bulerías* the public feels gay and wild, with his *tangos* frivolous and sensuous, with his *siguiriyas* serious and profound. What is more important, he seemingly has the ability to infect himself with the proper spirit of each dance, of turning himself on, no matter how many shows he has given that week or how listless he may feel before the performance. This is unusual in flamenco circles, and sets ANTONIO apart in that he is not only a great artist and *bailaor*, but a great showman as well.

When not on tour ANTONIO resides in his fine theater-equipped house in Madrid.

JOSE GRECO

(c. 1919 —

JOSÉ GRECO serves as an excellent example of the devastating effects of commercialism. When GRECO was with the companies of La Argentinita and Pilar López in the forties and early fifties, he was considered by the critical flamenco world as one of the finest *bailaores* of the period. He had everything: a slender, dancer's body and excellent carriage, the technique, the looks, the subtlety, the restraint ,the taste, the *duende*...

GRECO rose rapidly, and soon had the name and backing to form his own company, with which he undertook a heavy concert schedule, principally in the United States, playing everything from metropolitan luxury theaters to village high school gyms. After a few seasons of this, GRECO's fame reached unprecedented heights for a performer of Spanish folklore, surpassing even that of Carmen Amaya (within the United States).

But GRECO paid dearly for his fame. As his name grew his dance deteriorated; each year he was less effective. In my mind his trousers symbolize the change in his dance; it seems that as they became more satiny and flamboyant (i. e. skin-tight satin, champagne color, and the like), GRECO took on an airy, ballet style, and the characteristic virility and *duende* of his dance suffered badly. This deterioration was augmented by acrobatics and gimmicks, and with time GRECO became converted from a moving purist into a crowd-pleasing sensationalist.

GRECO is an excellent talent scout for his company, having over the years employed such fine artists as Rafael Romero, Manolita de Jerez, Araceli Vargas, Miguel García, Emilio de Diego, Pepe and Paco de Algeciras, and many others. During one period in the early fifties his company included the fine *bailaora*, La Quica.

Born in Brooklyn, New York, of Italian parents, GRECO began Spanish dancing at the age of seven. He studied in Spain during various periods, principally with El Estampío and La Quica. His early career included several years with the troupes of both La Argentinita and her sister, Pilar López.

EL FARRUCO

1988 Update: (c. 1936 —

There lives in Sevilla a little-known gypsy *bailaor,* called Antonio El Farruco, who, when he wishes, can demonstrate what this thing called the *baile flamenco* is all about. When fired up, El Farruco is perhaps *the* dominant *bailaor* in flamenco today.

What makes him so special? Superior technique? Physical appearance? Personality? It is none of these things; many *bailaores* outdo him on these counts. El Farruco does not bother much with dancing techniques, he is not a showman, and he is by no means handsome. He is, in fact, a little ugly, and heftier than is considered attractive for a male dancer. So what is it?

El Farruco steps on the platform casually, perhaps joking with the *cuadro,* perhaps playing a few nonchalant *palmas.* He looks like he is going to get by with as little effort as possible, two or three steps and back to the dressing room.

Suddenly, if you are fortunate enough to hit a good night, transformation. El Farruco takes command, fixing his audience with a penetrating look that demands complete attention. He makes a rapid movement signifying the beginning of his dance, and stops dead still, his eyes the only living part of his body. He remains thus for some seconds, and then slowly, meaningfully, moves only his arms. Suddenly the devil seizes him, his legs smash down with a force that only he possesses in the *baile,* he fakes a turn, and is again motionless. The audience is completely electrified, hanging on his every movement. His movements are few, the space in which he moves the absolute minimum. Although gypsy he never becomes frantic; he is free from all theater. He is primitive, a wild male animal pouring all of the force of raging instincts into a dance outwardly reserved, but inwardly teeming with *duende* and *cojones.* What makes El Farruco great cannot be learned; the dancer either has it or not, and only one in a thousand seems to have it. El Farruco has it in excess.

El Farruco was born Antonio Montoya in La Roda de Andalucía, a little town that lies between Sevilla and Antequera. His mother was a Moorish beauty from Agache, Morocco, his father a Madrileñan gypsy who made his living by dealing in horses and cattle in the fairs of Andalusia.

In El Farruco's words: "I was brought up on the open road, traveling from fair to fair with my parents. When a successful cattle negotiation was completed, I would dance at the ensuing celebration. When I was nine years old we were over in Extremadura, and my parents heard of a juvenile flamenco contest in Badajoz. They entered me, I won first prize (a box of condensed milk), and my professional career started.

"First I was contracted by a troupe called '*Galas Juveniles*' to tour Spain and North Africa, and after that by another youthful group ,'*Los Chavalillos de España*' (not Antonio and Rosario, who used the same name). Before long I was dancing in the company of Caracol and Lola Flores, and after that, at age eighteen, I went on a tour with Pilar López' troupe. We spent two years in England, during which time I learned an impressive amount of English: 'plee' (please) and 'tank you' (thank you). After Pilar I returned to Sevilla and settled down for a number of years, performing locally, marrying, and producing seven children. ¡*Ojú!*"

If the stories circulating about El Farruco have any basis in fact, his years in Sevilla have not been as tranquil as his words make them appear. His rumored private life could well serve as an excellent source for a first-rate romantic thriller, including brushes with the law, sundry love affairs and intrigues, and a liberal amount of tragedy. Perhaps that is the basis of Farruco's great dance — he has actually lived many of the emotions and moments he depicts.

As was the case with Manuel Torre in the *cante*, El Farruco is extremely erratic. He dances truly well only when, for some reason or other, he becomes possessed. It might be for someone in the audience whom he particularly regards, someone he knows will understand and feel his dance as much as he himself does; or it may be just because he feels in the mood. Many *aficionados* go night after night waiting for his great moment, much like bullfight addicts wait out someone like Antonio Bienvenida, and more often than not go away disappointed. Even in *juergas* El Farruco is likely to maintain his reserve; his greatness simply cannot be turned on and off as can the superficial dance of the majority.

Although FARRUCO's dance is highly respected by flamenco's knowledgeable *aficionados*, he has been forgotten by much of Spain's public due to the eight years during which he rarely performed outside of Sevilla. However, he is again beginning to travel about. He has spent recent periods in Torremolinos and in England, and in September of this year is going to begin a nine month tour of the United States with José Greco. All of this will undoubtedly cause his fame to spread, and will perhaps give his growing public a few rare glimpses of the true *baile gitano*.

ANTONIO GADES

(c. 1936 —

ANTONIO GADES, a young man recently launched to fame by his excellent dancing and acting in "*La Historia de los Tarantos*", is one of the most inspired *bailaores* dancing today. Surprisingly, I should add, for GADES' first love is acting. He enjoys interpreting character parts, as he did in "*Los Tarantos*", and feels that he is not at his best when merely dancing for dancing's sake. Thus he prefers dancing, be it classical or flamenco, in movies, plays, *zarzuelas*, *óperas*, and the like, within the confines of script and choreography.

Regardless of his preference, GADES' *tablao* flamenco dancing is both exciting and original. He is among the small group of *bailaores* who are blessed with uncompromised masculinity as well as an elegance of figure and movement, and an absolute grasp of flamenco's rhythms and counter-rhythms. He is not without ballet-type moments, however, such as his triple and quadruple turns, and an occasional slickness incongruous with his virile dance

Born in Elda (Alicante) of non-gypsy, non-artistic parents, GADES was taken to live in Madrid at the age of two, and there still resides. At the age of fifteen he joined the troup of Pilar López, with whom he spent eight years, and learned a vast amount about Spanish classical, regional, and flamenco dancing. During this period GADES also took advantage of the troupe's tours, studying other styles of classical dancing with *maestros* in Paris, Russia, and Italy. This classical study led to GADES' being appointed first *maestro* and choreographer in the Scala of Milan in 1962.

However, flamenco is taking up more and more of GADE'S time. After his film he was snatched up by the Corral de la Morería, and presently is fulfilling a lucrative contract at the New York World Fair with his flamenco troupe of fourteen.

Shortly before the beginning of the World Fair, GADES was married to the Spanish movie starlet, Maruja Díaz.

Future films? GADES has been approached concerning "*El Greco*", a film about the life of the painter, to be realized in Spain by Mel Ferrer.

Future flamenco? In view of all of GADES' activity, I shall be so rash as to predict that one had better see his flamenco dancing soon. Fame, fortune, and diversified commitments do not generally go hand in hand with uncontaminated flamenco. But there are exceptions...

COUNTRY GYPSY DANCING IN COMMERCIAL SETTINGS

At present there is a *cuadro flamenco* performing in the Cuevas de Nerja, in Madrid, that clearly shows the difference that I have attempted to point out between the country and the polished flamenco dance. This *tablao*, sparked by its artistic director, Sr. Portela, is experimenting with the presentation of authentic country flamenco, the type of spontaneous, primitive flamenco that is seen in private gatherings deep in Andalusia.

Their country-style representatives of the dance are three: Paco de Valdepeñas, Pepa Campos, and Felipe de Triana They dance the gay, light dances for which the country style is ideally suited, and come through with a type of dance thoroughly exciting and entertaining, while at the same time providing an excellent base of comparison between the country, and the more polished dancing of the rest of the show.

FRANCISCO CORTÉ ESCUDERO "PACO DE VALDEPEÑAS" is one of

the finest flamenco dancers I have seen. He is untrained in the sophisticated intricacies of footwork and stage polish, and he can do nicely without them, for Paco has a force and natural gypsy *gracia* that completely overshadows the academy-trained dancers who largely dominate the commercial scene. Paco's dance is the true flamenco dance: spontaneous, masculine, creative, unrefined, and above all, *natural* — Paco dances because he likes to dance, and in the way he feels like dancing, and has no need to move from pose to phoney pose as do most of the commercials.

Born a gypsy in Linares some forty-two years ago, Paco was taken to the wine-producing town of Valdepeñas at age seven, and there has made his way as a salesman of cloth. He did not turn to *tablao* dancing until some five years ago, when he was "discovered" at a *juerga* by the owners of Sevilla's Cortijo el Guajiro. From there he went on to Madrid's Torres Bermejas, and then to the Torres' sister *tablao* (same management), the Cuevas de Nerja.

Paco is proud of being part of the movement to introduce the pure, country dance to the *tablaos*. He is also proud of the flamenco accomplishments of the town of Valdepeñas, stating that even though they are well out of the flamenco sphere of influence, they have always figured prominently in the flamenco world in appreciation, and have even contributed a few fine artists, such as the *aficionados don* ALFREDO FILLOL, a guitarist of an upper class family praised by Fernando de Triana in his book, EL BOQUILLA, a singer of the *cantes de Chacón*, MARIO RIOPA, a singer *por soleares*, and perhaps the strongest of them all, ANTONIO DE VALDEPEÑAS, a professional *cantaor* renowned for his *soleares*.

Although Paco dances and sings only *por bulerías* and *rumbas* in the Cueva de Nerja *cuadro*, he dances all of the *bailes gitanos*.

Paco's dancing and even physical appearance are largely reminiscent of another excellent country-style dancer, Anzonini, a gypsy from Santa María who figured in this *cuadro* some months back. Like Paco, Anzonini, has dedicated his artistic life to *juergas*, fairs, and such, and only recently began performing commercially, at the urging of Sr. Portela. Anzonini's distinguishing feature is a large gap in his teeth that cannot be missed when he dances. In his early forties, Chonini can also be singled out as one of the great country-style flamenco dancers dancing today.

PEPA CAMPOS is a 62-year-old gypsy grandmother who was brought up from the port town of Santa María explicitly for this *cuadro*. It is her first experience at commercial performing, and she comes through beautifully.

Pepa sings and dances, and does both with such gypsy *gracia* that she is irresistible. She is a natural comedian, and her *bulerías*, *chuflas*, and *rumbas* are fine reminders of the authentic country flamenco and the gypsy genius for this art.

FELIPE DE TRIANA serves as a representative of the many unknown flamencos throughout Spain who dance and sing in an unprofessional, strictly non-commercial manner. Felipe knows a great deal of *cante* and sings it with purity, but his voice is lacking power and resonance; he can by no means be called a professional *bailaor*, as he knows only a few rudimentary steps; however, when Felipe sings and dances his gypsy *gracia* and natural flamenco bearing make him stand out from the commercials, at least for those who have experienced and lived the real thing, for Felipe and Paco and Pepa and the many others like them possess that evasive something that is the very nucleus of flamenco, that all-important something that so often withers and dies when mixed with polish and virtuosity, and is what, in the long run, separates the authentic flamencos from the theatrical showmen.

A 59-year-old gypsy from Triana, Felipe has been a behind-the-scenes *juerga* performer for years. He started out performing with JUAN EL TUMBA, a renowned dancer from Triana, of whom Felipe talks with reverence (El Tumba's son and grandson still live, and dance, in Triana).

OTHERS

There have been, and are, many other fine *bailaores*. A biography of each would be cumbersome, and is unnecessary in fulfilling the purpose of this book; those already discussed have played the most historical roles in flamenco's development, or have best served to illustrate certain points and trends.

Here space can be allotted, however, for brief rundowns on some of the deserving artists who have not been mentioned to this point.

Names of renowned artists that have filtered through from the past include: MANOLO PAMPLINAS, PACO CURRELA, ANTONIO VIRUTA, PACO CORTES, JEROMO ACOSTA...

EL FEO DE CÁDIZ (The Ugly One from Cádiz), brother of the gypsy singer Macandé, is remembered as a *"fenómeno"* of the flamenco dance. Particularly remembered are his unbelievable *pitos*, played with all five fingers of both hands. El Feo spent much of his life in Buenos Aires.

EL QUINO was a country-style gypsy *bailaor* who is still talked about in his native Morón de la Frontera.

ANTONIO DE TRIANA is another *bailaor* referred to as a *"fenómeno"*. How he must have danced to still be remembered so reverently, for Antonio disappeared from the Spanish flamenco world many years ago, to take up residence in Los Angeles, California. He has since been in various American movies in dancing roles. His daughter, LUISA DE TRIANA, is presently a prominent *bailaora* in the American scene.

RAFAEL ORTEGA (see Ortega family chart) is a renowned dancer who rose to fame in various companies, including those of Conchita Piquer, Custodia Romero, and Pilar López. He is the son of Manuel Ortega, a gypsy *cantaor* from Cádiz.

TOMÁS TORRE, the son of the great *cantaor*, Manuel, and PARRILLA, from Jerez, are two excellent country-style gypsy *bailaores* who occasionally perform in public. In their late fifties, both of these *bailaores* have a *gracia* in their dance that is only possessed by gypsies.

ALEJANDRO VEGA, when in his prime, was considered a fine flamenco dancer. He rose to fame in the companies of La Argentinita and Pilar López. Now in his fifties, he is still an active performer.

LUISILLO is a successful leader of a flamenco troupe. His dance is stylized and polished, as is his ballet choreography. He is Mexican.

Mexico-born ROBERTO IGLESIAS also has his own ballet. In his dance he appears to attempt to imitate the inimitable Carmen Amaya.

PEPE RÍOS, from Morón de la Frontera, is a fine country-style gypsy *bailaor*. In his thirties, he is related to Diego del Gastor.

MARIO MAYA is a highly-technical virtuoso of the male dance, as is EL GÜITO. In their early twenties, both have risen to fame in the past three years within Spain.

BAILAORAS

Only scarce data is available concerning many of flamencos' early *bailaoras*. A few of these I shall list first, together with whatever information is available, and then expound at more length about the better documented.

ROSARIO LA HONRÁ (Rosario the Honest One) is remembered as one of the finest dancers of the early *café cantante* period. She is thought to have been born around the year 1845.

JOSEFITA LA PITRACA (Little Josephine the Scrap) was called by Fernando de Triana the outstanding *bailaora* of her epoch. He mentioned particularly "the movement of her arms and her *gracia*". The *bailaora* La Macarrona also spoke of La Pitraca's fine reputation. From Cádiz, La Pitraca was born around the year 1855.

GABRIELA ORTEGA, a member of the illustrious bullfighting and flamenco Ortega family (see biography of Manolo Caracol and Ortega family chart), was an eminent *bailaora* in the *cafés cantantes* during the second half of the past century. Mother of the famed bullfighters Joselito and Rafael el Gallo, she hailed from Cádiz.

LA GEROMA was a *bailaora* and *cantaora* who spent years as a leading figure in the Café Silverio. She was the mother of Currito el de la Geroma, one of flamenco's great guitarists of the past, and wife of Juan el de Alonso, a *siguiriyero* renowned for his creativity and outstanding *cante*. Born in Jerez, La Geroma lived most of her life on Sevilla's Alameda de Hércules.

MARÍA LA CHORRÚA, remembered as a fine *bailaora*, was the aunt and first *maestra* of La Malena.

CARMELITA PÉREZ was a *bailaora* from an all-artistic family which included: Antonio Pérez, Sr. and Jr., both guitarists, and brother Manolo, a dancer. Carmelita danced in Sevilla's Café Burrero throughout most of her career. She was married to the singer Perote.

MARIQUITA MALVIDO, an accomplished *bailaora* and *cantaora* from the Jerez neighborhood of Santiago, made her professional debut at the age of six in the *café cantante* La Primera, in Jerez. Her career was short-lived due to her marriage to the *cantaor*, Fosforito.

LA MEJORANA

1988 Update: (c. 1862-1922)

One of the mainstays of Sevilla's famous Café Silverio was a gypsy dancing beauty, originally from Cádiz, called ROSARIO MONJE "LA MEJORANA" ("Sweet Marjoram", a plant similar to mint). Besides her excellent dance, La Mejorana is credited with two other monumental accomplishments: the innovation of the *baile por soleá* (1), and giving birth to two fine artists, Pastora Imperio, considered the supreme *bailaora* of the present century, and Víctor Rojas, a guitarist little remembered in Spain due to his long residence in Mexico City.

Fernando de Triana, who was obviously smitten by La Mejorana, if one can judge by the entire page in his book dedicated solely to her glowing beauty, tells of the gentlemen who used to arrive at the *café* long before show time in order to procure a strategic seat and perhaps a peek at Rosario's thighs. With dashing chivalry he claims that no one ever achieved this goal (if anyone ever did, no doubt Fernando was waiting outside of the *café* to waylay the culprit on his way home). In his description Fernando states that La Mejorana dressed beautifully, always with

---

(1) If flamencologists are right, and La Mejorana did first introduce the *baile por soleá*, it must not have caught on, or at least not widely, for dancers such as La Quica claim that the *soleá* was not danced until the second quarter of this century. Perhaps it enjoyed a period of popularity during the *café cantante* period, and then largely died out until resuscitated in this century.

a *bata de cola* and an accompanying *mantón de Manila*, and goes on to say of her dance that "she was not better than the best, but there was no one better than she".

Many dancers of old also sang, among them La Mejorana Fernando writes that when she sang the following *juguetillo* simultaneously as she danced, "many a Christian" would catch himself drooling with emotion:

Dormía un jardinero	A gardener *slept*
a pierna suelta:	*a deep sleep:*
dormía y se dejaba	*he slept and left*
la puerta abierta.	*the gate open.*
Hasta que un día	*Until one day*
le robaron la rosa	*they stole from him*
que más quería.	*the rose he loved most dearly.*

At the peak of her career La Mejorana fell in love with one of her many admirers, a famed bullfighter's tailor named Víctor Rojas. They married, and her career abruptly ended; a loss for *aficionados* of her day, but a great gain for succeeding generations who were able to relish the dance of her daughter, Pastora Imperio.

LA MACARRONA

(c. 1860 - 1947)

JUANA VARGAS "LA MACARRONA" is appraised by many as the greatest female flamenco dancer of all times. Others claim she was the greatest of her epoch, others that she was the greatest "within her style of dance". One thing is certain: she was one of flamenco's past greats.

LA MACARRONA, born in Jerez de la Frontera of gypsy parents, began dancing in the streets at the age of seven for tossed coins, accompanied by her singing mother and guitar-playing father. A year later she landed her first professional job, in Sevilla's Café de la Escalerilla, earning ten *reales* a night (two and one-half pesetas). However, her parents soon discovered that this amount could not support the entire family in the style to which they were accustomed, so LA MACARRONA was taken back to street dancing in Jerez. Within a few months she was "rediscovered" by a singer called El Mezcle, consequently being offered a more lucrative contract in Málaga's Café de las Siete Revueltas, where she remained two years.

During her first few years as a professional La MACARRONA was not taken very seriously; *aficionados* being what they are, they did not recognize her great possibilities until she reached a well-developed sixteen. It was then that she was contracted by Silverio Franconetti for his famous Café Silverio, where her dancing partner was another young dancing wonder, Lamparilla, and her contemporaries a veritable flamenco who's who, including Rosario la Honrá, Juana and Fernanda Antúnez, Antonio el Pintor, Fosforito, Chacón, Silverio, and so forth. From there LA MACARRONA went on to Sevilla's Café el Burrero and the Café Romero, in Madrid, by which time she was recognized as one of Spain's outstanding *bailaoras*.

Her fame spread, and LA MACARRONA was in demand all over Europe. She spent various long periods in Paris, and began priding herself on her "fluent French". The story is told of one of her arrivals at the Paris railway station. After boasting about her French to her traveling companions during the entire trip, she was naturally the one chosen to make all of the necessary verbal arrangements upon arriving, which she set out to do with glee. She lowered herself importantly from the train, and in her most sophisticated French began giving the porters a multitude of instructions. To her great dismay and irritation, they understood not a word, but she had a ready explanation: "It's not that my French isn't good, it's just that they've changed the damned language since I was here last."

LA MACARRONA nearly married a rich Madrid banker, but his family intervened at the last minute, "spoiling", as she put it, "my future". Another unfortunate occurrence, much later in her life, foiled her hopes of a leisurely and comfortable old age. House breakers stole all of her accumulated wealth, consisting of some 10,000 pesetas worth of cash and jewels, which was never recovered.

The loss of this relative fortune (in those days) was the cause of LA MACARRONA's having to dance, long after the *cafés cantantes* were closed and her fame dissipated, in the *colmaos* (flamenco taverns) and *ventas* of Sevilla until she was well in her eighties. Occasionally benefits would be organized in her honor when she was particularly desperate for money, or she would be hired for a few nights by visiting flamenco companies, but these instances were few and far between in her latter years. She did go on two tours during her last years, however, which bolstered both her morale and pocketbook considerably — in 1933 with La Argentinita's company, for her staging of *"Las Calles de Cádiz"*, and again in 1940 with the company of Conchita Piquer, for the staging of the same show.

LA MACARRONA danced the traditional style of dance, which is to say, the dance of the upper torso. She knew very little footwork, and rarely had to resort to it. Her arms and hands were full of grace, her *duende* exceptional. Fernando de Triana tells of the beautiful way she moved the *bata de cola*, and states that "everything that can be said about LA MACARRONA is not enough." Today, of course, she would undoubtedly be discounted as an incomplete dancer for, as we have discussed, footwork even within the feminine dance has attained such importance as to overshadow the more feminine aspects.

Juan de la Plata (*"Flamencos de Jerez"*) quotes a newspaper interview with LA MACARRONA which took place in Sevilla, in 1935, when she was a tired seventy-five-years-old. I shall print it here, as besides revealing the character and personality of LA MACARRONA, it is a good example of the *gracia* of gypsy communication.

"'Which artists have you liked best?'

"'Of the *bailaoras*, Rosario la Mejorana and Consuelo la Borriquera. There was another very good one, whom I did not see, called Josefita la Pitraca. Of the *cantaores* of before, now, and always ... the only one who has made me catch my breath has been don Antonio Chacón. Later... Manuel Torre. And now, I like them all. One has to live!'

"'Have you had students?'

"'A million. They have come in droves so I would teach

them the *baile*. But the only one who turned out really well was Teresita España. *¡Vaya salero!*'

"Sipping a *caña* (short beer) she added, sighing:

"'*Ya usté ve ahora! De cormao en cormao, esperando un arma güena que quiera acordarse de que existe er flamenco. Ni en los cafés nos quieren ya, cuando hemos sío siempre las reinas der mundo. Pero to lo acaba er tiempo. Las gentes están por las cosas modernas y er flamenco muere. Toavía queda arguna solera, pero poca, mu poca. Toavía hay quien no se divierte si no escucha un cante chipén o se le caen las lágrimas viendo una gitana darse una güerta con salero. ¡Pero son tan pocos! Los niños modernos, la juventú, nos mira como a cosas raras, sin pensá que hemos jecho yorá con nuestras gitanerías a tre generasiones.*'

"'And just look now! From tavern to tavern, hoping for someone to turn up who remembers that flamenco exists. They don't even want us in the *cafés* anymore, when we have always been the queens of the world. But time does away with everything. The public likes modern things, and flamenco is dying . There is still some *afición*, but little, very little. There are still those who don't enjoy themselves unless they hear a gay *cante*, or when a *baile* danced with *salero* brings tears to their eyes. But they are so few. The modern kids, the youth of today, look at us as if we were something rare, without stopping to think that we have made three generations cry with our *gitanerías*.'

"Again sighing, LA MACARRONA continued nostalgically:

"'Those times! Those men! Who would have guessed, when I performed in the streets of Jerez, that I would be famous in Paris!? Nor who would have guessed, when I was triumphing in Paris, that our art would die in the back rooms of taverns? That's life, *señó*, that's life...'

LA MACARRONA died in 1947, at the ripe age of eighty-seven, in her humble house near Sevilla's Alameda de Hércules. She died poor and forgotten, convinced that her beloved flamenco was also ceasing to exist. Had she lived ten years longer she would have seen the rebirth of flamenco, and could have died happy in the knowledge that her name has become a milestone in its history.

LA CUENCA

(c. 1860 - 1920)

It was about this time, during the height of the Golden Age, that the first *bailaora* went into direct competition with the male. TRINIDAD HUERTAS "LA CUENCA" donned men's clothing, concentrated on the masculine dances, developed advanced footwork, and caused a sensation in the flamenco world.

As LA CUENCA was the first woman to go masculine in her dance, she will have to bear the brunt of the results; setting the fashion for this type of thing, which has adversely affected the feminine dance, often to a disgusting point for those of us who still prefer our females feminine.

LA CUENCA, from Málaga, is said to have also played a fine guitar.

LA GAMBA

(c. 1860 - 1940)

ANTONIA LA GAMBA (Antonia the Shrimp) is remembered for two monumental reasons: one, for having been an excellent, fiery *bailaora* of the old school, and two, for having been the wife of the *cantaor* Manuel Torre.

LA GAMBA was a woman with a singular personality, capable of great brusqueness or of great warmth. This was also true of her dance, which contributed to make her one of the most popular dancers of her day. Caballero Bonald states, in fact, that her puzzling way of being, and her genius in her art, was comparable to that of her eccentric husband.

Even after her husband's death, in 1933 (LA GAMBA was over fifteen years older than Manuel Torre), LA GAMBA still attended, and even often danced at *juergas* and *fiestas* in Sevilla. Her days were spent wandering about the Alameda de Hércules nostalgically reminiscing with other old flamencos about days gone by, about flamenco's Golden Age and the roles that they had played in it...

FERNANDA AND JUANA ANTUNEZ

Jerez de la Frontera was an unequalled contributor to the feminine dance of the *café cantante* period. Jerez *bailaoras* who particularly stood out were five: Juana la Macarrona, La Malena, La Sordita, and the subjects of this biography, FERNANDA and JUANA ANTÚNEZ.

FERNANDA ANTÚNEZ (c. 1870-1940), a blond gypsy of considerable beauty, was the least accomplished *bailaora* of the two, although still one of the best of her day. She enjoyed great success throughout Spain and Europe, until retiring at an advanced age in Sevilla, there to sell flowers until her death at the age of seventy.

FERNANDA's last professional dancing was done late in her life, at the side of her beloved contemporaries and rivals, La Sordita, La Macarrona and La Malena. The four idols of an earlier epoch were taken by Encarnación López "la Argentinita" on a tour of Spain and Europe (*"Las Calles de Cádiz"*, 1933), in what must have been a wonderfully idealistic manifestation of the flamenco of days past.

Younger sister JUANA ANTÚNEZ (c. 1875-1935), besides being a superior dancer, was a dazzling gypsy beauty. She always had lines of admirers competing for her, to the point that several *señoritos* were on the brink of marriage (an act of some daring in those days, particularly within Spain with its sternly observed caste system).

JUANA began dancing as soon as she could walk, and won her first dance contest at the age of seven. Her dance is reputed to have been as majestic as her beauty, and won her success after success throughout Spain. She retired from performing, long before her sister, with fame and money, neither of which lasted long away from flamenco's platforms. Around the age of sixty she was forced to enter the Jerez home for the poor, where she subsequently commited suicide by throwing herself off the roof. Considerably before her death she showed marked signs of insanity.

LA SORDITA

(c. 1870 - 1945)

In good flamenco families several of the members participate, such as the family of the renowned *cantaor*, Paco la Luz. Paco had two extraordinary daughters, one a singer, María la Serrana, the other the *bailaora* JUANA VALENCIA "LA SORDITA" (the Little Deaf One).

LA SORDITA was a pure gypsy with a peculiar gypsy beauty and character. Fernando de Triana states that her dance was on the superb level of La Macarrona and La Malena, and that in the movement of her arms she exceeded all of the *bailaoras* of her day.

Although nearly totally deaf, it is said that LA SORDITA always maintained a perfect *compás*.

LA SORDITA danced until late in her life, performing in La Argentinita's *"Las Calles de Cádiz"* in 1933, and in Conchita Piquer's show of the same name in 1940.

As the reader may have noticed in this book, it is common in flamenco to refer to artists by their physical or mental defects. This is a strangely innocent, direct approach to life characteristic of uneducated classes the world over, but which seems particularly prevalent in Spain. Thus a deaf person is called "the Deaf One", if defective in the limbs, "the Cripple", if mentally deficient, "the Stupid One", if blind, "the Blind One", if subject to attacks of insanity, "the Crazy One", and so forth. The trait is practiced with such matter-of-factness that it appears that no slight is intended, although I cannot help but think that these terms must give some of the users a little flush of superiority, and serve to maintain the defective one in his proper slot in society's pecking system. Perhaps not...

LA MALENA

(c. 1870 - 1953)

It was a matter of opinion who danced better, LA MALENA

or La Macarrona, but it was almost universally agreed that these friendly rivals were the supreme *bailaoras* of their epoch.

Actually, their styles of dance, as they have been explained to me, were quite different. LA MALENA was more majestic in her dance, her passion and fire held more in check. Her manner of being was quieter, which was reflected in her beautiful, fluid, tranquil movement of arms and hands. The Macarrona's nature, and dance, were the opposite. She was more of a fireball, her dance full of gypsy temperament, more open and overwhelming. Both dancers apparently transmitted great *duende*.

LA MALENA, born in Jerez, grew to be a great gypsy beauty. She early turned to the dance, inspired by her first and only *maestra* her aunt, María la Chorrúa, and was soon dancing in the *cafés cantantes* of Jerez, Sevilla, and elsewhere, although she preferred to remain in Sevilla during long periods of time. Like nearly all of the flamencos of that period, LA MALENA fixed her permanent residence bordering La Alameda de Hércules, in Sevilla, and it took some coaxing to get her to leave for extended artistic engagements.

Like her contemporaries La Macarrona, La Sordita, and Fernanda Antúnez, LA MALENA was searched out and hired to dance in La Argentinita's *"Las Calles de Cádiz"* in 1933, and in Conchita Piquer's version of the same show in 1940.

LA MALENA followed the flamenco pattern of spending as she earned, and had to dance for a living until a year before her death. She died at the age of eighty-three, having spent over seventy years as a professional *bailaora*. She left life as penniless as she had arrived.

Presently LA MALENA's nephew, Eduardo de la Malena, a fine guitarist, lives in his aunt's old apartment on Sevilla's Alameda de Hércules. A niece, Maleni Loreto, is an excellent present-day dancer.

SALUD RODRIGUEZ

(c. 1870 - 1930)

SALUD RODRÍGUEZ "LA NIÑA DEL CIEGO" (Daughter of the Blind

One), had one burning ambition throughout her childhood: to dance the masculine dances as well as her heroine, La Cuenca. Thus SALUD equipped herself with *trajes cortos,* boots, and the other masculine dancing paraphernalia, spent numberless hours practicing her footwork, and eventually achieved her goal. She become in her dance what, through some glandular confusion, she was best suited to be from birth: a man.

SALUD, from Jerez, came from quite an artistic family. Her father was a blind guitarist of fame, Juan Manuel Rodríguez "el Ciego", accomplished in the accompaniment of both the *cante* and the *baile,* and four of her six brothers and sisters also became artists — three dancers and one guitarist, none of whom achieved much fame.

SALUD danced for a time in the Café Silverio, in Sevilla, but spent most of her career in Madrid. She was the early *maestra* and basic source of inspiration for one of the finest *bailaores* of this century: El Estampío.

PASTORA IMPERIO

1988 Update: (1890-1979)

My main interview with PASTORA IMPERIO, universally considered the finest remaining interpreter of the old school of feminine dance, took place in the summer of 1963 in her summertime *tablao* located just outside of Marbella, on the southern Spanish coast. The building was on the edge of the beach, and the sound of the surf, and the moonlight dancing on the waves, contributed to a Utopian mood as we watched her *cuadro* perform for nearly three hours.

PASTORA was as gracious as she was lucid about her likes and dislikes in present-day flamenco. As we watched various of her *bailaoras* dance she would comment that only remnants of the old-time dance still existed, the pure dance of the arms and hands and upper torso in general. "That", she went on, "was the true and difficult dance. Today the *bailaoras* cover up their defective hand and arm movements by using castanets, and their lack of imagination and inspiration by prolonged footwork. I recognize that the techniques of footwork and castanets are tedious to develop, but that is beside the point. Castanets should not be used in serious flamenco, and too much footwork for the *bailaora* is anti-aesthetic. Another crutch is prearranged dances — the great dancer does not need arrangements, but is inspired by the guitar, *cante*, and her mood of the moment. Today one views a dancer dance *por soleá*, for instance, several times, and each time it is danced in an identical manner. What boredom and lack of inspiration! I never permitted myself the luxury of dance arrangements, and neither did any of the other top *bailaoras*."

Pastora was born in the Barrio de la Alfalfa, in Sevilla, daughter of Víctor Rojas, a tailor for bullfighters, and Rosario Monje "la Mejorana", one of the great gypsy *bailaoras* of the *café cantante* epoch. Contrary to what one might think, Pastora claims that she did not learn her *baile* from her mother, nor from any teacher. She just began dancing, guided by her deep-rooted concept of the *baile flamenco*, a concept formed from living amongst, and constantly observing, such *bailaoras* as her mother, La Macarrona, La Malena, La Gamba, and others of the multitude of fine *bailaoras* who lived in Sevilla during her youth.

Pastora began dancing professionally in Madrid in 1911, in the now-disappeared Teatro Romea, as part of the *"fin de fiesta"*, a type of vaudeville show that was presented after a theatrical play. In 1915 she went overseas, first performing in the Teatro San Martín, in Buenos Aires, then proceeding on an extended tour of South and Central America.

What is little known about Pastora is her versatility as a performer. She began her career as a singer of *cuplés* (non-flamenco Spanish songs), and for years has been, and still is, an actress of legitimate theater. Her first experience as an actress was in the 1918 presentation of *El Amor Brujo*, in Madrid, expressly written by Manuel de Falla with Pastora in mind for the lead part. Her role was basically dancing, but her success in the acting parts was such that she determined to become an actress as well as a dancer. She has been acting on and off since, her last role a leading part in a Luis Escobar musical as recently as 1962.

However, flamenco has been the great love of Pastora's life. She had her own *cuadro* for many years which, she reminisces, "was quite a group". The lead guitarist was usually Ramón Montoya, the *cantaores* included, at one time or another, **Manuel Torre,** Aurelio Sellé, Canalejas de Puerto Real, Pepe Torre ... obviously nothing but the best.

Pastora remembers nostalgically when she and Ramón would step out alone on the stage, he to "spin a silver *soleá*" on his guitar, she to "weave an emotional web", creating, improvising, until the entire house was on its feet roaring its approval. It was good to hear her reliving her old successes, for with Pastora it was not the wishful thinking of a forgotten artist, but the reliving of an emotional moment. Every old *aficionado* who saw Pastora verifies her story, and then adds great eulogies of his own.

As if her other talents are not enough, Pastora is also blessed with an excellent business mind. Before opening her present *tablao*, El Duende, she managed her famous *venta* "La Capitana" from 1942-1954. At that time La Capitana, La Villa Rosa, and La Gran Taberna Gitana (now the Torres Bermejas) were the only flamenco centers of significance in Madrid, and three of the very few such establishments throughout Spain that helped keep flamenco alive during that difficult period.

Pastora, widowed a few years ago by the renowned bullfighter, Rafael el Gallo, is by no means retired, although she is well in her seventies. Together with her son-in-law, the retired bullfighter Gitanillo de Triana, she still manages El Duende, and manages it with energy and decision. As we sat together talking and watching the *cuadro* she would utter an occasional *olé* at something she particularly liked, while handling one or another of the problems that came up, such as hissing cavorting artists into silence. Once she became enthused over some part of our dance discussion and demonstrated the potential beauty of the *baile de brazos;* although she remained seated, her brief demonstration left no doubt as to the accuracy of her reputation.

Finally, at close to four a.m., Pastora excused herself and went home, having completed another flamenco-filled night in the many thousands of such nights in her long, illustrious flamenco career.

BALLET FLAMENCO

Around the turn of the century the *cafés cantantes* began closing down in earnest, and flamenco moved into theatrical "*fines de fiestas*" and other such vaudeville-type shows. A reasonable amount of purity was maintained in this unlikely atmosphere, as the *baile gitano* was still at a premium. But with the next logical step, the *ballet español* (large theatrical groups who perform a mixture of Spanish, classical, regional, and flamenco dances), *bailaoras* were replaced by *bailarinas* who also danced a little flamenco, and the flamenco dance became refined, stylized, civilized. These ballet companies traveled far and wide and were clamorously accepted, with the result that ballet flamenco was soon considered *the* flamenco. The authentic flamencos, the interpreters of the old-time *jondo* dance, found the transition all but impossible to make, and repaired, unwanted and outmoded, to the back rooms of *colmaos* and *ventas*. Authentic flamenco began dying, while ballet flamenco became big business, each year bigger, more contaminated, and more stylized. Save for an occasional theatrical effort at genuine flamenco, there was little hope...

The 1950's arrive. Some gentlemen in France inexplicably contract Perico el del Lunar to make an anthology of the *cante antiguo*. Perico, admittedly cynical about the undertaking ("I thought we would put the people to sleep, and told the record people so"), nevertheless locates some excellent old-time singers who still sing the *cante antiguo*, teaches a few forgotten *cantes* to younger *cantaores*, and comes up with a masterpiece of an anthology that has the startling effect of awakening international interest, particularly among the intellectuals, in the flamenco of old.

The *cante* begins reviving, the guitar is struggling ahead, but it is nearly too late for the dance. In the interim most of the masters of the old school have died away, and there are few left who can interpret and teach the authentic *baile flamenco*. Besides, the general public is ballet oriented, and are startled and a little revolted by unconcealed primitiveness. They want their flamenco in sophisticated, watered-down doses guaranteed to entertain, not involve.

The Two "Argentinas"

The ballet period of the Spanish dance was initiated by two now legendary figures who, curiously enough, were both born in Argentina, and whose artistic names reflected the place of their birth: Antonia Mercé "la Argentina", and Encarnación López "la Argentinita".

Although unrelated, these two non-gypsy dancers were similar in many ways. Both were debonair, bubbling women, which was reflected in their dance. The gay, airy dances were their forte, dances that they would move lightly through with apparently genuine smiles beaming from their faces. Both were virtuosos of the castanets, and both concentrated far more on Spanish classical and regional dancing than on flamenco. Both were charming women, and both died premature deaths while still actively performing.

La Argentina and La Argentinita introduced a new kind of refined, stylized flamenco, a type of flamenco quite unlike the primitive gypsy-inspired flamenco of old. Among flamenco artists this type of dance is referred to as *"baile flamenco estilizado"*, or "stylized flamenco dance".

ANTONIA MERCE "LA ARGENTINA"

(c. 1886 - 1936)

Antonia Mercé "la Argentinita", born in Buenos Aires the daughter of flamenco artists (according to Fernando de Triana), was generally considered the First Lady of the Spanish Ballet. Concerning her flamenco dancing there are widely varying opinions.

I have been told by more than one flamenco artist that Antonia Mercé never danced to guitar accompaniment. These statements have proven quite inaccurate, made either by ignorant artists, or, more likely, artists who side with Encarnación López in the eternal rivalry between the two, for Fernando de Triana actually printed in his book (p. 282) a program for a theatrical show that took place in Madrid, which read: *"Danzas a la Guitarra por* Antonia Mercé (Argentina), *"La Rosa"*, *"Soleares"*, y *"Tango"*, *acompañada por el popular guitarrista* Salvador Ballesteros." I am of the mind that a theatrical program cannot be logically discounted, although Fernando's statement that ANTONIA MERCÉ, in addition to being Spain's first *bailarina* was also its first *bailaora*, can be taken rather lightly due to the fact that LA ARGENTINA was instrumental in raising the money for the publication of Fernando's book. (How much of our written history has been influenced in similar ways?).

ANTONIA MERCÉ, called the "Queen of the Castanets", spent a good deal of her career in Paris, as did Vicente Escudero. Although their personalities and views of the flamenco dance clashed, they often worked together, and rose to fame largely together.

ANTONIA MERCÉ died in Bayonne, France, in 1936, the year the Spanish Civil War broke out.

ENCARNACION LOPEZ "LA ARGENTINITA"

(c. 1900 - 1945)

It is generally agreed that ENCARNACIÓN LÓPEZ JÚLVEZ had a better idea of flamenco dancing than Antonia Mercé, although she was also very sytlized in her approach.

Born in Buenos Aires, ENCARNACIÓN was early brought to Spain, and was raised in the San Sebastián-Santander area. She began dancing regional dances as a child, such as *la jota,* but did nothing in the flamenco vein until much later.

When LA ARGENTINITA formed her first ballet group she danced almost exclusively to the piano, but soon added to her repertoire the flamenco *rumba* and *tanguillo*. Finding that these dances enjoyed success, she began learning others, and by the end of her career was dancing an impressive repertoire of flamenco dances, all choreographed, including her innovation of *la caña*, which she was the first to dance.

According to Luis Maravilla, LA ARGENTINITA made her first trip to America in 1928, in company with her sister, Pilar López, the guitarist Luis Yance, and others. The troupe apparently caused a sensation in New York, and from that time, until her death seventeen years later, LA ARGENTINITA was considered the belle of the Spanish dance by New York *aficionados*. Her 1928 trip was the first of numerous highly successful tours which took LA ARGENTINITA to nearly all of the countries of North, Central, and South America.

In 1933, largely due to the inspiration and active planning of the great love of her life, the bullfighter Ignacio Sánchez Mejías (killed in the bull ring in 1935), LA ARGENTINITA innovated the first large scale theatrical attempt at authentic flamenco in a colorful, hour-long program called *"Las Calles de Cádiz"*. In a true search for authenticity she called out of retirement such old-time dancers as La Macarrona, La Malena, La Sordita, and Fernanda Antúnez, and rounded out the troupe with figures of the caliber of guitarist Manolo de Huelva (his one fling at theatrical flamenco), gaditano singer Ignacio Ezpeleta, a nearly black gypsy and fine singer who often stole the show with his sparking wit and gypsy mannerisms, the singer El Niño Gloria, one of the greats of his time, and so forth. The show attempted to bring to the stage, apparently with great success, the colorful life of the *barrio* Santa María, in Cádiz (see "Pericón de Cádiz" section for anecdotes concerning this most flamenco of neighborhoods). Each artist not only performed, but acted a role (policeman, prostitute, maid, *señorito*, shoe-maker, waiter, coachman, drunk, tourist, etc.), and it is said that the streets of Cádiz actually seemed to come alive on stage. As for the flamenco, it was apparently pure, and oftentimes even erupted into spontaneity. In the opinion of many, including my own, this type of show is the only manner in which authentic flamenco can be presented to the public.

ARGENTINITA's *"Las Calles de Cádiz"* was definitely the high point of theatrical flamenco. Since that time the graph would show an overall steady decline, marked by occasional rises and many dips.

ENCARNACIÓN spent much of her career outside of Spain. The United States, a country which she came to love next to Spain and Argentina, was the site of many of her triumphs, and also of her death. She began feeling faint on stage in the year 1945, and entered a New York hospital for a checkup. She died a short time later, of cancer.

Three years later the Metropolitan Opera House, in New York, paid LA ARGENTINITA the ultimate tribute. They erected a bronze statue of her, which stands beside those of the only two other artists who have been so honored: Pavlova and Caruso.

LA QUICA

1988 Update: (c. 1905-1970)

FRANCISCA GONZÁLEZ "LA QUICA", wife of the renowned *bailaor* Frasquillo, has earned a double distinction in flamenco: that of being one of this century's finest *bailaoras*, as well as an outstanding *maestra* of the *baile*.

QUICA's dance, marked by great fire and profundity, was based on the fluid movement of the arms, hands, and upper torso. Fernando de Triana praised her (1935) with the following paragraphs:

"Without a doubt she (La Quica) is the *bailaora* who possesses the most temperament today, and among those who truly know how to wear to best advantage the *bata de cola* and the *pañolillo de Manila*.

"Of her art I won't say anything, as I have already said that she is second edition of Frasquillo. And that's saying something!"

LA QUICA, a non-gypsy, was born and raised on Sevilla's *calle Feria*, near the Alameda de Hércules. She began imitating the dance that surrounded her nearly as soon as she could walk, and commenced informal lessons of classical and regional dances from an old maker of dancing shoes at the age of eight. Although she picked up a good idea of the flamenco dance from being in constant contact with it, she did not begin to dance it seriously until age eleven, when Frasquillo saw promise in her and began giving her free lessons. The following year she began her professional career, dancing in Sevilla's Café Kursaal and Teatro Imperial.

Upon reaching her fifteenth year, Frasquillo proposed that she join his company for a tour outside of Spain, an offer that became magnified into quite another type of proposal. In her words: "We foresaw so many difficulties, with me being a young virgin under the legal age and all, that we got married. That was the solution to everything, and we set out on tour."

QUICA's first dance partner was Antonio de Triana, father of the fine present-day *bailaora*, Luisa de Triana. As QUICA and Frasquillo rarely danced as partners, Frasquillo gave Antonio de Triana his first lessons so that he could dance with LA QUICA.

When asked what she danced in the early days QUICA answered:

"The only dances women danced then were por *alegrías, tangos,* and *tanguillos,* always using the *bata de cola.* Then with the years one or the other of us would innovate a new dance which was previously only sung, until arriving at today's large repertoire of dances. Unfortunately, the style of feminine dance has changed for the worse — most *bailaoras* today have lost much of their femininity. I don't even like to go to the *tablaos* anymore, excepting sometimes La Zambra, which still conserves something of the old-time atmosphere."

LA QUICA went on to talk of today's crop of young guitarists, whom she says are all but impossible to dance with unless one dances in the rehearsed, repetitious manner of modern flamenco. She tells of the last time that she gave a demonstration of the old dance. Two days before the event was to take place the guitarist hired for the occasion came to her for the customary rehearsals. QUICA, used to dancing in the spontaneous manner of true flamenco, asked the guitarist just one question before refusing to rehearse:

"Do you know how to accompany the *baile?*"

"Of course", answered the guitarist.

"Then why rehearse?", snapped back LA QUICA.

Why, indeed!

Since her last artistic tour, with José Greco in 1953, QUICA has devoted herself principally to her dance academy, located on the Plaza General Vara del Rey (number five), in Madrid, in which she has taught, at one time or another, nearly all of today's top dancers. She plays an accurate guitar, and accompanies most of her classes herself. Does she teach the old dance that she admires so much? The answer is yes and no. The System today is such that even LA QUICA has had to become somewhat commercially oriented. Most of her students are aspiring or full professionals, and she must teach them what the public wants to see, what the *tablao* and ballet managers demand from their dancers. Within these limitations QUICA's teaching is as pure as is possible.

QUICA's daughter, the well-known *bailaora* Mercedes León, also has a dance academy in Madrid.

PILAR LOPEZ

(c. 1906 —

PILAR LÓPEZ, sister of the legendary Encarnación López "la Argentinita", has been a leading figure of the Spanish dance for many years.

PILAR, born a non-gypsy in San Sebastián, learned most of her dance from La Argentinita. The sisters were inseparable companions, and shared their artistic successes, a good deal of the time outside of Spain, until the time of La Argentinita's death in 1945. In 1946 Pilar formed her own company, and has been on top since.

PILAR's flamenco dancing is feminine and quietly moving, tending towards the old style. Perhaps her most memorable achievements have been the excellent theatrical shows she has consistently produced over the years. She has a decided talent for forming fine male dancers in her company, wholly masculine in their dance (at least during their years with PILAR), although sometimes overly polished and stylized. Her discipline within her company must be exemplary, for even when PILAR dances with three of four of her *bailaores,* as during the golden days when her lead male dancers were José Greco, Manolo Vargas, Roberto Jiménez, and Alejandro Vega, the idea of a male-female relationship remains strong. The *bailaores* seem to be competing for the woman, not to see who is the best dancer. In my opinion PILAR is at her best in her theatrical mixed dancing.

Other than those mentioned, PILAR also strongly influenced the formation of Alberto Lorca, Antonio Gades, and others.

In keeping with theatrical tradition, PILAR's every move is

choreographed, designed for a one-performance audience — the antithesis of true flamenco, as must consistently be pointed out. Within this limitation, however, Pilar's dance appears far less stylized than that of many of her contemporaries, and she does achieve some fine moments. She does not, however, possess that indefinable something that makes for truly great flamneco dancing.

After all of these years of artistic success Pilar is not wanting. She presently resides in her mansion in Madrid. Her husband, Tomás Ríos, a musician and composer, is the general director of her ballet.

CARMEN AMAYA

(c. 1913 - 1963)

Carmen Amaya ... a magic name in flamenco. With her death, late in 1963 (November 19), flamenco lost a unique figure, an irreplaceable figure, a *bailaora* capable of creating her own style of turbulent yet deeply profound dance, so individual, so depending on the personality and genius of one fabulous *gitana* that it can never be adequately imitated.

To many, Carmen was *la única* (far superior) in the *baile flamenco*. To others, she represented a highly-talented phenomenon whose style of dance revolutionized the *baile flamenco*, whose example altered the very concepts of the old feminine dance. These critics, mostly old-time purists, accuse Carmen of having been the leading influence in defeminizing, to a degree, the dance of the *bailaora*. In effect, they say that Carmen unwittingly caused the emancipation of the feminine dance.

I would say that both of these points of view are based on the truth, depending on the period of which they speak, for Carmen's dance passed through two stages. The first might be referred to as the "masculine" period, the second, the "feminine".

The "masculine" period refers strictly to Carmen's early style of dance, which broke with many of the traditions of the old *baile flamenco*. Much of the tranquility, the absolute emphasis on femininity through fluid movement of the arms, hands, and upper torso was substituted by smashing, machine-gun footwork (CARMEN drove a foot through more than one platform), strength, drive, and hyper-charged excitement. More often than not CARMEN wore the masculine *traje corto*, or shirt and pants. She certainly was not the first to don the clothing of the *bailaor*, as we have seen, but was by far the most effective, for CARMEN had a body largely lacking in feminine curves, legs like steel, and a fiery, dominating nature (on stage) well-suited for the more driving, masculine type of dance.

It was with this type of dance that CARMEN came roaring out of Barcelona, some thirty-five years ago, to conquer the world. Conquer the world she did, and her instantaneous, overwhelming success caused many a *bailaora* to radically alter her dance in an attempt to climb on CARMEN's bandwagon. Soon every Pepita and Paquita were clutching *traje corto* jackets and grimacing fiercely in what degenerated into an all-out competition with the *bailaor*, a competition of masculine dancing techniques as meaningless as it was, and is, ludicrous. Why must it be that genius and originality are inevitably twisted and distorted through imitation? For when CARMEN danced, regardless of the style, there was truth, integrity, and beauty, for CARMEN was always genuine; she unveiled her personality through her dance. CARMEN danced CARMEN, without copying from other sources, and her dance, even during her early period, suited her (1). It does not, however, suit her imitators. CARMEN's dance was much too extreme, much too personal to be copied. When watching CARMEN's imitators one gets that embarrassed feeling, that urge to turn away, for the result is almost inevitably misplaced movements, unfelt turbulence, a complete lack of originality — in a word, utter chaos. Fortunately, CARMEN spent long periods of time outside of Spain, and her influence within Spain did not become as wide-spread as it might have.

CARMEN gradually began outgrowing her masculine type of dance. As she matured she began altering her style, adding more

---

(1) Pilar López summed it up well when she said that she has never been able to stand *bailaoras* in pants, with the exception of Carmen Amaya. Carmen was always the great exception!

elements of femininity, more ruffles, more flowing arms and hands, more tranquility, a more subtle fire and passion and a suppressed sensuality formerly lacking. It was a struggle at first; her public had had a taste of CARMEN the spitfire, and CARMEN the complete *bailaora* had to fight for recognition. The public demanded, even up to the time of her death, the CARMEN of old; fire, flashing turns, wild movements, footwork and *pitos* the equals of any man, a sensational, roaring twenties brand of flamenco that the public could sit back and enjoy without having to employ thought or subtler emotions.

But CARMEN persisted, and with time her dance achieved true greatness in both the traditional and revolutionary sense, a greatness fortunately captured in the outstanding movie *"La Historia de los Tarantos"*, filmed only a year before CARMEN's death. In this movie CARMEN's dance is age-old and yet highly personal, giving vent to her consuming fire and passion while remaining overwhelmingly feminine.

CARMEN was born in the very setting of *"La Historia de los Tarantos"*, the gypsy neighborhood of Somorrostro, on the outskirts of Barcelona. By the age of four she was dancing what could be called professionally in the waterfront taverns of Barcelona, as well as in an occasional theater. This was arranged by her father, El Chino, who accompanied her on the guitar, and set the stage for his complete domination and exploitation of his daughter until his death. (There is nothing unusual in this; it is a father's privilege, according to gypsy customs). At seven years CARMEN was called *"La Capitana"* (the Captain, or leader), and was dancing a great deal in theatrical *"fines de fiestas"*. At age ten CARMEN's aunt, La Faraona, a famous Granadinan *bailaora*, took CARMEN to Paris to perform in the show of Raquel Meller, together with CARMEN's sister, María, and the guitarist Carlos Montoya. CARMEN completely stole the show, according to Vicente Escudero, and was ultimately dismissed by Raquel due to artistic jealousy. At this age CARMEN was already performing in *cuadros* with such artists as Manuel Torre, Tomás Pavón, and La Niña de los Peines.

CARMEN enjoyed talking about her family and active childhood. She used to claim, with considerable family pride, if doubtful accuracy, that her grandfather, Juan Amaya Jiménez, a gypsy from the caves of the Sacro-Monte (Sacred Mountain), in Granada, was the *bailaor* who innovated the *baile por jaberas* (which, she explained, was a form of the *soleares*), and also the *bailes "por agua"* (water dances), according to CARMEN the old name of the present-day *alegrías*. Her parents were also from Granada's Sacro-Monte, her father a *tocaor*, and her mother a *bailaora* "who was never permitted to dance outside of the family circle — my father was too jealous."

"My mother married at the age of fourteen, and had ten children. Paco is the oldest. Of the ten, only six lived, all of us flamenco artists. Our family name is Amaya and Amaya, because both my mother and father are Amayas."

CARMEN liked to tell of her childhood dancing, when she was "spurred on by gnawing hunger." Her problem in the early days was not a lack of clamouring public, but the police, who did their best to prohibit her from dancing due to her extreme youth. She remembered one theatrical show in Barcelona that was raided by the police precisely because she was performing at the tender age of four.

"My father ran for a taxi to have waiting at the stage door, and I ran backstage looking for a hiding place. You'll never guess where I hid — under the overcoat of the *cantaor* José Cepero! He was a big man, and I a tiny tot, and he held me inside his coat with one hand while the police searched in vain. ¡Ozú!

"Another time I was dancing in the Spanish pavillion of the Pueblo Español, in Barcelona's International Exposition (1929 — CARMEN was sixteen). I was still very young. The job of the artists was to entertain the guests of the pavillion, who always responded with presents, as is natural. One day a very plainly-dressed man entered, who looked pretty low on money. The other artists wouldn't go near him, for fear of dancing gratis, but I went anyway, against all of their advice and protests. I danced for him for some time, with all of the other artists laughing at both the poor man and me. He took all of their joking and laughing with a kindly smile.

"Sure enough, when he left all he gave me was a very humble

'thank you' but I didn't mind; he had been enchanted with my dance, and that was pay enough. But the other artists couldn't understand this, and didn't tire of pulling my leg...

"But an hour later you should have seen their faces fall. Some men delivered to me a huge basket full of wines, hams, preserves ... thousands of pesetas worth of delicious things.

"Inside the basket was an envelope containing five hundred pesetas, and a note from the nice man for whom I had danced. The man expressed his sincerest admiration for my dance, but the letter head was what stunned us all. The man, who had been disguised to avoid attention, had been none other than El Infante Don Carlos de Borbón, brother of the King of Spain!!"

Just after her round of triumphs at the Barcelona fair, CARMEN left for Buenos Aires to fulfill a six-months contract. Her success was enormous; when she returned to Spain a full eleven years later she was a rich woman, replete with money, jewels, a ranch in Buenos Aires, the former Hollywood home of Diana Durbin, presents from the president of the United States, Franklin Delano Roosevelt, and a vast hemisphere just awakening to the thrill of flamenco and eager to pay any amount to lure CARMEN back.

CARMEN was torn between two desires. While she was tempted to return to the land of plenty, where she was treated like a gypsy goddess, she did not want to leave her beloved Spain again. The issue was quickly decided by her father, who was not about to play Spain for peanuts when such an abundance of green was available on the other side of the ocean. He did, however, compromise with CARMEN. She could not stay in Spain, but they could take a sizeable chunk of the Spanish population back with them to keep them company. Thus they rounded up some forty-odd gypsies, nearly all members of the family (tribe), and CARMEN had her first troupe.

Off they went to America, probably the most colorful flamenco troupe that has existed in modern times, to make and spend fortunes, and create legends. CARMEN was delighted with this turn of events, apparently unconcerned that they spent as much, or more, than they made. She has been described as "generous to a fault", and "completely unimpressed with material possessions", which seems to have been absolutely true. Besides, her father handled the money and made the arrangements, and kept CARMEN largely in the dark about these "masculine affairs".

Alfredo Mañas recounts some of the stories of this troupe, told to him by various of its members. One is about CARMEN's father, El Chino, and the guitarist, Sebastián Pelao. El Pelao did not know how to write, and signed hotel registers with a fingerprint, planting an inked finger on the sheet and twisting in his print slowly and carefully, much to the astonishment of sophisticated hotel clerks. After one such operation he turned to El Chino and stated gravely:

"Look, Chino, each day I write better..."

One of the gypsy women of the troupe still recalls nostalgically:

"All forty of us gypsies went together everywhere. Sadness didn't exist for us. After doing three theater shows we continued the *fiesta* amongst ourselves. We didn't stop singing and dancing throughout the whole trip!"

CARMEN, so they say, returned from this tour empty-handed.

A story is told in Mexico about the time CARMEN was hired to perform in a night club in Mexico City. She was in Spain at the time, and was instructed to bring a small troupe with her. When the time of embarcation was drawing near, the owner wrote and asked CARMEN how many boat tickets should be taken out. The answer came back: twenty-six!

This was about three times the number of artists anticipated, but the owner reasoned that, although the cost of passage would be excessive, the club would be getting a fabulous show, and would be getting three times the number of artists for the pre-arranged priced. So the twenty-six tickets were purchased with nary a flinch.

The expression on the owner's face must have been quite something when the boat docked. The only members of CARMEN's immediate family that had been left behind were the *burros*. The grinning tribe came in all sizes and ages, and only about one-half could be considered artists, even with the wildest stretch of the imagination. Of this one-half, only about another one-half were competent artists.

And that was only the beginning. It seems that there were frequent moments of tension between CARMEN's sisters and brothers and their husbands, wives, and lovers, which oftentimes resulted in bruises and black eyes, refusals to work, and temporary disappearances of one or another artist. Things got so bad that on any particular night only about eight or nine of the twenty-six "artists" would show up to perform.

The situation sounds pretty disastrous, but, fortunately, has an ending as unlikely as the beginning. CARMEN, with her wondrous art, turned the potential fiasco into a smashing success. Crowds poured into the club, money rolled in, and everyone ended up happy and good friends.

Another time CARMEN became fed up with family difficulties of the type outlined above, and called off a tour of the United States during the intermission of one of the performances. She merely walked out on stage and told the people that the show was over and that they could obtain refunds at the box office (without the theater manager's knowledge), disbanded the troupe, and flew off to Mexico City.

The repercussions of this impetuous act were minimal. CARMEN's dependability rating suffered a bit, and she lost one of the most important agents in the United States, although they remained friends — CARMEN's winning personal charm always had to be considered apart from her impulsive gypsy behavior.

After years of reputed courtship with the guitarist Sabicas, CARMEN finally married another guitarist, Juan Antonio Agüero, a few years ago. This man firmly set about improving CARMEN's affairs, one of his first acts being to dismiss most of CARMEN's family from the troupe, as well as all hangers-on and aides-de-camp. He introduced formality and a degree of frugality, and CARMEN began to prosper.

CARMEN found herself in these circumstances when her illness struck. She had recently returned to Spain and purchased a picturesque home in Bagur, near Barcelona, that contains an old Arabic watchtower. Her movie *"La Historia de los Tarantos"* was about to be released, and she was contendedly settling down to her first authentic home life in years.

Then one day during a performance CARMEN passed out on stage. Doctors found that her kidneys were not eliminating the toxins sufficiently, and told her that she must never dance again. (CARMEN had apparently had this defect since childhood. Her physician stated that CARMEN's unbelievably energetic dance saved her from death as early as in her teens, as the toxins found release through her sweat glands). CARMEN accepted this ultimatum bravely, saying that even if she could not dance, she would go on stage and play the *palmas*, sing, or whatever. She stated that she would not wholly retire until she could no longer mount a *tablao*.

Less than a month later CARMEN died in her home in Bagur. Few personalities have been so widely mourned, both internationally and in Spain, as was CARMEN, and certainly none in the world of flamenco. As far as I can ascertain, CARMEN had no enemies. She was beloved by one and all. Her acts of generosity are legendary, such as the benefits to which she donated her services, sometimes to points halfway around the world, paying the troupe's salaries and traveling expenses from her own pocket. One of these acts of charity provided a school for the children of the neighborhood of her birth; to demonstrate its appreciation, the *barrio de* Somorrostro is raising a statue of CARMEN in its main *plaza*.

Several phonograph records, featuring CARMEN and her troupe, are on the market. Probably the most excellent is her Decca release "The Queen of the Gypsies", which captures CARMEN's fine singing and footwork superbly, as well as the inspired playing of Sabicas at his most flamenco. Other good ones are "Flamenco", also a Decca release, and an earlier Decca featuring the singing of CARMEN and her sister, Leonor, and the playing of brother Paco. For admirers of CARMEN, and lovers of flamenco in general, these records are valuable. Her last movie, "*La Historia de los Tarantos*", is an absolute must!

ROSARIO

(c. 1914 —

FLORENCIA PÉREZ PADILLA, better known as "ROSARIO", has been an international figure of the Spanish dance for well over a quarter of a century.

ROSARIO's name is inevitably linked with that of Antonio, and well it should be. ROSARIO and Antonio, both native *sevillanos*, took their first dance lessons together with Sevilla's Realito, and formed a dance team that lasted a phenomenal twenty-two years (1930-1952). During those twenty-two years "*Los Chavalillos de España*" performed in a multitude of continents and countries, always with great success, ultimately becoming the most famous and acclaimed dance team in the history of the Spanish dance.

ROSARIO has spent her life in the atmosphere of the Spanish ballet, and her flamenco, as is natural, is ballet flamenco. That is to say, stylized and choreographed. As a solo flamenco dancer ROSARIO is perhaps at her best in the gay *bailes*, such as the *tanguillos, rumbas, tangos*. She has a special impish appeal in these dances both original and catching.

Since breaking with Antonio in 1952, ROSARIO has formed her own ballet on fifteen different occasions, in which she acts as promoter, director, choreographer, and star . During her career she has appeared in six movies in the United States, and three in Spain, and has been decorated several times for her brilliant artistic career and for furthering the good name of Spain.

Amid much fanfare ROSARIO again appeared with Antonio during his 1962 theater stand in Madrid, several times in 1963, and even more often, to date, in 1964.

REGLA ORTEGA
(c. 1919 —

REGLA ORTEGA, another member of the famed Ortega family (see biography of Manolo Caracol and Ortega family chart), has the reputation of being one of the finer dancers of this century. She is one of the more complete *bailaoras* in the sense of repertoire. Her dance is often highly technical.

It is said that had REGLA been blessed with the beauty to enhance her artistic talents, she would have achieved far more success in the commercial flamenco dance.

Today REGLA is largely devoted to teaching the dance in her Madrid academy, to the accompaniment of her guitar-playing husband.

ROSITA DURAN
(c. 1920 —

Jerez-born ROSA DURÁN, gypsy niece of the *siguiriyero* Diego el Marrurro, is one of the few interpreters of the traditional *baile flamenco* remaining today. ROSITA emphasizes the dance of the arms, hands, and upper torso; her movements are slow and fluid, such a relief from the windmills and hysteria of the modern flamenco dance. Her footwork is also accomplished, although often overly-extended.

Among ROSITA's large repertoire of dances one stands out in my mind; her interpretation of the rarely danced *peteneras*. She dances this dance with a black *bata de cola* and a black *mantón de Manila*, and a gravity truly moving. That is, the first one or twice that it is seen, for ROSITA is inexplicably among those who dance unvarying arrangements for years at a time (the almost inevitable drug of commercialism, as we have discussed).

ROSITA made her artistic debut in the 1935 flamenco program, presided over by La Argentina, that raised money for the publication of Fernando de Triana's valuable book *"Arte y Artistas Flamencos"*. She went on to study the dance with another famous *jerezano*, Juan el Estampío, before moving into the international flamenco scene. Some twelve years ago ROSA became the leading figure in Madrid's La Zambra, where she is still the reigning queen.

ROSITA owes much of her knowledge of the dance to her longtime accompanist in La Zambra, Perico el del Lunar. Perico, a student of all of flamenco's facets, showed ROSA many old-time dances and ways of dancing that he had absorbed during his long career, which have become the very base of ROSA's dance. Her favorite accompanist now, naturally enough, is Perico's son, a youth who possesses much of his late father's knowledge and *toque*.

ROSITA was the *protégée* of two fine Jerez *cantaores*, Isabelita de Jerez and José Durán. She was later betrothed to José Durán, and recently widowed.

ROSITA, certainly one of the outstanding *bailaoras* dancing today, is presently performing at the New York World's Fair with other members of La Zambra's *cuadro*.

LOLA FLORES

(c. 1924 —

LOLA FLORES is a refreshing figure in today's flamenco world of studied arrangements and stagnation. LOLA is a flamenca by instinct. She has never bothered much about actually learning how to dance, and she consequently rarely uses dance arrangements, knows only the most rudimentary footwork — and that is all she needs.

LOLA's dance is completely unorthodox, she is not even seriously considered a dancer (she is a singer and overall entertainer in the Spanish vein), yet there is no dancer dancing today who can put more *duende*, more fire, or more basic, unsophisticated flamenco creativity into her dance than she.

Born in Jerez de la Frontera, LOLA, a non-gypsy, learned her basic formation as a dancer and an artist from the guitarists Javier Molina and Sebastián Núñez, and the dancer María Pantoja, all of Jerez (1). Her first organized tour was in 1940, headed by Javier Molina. Not long after she teamed up with Manolo Caracol, and together the two spectacular artists with explosive temperaments rose rapidly to nationwide fame. They stayed together some years until an inevitable split, at which time each formed his own company. Since then LOLA's genius has gained her international fame, as has her well-known private life, which has caused delighted gossip over every back fence and along every telephone wire in Spain.

---

(1) It is not unusual that beginning dancers are instructed by experienced guitarists, accustomed to the *baile* through long years of accompanying. This is due to two reasons: a shortage of dance instructors, especially in the provinces, and the simple economy of having the instructor and accompanist one and the same person.

Recently LOLA married the guitarist Antonio González "Pescadilla", who is now a very adequate member of LOLA's company. Other than their shared artistic successes, they have set about having children at the respected Spanish rate of three in four years. When not on tour, LOLA and family rotate between their winter residence in Sevilla and their summer home in Marbella.

MALENI LORETO

(c. 1934 —

MALENI LORETO, a niece of the celebrated *bailaora*, La Malena, dances beautifully the style of dance that made her aunt one of flamenco's most famous dancers of all times: the dance of the upper torso.

A green-eyed, nearly blonde gypsy beauty from Sevilla, MALENI has a naturally graceful and flamenco play of arms and hands, and is not afraid to use them (of course, many spectators, hopped-up on flamenco *rumbas* and *bulerías*, find her dancing dull). When she dances *jondo*, she *is jondo*, with no concessions granted to the less sensitive public. Her type of dance cannot be turned on at will, however, and she is not always at her best in commercial surroundings. But when inspired, she has a *duende* possessed by few.

MALENI is also an accomplished dancer below the waist, although her footwork is held strictly subordinate to her dance of the upper torso. A long-time professional *bailaora*, MALENI presently resides in Madrid.

LUCERITO TENA

(c. 1936 —

LUCERITO TENA, Mexican by birth, Spanish by ancestry, is one of the *baile's* finer young virtuosos. Her footwork and castanet playing are impeccable, her *pitos* good, her dances flamenco, her movements free from the foolishness found in so many present-day dancers, and her overall effect ... extremely professional.

LUCERITO is perhaps the most widely accomplished Spanish dancer dancing today. Her impressive diversity is due to the following: eight years of classical Spanish dance instruction, beginning at the age of four, under Emilio Díaz; six years of Russian classical instruction under Nina Shestakova; and two and one-half years with the company of Carmen Amaya. All of this training gives LUCERO the background for her unusual, and quite astonishing, concert activity, which includes:

1) Eighteenth century *zapatilla* (*boleras*, etc.).

2) Spanish regional (*jota, seguidillas manchegas, sevillanas,* etc.).

3) Spanish classical (Falla, Turina, Albéniz, etc.).

4) Classical, in which LUCERO's castanets are the solo instrument in a chamber group playing such masters as Bach, Scarlatti, etc., and in which she both dances and plays Debussy.

5) Concerts of eighty-piece symphonic orchestras, in which LUCERO solos with her castanets.

6) Flamenco.

LUCERITO's flamenco is of the modern brand that uses a great deal of castanets, prolonged, intricate footwork, and long, meticulously worked-out arrangements, rarely varied, with the rest of the *cuadro*. In spite of her technical preoccupation, however, LUCERO's flamenco dancing is moving, especially until one becomes overly-familiar with her arrangements, for LUCERO puts a great deal of herself into her dance. In addition, she is extremely accomplished in all phases of the dance, from the waist up as well as from the waist down.

LUCERO, a charming woman, is definitely on her way up. If her dedication remains at its present pitch, there is no doubt that she is fully equipped to head her own Spanish ballet company, and thus remain in the foreground for years to come.

For well over a year LUCERITO has been the featured dancer in Madrid's Corral de la Morería and has, as well, given several recitals, of the type outlined above, in various of Spain's capitals.

LUISA MARAVILLA

(c. 1939 —

Luisa Maravilla, a *madrileña* whose ancestors hailed from Ronda, ranks among the purest and finest of today's *bailaoras*.

Luisa emphasizes the traditional dance of the arms, hands, and upper torso with a fluidity, grace, and beauty too rarely seen in today's frenzy of movement. As such, she is opposed to the use of castanets in all serious flamenco dancing, in that they definitely hinder, as we have previously discussed, the proper interpretation of this type of dance.

Luisa's dance is traditional enough so as to actually seem unorthodox in commercial surroundings. There are moments when she will remain motionless for thirty seconds or longer, moving only her arms and hands, her face reflecting a true, profound absorption in her art. Her dance contains great temperament, but a refined temperament free from the commonplace bumps and grinds and other vulgarities that so besiege and belittle the *baile flamenco* today.

Luisa dances all of flamenco's dances, but by temperament and preference tends towards the slower, more *jondo* dances — the *siguiriyas, soleares, taranto,* slow *alegrías* and *tangos* — when the true majesty of the dance from the waist up can be properly executed. Her footwork, also well-developed, is usually kept in the proper proportion to the rest of her dance, although occasionally it becomes overly-prolonged and may detract somewhat from the dance.

Luisa's traditional style of dance has developed considerably in the past few years. From a product of dance academies, replete with castanets, dance arrangements, and such, only a few years ago, she has come a long way, in large part due to her opportunity to spend a number of years in the still traditional flamenco atmosphere of the province of Sevilla. In her words:

"Among the gypsies, whether in a cave christening or marriage, or at the traditional '*Potaje de la Hermandad de los Gitanos*'

(1), which annually brings together such gypsy artists as Juan Talegas, Antonio Mairena, La Fernanda and La Bernarda de Utrera, Diego del Gastor, and so forth, I found such emotion that I recognized the confinement and frustration of arrangements.

"At my first *Potaje*, with Diego del Gastor accompanying me, I found a release in spontaneous dancing that simply does not exist in academic, arranged dancing. I just let myself go, dancing exactly as I felt like dancing, and found myself lost in the music, drunk with rhythm and emotion. When I finished dancing it was like awakening from a dream ... or like I had been drifting around in a high fever, only half conscious that the one dancing was I.

"That was perhaps my most memorable moment in the dance. The gypsies went wild, made me sign the announcements of the *Potaje* and the wooden spoons with which we ate it, and told me that only a person with gypsy blood could possibly dance like that. From then on I was considered one of them, which is the finest artistic compliment that can be paid.

"At any rate, it was in that atmosphere that I learned what true flamenco dancing can be. My present problem is, of course, that it is not as suitable for the *tablaos* as the frenzied dance of today. The difference is significant, much the same, for instance, as the difference in the bullfighting styles of Antonio Ordóñez and El Cordobés. One appeals to the initiated, the other to the public at large.

"And once one has tasted the true, spontaneous flamenco dance, it is difficult to return to *tablao* dancing with its deadening routine."

Nevertheless, LUISA occasionally accepts commercial offers, but consciously avoids becoming caught up in the System. Her philosophy helps her out: "I have always believed that the public is capable of appreciating good flamenco if only given the opportunity."

---

(1) A «*potaje*» is a garbanzo bean, vegetable, meat dish. The *potaje* referred to is an annual gathering of gypsies from the Utrera-Sevilla area, at which *potaje* is served. The objective of the *fiesta* is to raise funds for the gypsies' Holy Week religious procession, as well as for charity.

As of this writing LUISA is dancing in Manolo Caracol's *tablao*, Los Canasteros, in Madrid.

LA CHUNGA

(c. 1940 —

MICAELA FLORES AMAYA "LA CHUNGA" (gypsy for the "Ugly One") presently holds the distinction of being flamenco's top box office attraction. She is also one of today's finer young *bailaoras* but, unfortunately, a far cry from the dancing *ingénue* of a few years ago.

LA CHUNGA's curious story is perhaps simply that of lost innocence. But no, it is more than that ... it is also a story of a close-minded society insisting upon conformity, a hypocritical society avoiding and fearing truth and naturalness.

The story starts in Barcelona. LA CHUNGA, a beautiful artist's model in her early teens, began attracting local attention with her little-girl dance, as natural and pure and gypsy as she herself. Through her artist-employer she came to the attention of the grand old *bailaora*, Pastora Imperio, who happened to be looking for a young dancer in Barcelona at the time.

Pastora saw the great promise, and made LA CHUNGA her *protégée*, correcting what was necessary, always avoiding superficiality. They concentrated on the arms and hands and carriage, completely ignored the feet, encouraged her instinctive sense of rhythm, and accomplished what I am sure Pastora wanted: a *bailaora* to dance in the ancient style of true flamenco.

When LA CHUNGA was ready, Pastora introduced her into Madrid's Corral de la Morería. LA CHUNGA knew little more than the *rumba gitana* at that time, but she danced it in such a way as to draw more applause than the headliners. Most professionals scoffed, giving LA CHUNGA credit only for her natural beauty, but discrediting her dance. No footwork. No repertoire. After all!

LA CHUNGA began learning other *bailes* through observation, and could soon dance her unorthodox versions of the *soleá, siguiriyas, bulerías,* and *tientos*. About this time a Hollywood producer wrote LA CHUNGA's agent, attempting to sign her up for a movie — the producer had seen her in the Corral and had been completely betwitched. CHUNGA's agent thought it a joke and ignored the letter, for even her agent did not believe in her primitive dance. The producer persisted, however, contacting LA CHUNGA directly, and she was off to Hollywood (1955).

After the filming of the movie (Robert Taylor, star; LA CHUNGA danced a cabaret dance), CHUNGA traveled to New York for a first meeting with her aunt, Carmen Amaya, with whom she stayed for several months. Carmen arranged for LA CHUNGA to dance in El Patio, in Mexico City, and CHUNGA had her first starring opportunity.

In Mexico City LA CHUNGA continued pleasing her audiences. Her *jondo* dance (as distinguished from her *rumba*) was out of the past, almost religious, completely unlike the agitated, virtuoso dance that surrounded her. She was still dancing with such simplicity that she had no standard dance outfits, but wore gypsy blouses and skirts and danced barefoot. The pros continued scoffing, and told each other consolingly: "No footwork".

While in Mexico, however, she and her manager began submitting to the pressures of the System. "If she is to dance professionally," they were told, "if she is to carry several numbers by herself, she must dress up her dance, offer more variety, wear beautiful costumes, insert footwork, or otherwise the public will soon become bored." From the professional point of view they were, of course, right. LA CHUNGA's purity and simplicity were suited for a gypsy campfire or cave, or a little country inn filled with true *aficionados*, but not for a good-time night club or theater crowd. Such a crowd goes to be entertained, not to become emotionally involved, and they demand variety. LA CHUNGA's primitive dance was suited for one or two numbers in such an atmosphere, but had to be sophisticated if she were to carry a starring role.

A gradual but total submission. Dance lessons, set dance arrangements ("discipline", as the pros call it), expensive costumes, shoes (1), more make-up, more gimmicks, more this, more that, until LA CHUNGA began looking like the others — in some ways superior (arms, hands, carriage), and in some ways inferior (footwork). But no longer truly distinctive (society takes its toll).

Artistically this is where LA CHUNGA stands today. She is no longer the shining hope of the purists, but better accepted among the rest. We cannot lose sight of the fact, however, that even in this diluted form she remains one of flamenco's outstanding *bailaoras*, for there are very few who possess the basic qualities in which she is so well grounded: the arms, hands, carriage, and essential instincts.

LA CHUNGA retired from her active professional career when she married, in 1961, at the age of twenty-one. After the birth of a baby she began to reappear in lucrative situations — movies, high-class night clubs, television ... As a rule her movie dancing, directed by the unknowing, is mediocre, her luxury club dancing, so out of atmosphere, uninspired. Recently, however, LA CHUNGA's performance on a Spanish TV benefit program showed clearly that she has not lost a hard core of pure dance possessed by few in the *baile flamenco* today.

Born in Barcelona's gypsy outskirts, LA CHUNGA presently resides with her producer husband, and baby, in Madrid. Her sister, La Chunguita, is a copy of LA CHUNGA's younger days, but to date lacks the genius that sparked her sister's *baile*. La Chunguita is presently dancing the Spanish *tablao* circuit.

---

(1) La Chunga rose to fame dancing barefoot. Is this due to some old gypsy ritual or unwritten law? The answer is simple: the unwritten law is necessity. The poor gypsies consider common shoes a luxury (less now than in years past — their standard of living has risen), and higher-priced dancing shoes are out of the question. In addition, shoes are usually somewhat of a handicap for gypsy *juerga* dancing, which nearly always takes place on the dirt floors of caves or humble houses, or in unpaved streets and fields. The third factor to take into consideration is that footwork requires training, and the huge majority of the flamencos, be they gypsies or andaluces, do not train for their flamenco. Flamenco is simply a part of their lives, much as is eating and sleeping.

Thus La Chunga, from the traditional point of view, was being more authentic, or at least realistic, when dancing barefoot. However, the professionals and sophisticated public have developed their own rules for flamenco dancing, which include shoes and training. They observe these rules religiously, and chide and laugh at those who do not. La Chunga now wears dancing shoes.

OTHERS

There have been, and are, many other fine *bailaoras*. A biography of each would be cumbersome, and is unnecessary in fulfilling the purpose of this book; those already discussed have played the most historical roles in flamenco's development, or have best served to illustrate certain points and trends.

Here space can be allotted, however, for brief rundowns on some of the deserving artists who have not been mentioned to this point.

LA FARAONA, a widely renowned gypsy dancer from the caves of Granada, was one of Carmen Amaya's many relatives (aunt) from that area. She was a fiery interpreter of many *bailes,* specializing in those of Granada.

RITA ORTEGA, still another of the famed Ortega family (see Ortega family chart), was a leading dancer during the first half of this century. Presently in her late seventies, she resides in Sevilla.

MARÍA LA FLAMENCA's *bulerías* and ten-finger *pitos* are still remembered with awe by the *bailaora* La Quica. María was from Málaga, and danced largely during the first quarter of this century.

PASTORA MORENA VARGAS "LA POSAERA" is one of the few remaining interpreters of the old style feminine dance. Presently sixty-eight years old, La Posaera still makes her living in Sevilla's after-hours *juerga* establishments.

LA PAULA, now in her sixties, is a gypsy dancer renowned for her *bulerías*. She is a long-time resident of Málaga's flamenco district, the Calle de los Negros.

LOLA MEDINA is another highly-respected gypsy dancer from Granada, today nearly wholly retired. Lola was considered the finest dancer of the *zambra* of her epoch. Although she spends most of her time in Torremolinos, Lola still maintains one of the most picturesque caves of the Sacro-Monte.

FERNANDA ROMERO is perhaps the outstanding example of the disastrous results that can be achieved by those who imitate Carmen Amaya.

FLORA ALBAICÍN is a fiery *bailaora*, formerly the dancing partner of Roberto Iglesias.

CARMEN ROJAS rose to fame as Antonio's partner, is today among the best *bailaoras* dancing. Her light dancing is extremely reminiscent of that of Rosario, with much of the same impish quality. Although flamenco, Carmen's dance is of the stylized type.

TRINI ESPAÑA, from Sevilla, is one of today's more impressive *bailaoras*. Her dance is moving and flamenco, although she practices the usual commercialisms: castanets, overly-prolonged footwork, ending almost all of her dances, even the *siguiriyas, por bulerías*, and so forth. She is in her late twenties.

CARMEN CARRERA, like Trini a Sevilla-born non-gypsy, is another of today's finer young *bailaoras*. Carmen has a style of dance perhaps less fiery than Trini's, but which is compensated for by increased majesty. She employs the same commercialisms as Trini, as do nearly all of the young *bailaoras* today. On stage, Carmen is in appearance the world's conception of a flamenco dancer. Unfortunately, she is due to retire soon (marriage).

MARÍA ALBAICÍN, from a respected bullfight and flamenco family, has risen to become one of flamenco's most highly-paid and highly-regarded *bailaoras*. Madrid-born, María started her career some three years ago, in the Corral de la Morería, knowing only the barest essentials about the flamenco dance. Thas was all she needed: her great personal magnetism and widespread publicity did the rest. María merely moved from pose to pose, but each pose was poster perfect. Today, in her early twenties, María is a far more accomplished dancer, although strictly a routinist.

MANOLI VARGAS is an excellent example of personality and sex appeal capturing the imagination of the public. For years Manoli, a dancer in her early twenties well on her way to fame and fortune, danced only one dance well: the *rumba gitana*. With her *rumba* Manoli electrified her audiences, and on the strength of it recently won an international dance prize in France. However, Manoli has been learning other dances with Sevilla's fine dance instructors, Eloísa Albéniz and Enrique el Cojo, and has improved immensely in her other dances. Her main problem now seems to be in limiting her dances — instead of the ideal three to four minutes a dance should take, Manoli often goes on for eight or nine minutes. A dance of this length is boring no matter how well it is danced.

JUANA LORETO, a non-professional dancer from Utrera in her twenties, caused a sensation with her unschool gypsy dance in the 1964 Morón de la Frontera "Gazpacho".

TATIANA is a young Venezuelan *bailaora* of great promise. She is presently dancing in many of the flamenco festivals that are being organized around Andalusia, often at the side of her mentors, Antonio Mairena and Juan Talegas, as well as in Spain's *tablao* circuit. Tatiana dances well the slow, fluid dance of the upper torso, and has an appealing flamenco bearing. At present she is prone to inject into her dance such incongruous elements as highly suggestive grinds, which tend to water down the effect of her dance, but she may well outgrow such silliness as her dance matures.

THE GUITAR

THE SPANISH GUITAR

Before confining ourselves to the flamenco guitar, let us look briefly into the development and history of what is known as the Spanish guitar (1).

The Spanish guitar is the direct offspring of, principally, the *guitarra latina* (Latin guitar) and, secondarily, the *guitarra morisca* (Moorish guitar), both of which are generally believed to have descended from the ancient *kithara asiria* (Oriental zither).

First let us attempt to trace the *kithara asiria*. José de Azpiaza, in his book *"La Guitarra y Los Guitarristas"* (Buenos Aires), makes the observation that we must look to Egypt and Babylonia for the earliest stringed instruments, including the zither, from whence they passed on to Syria, Persia, India, and the Middle and Far East in general. He bases this assumption on diverse archaeological finds, principally in Egypt, singling out in particular a bas-relief, dated at 3500 B.C., discovered in the tomb of one of the Kings of Thebes. This bas-relief, now in the museum of Leyden (Holland), includes an instrument somewhat resembling today's Spanish guitar. Sr. Azpiaza also states that around the time 800-1000 B.C. the

---

(1) Vidal Benito Revuelto, in his pamphlet *«La Guitarra»* (*Temas Españoles*), outlines the development of the guitar in Spain with particular clarity, quoting from the writings of such musicologists as M. Schneider (*El Hombre y la Música*), San Isidro (*Etimologías*), H. Angeles (*Gloriosa Contribución de España a la Música Universal*), Emilio Pujol (various works), Levi-Provençal (*La Civilización Arabe en España*), Al-Saqundi (*Elogio del Islam Español*, translated into Spanish by Emilio García Gómez), Menéndez Pidal (*Poesía Juglaresca y Juglares*), Archpriest of Hita, Sainz de la Maza (*La Guitarra y su Historia*), Juan Carlos Amat (*Guitarra Española y Vándula en Dos Maneras de Guitarra, Castellana y Cathalana, de cinco órdenes* — 1572), Juan Bermudo (*Declaración de Instrumentos* — 1555), and others.

Egyptians possessed an instrument greatly resembling the modern guitar. This instrument could easily have been the previously mentioned *guitarra morisca*, or one of its predecessors in its development from the *kithara asiria*. However, in view of continued archaeological discoveries, no date or place can be irrevocably pinpointed concerning the origin of any of the ancient stringed instruments. The recent discovery by an English archaeologist, Miss Kathleen Kenyon, determining that the city of Jerico was teeming with life as far back as 6800 B.C. (Time, Dec. 13, 1963), makes the first Egyptian dynasty (3400 B.C.) seem relatively modern. In truth, the family tree of stringed instruments, in all of its rich variety, is as vague as civilization's early history. Perhaps the only data available to sustain the belief that the guitar is descended from the ancient *kithara asiria* is the similarity and progression of the zither-guitar terminology in various languages, and the corresponding similarity and development of the instruments represented by the terms, as follows: *qitâra* (Chaldea — an ancient region in Southwest Asia, on the Tigris and Euphrates rivers), *quitar* (Arabic), *sitar* (Hindi), *kithara* (Greek), *cítara* (Spanish), and *guitarra* (Spanish).

If we wish to follow the popular theory that the guitar was derived from the *kithara* (there is no good reason not to), the guitar's development in Spain can be traced in rough outline. It is generally agreed that the *kithara asiria* (then called the *kithara romana*) was introduced into Spain during the time of the Romans, sometime before the birth of Christ (1). The *kithara* flourished in Spain until the fall of the Spanish Roman Empire (fifth century), at which time it fell largely into disuse until the invading Visigoths were firmly established on the peninsula. The Visigoths set about reviving the old Roman culture, and the *kithara* again emerged. In the VII century San Isidro wrote of wandering minstrels singing and accompanying themselves on the *kithara* (he also states that the musical centers of Spain at the time were Sevilla, Toledo,

---

(1) In my opinion it is more likely that visiting Hindu musicians introduced the *kithara asiria*, or similar instruments, into Cádiz before the coming of the Romans, probably during the reign of the Greeks (c. 500-250 B. C.), as discussed in the Dance Introduction.

and Zaragoza). It was around this period that the *guitarra latina*, an instrument containing four sets of double strings and which resembled a small version of the present Spanish guitar, was developed in Spain, presumably, as we have stated, from the *kithara romana*.

Meanwhile, in the Middle East the *kithara asiria* had long ago inspired the family of the *guitarra morisca*, an oval-shaped, three-stringed instrument introduced into Spain with the eight-century Moorish invasion. It is thought that the only significant characteristic that the Latin guitar borrowed from the Moorish guitar, in its development into the Spanish guitar, was the idea of the single strings in place of the formerly-used sets of double strings.

So by the ninth century there existed in Spain guitars not unlike those we play today, but until the troubadour period (eleventh through the thirteenth centuries) the guitar was not widely introduced to the general populace. Little structural change of any significance took place in this guitar until the sixteenth century, when Vicente Espinel began using a fifth string (1). With this development the Spaniards finally seemed to feel that the guitar was their instrument, and it was then that the *guitarra latina* was rechristened the "Spanish guitar". Two centuries later the final radical development as made, which was the addition of the sixth string by fray Miguel García, a monk also known as Padre Basilio, an excellent classical guitarist and the guitar instructor of King Carlos IV, Queen María Luisa, and the famous concert guitarist, Dionisio Aguado.

Thus, except for its growth in size and quality, by the latter third of the eighteenth century the Spanish guitar was as we know it today.

Now that we know something of the development of the guitar, let us look into the development of the music. According to Levi-Provençal (*La Civilización Arabe en España*), the great tradition of Andalusian music was molded together and developed in the

---

(1) This was not Espinel's invention, as guitars had existed previously with five strings. Espinel merely made the fifth string fashionable. Many musicologists express the belief that the famous Ziryab himself first innovated the use of the fifth string in the ninth century.

Cordovan conservatory of music established and directed by the Mesopotamian musician, Ziryab, in the ninth century A. D. (Ziryab arrived in Córdoba in 822 A.D., in his early thirties, and remained there the rest of his life). What Ziryab must have done was gather, and become proficient in, the Andalusian folklore of that period, which was, of course, highly Oriental in nature, and conserve and teach it to attending minstrels and nobility in his conservatory. As he had spent years in the courts of Bagdad, and was the supreme musician of his time, he undoubtedly added to, and purified, what he found. Ziryab, in fact, is credited with having played *the* major musical role in making Andalusia the outstanding cultural center of the world at that time.

When did flamenco enter the picture? Frankly, we do not know. It is supposed, as we have seen in the *cante* and *baile* sections, that a type of flamenco has existed for centuries, slowly developing into the flamenco we know today, but as this music has not been popularly called "flamenco" until relatively recently there is no way of knowing when the seed was sown. We have seen that the guitar was in the hands of the Spanish people as early as the ninth century, and we know that the minstrels used it to accompany their singing. In the fourteenth century the Archpriest of Hita talks about the musicians *"rasgueando"* the guitar, and in the fifteenth century Bermudo writes of the common lower class use of the guitar in simple accompaniment, utilizing *rasgueados* and picking with the fingers. After that the "Andalusian style (school)" of playing is mentioned in the literature of various periods, but the first concrete mention of the flamenco guitar is not dated until the first third of the nineteenth century.

THE FLAMENCO GUITAR

Back in the years 1800-1835, when the flamenco guitar began attracting some attention and finding its way into print, flamenco guitarists were extremely scarce . This was due to several factors: the *cante* was traditionally sung without guitar accompaniment, or at least this had been the case during a sufficient number of years as to become tradition; flamenco was a peasant art, and few peasants could afford the luxury of a guitar before flamenco became financially profitable for artists; guitarists were secretive with their material and generally unwilling to teach, often making it necessary for aspirants to teach themselves, especially as few could afford formal lessons (up until a few years ago secrecy was so widely practiced that guitarists would usually refuse to play what they considered their "good" material in the presence of other guitarists; there have even been cases of fathers refusing to teach their sons).

The playing of this period is usually described as "primitive and limited". This is perhaps a misleading statement, and as such deserving of clarification. By "primitive" playing is meant an accompanying type of playing free from flourishes and superficiality. However, do not be mislead into thinking that primitive necessarily means easy. The *falsetas* played then were based on the thumb, and a good thumb can move at a breath-taking pace. Take the example of our present-day Manolo de Huelva, who accomplished with his thumb, when in his prime, what more sophisticated guitarists spend a lifetime trying to do with five fingers.

Not to mention the accepted fact that the thumb is infinitely more flamenco. "Limited" signifies that the guitarist of that period usually knew how to accompany only the *cantes* and *bailes* of his particular region of Andalusia, as he rarely ventured far from his place of birth.

These limiting factors to the development of the flamenco guitar began to disappear with the opening of the *cafés cantantes* (1842 on). Professional guitarists hired to play in these *cafés* had to radically expand their horizons. For the first time singers and dancers from all regions of Andalusia gathered under one roof, and the guitarist was faced with the monumental task of accompanying all of the difficult styles of *cantes* and *bailes*. Simultaneously, guitarists began refining their playing, discovering the potential of their instruments while they wiled away the monotonous hours of work. As their playing progressed, they began to assert themselves, and soon, inevitably, a few began competing with the singers and dancers. They invented all manner of crowd-pleasing techniques as a way of garnering recognition and attention, which eventually resulted in the arrival of the first flamenco guitar soloist.

Flamenco's first guitar virtuosos caused a minor sensation in the flamenco world. Soon each *café cantante* had its soloist, who was paid more and earned greater fame than the mere accompanist. Needless to say, within a short period there were many more aspirants than solo chairs available, and competition became fierce; — soloists began attempting all manner of tricks to capture the fancy of the public, such as playing behind their backs, over their heads, with a sock or a glove on one hand or even both hands, and so forth. Since that time, the ranks of the dedicated accompanists have dropped to a fraction, while the number of soloists has grown out of all proportion. This has produced an ironical situation today; the truly great accompanist has become so scarce that conscientious singers and dancers hold him in much greater esteem than the fanciest of soloists. As I have been told innumerable times by today's singing and dancing greats, guitar fancy-Dans are a dime a dozen, but outstanding accompanists that help, and oftentimes even direct, a singer or dancer are each year becoming a greater rarity.

The question arises, why cannot a guitarist be a soloist *and* a great accompanist? He can, and some do, but due to two basic human traits, laziness and the overpowering desire to show off, he rarely does. Strange as it may seem, with today's record players, tape recorders, and similar gadgets, it is more comfortable to sit in the privacy of one's home and practice to become a virtuoso than it is to become an accomplished accompanist. The astute guitar *aficionado* can pick enough material for a lifetime off records, practice six hours a day, and in time be acclaimed a virtuoso. The fact that he is completely ungrounded in his "art", that he can become a virtuoso without truly understanding anything about flamenco, and feels it even less, seems to be of no importance. Learning to accompany well is far more difficult, for the truly great accompanist must *know how to sing and/or dance everything that he accompanies.* Only by possessing this complete knowledge of each *cante* and *baile* can the accompanist throw himself into creative accompanying; the melody, *compás*, chording, and phrasing must be second nature so that he can devote himself to such subtleties as anticipating the inventive flights of the singer or dancer, and enhancing to the fullest each moment of the *cante* or *baile*. It is not surprising, then, that the outstanding accompanist will play badly when accompanying mediocre or bad artists. Accompanists of the stature of Manolo de Huelva, Melchor de Marchena, or Diego del Gastor will often merely stop playing when confronted by ignorant or impure performances on the part of the leading artist. I have heard both Manolo de Huelva and Diego del Gastor not only stop playing under these circumstances, but sing the *cante* properly for the benefit of the offending *cantaor*. On one occasion Manolo de Huelva not only stopped and sang the *copla*, but then played it, then created around it, and was soon off on a binge of playing. The offending *cantaor* was not heard from again, in fact was completely forgotten in the fabulous playing of Manolo.

The accompanist's task is further complicated in that each singer will sing the same style of the same *cante* a little differently each time, each dancer of category will improvise a new version of a particular dance each time he dances it, and the great accompanist has to instinctively follow their moods and caprices. It takes years and great patience, even for a natural, to achieve this knowledge and sharpen this instinct. Today only in private gatherings will one see this beautiful, spontaneous coordination between artists. In all commercial places they not only rehearse all numbers to over-perfection, but they tend to condemn as "primitive and backward" any artist who wishes to improvise his own *cante, baile,* or accompaniment. In the words of the *bailaora*, La Quica: "If each artist knows what he is about, if he knows how to dance, sing, or accompany, rehearsals are unnecessary." La Quica, of course, is referring to the élite. For the large majority of flamenco artists, rehearsals are an absolute necessity.

Even the virtuoso who goes out of his way to learn the proper accompaniments, and wishes to accompany well, is likely to have great difficulty subjecting himself to a subordinate position. More than a virtue, his virtuosity is likely to be a burden. As Federico García Lorca pointed out in one of his lectures (*"Obras Completas"*, p. 1541):

"The guitar, in the *cante jondo,* must limit itself to keeping the rhythm and following the singer; the guitar is a base for the voice, and must be strictly subjected to the will of the singer.

"But as the personality of the guitarist is often as strong as that of the *cantaor,* the guitarist must also sing, and thus *falsetas* are born (the commentaries of the strings), when sincere of extraordinary beauty, but in many cases false, foolish, and full of pretentious prettiness when expressed by one of those virtuosos...

"The *falseta* is now traditional, and some guitarists, like the magnificent Niño de Huelva (Manolo de Huelva), let themselves be swept along by the voice of their surging blood, but without for a moment leaving the pure line or, although they are maximum virtuosos, displaying their virtuosity."

Pretentious virtuosity is as badly considered in Hindustani music, so closely related to flamenco in feeling and form (and likely the very foundation of flamenco), as it is in flamenco. The following passage from the booklet "Music and Dance in Indian

Art" (Edinburgh International Festival, 1963) relays in no uncertain terms the feelings of Indian purists on this subject:

"Indian classical music is played *ex tempore*, and the executant is also composer. The musician's skill is supposed to be specially directed towards exhibiting the full beautiy of the *ragas* (for our purposes "*ragas*" can be translated as "*toques*"), rather than to displaying his virtuosity . There is a story told of a certain immensely skillful and vain musician who, one night in a dream, was taken by the Lord Shiva (The Destroyer in Hindu theology) on a journey. The two entered a palace where there lay about in pools of blood in every room the hideously chopped and mangled corpses of divinely beautiful men and women. The musician, full of indignation, urged that everything should be done to find the maniac who had committed this crime. Lord Shiva answered: 'These beautiful people are the *ragas*. You are the criminal.'" (Viewed in this light, it is impressive to think of the slaughter, stench, and waste of beauty to be found in flamenco's great palaces).

According to Cynthia Gooding, the guitar virtuoso Sabicas once stated that the flamenco guitarist is not ready to play solos until he has undergone a forty year apprenticeship, the first twenty in the accompaniment of the *baile*, the second twenty in the accompaniment of the *cante*. Grossly exaggerated, yes, and certainly not the route taken by Sabicas, but nevertheless a point well made, because without a complete knowledge of the backbone of flamenco, its rhythms, *compases*, traditions, the complete structure of its dances, and more important, its *cantes*, the guitarist does not have the necessary background to become a true creator in his *toque*. Creation is the ultimate in flamenco. There is little merit in interpreting more or less well the creations of others. The merit arrives, the greatness arrives, only when the guitarist can create his own truly flamenco material, the culmination of this creativeness being when he can spontaneously improvise as he plays. Only then, and with the condition that his playing transmits *duende*, is he a great flamenco guitarist.

How many flamenco guitarists today possess the qualifications for greatness as outlined above. A handful, at best. In this sense the flamenco guitar has fallen badly in modern times. In the past the major consideration was creativity. Copying from others was a shame-faced admission of mediocrity — a guitarist without his *"propio sello"* (distinctive material, and style of playing), regardless of how well he played the creations of others, was poorly considered.

Distinctiveness in playing styles even extended to regions of Andalusia. Until as recently as forty years ago there existed immediately recognizable styles of playing from Cádiz, Jerez, Sevilla, Córdoba, Granada, Morón de la Frontera, and so forth. Like in the *cante*, the styles of *toque* from these regions were adopted by the guitarists native to those regions, who, in turn, if they were to be considered outstanding, created their *"propio sello"* within the style of the region. There was also a basic difference between the *andaluz* and the Madrid *toques*. *Tocaores* from the North were generally more interested in technique and flying fingers, while those from Andalusia were more flamenco, basing their *toque* on the thumb and good accompaniment.

Today the flamenco guitar is universal. One hears identical playing in Sevilla, Cádiz, Madrid, London, New York, Hong Kong, and points east. Source — phonograph records, of course.

Another interesting phenomenon, which many *aficionados* will have noticed, is the flexibility of the *compás* in solo playing. This is due to several reasons, other than ignorance of the proper *compás*. First of all, most old-time accompanists do not take solo-playing at all seriously. To them, flamenco without the *cante* or the *baile* is incomplete, like food without wine, and they toy with their solo numbers, often in a tongue-in-cheek manner. Why bother to keep the *compás* if no one is to sing or dance? Thus they will discard the *compás* for the achievement of effects, or merely to enjoy the freedom gained by dropping the *compás*. Ramón Montoya was this way, as is easily discernible from a comparison of his solo and accompanying records. In his solo playing Ramón's *compás* was cloudy at best, and oftentimes nearly non-existent. In his accompanying, it was always perfect. Ramón, grounded in the school of accompaniment, simply did not take his solo playing seriously — to him it was merely a means of diverting himself, and of showing off. Many old-time accompanists refuse to waste their time on solo playing or, if pressured into it, do so reluctantly. Such is the case today with Manolo de Huelva, Diego del Gastor, Melchor de Marchena, and others, and was the case with most of the guitarists of the past who devoted themselves to accompanying.

Today solo playing, and the *compás* within it, is taken much more seriously by young guitarists, and accompaniment is the art that is suffering.

A special effort is made in "The Art of Flamenco", and in this book, to emphasize the wide difference between the old-style and modern styles of flamenco guitar-playing. Please bear with me once more as I go over this familiar terrain; it is absolutely necessary that the reader understand this difference in playing styles if he is to understand something of flamenco and the flamenco guitar.

The old-time (*jondo*, authentic, direct, primitive, true, or however one wishes to call it) school of flamenco guitar-playing, in its deceptive simplicity, is a style in which the transmission of *duende* is paramount. It is a very soul-satisfying and serious business for the guitarist, much as was the early singing of the blues and spirituals; the interpreter undergoes an emotional experience, as do sensitive listeners. It is music for the minority, and can only be truly experienced at close quarters.

With exceptions, *jondo* guitarists are not advanced technically, in comparison with concert flamenco techniques. We have seen that it is preferable that they are not, as the *duende* thrives in primitive playing. Also, as technique is not of great importance, *jondo* playing has another obvious advantage: the guitarist does not have to spend hours each day in constant practice, but picks up the guitar when he feels like it, and plays what he feels like playing. He consequently creates more of his own *toque* as, unlike concert guitarists, he is not concerned with perfecting particular arrangements. Only in this way is the flamenco guitar a companion, instrument of expression, and conveyer of true, meaningful beauty.

The modern (concert, technical, new, atomic, nervous, etc.)

style of flamenco guitar-playing, on the other hand, is forever demanding and basically frustrating. The guitarist, no matter how advanced, never completely dominates the concert flamenco guitar; he becomes a slave to it. His guitar, constantly nagging, seems to say 'practice me, you bastard, practice me, four, six, eight hours a day, or you'll never catch up with Sabicas or Escudero or Vélez or Serrano. You'll be second rate, a failure, your children won't eat. Practice, *venga,* get flashier, faster, screw the emotion, that doesn't sell, add some more notes to that *falseta,* do away with that silence; scales, exercises, let's run over that same *soleares* for the 3,000th time, not flashy enough, more left hand up the neck that gets'em, put on that Sabicas record Jesus Christ how does he do it, he must never let up practice practice PRACTICE...

Exaggeration? I am afraid not. No matter how dedicated the concert flamenco guitarist, how starry-eyed he starts out, after a number of years of this he almost always ends up secretly abhorring the flamenco guitar. In time he becomes horribly bored with flamenco, and to offset this boredom begins mixing in classical music, international folklore, Autumn Leaves and the St. Louis Blues, anything different or exotic that might temporarily rekindle his interest. The long hours of compulsory daily practice, grind, repetition, perfection methodically kill whatever feeling he may initially have had for flamenco, and he is left only with an immense ocean of unconquerable, meaningless notes. True, it is the means to an end: fame and fortune for the exceptional, a way of living for the rest. But that is about all.

Outside of Spain the flamenco guitar is enjoying a great surge of popularity. The heroes of this movement are mostly flamenco's traveling *concertistas,* whom we have just discussed, and the impression understandably grasped by most *aficionados* in countries such as the United States, England, and so forth, is that the concert flamenco guitar is *the* flamenco guitar. As we have seen, any resemblance between the concert flamenco guitar and traditional flamenco is mostly superficial and often downright accidental. However, the surprising and gratifying response to my first book, "The Art of Flamenco", is making it clear that many *aficionados* in those countries instinctively felt that there must be more to the flamenco guitar than what they heard from the virtuosos. Others, having invested their money, time, and devotion in modern flamenco, refuse to recognize that flamenco offers two roads: one to the heart, the other to the brain. Rarely do the two roads meet.

Incidently, in the preceding paragraphs I am *not* advocating that the less a guitarist plays his guitar the more *jondo,* or better, he becomes. Not at all. A *jondo* guitarist often plays his guitar, for pleasure, nearly as much as a concert guitarist, indeed may become extremely accomplished technically, may conceivably become a virtuoso, but a virtuoso who has the instinct, will, and integrity to *control his virtuosity.* Controlled virtuosity is perhaps the most important requisite for today's advanced flamenco guitar. It certainly appears to be the most difficult to master!

Guitar-playing readers may be disappointed at the brevity of the guitar section, as compared to the *cante.* It must be kept in mind that the guitar has played a much smaller role than the *cante* in flamenco's development. With the exception of the *rondeña toque* (a form of the *taranto*), all of flamenco began with the *cante* or the *baile.* This was partly due, as we have discussed, to the prohibitive expenses of a guitar and formal instruction, and the secrecy of old-time guitarists and their unwillingness to teach, which resulted in most flamenco sessions of old being conducted without a guitarist (this still holds true in Andalusian villages today). In view of this, it is not strange that the development of the flamenco guitar has been in the hands of a few until recent times.

FRANCISCO RODRIGUEZ MURCIANO

(c. 1795 - 1848)

The first significant flamenco guitarist, chronologically speaking, that I have run across in my investigations is Francisco Rodríguez Murciano, a guitarist who lived in Granada during the first half of the last century. Eduardo Molina Fajardo, in his book *"Manuel de Falla y el Cante Jondo"*, tells how Murciano so inspired the Russian classical composer Glink that the composer spent days listening to MURCIANO play, attempting to jot down his rhythms and *falsetas*. The experience inspired one of Glink's subsequent works.

MURCIANO had at least one of his *toques*, a *malagueña*, published in a *"Colección de Aires Populares para Guitarra"*.

EL MAESTRO PATIÑO

1988 Update: (1829-1902)

One of the principal guitarists of the early *café cantante* period was *el maestro* PATIÑO, a gypsy *tocaor* from Cádiz. PATIÑO was convinced that the guitar's only function was to accompany the *cante,* at which he excelled. He first came to the attention of the general public in Sevilla's Café de los Cagajones (Café of the Horse-dung) around the years 1850-1860, where he played until the *café* closed its doors. He then returned to Cádiz and dedicated himself to giving lessons.

Although PATIÑO was opposed to solo playing, and taught only accompaniment, his most famous student, Paco el Barbero Paco the Barber), did not feel the same way. Paco worked hard on guitar techniques, eventually excelling his instructor in virtuosity, although not in accompaniment, and went on to become flamenco's first guitar soloist.

ANTONIO PEREZ

(c. 1835 - 1900)

ANTONIO PÉREZ' artistic career pretty well paralleled that of *el maestro* Patiño. PÉREZ was also a dedicated accompanist, first gaining some fame in a Sevilla *café cantante* where he played until the *café* closed down. He then retired from active artistic life and dedicated his talents to teaching in his native Sevilla. PÉREZ did not accompany the *cante* as well as Patiño, but was an extraordinary accompanist of the *baile*.

Pérez turned out many excellent students, all accompanists, including: Juan el Jorobao, Pepe Robles, Manuel Pozo, Monterito, Antoñito González, and his son, ANTONIO PÉREZ.

ANTONIO PÉREZ grandson, also named Antonio Pérez (c. 1890-1957), carried on basically the same school of *toque* started by his grandfather and passed on to him by his father. That is to say, PÉREZ' grandson concentrated on accompanying, and his playing was basically thumb-driven. He performed for some years in Madrid's La Zambra, until the time of his death.

PACO EL BARBERO

(c. 1840 - 1910)

According to Fernando de Triana, FRANCISCO SÁNCHEZ "PACO EL BARBERO" was the first guitarist to play flamenco guitar solos in commercial surroundings, and can thus be credited with preparing the ground for the evolution of the solo flamenco guitar (1).

PACO, a barber from Cádiz, was the most famous student of *el maestro* Patiño. He was extremely interested in developing his guitar techniques, and in time excelled his instructor in virtuosity. PACO also became a good accompanist, although not of the caliber of Patiño. During the long hours of practicing his guitar techniques PACO began running *falsetas* together and filling in the singer's melody line (as discussed in the footnote), and soon found himself playing guitar solos that captured the fancy of *aficionados*. He was

---

(1) The solo flamenco guitar was developed directly from the *cante*. The first soloists were specialists in the accompaniment of the *cante*, and their solos were played much as a singer would have sung them: the guitar filled in the melody normally sung by the singer, and traditional *falsetas* were inserted at appropriate points exactly as they are in the accompaniment. Another form of solo omitted all, or part, of the singer's melody line, and merely ran together the *falsetas* normally played in the accompaniment. Most solos heard today still follow, or are elaborations of, these formulas; indeed, the more the guitarist understands the overall scope of flamenco the more obvious it becomes that the solo flamenco guitar is still solidly based on the *cante*. The obvious exception to this, of course, is today's outcropping of the virtuoso flamenco guitar that is energetically striving to liberate itself from the confining main body of flamenco. This phenomenon is succeeding remarkably well in becoming a separate art in itself, only vaguely based on flamenco, and even now needs to be referred to as «international», «progressive», or, more descriptive, «guitar stylings *a la flamenca*». In time, the surname «flamenco» will probably be altogether dropped from this branch of the flamenco guitar as it completes its fusion with jazz, classical and popular music, and international folklore into a sort of universal art, in which nations, boundaries, regions, and traditions are democratically left behind.

hired, basically as a soloist, in various *cafés cantantes*, and enjoyed popularity and success, finally becoming so prosperous that he was able to retire and open his own *colmado* (flamenco type of tavern) in Sevilla. The *colmado* proved very lucrative, and PACO returned only once to the artistic scene, at the opening of a Madrid *café cantante*, in 1886, owned by friends.

PACO EL BARBERO also taught a few students, the most prodigious of whom were Javier Molina and Antonio Sol. The latter, after gaining fame throughout Andalusia, died at a young age while at the height of his abilities. Javier Molina went on to become one of the great guitarists in flamenco's history.

PACO LUCENA

(c. 1855 - 1930)

The first "phenomenon" of the flamenco guitar, according to Fernando de Triana and other flamencologists, was FRANCISCO DÍAZ "NIÑO DE LUCENA", or "PACO LUCENA". PACO LUCENA was unique in that he not only became extremely proficient in the traditional guitar techniques, but introduced into his playing classical techniques formerly not used in flamenco guitar-playing. Old-timers calculate that these techniques were probably the *picado*, three-fingered arpeggio and tremolo, and a slightly increased scope in chording, innovations that were enough, in those days, to dazzle all concerned.

PACO LUCENA was born in Lucena (Córdoba), a town on the very rim of flamenco territory, the son of a farm hand. PACO was early attracted to the guitar, and contrived to become an apprentice to a barber who was a flamenco guitar *aficionado*. Before long, he had exhausted the barber's repertoire, playing what he learned with better style and technique than his *maestro*. PACO was then befriended by a local marquis, a classical guitar *aficionado* who knew something of flamenco, and who soon taught PACO his entire flamenco repertoire. While studying with his marquis friend, PACO also had ample opportunity to observe his classical techniques, and began experimenting with them in his flamenco playing.

Before long PACO was feeling like quite the artist, until one day he was asked to accompany a singer and dancer who came to LUCENA without their accompanist. After a few starts and stops he realized that to date he had not been taught the basics: the *compás* of the various *cantes* and *bailes*, and their appropriate accompaniments. It was then that he tucked his guitar, a present from the marquis, under his arm and headed deeper into flamenco country.

PACO went due south to Málaga, the nearest city of flamenco importance (then studded with eleven *cafés cantantes*). He found a job with a barber who luckily happened to be a great *aficionado*, and who encouraged PACO in his playing and took him around to the *cafés* at night so that he could study the professional guitarists and their accompanying. Before long PACO got his break. The guitarist in one of the cafés got sick, and there was no one at the time in Málaga to replace him. PACO's boss learned of the predicament and quickly suggested that PACO be given a trial. He was, and to everyone's surprise he accompanied reasonably well. He learned fast, and by the time the sick guitarist, Paco el Aguila, returned, PACO LUCENA had earned himself a job as second guitarist

Now I believe that EL NIÑO DE LUCENA, a nickname given PACO by his boss, don Salvador, to replace his former handle "Len tejo", would have risen to the top in most any profession he had chosen, for besides his great natural talent for the guitar, he was blessed with a great and natural *cara dura* (hard face). PACO was a real pusher. The tradition is that the second guitarist remain well in the background when it comes to playing *falsetas*, or getting flashy in any way; this is the sacred privilege of the first guitarist. That did not stop PACO, however. Time and again he cut in with sparkling *falsetas;* as the management chose to ignore the unwritten rule, there seemed to be no way for the other artists to stop PACO other than to put poison in his beer. Finally the first guitarist decided to put the young whippersnapper in his place. Amid much tittering and applause he played an entire accompaniment wearing a glove on his left hand. Undaunted, PACO the Hard Face stepped forward, breaking rules right and left, removed a stocking, placed it on his left hand, and ripped off a hot solo. Pandemonium!

From that day on, PACO rose rapidly. Everyone wanted to see the new guitar sensation, reputedly waiting for him to replace that stocking with a shoe. But again PACO was equal to the situation. Instead of more fancy tricks, PACO gave the public some fancy guitar work the likes of which they had never seen. Soon he was an attraction in the mecca of the *cafés cantantes*, the Café Silverio, in Sevilla, from where he went on to great fame throughout Spain.

PACO LUCENA became, in time, an accomplished accompanist, but his first love remained the solo guitar, for which he had a fine creative talent. Although his playing was revolutionary for his time, there is, however, evidence that it was basically *jondo*. He introduced various techniques, as we have seen, but even his solos were built around the traditional thumb and *rasgueado*. It is possible to visualize this through the direct line of playing of the PACO LUCENA school of guitar, which has remained in the town of Morón de la Frontera, due to the fact that PACO LUCENA's outstanding disciple was an *aficionado* from Morón, José María Alvarez "el Niño de Morón". El Niño de Morón played with an ease and creativity equal to that of his *maestro*, and strived to maintain intact the playing style of PACO LUCENA. He in turn passed on his knowledge to Pepe Naranjo y Olomo, another non-professional from Morón de la Frontera who was the guitar idol of flamenco, in the *jondo* style, some decades ago. Pepe Naranjo's influence has been passed on to another non-professional from Morón, Diego del Gastor, who still carries on at least remnants of the PACO LUCENA tradition, and is one of the great *jondo* guitarists of our time.

PACO LUCENA was most renowned for his solo creations within the *rosas* (*alegrías en mi*), many of which are still played by Diego del Gastor.

H A B I C H U E L A

(c. 1860 - 1935)

JUAN GANDULLA 'HABICHUELA" (Kidney-bean), a gypsy from

Cádiz, ranks among the finest accompanists remembered of both the *cante* and the *baile*. Like his instructor, *el maestro* Patiño, HABICHUELA played in the primitive style, and had a thumb that was the envy of his fellow guitarists. His knowledge of the *cantes* and *bailes* was wide and unfailing, and while he lived he was the preferred accompanist of many of the leading artists.

Fernando de Triana wrote that the "notes of HABICHUELA's guitar became converted into tears, such was the emotion of his playing". I can personally vouch for the accuracy of Fernando's statement. I have been fortunate enough to learn some of his *granaína falsetas* that have been passed down, which are the most flamenco and beautiful of the multitude of *granaína falsetas* that I have heard.

The present-day guitarist, HABICHUELA, from Granada, is not related to the subject of this biography.

JAVIER MOLINA

(c. 1868 - 1956)

Jerez-born JAVIER MOLINA was one of the top four or five flamenco guitarists of the last one hundred years. Born in 1868, JAVIER was playing well at the age of seven, began playing professionally at the age of eight, and was maintaining his family by the time he was twelve. At the age of seventeen he, his brother, and another youngster, Antonio Chacón, left Jerez to conquer Spain (in his autobiography, "*Javier Molina, Tocaor y Jerezano*", JAVIER tells of their adventures in the lively flamenco life of those times). Before long they were all snapped up by Sevilla's active flamenco life, and JAVIER became one of the featured guitarists in the Cafés Silverio and Burrero during the twenty years of their fullest bloom.

The few formal guitar lessons JAVIER ever had were with Paco el Barbero, flamenco's first soloist. JAVIER was therefore initiated in what was then considered the "*flamenco moderno*", to which he contributed, during his long lifetime, an unending number of creations from his fertile mind. But at the same time that JAVIER was contributing creatively to the development of the guitar as a solo instrument, he was maintaining the traditional school of accompaniment. JAVIER accompanied beautifully even the most difficult and obscure of the ancient *cantes* and *bailes*, and for this reason, more than for his solo playing, he was in constant demand during his entire sixty-five years as an active professional guitarist.

JAVIER's playing is said to have contained such *duende* and beauty that he was universally referred to as the *"Brujo de la Guitarra"* (Sorcerer, or Wizard, of the Guitar). He accompanied all of the great singers and dancers of his time, and started an impressive list of guitarists on the way with their first lessons, including Currito el de la Geroma, Perico el del Lunar, Niño Ricardo, Moraíto de Jerez, and many others, as well as instructing the *cantaores* Enrique el Mellizo and Enrique Ortega in the mysteries of the guitar. Ramón Montoya, who heard JAVIER in the *cafés cantantes* of Sevilla, admired him greatly, and stated that JAVIER had a strong influence in his development. Ramón went on to become the principal rival of JAVIER for a number of years, with one very marked, and universally agreed-upon, difference: JAVIER was less flashy and far more earthily flamenco than Ramón.

JAVIER's stage was almost always the *cafés* and *juergas*. He only went on two theatrical tours, once in 1926 with the Niña de los Peines, Estampío, and other artists, and once more in 1940 with a group that included the beginning Lola Flores. After his 1940 tour Javier, then seventy-two, retired and returned to Jerez de la Frontera to spend his last days. Much to his consternation JAVIER's last days dragged out sixteen years; as was customary, JAVIER had spent his artistic earnings as he received them, and he had to rely on poorly-paid guitar lessons for his livelihood during those last years.

After his death, the city of Jerez honored JAVIER by placing a commemorative plaque on his house. This unusual act has been done in memory of several Jerez flamenco artists, including Manuel Torre and Antonio Chacón. This, in my opinion, speaks very highly of the *aficionados* of Jerez de la Frontera, and is still another sign of today's resurgence of flamenco.

ANTONIO MORENO

(c. 1872 - 1937)

ANTONIO MORENO, in his prime during the first quarter of this century, was one of flamenco's leading accompanists of the *baile*. From Sevilla, he was the preferred accompanist of the *bailaora*, Juana la Macarrona.

MIGUEL BORRULL

(c. 1880 - 1940)

MIGUEL BORRULL (*padre*), born in Valencia but a resident of Barcelona much of his life, was one of the finer guitarists around the first quarter of this century. He had a vicious thumb, and was an excellent accompanist. His son, MIGUEL BORRULL (*hijo*), a more modern-style guitarist who mixed in overdoses of *picado* into otherwise fine playing, was one of the preferred accompanists of Manuel Torre.

MIGUEL (*padre*) was the owner of the Villa Rosa, a still-existent flamenco tavern in Barcelona's Barrio Chino.

AMALIO CUENCA

AMALIO CUENCA was an extremely popular guitarist during the first quarter of this century, although due more to his outgoing personality than his playing. AMALIO had a scant knowledge of accompanying, and was not taken too seriously by his flamenco contemporaries. He did, however, play an accomplished solo guitar.

AMALIO spent a good deal of his time outside of Spain, as he was owner and manager of a flamenco establishment in Paris. He was one of the guitar judges at the 1922 Granada contest of flamenco.

RAMON MONTOYA

(c. 1880 - 1949)

RAMÓN MONTOYA, born in Madrid of gypsy parents, has been

without a doubt the most famous and trend-setting guitarist in flamenco's history. He was the first really adept virtuoso for virtuosity's sake, and his fertile mind blossomed with creativity, the combination of which made his playing, probably more than that of any guitarist before or since, the very foundation of the modern style of the flamenco guitar. Thus Ramón's role in the development of the flamenco guitar was similar to the role played by Antonio Chacón in the development of the *cante*.

Aficionados might question my last statement, saying: "And what about Paco el Barbero, Paco Lucena, Javier Molina? These guitarists were founding the modern school before Ramón arrived on the scene, they had creative minds, they were virtuosos in their own right." All of this is true. RAMÓN cannot be called the father of the modern style, but it can be said that he took the *toque* of these guitarists which, although exploring into the modern, was still basically primitive, and replaced much of what was left of the primitive with even further virtuosity.

RAMÓN was a great admirer of the classical guitar, to which he was introduced through the playing of Tárrega and Miguel Llobet, and he consequently enlarged upon the classical techniques first introduced into flamenco by Paco Lucena. RAMÓN's contributions included a four-finger version of the classical three-finger tremolo, arpeggio intricacies, increased emphasis on the *picado*, and a left hand far more complex than anything dreamed of in flamenco previously. Oh yes, and one more thing not so classical in nature: speed.

Because of this strong classical drive and preoccupation with virtuosity, RAMÓN's early playing began losing its gypsy urgency. It cannot be denied that RAMÓN's playing was flamenco, but it was sophisticated flamenco, and the very meanings of the words "sophisticated" and "flamenco" are incompatible. In listening to RAMÓN's playing, I sometimes find myself thrilled by passages that strike a deep chord, but this feeling is too often lost in a maze of unnecessary fancy work. One can detect the great tradition in RAMÓN's playing, but it is rarely like it can be with others, when the very odors of *juergas* and gypsies and cave dwellings seem to permeate the room, when bubbling gaiety or profound sadness issues from the tremulous strings.

It is tragic, in a way, that in RAMÓN's last years he himself recognized the inadequacy and pointlessness of most of his artistic life. He was able to look back and clearly understand that nearly all of his artistic life had been spent in impressing the world with his virtuosity, in being the fastest, flashiest, and trickiest of them all. He began remembering his early *jondo* playing with sharp nostalgia, and in his last years he was again a magnificent mixture of depth and controlled virtuosity. He tried to call out that this was the way the guitar should really be played, but it was too late. By that time RAMÓN had thoroughly and irredeemably launched the modern style of flamenco guitar-playing, and his late resurgence of *duende* was lost in the noisy jumble of nervous notes issuing from flamenco's ever-growing number of virtuosos.

RAMÓN began playing the guitar around the age of ten on a small, cheap guitar he bought in a Madrid bazaar (undoubtedly in the "Rastro"). He picked up pointers from every source, but mostly from the street musicians that were not uncommon in those days. RAMÓN's father was also a guitarist, but was possessed by the instinct for secrecy and refused to teach his son what he knew; he would hide in another room, and RAMÓN had to catch what he could through the thin walls.

Soon RAMÓN began frequenting Madrid's Café de la Marina. There he observed the hand positions of, and listened to, the Marina's first guitarist, El Cañito, and made such rapid progress that by the time of El Cañito's death RAMÓN was prepared to step into the first guitarist's chair. He remained there eight years, by which time he had established himself as one of flamenco's promising young virtuosos.

During his career RAMÓN accompanied virtually all of flamenco's great *cantaores* and *bailaores* of the period. He was an accomplished accompanist, and a favorite of such singers as Antonio Chacón and Aurelio Sellé. RAMÓN was more flamenco in accompanying than in his solo playing, kept on the right track and under control by the presence of the singer. However, even in his accompanying much of the depth was lost, both to the guitar and the overall *cante*, due to unfeeling virtuosity. He had an unusual style of accompanying, nearly devoid of silences. Even in his accompaniments of the *malagueñas, tarantas,* and the other *cantes de Levante,* when the guitar is usually silent during the non-rhythmical flights of the singer (until the singer returns to certain traditional notes within the structure of the *cante*), RAMÓN generally kept up an incessant, always accurate accompaniment. This type of accompaniment, certainly a proof of RAMÓN's excellent knowledge of the *cante*, could only be done, of course, with exceptional *cantaores* with whose *cante*, style, and personality RAMÓN was well acquainted. Whether it improves or detracts from the *cante* is a matter of opinion.

RAMÓN has been one of flamenco's great creators, one of the most significant in flamenco history, and certainly *the* most significant within his style of playing. Paradoxically, he had an extremely bad ear for catching the *falsetas* of others. I have talked to guitarists who claim that they have actually tried to teach RAMÓN *falsetas* that he particularly liked, but to no avail; after much effort RAMÓN would finally give up attempting a note-for-note imitation, sit back and listen to the *falseta* once or twice, and then improvise his version of the *falseta* that usually turned out "far more involved and complex than the relatively simple *falseta* he was unable to grasp." RAMÓN was simply born a creator, not an imitator.

Many flamenco guitarists claim that they studied with RAMÓN. I have been led to believe by reliable sources that these statements are not absolutely accurate. It seems that RAMÓN was an egomaniac, needing the applause and approval of others while, at the same time, proving himself superior. Thus he liked to play for other guitarists or, better said, to dazzle other guitarists, then look up beaming and say: "Bet you can't do that. Only RAMÓN can play that *falseta* with that air. Go ahead, try it." Of course, few guitarists were adept enough to pick up the *falsetas* that RAMÓN raced through, and when asked to slow down and teach them, RAMÓN would become very crafty and teach them with a faulty *compás* or inferior chording or phrasing, if he would deign to teach them at all. He was apparently much more at ease instructing beginners, whom he knew could not play his creations properly.

As stated in the introduction to the guitar section, RAMÓN was schooled in accompaniment, and did not take his solo playing seriously. During most of his career he considered the solo flamenco guitar only as a fine means of showing off his domination of the guitar and his creativity, but it did not move him — thus his indifference to the *compás* and the *duende* in his solo playing (friends of RAMÓN state that when he soloed, it was useless to try to play accompanying *palmas* — the *compás* was simply too erratic. When accompanying, on the other hand, his *compás* was unfailing). RAMÓN was moved in flamenco only by inspired accompaniment of equally as inspired *cante* or *baile*, and during the most pretentious part of his career even that did not reach him.

RAMÓN was a serious man and a dedicated artist. He took little part in the horseplay and back-biting so characteristic of much of flamenco. He left many records, both solo and accompanying. Two American record companies, both presently out of business, have perhaps published the most extensive collections of his old records to be found on 33 rpm's (Philharmonia and Stinson).

RAMÓN did not suffer a decline in his playing during his last years, which happens with most guitarists. To the contrary, he played the best flamenco of his lifetime during those years. His death, in Madrid in 1949, was widely mourned by the entire flamenco world. Perhaps not everyone agreed about the merits of his playing or his contribution to flamenco, but everyone had to agree on one point: one of the great geniuses of the flamenco guitar had quietly left the scene.

LUIS YANCE

(c. 1883 - 1938)

LUIS YANCE was another accomplished guitarist of the modern Ramón Montoya school. Luis Maravilla tells of YANCE's sensational acceptance in New York, when he accompanied La Argentinita there in 1928. Offers poured in to him from various parts of the

United States, but YANCE turned them all down. His only desire was to return to Spain.

LUIS MOLINA

(c. 1885 - 1925)

LUIS MOLINA, like Ramón Montoya born in Madrid, was beginning to be considered a serious rival to Ramón in the fast new school of flamenco guitar playing when he was killed in an automobile accident in 1925.

LUIS' playing style was strongly influenced by that of Ramón — much use of *picados* and *arpegios* — although tending, so it is said, more towards the *jondo* than did Ramón, at least at that point in Ramón's career. LUIS was also a prolific creator.

Besides his solo aspirations, LUIS was an excellent accompanist, one of the favorites of such artists as Antonio Chacón, Antonio el de Bilbao, and many others.

MANOLO DE HUELVA

1988 Update: (1892-1976)

How does one begin to talk of the wondrous MANOLO DE HUELVA? Perhaps by stating that the has quietly, semi-secretly reigned as flamenco's supreme guitarist for a half a century? Or by stating that in the eyes of many knowledgeable *aficionados* and artists he has been the outstanding flamenco guitarist of all times? Truthfully, a separate volume, accompanied by tapes or records demonstrating MANOLO's evolution as a guitarist, which could only be played by MANOLO himself, would be perhaps the only way to begin to give MANOLO his due. This, I fear, cannot be accomplished; MANOLO himself has seen to this by his elaborate, unbending covertness, his lifelong refusal to play anything that he considered to be of true value in the presence of any type of machine, often including the human.

MANOLO especially dislikes playing when other guitarists are present. How many professional guitarists have actually heard MANOLO cut loose? Very, very few, but those who have consider the occasion as having been sacred. Andrés Segovia has, and has called MANOLO the greatest living flamenco guitarist. Segovia became so inspired, in fact, that he devoted the major part of a thesis to MANOLO DE HUELVA. Melchor de Marchena has, and proclaims MANOLO the greatest guitarist he has ever heard. This covers some ground, including Ramón Montoya, Javier Molina, today's virtuosos, and Melchor himself. Many singers and *aficionados* have, and they unanimously agree that in the accompaniment of the *cante*, and in the transmission of pure flamenco expression, MANOLO is far off by himself.

Just what makes MANOLO's playing so exceptional? To start with, he has the best thumb and left hand in the business. He is flamenco's most original and prolific creator. He has a vast knowledge of flamenco in general and of the *cante* in particular, which causes his *toque* to be unceasingly knowledgeable and flamenco. He is blessed with the same genius and *duende* for his art that separated Manuel Torre from the pack; as was the case with Torre, when MANOLO DE HUELVA becomes inspired his playing drives *aficionados* to near-frenzy, striking the deepest human chords with overwhelmingly direct force.

As is so rarely the case, MANOLO's playing, when he is fired up, is truly spontaneous; he plays from the heart, not the head. His *toque* is full of surprises, of the unexpected. His manipulations of the *compás* are fabulous, his lightning starts and stops at once profound and delightful. He is a guitarist (this is important) *impossible to anticipate* — his genius flows so spontaneously that often not even MANOLO knows what is coming next.

MANOLO was born MANUEL GÓMEZ in Río Tinto, a picturesque little village in the province of Huelva, in 1892. He began fiddling with the guitar at the age of seven, accompanying the local *fandanguillos.* He soon developed a consuming love for the flamenco guitar, and his early apprenticeship in his father's tailor shop was discarded with relief when MANOLO decided to turn to flamenco for a living. While still in his teens he left Río Tinto for the flamenco activity of Sevilla.

Pepe Torre tells of the day, over fifty years ago, when Manolo showed up in Sevilla's Alameda de Hércules, a battered guitar under one arm, declaring with youthful enthusiasm that he wanted to become the greatest *cante* accompanist of them all. Coming from a *payo* this was a meaty desire, and Manolo was tolerantly told to play. Play he did, showing such exceptional promise that he was accepted into the inner circle, and was soon accompanying such *cantaores* as Manuel Torre, Tomás Pavón, La Niña de los Peines, and the other greats of the period. Manolo progressed rapidly, and by the time he reached his early twenties his *toque* was mentioned with awe in the flamenco world. He had everything; a naturally flawless *compás* that was equalled by no one, a driving, extremely flamenco way of playing, great *duende*, and the sixth sense that permitted him to anticipate the singers, without which an accompanist is lost. *Cantaores* began calling Manolo first, before Javier or Ramón or any of the others. Soon Manolo was known as the top man.

Wide-spread fame followed, and opportunity began bugging Manolo. He wanted no part of it. As I wrote in "The Art of Flamenco": "His (Manolo's) hatred of being plagiarized is basically what prompted him to renounce nearly all playing commitments other than private *juergas*. He not only declines numerous record-making propositions, but he dislikes, and often refuses, to play in front of a guitarist whom he considers musician enough to copy his material. The singular Manolo has become a legendary figure as much for his extraordinary playing as for his eccentricities. He frequently used to lock himself in a hotel room with his wife and a bottle, and play up a storm for their private pleasure. As this idiosyncrasy became known, people used to gather outside of his hotel room hoping to hear him during one of these sessions (which have been described to me as "unbelievable") when he could really let himself go. He also seems untouched by the lust for money or fame. On many occasions he has refused to play for private *juergas* that offered him four to five thousand pesetas, unheard-of sums for a guitarist in Spain, only later to accept ten times less to play in a gathering that was to his liking. He has also been frequently known, during the course of a *juerga*, to wordlessly pack up his guitar and walk out, refusing all payment, when his audience did not pay proper respect to his art."

Many other colorful stories are told about and by MANOLO, such as the time, some thirty years ago, when MANOLO deigned to play for La Argentinita's *"Las Calles de Cádiz"* on the condition that a special cage be made that rendered him invisible to the public. MANOLO got his cage, only to walk out, sick of the whole theatrical business, before the theatrical season was completed. Or the letter that MANOLO received from Sabicas, inviting him to join Sabicas in cutting a record of guitar duets. MANOLO felt highly insulted, firstly because Sabicas should consider himself in the same class, and secondly that he should be propositioned to play such nonsense as flamenco guitar duets. On the other hand, upon asking MANOLO whom he liked best of the modern guitar virtuosos, he instantly replied that Sabicas presently has the best *compás* in the business (next to his own). That is as far as he would commit himself.

Technically, MANOLO relies on his blindingly fast and accurate thumb and left hand for most of the astounding effects he achieves. His entire right-hand technique is subordinate to his thumb: that is to say, his right hand is held in such a posture as to give the thumb complete freedom of movement (see photo). His other techniques? When he wishes, his *picado* is unexcelled and his arpeggios are sound, although he uses them sparingly. His *rasgueados* are excellent. Little is known of his *trémolo*, as he holds this flowery technique in great contempt.

Generally speaking, MANOLO is above being included in the eternal *payos* versus gypsies rivalry. Knowledgeable gypsies and non-gypsies alike hold him supreme. There are those gypsies, however, who will close-mindedly state something to the effect that as MANOLO is not gypsy, he cannot play the *toque gitano* (this statement is invariably made by those who have never heard him play).

The gypsies like to believe that flamenco surges exclusively through *their* veins. It is impossible to explain that environment is what counts (were it not, someone would long ago have begun selling pints of gypsy blood to *payo* aspirants). It is easier to trick them by appearing to drop the subject, letting a few minutes tick by, and then casually ask what they think of various artists, remembering to sandwich in the names of *payos* like Silverio Franconetti, Salvaoriyo, Aurelio Sellé, Antonio Chacón, El Niño de Almadén, La Quica, Frasquillo, Antonio de Bilbao, Paco Lucena, Antonio, and so forth, between those of various gypsy artists. As they do not usually know just who is gypsy and who is not, they almost invariably slip up. Then pounce!

How do people react personally to the eccentric MANOLO DE HUELVA? With admirers he is extremely amicable; with other guitarists crafty and condescending; with singers, unless their knowledge of the *cante* equals his, oftentimes crude and heartless — not infrequently he runs out of patience with a mediocre singer, tells him in no uncertain terms that he knows not what he sings, and refuses to play further for him. This is when MANOLO can best be heard, for it is then that he launches into his finest playing in a demonstration of just what flamenco really is.

MANOLO has also had considerable classical guitar training, and sometimes enjoys experimenting. I have not personally heard any of this type of playing from MANOLO, other than his thoroughly flamenco renditions of two Spanish classical pieces, but I have been assured by knowledgeable *aficionados* that his flamenco interpretations of Bach, Scarlatti, and other composers are astounding. They say that his left-hand during these flights would be the envy of any classical guitarist (as a matter of fact, MANOLO's left hand has been marveled at by Segovia), as would his imagination and intimate, spontaneous knowledge of the guitar.

As is to be expected, MANOLO's playing is flagging with age. He is not the same flawless, hard-driving MANOLO of ten or fifteen years ago, and, I am constantly assured, is far inferior to his peak of thirty and forty years ago. A seventy-some-year-old cannot maintain the same pace in an art like flamenco. But it must be kept in mind that even a declining MANOLO DE HUELVA is still worth his weight in gold; because he does not play like before does not mean to say that he does not still play brilliantly during the rare occasions when his old hands, and eccentric mind, loosen up.

Many years ago, before he raised his permanent guard, MA-

NOLO cut a few records, "none of which", he states, "is worth the whatever-it-is it's printed on." They insisted that he accompany some singers, and accompany he did, keeping the *compás*, throwing in a *falseta* or two, but certainly not displaying what he is capable of. MANOLO was not to be that easily tricked.

It is a shame. Had MANOLO cut solo records, had he permitted other guitarists to imitate him, it is probable that the route taken by the modern flamenco guitar would have been radically altered.

MANOLO lives with his wife in a little pension on Madrid's Plaza Santa Ana. He has lived there "temporarily" for seven years, always intending to return to his home in Sevilla, which he still maintains on the Alameda de Hércules. But the flamenco activity of Sevilla is in such a state that MANOLO cannot afford to go back.

After all of these years of being flamenco's paramount guitarist one would imagine MANOLO to be comfortably retired. Nothing is further from the truth. MANOLO must still play for his bread. Until recently he maintained the following schedule: around ten-thirty in the evening he entered Madrid's Villa Rosa, where he sipped a wine or a coffee until the taxis took the artists out to the Venta Manzanilla. There he stayed, some nights playing for private parties, some nights not, until dawn and often well into the sunlight hours. That was rough enough for a man over seventy, but now things are rougher. Both of those establishments have closed down within the last few months, and work is scarce. On top of it all, MANOLO's health is failing.

In the midst of these difficulties one opportunity has been accepted by MANOLO: a six-month stint at Madrid's La Zambra, his first such commercial performing in nearly thirty years. When this contract is completed, in October, MANOLO tentatively plans to return to his home in Sevilla. (In La Zambra MANOLO accompanies Pericón de Cádiz in two nightly numbers, displaying, needless to say, nothing of his fabulous *toque* — enemy ears may be listening!).

THE BADAJOZ FAMILY

Few artists of note have come from unlikely Badajoz, a city

outside of the sphere of flamenco influence. In fact, to my knowledge only five *badajocenses* have made a name for themselves: Porrina de Badajoz, whom we discuss in the *cante* section, and a family of non-gypsy barbers who have all turned to the guitar for a living — MANOLO, PEPE, JUSTO, and ERNESTO DE BADAJOZ.

The late MANOLO DE BADAJOZ (c. 1892-1962) died at the age of seventy-one after a paralizing sickness of some years duration. During the prime of his playing (1925-1950), Manolo was considered one of the finest accompanists of the *cante*. He was the chief guitarist of the Regal Record Company, and made an infinity of records accompanying all of the greats of the *cante*. Apart from the record company, Manolo made his way at private *fiestas*, as his personality and playing style did not suit theatrical flamenco.

The mainstay of Manolo's playing was a rapid, hard-driving thumb, an infallible *compás*, and an excellent knowledge of the *cante*.

Brother PEPE DE BADAJOZ, seven years younger than Manolo, was the first of the family to leave the Badajoz barber shop and try his hand at the professional flamenco world. Arriving in Madrid in the early 1920's, Pepe played *juergas*, looked and learned, and made a name for himself. In 1927 he made his first trip to America, accompanying the dancer María del Albaicín, sister of the bullfighter Rafael, aunt of the present María Albaicín. It was at this time that Pepe convinced Manolo to come to Madrid, to replace him as accompanist at Regal Records.

Before long Pepe joined the troupe of La Argentinita, remaining with her, on and off, during a period of several years. The outbreak of the Spanish Civil War (1936) found Pepe with Argentinita's troupe in Buenos Aires, where they spent the war years performing amongst such artists as Carmen Amaya, Antonio, Rosario, and many more. Leaving La Argentinita in 1940, Pepe spent some time touring America, lived several years in Mexico City, and finally returned to Spain in 1946. Since that time Pepe has played mostly for *fiestas* and *juergas*, and has cut several records, both solo and accompanying singers.

Pepe's style? Tending toward the modern, with outcroppings of the old. He is an excellent and much sought-after accompanist of both the *cante* and the *baile,* having accompanied most of the great in both fields. His technique does not compare with that of modern virtuosos, nor is that one of Pepe's ambitions. Pepe maintains the old school belief that outstanding accompaniment is far more valuable than virtuosity. Pepe is, nevertheless, an accomplished technician.

Today Pepe concentrates on *juerga* and *fiesta* playing, which keeps him as busy as he chooses. He also gives occasional lessons. He resides, since 1946, in Madrid.

The third and youngest brother, ERNESTO, arrived in Madrid from the Badajoz barber shop in 1956. A lesser guitarist than his brothers, Ernesto plays for private gatherings.

JUSTO DE BADAJOZ, Manolo's son, born around the year 1927 in Badajoz, has lived most of his life in Madrid. Today considered one of flamenco's better guitarists, Justo has exceeded his father and uncles in guitar virtuosity, and with such a source of knowledge at his disposal, he has a wide knowledge of the flamenco guitar. Justo's playing does not in the least resemble that of his father; it is, in fact, the opposite. While Manolo's was hard-driving and flamenco, Justo's tends towards a softer type of modern style, seemingly with a strong classical influence. His technique is well-developed and clean.

Justo travels a great deal with troupes outside of Spain, although his permanent residence is still Madrid. He has cut several records, including one longplay of solos.

PERICO EL DEL LUNAR

(c. 1894 - 1964)

PEDRO DEL VALLE, better known by his artistic name "PERICO EL DEL LUNAR" (Pete, he of the Mole), so-called because of a prominent mole which was removed some time ago, was a Jerez-born, non-gypsy *tocaor* who possessed as vast a knowledge of the *cante,* and its accompaniment, as any guitarist of this century.

Born in 1894, PERICO spent fifty-eight of his seventy years playing the guitar. He has accompanied most of the great *can-*

taores and *bailaores,* including Manuel Torre, the old Fosforito, La Niña de los Peines, Pepe de la Matrona, Vicente Escudero, Carmen Amaya, Antonio Chacón, with whom he spent several years, and many others. But his entire professional career was perhaps highlighted by his noteworthy showing of knowledge and heart in the famous anthology on which he was not only the sole accompanist of thirty-three different *cantes,* but also had to teach many of the *cantes* to the *cantaores* who sang them on the records (1). Thus PERICO's curiosity and quest for knowledge about his chosen art surely saved some of the more obsolete *cantes,* and their accompaniments, from passing out of existence.

Fernando de Triana recognized this investigative trait in PERICO way back in the early 1930's, when he wrote: "Perico is a master accompanist, dedicating much of his time to learning the oldest *cantes* and their accompaniments, rather than taking part in the race for monotonous velocity which makes up the modern school of the flamenco guitar."

Lesser recognized was PERICO's vast knowledge of the *baile,* which he loved nearly as much as the *cante.* PERICO delved deep into the old-time dance, and passed his knowledge on to whoever was interested. He was directly responsible for the excellent *baile* of Rosita Durán, for instance, for whom he has been both a teacher and an inspiration.

PERICO was first taught the guitar by his father, and later, principally, by Javier Molina. His early playing was also strongly influenced by Ramón Montoya, which can be clearly seen in PERICO's early records accompanying Antonio Chacón. These records would be a revelation to PERICO's detractors, who label his playing as "too primitive"; at one time PERICO sounded a great deal like Ramón, although PERICO played, for my taste, with more force. But this was not the real PERICO; the *toque* he truly admired and felt at home with was more primitive. Perhaps prompted in part by an injured tendon in his right hand, which never healed prop-

---

(1) Westminster Anthology of Cante Flamenco, in the USA and England. Hispavox in Spain. The French edition won the 1955 outstanding record award in Paris. The same anthology was done with forty-one *cantes* in Mexico, also organized, inspired, and accompanied by Perico.

erly, he reverted to his early *toque*, and never for a moment regretted it. He had only to listen to the machine-like playing of many of his contemporaries to reinforce his feelings on the subject. In PERICO's words: *"Tocan limpio, tocan rápido, pero no dicen ná."* (They play cleanly and fast, but express nothing). PERICO was fully qualified to make this statement, for his playing *"decía tó"* (expressed everything). In the expression of *duende* PERICO was unexcelled.

As great as his feeling for flamenco was his creative ability. PERICO was one of the old-time guitarists who developed his *"propio sello"*, characterized, in his later years, by the deceptive simplicity and great expressiveness of his creations.

As a person PERICO was as fine as his *toque*. He had an unceasing love for flamenco that surmounted even his last years of suffering from cancer, years when PERICO rarely left his Madrid apartment in the *barrio de* Lavapiés. His death, on March 27, 1964, was a great loss for pure flamenco.

PERICO's son, also Pedro, has taken over PERICO's long-time job at La Zambra, and is filling his father's shoes nicely. Young Pedro, in his twenties, can sound exactly like his father when he wishes, which is when he is at his best. He accompanies well indeed, and is certainly one of the finest young guitarists playing today.

VICTOR ROJAS
(c. 1894 —

VÍCTOR ROJAS, brother of the great gypsy *bailaora*, Pastora Imperio, still clings to the primitive style of flamenco guitar-playing much as his sister clings to the old school of dance. As a youth VÍCTOR studied with Luis Molina, whom he says was an outstanding accompanist and guitarist. Accompanying is also VÍCTOR's forte.

Although VÍCTOR performs from time to time in Spain, more precisely in El Duende, he has resided long years in Mexico City, the old *maestro* in a group of guitarists which includes: Málaga-born PACO MILLET, in his late fifties, first guitarist for the Tarriba Ballet;

Manuel Medina, an accomplished Mexican guitarist of the modern school; and Julio de los Reyes, Mexican-born of Spanish parents, one of today's promising young guitarists, presently playing out of Los Angeles, California.

CURRITO EL DE LA GEROMA

(c. 1900 - 1934)

Currito el de la Geroma is universally remembered not only as a *"fenómeno"*, but as a *"genio"* as well. For Currito was outstanding in all phases of flamenco: as a singer, dancer and guitarist.

What made Currito the most famous was his excellent accompanying, and guitar-playing in general. Fernando de Triana wrote that Currito's playing drew the best out of the singers. Pepe Torre says that although there were guitarists technically better than Currito, he knew of none with whom he would rather sing. To quote Pepe: "Curro was truly a great flamenco guitarist. His manner of playing, his creations, his *duende,* were flamenco to the core. He has been one of the few true geniuses of the guitar."

Melchor de Marchena ranks Currito alongside of Manolo de Huelva and Javier Molina as the three top guitarists that he has heard.

Curro was the son of the renowned *siguiriyero* and guitarist, Juan el de Alonso, and of the equally as renowned dancer and singer, La Geroma. He studied the guitar with his father, and also a little with Javier Molina, then went on to teach himself, developing his *"propio sello"* despite his relative youth. He was particularly renowned for his fabulous thumb, which he undoubtedly developed to an even greater degree due to one of the fingers of his right hand being left useless by a knife accident.

Currito lived his short lifetime amidst the lively flamenco activity of Sevilla's Alameda de Hércules. His talent was entirely directed towards *juergas,* excepting for one year-long tour with the company of Pastora Imperio. He died, according to old-time flamencos, from the *"vicios de mujeres y alcohol"* (vices of women and drink). His exploits with women were legendary, as was his compulsive drinking; CURRITO used to complain that alcohol had no effect on him, and he consumed the entire contents of bottles of *cazalla* at a sitting before he could achieve the proper glow. As was inevitable, his body failed him when he was at the prime of his artistic career, and one of flamenco's true geniuses was prematurely removed from the scene.

ANTONIO AND ESTEBAN SANLÚCAR

Fernando de Triana, in 1935, predicted the artistic success of ESTEBAN DELGADO, EL NIÑO DE SANLÚCAR. At that time ESTEBAN was an unknown, preparing to embark upon his career. Embark he did, and he has since fulfilled Fernando's expectations.

ESTEBAN is a virtuoso, although his playing has retained more touches of the old than is true of most modern-style guitarists. He is also an accomplished classical guitarist. Many years ago ESTEBAN moved to Buenos Aires, where he reigns as *maestro* in a lively flamenco atmosphere. Like Sabicas, ESTEBAN has never returned to Spain. He is presently in his fifties.

Older brother ANTONIO (DELGADO) SANLÚCAR, who also plays an excellent flamenco guitar, stayed on in Spain, and has managed to eke out a living as a professional guitarist in the Sevilla area. ANTONIO told me recently that times have become increasingly rough since the closing, by law, of the flamenco activities of the Alameda de Hércules area some years ago. Most of Sevilla's artists, such as Manolo de Huelva, went to Madrid, and the rest began frequenting roadside *ventas* on the outskirts of Sevilla. ANTONIO SANLÚCAR can still be found nearly every night at Marcelino's, just out of Sevilla on the highway to Cádiz.

ANTONIO has a fine reputation as an accompanist of both the *cante* and the *baile*, while ESTEBAN has branched out more as a soloist. Both brothers were born non-gypsies in Sanlúcar de Barrameda (Cádiz).

CARLOS MONTOYA
1988 Update: (1903 –

CARLOS MONTOYA. What contradictory reactions that name

evokes. For thousands of record and concert fans he is Mr. Flamenco Guitar. When brought up in a professional conversation, however, he is nearly always dismissed with a shrug.

This contradiction again points out that in flamenco, as in all arts, one's tastes must be cultivated. This is further complicated by the fact that even within the professional flamenco world there are widely varying opinions due to the existence of the two schools, the traditional and the modern.

However, the general feeling in the professional world against MONTOYA runs, I believe, deeper than this. There is without doubt a great deal of envy at MONTOYA's long reign as the world's busiest concert flamenco guitarist, his countless records, and, in general, his lucrative status in having been the United States' fair-haired boy of the flamenco guitar for the past twenty years. And, of course, his acceptance into, and lionization by, New York society.

Let us attempt to examine this man's playing impartially. We must start by saying that his playing is unique; a few notes from any of his records serve to identify him. The fact that he has his own "*sello*", then, is definitely a strong point in his favor.

Born into a family of gypsy artists, CARLOS' playing is based on that of his uncle, Ramón Montoya (CARLOS denies this). However, CARLOS plays in a more primitive, country-gypsy fashion than did Ramón. Perhaps the most fascinating facet of CARLOS' playing is his extraordinary mixture of good and bad taste. His playing often contains an undeniable gypsy drive and *duende,* only to be too quickly destroyed by some absurdity, some flashy, misplaced *picado* or sixty seconds of continuous *ligado.* This could very easily be attributed to the non-flamenco atmosphere in which CARLOS lives, which seeks, and applauds, his flash, and lets his moments of genius go unrecognized. Few artists will long insist upon the less popular; it is necessary to live where true flamenco is recognized and appreciated (such places are becoming increasingly difficult to encounter, even in Spain).

We can perhaps be aided in our discussion by referring to one of MONTOYA's solo records. One of his first, on a Montilla label, is the best of his that I have come across. Unlike most of his records, here CARLOS shows that his playing is well-grounded when he wishes. On this record: his *bulerías* are unusual, very choppy, and oftentimes truly gypsy; in his *café de chinitas* he relaxes and lets simplicity, and consequently *duende,* seep through; his *sevillanas* are good, his *granaínas* mediocre; with parts of his *tientos y tanguillos* he would have a gypsy gathering in the palm of his hand, particularly his *tientos;* his *soleares,* after a nice start, degenerate into an emotionless, repetitious, monotonous mess, rushed and disjointed, probably the worst effort at *soleares* that I have heard issue from a professional; the *rondeña,* a potentially beautiful piece, starts well, but is soon ligadoed to death — the whole effect turns out much nicer than the *soleares,* however; the *malagueñas boleras* and the *fandangos* and *verdiales* had me nodding, to be snapped fully awake again by the *rasgueados* of a *farruca* possessed of little of the majesty traditionally characteristic of this misunderstood *toque.*

Conclusions? MONTOYA is more at home with choppy, fast, light *toques,* out of his element with the *toque jondo* if we are among those who believe that it should be played in a *jondo* fashion.

Is MONTOYA a virtuoso? Somewhat, but not exceptional. He has a good *thumb, rasgueado, picado,* and *ligado.* His style of playing does not make much use of arpeggios, and it is a shame he does not do likewise with his tremolo. His playing falls short of that of the virtuosos, but has advanced well beyond the primitive stage. An overly-simplified summation of his playing might read: MONTOYA makes ostentatious use of a primitive style of playing, which too often destroys the purity of his *toque* and the *duende* I believe to be inherent in him.

MONTOYA has lived for years with his American wife in New York City. He gives concerts tirelessly the world over, and is equally prolific in his record-making. He is undoubtedly the most widely known flamenco guitarist, in an international sense, in the world today.

Two observations of interest: 1) CARLOS' accompanying is superior to his solo playing; 2) he keeps his guitar tuned well below normal pitch, and has his guitars constructed so that the strings nearly rest upon the finger board, both of which factors make for extremely light action.

Some time ago MONTOYA ran out of recording companies with whom he could repeat his same tireless *toques,* and he turned to new gimmicks, such as his record of combined flamenco-jazz (the flamenco guitar backed up by a jazz combo). Bad taste? Of course, but what the hell — it will probably prove trend-setting!

ROMAN EL GRANAINO

(c. 1905 —

ROMÁN EL GRANAÍNO, gypsy-born in Granada, proudly conserves a relatively old style of *toque* that goes largely unappreciated today. Like a true *gitano,* he prefers the *toques a compás (soleá, siguiriyas, bulerías, tangos,* etc.). His old-style *bulerías a golpe* are particularly unusual and impressive.

ROMÁN's *toque* is largely based on that of his father (with touches of Ramón Montoya), although ROMÁN has added to it and innovated around it, and in so doing has formed his own style. ROMÁN enjoys talking about his father, Salvador (c. 1875-1940), a guitarist born in the village of Asastrigo, in the Alpujarra mountains (the region so well captivated by Gerald Brenan in "South from Granada"). ROMÁN says that in the style of the old-time flamenco guitarists, his father created his *"propio sello",* and went on to say: "Guitarists of old were ashamed to copy from others. Creativity was a major and common virtue in those days.

"My father moved to Granada at an early age, where I was born. During his career he accompanied such artists as Manuel Torre, La Macarrona, La Malena, Enrique el Jorobao, Antonio de Bilbao...

"My older brother, SALVADOR, was also a fine guitarist, but died at a relatively young age from drinking. In those days the flamencos drank *cazalla* (a strong type of *aguardiente)* by the water-glass full, not wine like they do today. Many flamencos of old died from the *vicios* (vices) of women and drink."

ROMÁN continued:

"We must distinguish between playing and executing a *toque.* Today many guitarists execute, but very few play. To play one must give of himself ... put soul into his playing. Too much technique and showmanship defeat this objective."

Some of ROMÁN's miscellaneous observations:

"Before the women danced. Now they are only machines...

"Francisco Yerbagüena has been the greatest singer of *granaínas*...

"Before, the gypsy mixed with no one, like the Chinese and the Moors. Today it is different...

"Good guitarists? Ramón in his last years; Currito el de la Geroma was outstanding in the *toque*, *baile*, and *cante*, all three — a true genius of flamenco; Javier Molina was also a *genio*; Antonio Sol was a *fenómeno*, but died young; today Manolo de Huelva is extraordinary, the best; Sabicas is the finest technician, but as for *duende*..."

ROMÁN's entire family is involved in flamenco ... singers, dancers, guitarists, all presently Madrid-based. ROMÁN himself owns a little house in a Madrid suburb, but spends a great deal of time on artistic engagements outside of Spain. He has this to say of the non-Spanish public:

"The foreign public appreciates the true flamenco more than the Spanish public. It is far more rewarding, both artistically and monetarily, to perform outside of Spain. Except for the non-flamenco atmosphere, of course..."

DIEGO DEL GASTOR

1988 Update: (1908-1973)

DIEGO AMAYA FLORES "DIEGO DEL GASTOR" is an exemplary gypsy and flamenco, unique in many ways. He has the heart of a poet, and loves nothing more than long sessions of reciting and creating poetry over bottles of red wine (his and his friends' interpretations of García Lorca - put many a professional reciter to shame). He is a true bohemian, free from the lust for money or fame, content with his simple village needs of food and wine. He is a born gentleman, incapable of unprovoked offense, free from the close-minded arrogance so commonly found in flamenco artists.

He has a grand heart, always helpful, generous to a fault. And, as if this were not enough, he is one of flamenco's few remaining guitarists who yet understands, and plays, true flamenco.

The reader will ask, what is so unique in Diego's playing? Let us attempt to construct an answer to this. First of all, when playing seriously, Diego foregoes all superficiality or ostentatiousness. Unlike the majority of guitarists, his instinct is to unfold the mysteries of the flamenco guitar and of the heart, not to show off. In Diego's playing, each note is meaningful, each *toque* a primitive, urgent soul-summons. It is this particular gift, possessed by Diego and so few others, that makes the art of flamenco, or any art, worthwhile.

Meaningful creation is another of Diego's gifts. His creations, oftentimes spontaneous, are a source of inspiration for all guitarists who come in contact with him, regardless of their fame or name. When listening to an inspired Diego, one must resign himself to the fact that many of the fabulous *falsetas* that issue from his guitar will never be heard again. Although in a way this is a pity, at the same time it is a basic contributing factor to the splendor of flamenco.

Diego is not overly-concerned with technique. Sometimes weeks go by without his playing a note other than in *juergas*. He seems to have trained his hands to a necessary point of being able to properly interpret whatever he wishes to interpret, and he is quite content to let it go at that. However, his technique is neither sloppy nor deficient. To the contrary, each note issues crystal clear, and when warmed up his playing often reaches a point of extreme difficulty. Technique is just another of his natural talents.

His hands are hard, and his touch is hard. When Diego plays, guitars come alive, seemingly responding to his authority. His style of playing is old; his *bulerías*, for instance, are played as they were fifty years ago, not in the more showy manner of today. His *toque jondo* is slow, his phrasing beautiful and full of *duende*. In the old manner, Diego will occasionally sacrifice the *compás* in order to accomplish some particularly meaningful passage in his solo playing. Instead of interrupting the *toque*, as is often the case with other guitarists, these moments in the hands of Diego flow naturally, and even seem to lend further expression to his playing.

DIEGO plays fine guitar solos, but strongly prefers accompanying. Juan Talegas states: "When Diego begins playing, it is impossible to contain oneself. One must sing. This reaction is initiated by only a few exceptional guitarists." All singers who have been accompanied by DIEGO (and dancers) marvel at the ease with which they can sing with him. Pepe Torre compares Diego's playing with that of Currito de la Geroma. He says: "There is such *duende* in their playing that one sings well despite oneself!"

DIEGO's most brilliant *toques*, and those he prefers, are the *siguiriyas, soleares,* and *bulerías.* This is natural, as those are the *cantes* most widely sung in the Sevilla-Morón area, and those that DIEGO accompanies a vast majority of the time. However, DIEGO plays a host of other *toques*, and has, in his day, played considerable classical guitar music (1). But he is not a complete flamenco guitarist in the modern concert sense of the word, in that he has not taken the trouble to work out solos in *toques* that he does not take seriously, or that are not traditionally solo numbers, such as the *verdiales, fandangos, malagueñas, rumba,* and so forth. Because of this he is sometimes described, in concert circles, as "exceptional but *corto*" (not complete in flamenco's repertoire), much as Juan Talegas is described in the *cante*. The truth is, within one week DIEGO could be playing solos in all of flamenco's *toques* if he so desired. "But why bother," he reasons, "if these *toques* do not inspire one to play them as solos. I much prefer to be *largo* (complete) in my preferred *toques*."

DIEGO was born in Ronda, but at an early age moved to Gastor, a village near Morón de la Frontera. His father was a wealthy gypsy cattle dealer and owner of several businesses in both Gastor and Morón, and DIEGO grew up in these two towns. Both DIEGO's father and mother sang well, although not professionally due to the lack of need, and DIEGO early gravitated to-

---

(1) Manolo de Huelva, Diego del Gastor, Esteban Sanlúcar, Luis Maravilla, and others could well serve as the base for an excellent argument against the general belief that flamenco guitarists are hampered by any knowledge of the classical guitar. I would say that as long as the two are kept separate in one's playing, and the flamenco strongly predominates, no harm seems to be done. Of course, one must guard against classical techniques and hand positions creeping into one's flamenco playing.

wards the flamenco guitar. His prime inspiration was the great Pepe Naranjo, although DIEGO also found inspiration in other guitarists among the then abundant flamenco population of the Morón area.

As DIEGO began playing in the active *juerga* life of that period, he became known as a moving and knowledgeable guitarist, and as an extremely eccentric personality. This eccentricity was mainly based on one thing: DIEGO's complete lack of ambition, his total indifference to fame and fortune. DIEGO played when he felt like playing, and many were the lucrative *juergas* that DIEGO turned down because he did not like the singer, or felt that the gathering would not truly appreciate or understand his art. Above all, DIEGO balked at condescending *señoritos;* he knew that he had more dignity in his little finger than they in their misguided entirety, and he would not serve the more offensive of them for any amount of money. DIEGO also made a point of refusing all contracts for extended periods after his one experience in such a venture with the singer Manuel Vallejo, in the 1930's (offers from flamenco companies still pour in to DIEGO, in hopes that he may change his mind). He feels that this type of rehearsed activity is the antithesis of good flamenco. Today he is more reluctant than ever to leave Morón for any length of time due to the failing health of his aged mother.

Nearly as many stories are told about DIEGO's eccentricities as are told about Manolo de Huelva. Such as DIEGO's refusal to accompany Antonio Chacón simply because he did not like Chacón's falsetto voice nor his style of singing — this when Chacón was called the "Emperor of the *Cante*", and it was considered a great privilege to be chosen to accompany him! Or the story Juan Talegas tells of DIEGO's first decent guitar. In Juan's words:

"Like now, Diego used to be our favorite accompanist, except for one thing; the guitar that he played was so inferior and beat up that it could not even be tuned properly. So we decided to organize a *juerga* and present DIEGO with a fine guitar. If I remember properly, it was a Santos Hernández. Everyone chipped in, and what a *juerga* that was. Diego was like a child with a new toy, and played and played and accompanied us all like never before. Finally, late at night, he grew tired of playing and wanted to rest, but couldn't find a safe place to put his guitar, as none of us had thought of buying a guitar case. DIEGO solved the problem by locking it in our car outside. He rejoined the gathering jubilantly, and amidst the ensuing drinks and merry-making completely forgot the existence of the guitar. At *juerga's* end, still unusually exuberant for some reason he could not quite recall, Diego danced out to the car, hurled himself drunkenly into the back seat, lit atop his beloved Santos and smashed it into pieces. The guitar never could be properly repaired, and was the last good guitar, to my knowledge, that Diego has owned."

Certainly one of the most charming of DIEGO's gifts is that he, like his *toque,* never becomes boring. When he tires of playing he turns enthusiastically to poetry, or any number of other interests. After having known him for three years, I was amazed one night to hear him begin singing, and singing well, the old *cantes* of his parents and other *cantaores* of the past. Once started, DIEGO is also an entertaining storyteller. He is a tireless reader, and enjoys literary discussions. He is one of the numbered gypsies left in Andalusia who can still talk *caló,* the Spanish-gypsy language, although he has forgotten much of it due to lack of usage. Above all, his ideas about flamenco are worthy of close attention.

DIEGO lives with his mother in upper Morón de la Frontera. The town is full of his relatives, including three nephews whom DIEGO is instructing in the guitar. One of these, Paco del Gastor, has developed into an excellent guitarist in his own right. Paco's uncle, Francisco "el Mellizo" (DIEGO's brother), also has a fine reputation as a guitarist.

DIEGO is presently undergoing considerable lionization by non-Spanish guitar students who read of him in my first book, "The Art of Flamenco". These disciples are flocking to Morón de la Frontera from as far off as California, hoping to study with DIEGO. Unfortunately, DIEGO detests formal teaching or timetables of any kind. His day consists of tireless reading, walking, talking, drinking, and *juergas.* He will not refuse to teach — he is incapable of refusing a friend or true admirer anything. Instead, he will set an hour for the lessons, fully intending to go through with it. Of course, something comes up. Many are the students who arrange for daily classes, only to go day after day without a glimpse of DIEGO; the dullness and routine of teaching is simply beyond him.

Nevertheless, DIEGO should be listened to by all serious guitar *aficionados*. My advice is to spend the lesson money in *juergas*, and hear, and absorb, DIEGO and his atmosphere at its best. This proves infinitely superior to formal lessons, and will put the serious student into contact with one of the few remaining outposts, and guitarists, of true flamenco.

NIÑO RICARDO

1988 Update: (1904-1972)

MANUEL SERRAPI "EL NIÑO RICARDO" can be singled out as the guitarist who has perhaps most influenced the development of the modern flamenco guitar since Ramón Montoya. From his fertile mind has blossomed a distinct style of playing immediately recognizable as RICARDO, which is eagerly imitated wherever the flamenco guitar is played. As is only fitting, RICARDO's genius has made him an idol in the eyes of countless followers.

RICARDO possesses a vast knowledge of the guitar. One of his students has told me that RICARDO encourages his students to select any string and fret on the fingerboard as the base and starting point for whatever *toque* they wish to request, and RICARDO will improvise from this base intricate *falsetas*, playing on for as long as desired.

Within the complex stylings of modern concert flamenco, RICARDO's creations are sometimes very flamenco, always imaginative, and certainly very difficult. Some of his compositions have been played so often as to become flamenco standards, if such a non-flamenco occurrence is possible. How is his playing? His undeniable virtuosity is marred by one failing; his flying fingers cannot keep up with his racing imagination (nor could anyone's). As he plays his mind is skipping along at one hundred per, inventing all kinds of impossible situations that he cannot execute to the fullest. Consequently his playing often sounds sloppy and inconsistent. Also, RICARDO considers his own playing secondary to his vast knowledge of flamenco and his creative ability, and he does not devote the necessary number of hours to practice that his style of playing demands. In addition, he is a very busy man, nearly always on tour, which limits an artist's practice time considerably.

A more serious failing in RICARDO's makeup is that his intricate style of playing presents an obstacle through which little *duende* can seep. His playing is exciting, musically fascinating, sometimes beautiful, but not generally emotional to the extent that RICARDO would be capable with a less complex style of playing.

Born a non-gypsy in Sevilla, RICARDO began his professional career as a youthful accompanist, second guitarist to Antonio Moreno in Sevilla's now disappeared Salón Variedades. From there he moved over to the Café Novedades, and the opportunity to play under the tutelage of the great Javier Molina. With this solid background, RICARDO went on to develop his own style and material, which became increasingly complex as years passed.

RICARDO is an accomplished accompanist, although his talents along this line have largely gone to waste in recent years. From his early great days of accompanying such singers as La Niña de los Peines, Tomás Pavón, Manuel Torre, and others of similar stature, RICARDO became caught up in the lucrative commercial web and has found himself playing long periods with the companies of such singers as Juanito Valderrama, Angelillo, and, as if reaching the ultimate in this trend, Antonio Molina. Meanwhile, he has cut many records, and published considerable sheet music of simplified flamenco arrangements. He has had many students, some of whom have gone on to fame (most notably Mario Escudero). His favorite student today is, understandably, his son, a lad in his twenties who now travels with his father as second guitarist.

NIÑO RICARDO is an agreeable man with a fine sense of humor, as can be seen by a story he tells concerning the guitar-maker, Santos Hernández. It seems that just after the Spanish Civil War RICARDO was in France, and desired one of Santos' guitars. He wrote the great craftsman ordering a new one, offering to pay for the guitar with high-grade Spanish olive oil, which was impossible to find in Spain at that time. Santos agreed, made the guitar, and sent it to RICARDO after having received his payment of oil.

The guitar arrived, and much to RICARDO's distress was far inferior to the usual Santos masterpieces. RICARDO tore off an indignant letter telling Santos that he found the guitar entirely unsatisfactory.

A few weeks later Santos' reply came: "A shame you find the guitar unsatisfactory. The olive oil was excellent!"

RICARDO is a long-time resident of Sevilla, where he maintains a house near the Alameda de Hércules. RICARDO rarely gets home for any length of time, however, due to his constant artistic commitments.

PEPE MARTINEZ

1988 Update: (1922-1985)

And now we arrive to the self-proclaimed "king of the flamenco guitar". In this corner, PEPE MARTÍNEZ!

Any truth in this, you ask? Let us look into it.

PEPE MARTÍNEZ, a non-gypsy, is definitely one of flamenco's top virtuosos, with an added advantage over most of them: he has learned to control his virtuosity. He is not above slowing down so as to be able to savour the beauty of the guitar; he is capable of playing passages of great simplicity; his *toque* is tasteful, slow, melodic, flowing, lyrical, and ofttimes truly lovely. He is a complete *tocaor* in that besides his solo playing he is an excellent accompanist: knowledgeable, and willing to take a back seat to the singer or dancer. And his *toque* is quietly moving, possessed of a subtle *duende* throughout.

So far it sounds like PEPE's proclamation may be true. Is there anything lacking? Just one thing — force (or to use the Spanish term: *"cojones"*). PEPE's toque is too evenly subdued — it lacks moments of power, of passion, of evil. His style is that of an eighteenth century romantic novel, full only of beauty and repose, where everyone is gracious and hunger does not exist. To round out this basic lack in his *toque* PEPE would not have to be another Melchor de Marchena, whose *toque* is all passion, love, hate, lust, and four-letter words. There are others who play in basically the same style as PEPE, and manage to achieve something more of realism. The problem seems to be that PEPE is temperamentally a classical guitarist.

Another obstacle blocking MARTÍNEZ' desire to be the top man is his lack of a *"propio sello"*. He is capable of creation, but as yet not of a thoroughly distinctive style of playing such as is possessed, for instance, by Manolo de Huelva, Melchor de Marchena, Diego del Gastor, Sabicas, Niño Ricardo, and Moraíto (among others). If one was ignorant of who was playing, it would be difficult to tell MARTÍNEZ from countless others.

Something of MARTÍNEZ' views on flamenco can be understood through his utter devotion to Pepe Marchena, whom he proclaims "today's greatest *cantaor*". Pepe Marchena wholeheartedly agrees. These two friends certainly represent a cozy union of styles and egos...

PEPE MARTÍNEZ rarely plays in Spain's commercial flamenco centers. He considers them beneath himself and good concert flamenco. Instead, he spends extended periods in England, where his playing is devoutly and silently heard. His Spanish activies include recordings, both as a soloist and an accompanist, and guitar instruction in his home in Sevilla.

SABICAS

(c. 1913 —

As of this writing it is fashionable to criticize the great virtuoso, AGUSTÍN CASTELLÓN "NIÑO SABICAS". He has cut many too many records, some of them strictly commercial, a lot of them trash. He is definitely following the route of the purloined purse with great energy and, it seems, nary a backward glance, and in the process he is picking up quantities of detractors. Like so many worshipers whose idol has fallen, these detractors do not spare the whip; as far as they are concerned, everything that SABICAS does nowadays is to be blindly condemned.

In a way they are right. It is acceptable and even understandable that the mediocre go this route, but when one of the great flamenco talents of all times falls prey to the system, it is more difficult to tolerate.

Nevertheless, it cannot be overlooked that, for whatever it is worth, SABICAS is still the king of the concert flamenco guitarists. Recently one little-versed *aficionado* told me that the playing of an up-and-coming concert guitarist, Juanito Serrano, makes SABICAS look like an amateur. This, of course, is ridiculous. There has never been a guitarist, presently or in the past, who can excel SABICAS in mastery of the concert-style flamenco guitar.

What makes SABICAS stand out? There are four major factors in his greatness. The first is his unbelievable technique. All of the flamenco guitar techniques in use today have been developed by SABICAS to a high state of perfection. The second consists of the fact that SABICAS is one of flamenco's great creators, ranking alongside Ramón Montoya, Javier Molina, and Niño Ricardo as a contributor to the modern, concert school. The third is SABICAS fabulous sense of *compás,* recognized by Manolo de Huelva as foremost among present-day guitarists. Especially in his accompanying (i.e. SABICAS' records with Carmen Amaya), SABICAS makes one want to leap to his feet and dance. The fourth is SABICAS' outstanding accompanying, for which art he has a profound instinct. Only one major factor is questionable: his *duende.* SABICAS *has duende,* but as I must not tire of repeating, the concert flamenco guitar largely defeats whatever emotion is felt by the guitarist. In this, SABICAS is no exception, although touches of *duende* do seep through at times (again, SABICAS' solos on the Carmen Amaya discs, and pieces of some of his others). Mostly, however, after listening to SABICAS or any of the other moderns for a short period of time, the notes go tinkling away as one's thoughts run astray. It is only when true emotion is being expressed that the listener is caught up and not released until the guitarist stops playing This last factor, which must be possessed in flamenco if one is to achieve ultimate greatness, will, I am afraid, forever escape flamenco concert guitarists of the modern school.

SABICAS was born a gypsy in Pamplona, a most unflamenco town in northen Spain. His nickname was reputedly derived from his childhood mispronunciation of *"habas"* (beans) into *"sabas"*, to which the diminutive *"sabicas"* was applied. Fernando de Triana describes SABICAS as a child prodigy, and says that at the time of the publishing of his book (1935) SABICAS was one of the great guitarists of Spain. Fernando goes on to tell some anecdotes of SABICAS' childhood, which I shall briefly relate here: according to Fernando, when SABICAS was just a child of five, he used to spend hours listening to a neighbor play and replay his limited repertoire, until finally SABICAS knew it all by heart. SABICAS said to himself. 'Had I a guitar, I would play all of that and a lot more', and he began pestering his parents to buy him a small seventeen-peseta guitar. His parents eventually gave in, and SABICAS set about teaching himself to play the compositions of his neighbor. This was soon accomplished, and SABICAS sought new worlds to conquer. He tried Pamplona's best guitar instructor, only to find that he already played more flamenco than this guitarist. There was nowhere else to turn but to phonograph records, which he did with zeal.

SABICAS made progress, and at age ten made his professional debut with the company of La Chelita, a popular singer, in the El Dorado theater in Madrid. He was presented as a boy prodigy, wearing short pants, and caused something of a sensation. It was then that he was first called a *"fenómeno"*, a description still universally used when referring to SABICAS.

SABICAS rose rapidly, and became featured guitarist in a number of companies. When the Civil War broke out, SABICAS left Spain, and for some reason has never returned. Whether for political or personal reasons, we can only speculate.

After a time SABICAS made his permanent residence in Mexico City, where he did not fare as well as might be expected. He could not leave Mexico for long for fear of having difficulty re-entering (political red tape), and had to content himself in Mexico City with two or three concerts a year, playing for visiting flamenco companies, and teaching. According to one friend of his, during some periods of his nearly twenty years in Mexico SABICAS lived in near-poverty. His always successful concerts, and the tours he made with his own company and with that of Carmen Amaya, were the highlights of his Mexican existence.

After various playing engagements in New York with Carmen Amaya, SABICAS was finally able, around the year 1957, to enter the United States permanently. Once there, he took the United States by storm, and his problems were solved.

SABICAS' family includes a guitar-playing brother, Diego Castellón, whom SABICAS has included in several of his records.

Concerning SABICAS' records, incidently, various rumors abound that point out the absurd limits to which rivalries, artistic envy, and *aficionados'* gullibility and hero-worship can reach. Many students and admirers of Mario Escudero, for instance, claim, straight-faced, that Escudero has cut all or most of SABICAS' records for him, as SABICAS is not capable of such fine playing (I wonder if Mario also plays SABICAS' concerts in disguise). SABICAS fans, on the other hand, retort that SABICAS cut both parts of the SABICAS-Escudero record of duets. Escudero fans, enraged, stamp their feet and cry that SABICAS has never created a note in his life, that he stole all of his material from old Manolo de Huelva records. The latter statement is truly a masterpiece of hard-headed ignorance, for 1) Manolo never cut solo records, and his few accompanying records contain only an occasional *falseta,* and 2) Manolo's style of playing and type of material is completely unlike that of SABICAS. Each has his *"propio sello"*, and their *toques* differ like night and day. (How complicated we humans make life!)

SABICAS presently lives in New York City with his family.

MELCHOR DE MARCHENA

1988 Update: (1913-1980)

Words cannot describe the masterful, old-school playing of MELCHOR DE MARCHENA. I recently asked him what he considered *the* essential in flamenco guitar-playing. He replied in his manner, rough, to the point: "To play from the soul."

And play from the soul he does. His *siguiriyas*, particularly, are played with a force, emotion, and primitive poetry that I have never heard excelled, and rarely approached. Each note seems torn from him, and with equal strength enters the guts and heart of the sensitive listener. MELCHOR is the Caracol of the guitar: a needing animal howling his lament, making the flamenco of the fancy boys seem like the foolish patter of children.

MELCHOR, born of gypsy parents in Marchena, a town near Sevilla, claims that he never had formal guitar lessons, but learned by listening and watching. To whom, in particular, did he listen? The guitarists that MELCHOR holds supreme have been three: Javier Molina, Currito de la Geroma, and the greatest of them all (in MELCHOR's words), Manolo de Huelva. MELCHOR has been one of the privileged few to hear Manolo de Huelva at his best, and he says that it is a "sublime experience." Coming from a guitarist of MELCHOR's stature, *duende*, and philosophy, that is the supreme compliment.

Although MELCHOR has, against his better judgement, cut solo records, he is at his best accompanying. Particularly accompanying the *cante gitano*. He is an accompanist that brings out the best in the singer, and is therefore very much in demand. To quote Manolo Caracol: "If the singer is capable of singing well, he must sing well with Melchor de Marchena!"

MELCHOR's style of playing is unusual, full of meaningful silences and profound, instantaneous changes of emotional context. Certainly it is not soothing, nor is it usually lyrical, beautiful, nor melodic — it simply has guts and *cojones*, the most *macho* guitar I believe that I have ever heard. As such, it is at complete opposites with the styles of such guitarists as Pepe Martínez, Mario Escudero, Luis Maravilla, etc. It is gypsy like the gypsies dream of being, like the gypsies of García Lorca. If one wishes to play a gypsy guitar, one can follow no better man.

As the gypsy *toques* turn *andaluz* in the hands of Pepe Martínez, so the *toques andaluces* turn gypsy when played by MELCHOR, much as the *tarantas* or *malagueñas* turned gypsy in the mouths of Manuel Torre and the Niña de los Peines (this distinction between the *andaluz* and gypsy feeling and style of delivery is often overlooked, and is perhaps the major contributor to the confusion and misunderstanding within flamenco). When played by MELCHOR, the *malagueñas, tarantas,* and similar *toques* lose something of their melodic flow, but gain in strength; vitality is largely substituted for ornamental prettiness. This is not to say that MELCHOR's playing does not have its beautiful moments. At a twinkling and within the same *toque* MELCHOR confronts beauty, death, hate, love, hope, cruelty, and for this reason his playing is so alive and real — it embraces the whole flood of constantly-changing human emotions (1).

MELCHOR has had the hands, instinct, and good taste to achieve an important goal: controlled virtuosity. His techniques are all well-advanced when he wishes to bone up and use them, which is generally just to the extent of achieving his desired *toque*. Rarely does he use them in a pointless and show-offish manner. Exceptions to this, as far as MELCHOR is concerned, are his sometimes use of the tremolo and his solo playing, both of which he disdains. He firmly believes that flamenco should be free from all ornamentation, and that the flamenco guitar's prime function is to accompany.

Creative ability? Definitely. MELCHOR has one of the most creative minds in flamenco, as is obvious when listening to him. Much of his *toque* is completely unique in the world of the flamenco guitar, which, combined with his unusual style of playing, gives him a thoroughly distinctive *"sello"*. He is also one of the great spontaneous innovators of our time.

When Sevilla's flamenco life was largely closed down some years ago, MELCHOR joined the migration of artists to Madrid, where he still resides. He has been the long-time companion and accompanist of Manolo Caracol, and it is in Caracol's Los Canas-

---

(1) There are presently two anthologies available outside of Spain that demonstrate excellently the *toque* of Melchor, and the above-mentioned qualities I attribute to his playing. They are: 1) «A History of *Cante Flamenco*». Top Rank International. Manolo Caracol, singer, Melchor de Marchena, guitarist; 2) «An Anthology of *Cante Flamenco*». London Records. Features various excellent *cantaores* and guitarists, and shows just how clearly Melchor's playing stands out.
Both of the anthologies are extremely valuable as much for the *cante* as the guitar. Melchor's playing in them far surpasses that of his solo records

teros where he is presently playing (MELCHOR is completely out of place in a commercial atmosphere).

A fitting close to MELCHOR's biography is his following outspoken statement, which well sums up the feelings of the purists concerning the modern flamenco guitar trend:

"The flamenco guitar, in its great advance in virtuosity, is losing its vitality and soul. As such, it is becoming a great big, fancy nothing!"

LUIS MARAVILLA

(c. 1914 —

One of flamenco's finer guitarists is Sevilla-born LUIS LÓPEZ TEJERA "LUIS MARAVILLA". A half-century old, LUIS has been playing professionally for thirty-eight years, and in that time has become one of flamenco's most knowledgeable accompanists and soloists.

LUIS particularly excels in accompanying. He accompanies with ease, leading the singer or dancer beautifully but subtly, never competing. His style of playing is melodic and flowing, reminding one of days and memories long past, and is full of exquisite, imaginative touches lost to many present-day guitarists in their race towards virtuosity. In his accompanying more than in his solo playing LUIS has known how to develop a controlled virtuosity which conserves and encourages the intrinsic beauty of the guitar. This talent is portrayed particularly well on records in LUIS' accompaniments of Jarrito Montoya, above all in the *cantes de Levante*.

The very qualities described above have prompted some criticism of LUIS. Many critics believe LUIS' playing too beautiful and subtle, not "flamenco enough". This is a valid criticism if they are talking strictly about the gypsy *toques;* LUIS' playing perhaps lacks a bit in the primitivism necessary in these *toques*. However, LUIS' style and temperament are ideally suited for the *toques andaluces*, which he plays with exceptional feeling and *duende*.

The son of the non-gypsy *cantaor*, Niño de las Marianas, LUIS began his career known as "Marianas hijo" (son of Marianas), later adopting his present artistic name. When only eight years old LUIS decided to surprise his father, and secretly began learning the guitar under the tutelage of Marcelo Molina, a *tocaor* who was a close friend of the family. When LUIS revealed his newly-acquired skill, his father was indeed surprised and not a little delighted. LUIS had made such rapid progress that by the age of twelve he was ready to make his first professional appearance, which was in none other than the famous 1926 *Llave de Oro* Contest of the *Cante*, in Madrid. Two years later LUIS won the "*Copa de Oro* Ramón Montoya" in a guitar contest in Madrid's Teatro de la Zarzuela, and was on his way in the flamenco world.

After playing about Spain for several years, LUIS, in 1932, traveled to Buenos Aires, where he met and married his wife, the dancer Pilar Calvo. They formed a company and toured America, ending up in New York in 1936, where they waited out the Spanish Civil War. Upon returning to Spain LUIS played for most of the famous singers and dancers of the day, remaining the longest with the Company of Pilar López (1946-1956). Among the many highlights of his active professional career, two in particular stand out for LUIS: his playing the lead guitar in the movie "*Duende y Misterio del Flamenco*" (in English called only "Flamenco"), and the 1952 French prize for the best record of the year ("*Penas y Alegrías de Andalucía*", singer Pepe Valencia, guitarist LUIS MARAVILLA).

LUIS also has a very active interest in the classical guitar, having studied three years with Miguel Llobet. However, it will never replace flamenco for him. To quote LUIS: "I enjoy the classical guitar greatly, but my first love will always be flamenco. Flamenco's excitement and *duende* have never become lost to me."

Presently LUIS is semi-retired from professional flamenco life. He tired of the constant travel and late hours, and after leaving the company of Pilar López, in 1956, he opened his own guitar shop in Madrid, where he teaches, and sells guitars and other accessories. He does, however, accept occasional playing commitments when they are especially attractive to him,

TRIGUITO

(c. 1914 —

I have admired JUAN GONZÁLEZ "TRIGUITO" (Sprig of Wheat) since first seeing him perform in La Zambra some years ago. He is a guitarist who truly enjoys his art. As he accompanies the *cuadro grande* his playing is serene enough until the performance of one of the *cuadro* particularly inspires him. Then he becomes like a man possessed: his eyes light up, and he perches on the edge of his chair, thoroughly alert. Lightning movements of his guitar mark rhythmical accentuations, he smiles, frowns, bobs, weaves, but somehow suppresses his obvious desire to leap to his feet and join the dancer. He is a man, I am sure, who rarely becomes bored with his art.

TRIGUITO, Sevilla-born, part gypsy, has long been considered one of flamenco's top accompanists. By the age of ten he was tagging after flamenco's finest singers in Sevilla, listening and absorbing, learning the *cante* and *baile* as well as the *toque*, as he knew a good accompanist must. Not long after he was earning his living in the highly competitive world of flamenco.

"Don't think flamenco then was like it is now," he muses. "Now the academy-trained youngsters, with or without talent, can find work in any number of clubs or *tablaos*. In the old days only those of us who truly loved, and lived, our art lasted long as professionals. There were almost no commercial flamenco places, and we had to rely entirely on *juergas*, going from *venta* to *venta* and fair to fair. And artistically we had to produce. ¡Vaya! The *señoritos* in those days knew more about flamenco than most of the artists. They used to call seven or eight of us into a room and test us. Those of us who knew what we were about stayed, the others were dismissed as incompetents. Not like today, when a singer can sing a *rumba* and a *fandango* and walk away with a thousand pesetas. Today, in fact, the *señoritos* and public in general actually prefer *rumbas* to *siguiriyas* and *soleares*. How times change!

"Back around the late 1920's and early 1930's some of the best flamenco activity was down on the coast — Málaga, Algeciras, La Línea — and I used to spend long periods of time in that area. I'll never forget one fabulous gypsy singer from La Línea, called Macandé (born in Cádiz — c. 1887-1942). Fabulous, that is, during his periods of lucidity, for he was almost completely insane. *Señoritos* used to wait for the news that Macandé had cleared up, and then start an impromptu *juerga* that would usually last until Macandé clouded over again. How that man sang! And what trouble he got into when the craziness hit him!

"One time in Málaga various of us artists were in the home of a *señorito*, all sitting around in a little house built of wine crates in the middle of his living room. I imagine that sounds strange. The wine crates were a favorite way of limiting the length of a *juerga*. It lasted until all of the wine from the crates was consumed, which sometimes took a week or more. People left once in a while to sober up, and then returned, and new artists and *aficionados* would keep coming to liven things up. At any rate, Macandé was there, and began having an attack. He would get a wild look in his eyes, which was a signal to leave him alone; at those times he rarely recognized anyone, and was liable to be violent.

"This particular time he attached two razor blades to a piece of wood, and went out looking for some imaginary enemy. Around the streets of Málaga he went, brandishing his makeshift weapon, until a *guardia* was finally called. The *guardia* demanded that Macandé give him the weapon, but Macandé became very coy and hid it behind his back, like a child. This infuriated the *guardia*, and he took Macandé to the station to teach him a little respect. We found out about it, however, and rushed over before the proceedings began.

"'This is Macandé, the *cantaor*,' we told the police.

"Their attitude immediately changed.

"'You mean the famous one, from La Línea.'

"'The very one.'

"They turned to Macandé: 'You had better be Macandé, and you had better sing damn well.'

"Macandé got the point, and started singing *por siguiriyas*.

The *guardias* listened in astonishment. When Macandé had finished they implored, not demanded, that he continue singing. Wine was brought, and by the end of the evening the *guardias* all chipped in and gave Macandé a goodly amount of *pesetas*, together with their blessings.

"Another time we were in a little town in the mountains behind La Línea, waiting to perform in a little theater. Much to our distress, Macandé began getting his wild look, and soon went off looking for his eternal enemy, who turned out to be no less than a sergeant of the *guardia civil*. Before we knew what he was up to, Macandé maneuvered across the *plaza* and up to where the sergeant was sitting reading his newspaper. With a triumphant swoop Macandé tore the paper from the hands of the bewildered sergeant, and began vigorously cussing him out for some imaginary wrong he had done. The sergeant looked confused for a moment, but quickly recovered. Before we had time to intervene the sergeant had picked Macandé clean off the ground with one burly hand, and was carrying him off to the commissary. Needless to say, he had blood in his eye.

"Up we finally rushed:

"'Sergeant, sergeant, this is Macandé el Loco. He's having an attack of craziness.'

"'Macandé the *cantaor*, from La Línea?'

"'The very one.'

"Then we went through much the same as we had the other time in Málaga. Macandé sang, and the anger of the police changed to respect, and then to amazement. Macandé was ultimately given a handsome present, and escorted to the theater.

"Had Macandé been sane, or at least a little more so, he could have made fortunes and been famous. As it was, he couldn't have cared less about either. Sometimes he would throw his earnings away, off bridges and such, as if the money was contaminating him. He finally died, completely crazy, in an insane asylum (1), leaving behind his mute wife and two mute children."

---

(1) Rafael el Aguila (the Eagle), a fine guitarist from Jerez, was interned in the same asylum in Cádiz as Macandé during part of Macandé's stay. The two brought off some fine flamenco, according to attendents and visiting friends.

TRIGUITO was just getting warmed up.

"In Málaga I used to play a lot for Manuel Torre, also a very eccentric man, but completely normal alongside of Macandé.

"Manuel loved Málaga, and had many good friends and admirers there. Sometimes on a whim he would run down to Málaga from Sevilla on the train, no small journey, as you know. Once I remember that he made the trip just to pick up a canary and two balls of cheese, of a special kind that he liked. Sometimes, if nothing was going on, he would go back that very night on the train. Usually, though, he would be kept there in continuous *juerga* for days and maybe even weeks.

"I remember once, in 1932, shortly before Manuel died, when we performed in the *plaza de toros* of Vélez-Málaga, during their fair. The public was quite a bit more demonstrative then, and, much to everyone's amazement, they actually started rioting over one of Manuel's verses that went:

Engarzá en oro y marfil	Mounted in gold and ivory
cruz que tú llevas al cuello,	the cross you wear at your
engarzá en oro y marfil,	[throat
déjame abrazarme a ella	mounted in gold and ivory
y después crucificarme a mí.	let me embrace it
	and afterwards be crucified...

"The people were then violently anti-religious, and the effect of Manuel's *copla* was instantaneous. The crowds thought that Manuel was preaching to them, and they came pouring out of the stands to get him. The guards poured into the ring to stop them. In the meantime Manuel and I crawled underneath the platform and waited it out.

"Manuel said once: 'Triguito, crawl out and see how things are going.'

"I was young, but not that young: 'Crawl out yourself, *sin vergüenza.*'

"Crowds were really tough then. When they didn't like a singer they would literally boo him off stage. They didn't necessarily have good taste, but they knew what they liked. I often got stuck with a singer called El Americano, who sang terribly. We never lasted more than three minutes, and back to the corner bar. In fact, it got to the point that singers would purposely sing badly so as to spend less time performing.

"Manuel Torre ... ¡qué tío! Manuel never went looking for *juergas*, the *señoritos* always went for him. When he was uninspired, as was usually the case, the *señoritos* would look for a solution:

"'Manuel, whom do you want us to call?'

"More often than not Manuel would ask for a half-crazy gypsy singer from Utrera called Araujo, who imitated Manuel's *cante*. This man had the ability to turn Manuel on because he imitated Manuel so badly. Finally Manuel would have to break in:

"'That's not how it goes, Araujo. It's like this...'

"And, if we were lucky, Manuel would be off. Araujo was considered really rare, mainly because he had the nerve to imitate Manuel's *cante* in the presence of the *maestro*. In fact, there was a refrain that went: 'One has to be *loco* to attempt to imitate Manuel Torre'. It simply was, and is, impossible.

"The Andalusian flamencos in those days threw every cent they earned into drink, gambling, women, and *juergas*, and therefore rarely had money for such non-essentials as clothing, shoes, and such. Even Manuel Torre went around in old clothes and *alpargatas*. There were exceptions, however, most notably don Antonio Chacón and Ramón Montoya.

"They still tell of the *fiesta* given by don Alvaro Domecq in his *bodega* in Jerez. When it came time for the entertainment the people began looking around for the flamenco performers — they could always be spotted in such a gathering by their tattered clothing. This time they were fooled, however, for there was Chacón, seated next to don Alvaro, looking every bit a rich banker in his elegant dinner clothes, with diamonds on his fingers that had been causing much awed whispering. And Ramón, similarly dressed. The people, when they found out that these were the flamenco entertainers, were dumbfounded, and even more so when Chacón commenced singing in perfect Castilian Spanish.

"However, not even Chacón could beat the System. He died in complete poverty."

Triguito went on to say that Pepe Marchena was largely responsible for raising the standard of living of the professional flamencos. He was the first to begin organizing theatrical shows, during the years 1922-1930, which laid the groundwork for the increasingly ample employment and higher wages now enjoyed by flamenco artists. This movement, of course, also caused the decadence and decline of the pure art of flamenco, and caused much of the color of the old flamenco way of life to disappear. The phrase about "can't have your cake and eat it too" seems to pretty well apply here.

Triguito has spent the past eight years in La Zambra, the lead guitarist in the large *cuadro*. He is a guitarist who believes that accompanying well is the ultimate in flamenco, although he also admires well-phrased solos that "say something". Niño Ricardo, he believes, is sublime among the present-day moderns.

Triguito resides with his family in an apartment near Madrid's *rastro* section.

JUAN GARCIA DE LA MATA

(c. 1920 —

Juan García de la Mata is a talented guitarist accomplished in both the classical and flamenco fields. He formerly taught the classical guitar in Madrid's conservatory of music, while earning most of his livelihood from his flamenco playing.

I last heard Juan several years ago when he was the featured guitarist of Rosario's Ballet, in which he played, movingly and well, both classical and flamenco solos, as well as accompanying Rosario's dancing. His playing is of the modern style.

Some time ago Juan moved to New York, where he still resides. As of this writing he is the featured guitarist in the flamenco room of the Chateau Madrid, in New York. He is also one of New York's more popular guitar instructors.

MORAITO DE JEREZ AND MORAITO CHICO

Perhaps the outstanding brother team of flamenco guitarists today is MANUEL MORENO "MORAÍTO DE JEREZ" and JUAN MORENO "MORAÍTO CHICO". Gypsy sons of a Jerez *cantaor* known as El Morao, both brothers acquired their guitar foundation from one of the finest guitarists flamenco has known, Javier Molina.

"Dynamic" is the word to describe older brother, MANUEL MORENO. He has a drive and force in his playing equalled by few, a superior sense of the *compás*, and is well-advanced technically. In fact, MANUEL is one of today's outstanding virtuosos and *tocaores*.

If anything, MANUEL has just the opposite problem from that of Pepe Martínez. While Pepe is overly subtle and refined, MANUEL is just too unceasingly dynamic. His playing is oftentimes very similar to that of Melchor de Marchena, except that MANUEL largely lacks the subtle touches and changes of expression contained in Melchor's playing. This forceful trait, however, helps make MORAÍTO's playing truly distinctive. That, combined with his creative ability, has given MORAÍTO his *"propio sello"*.

In listening to MORAÍTO's playing it has occurred to me that he has drawn inspiration from two little-tapped sources: Diego del Gastor (especially in many of his *bulerías falsetas*) and Manolo de Huelva. Many of MORAÍTO's playing traits are reminiscent of those of Huelva — his gypsy starts and stops, and unusual manipulations of the *compás*. Although his playing is dissimilar in many ways, MORAÍTO can perhaps be singled out as today's guitarist whose playing most closely resembles that of Huelva.

However, MORAÍTO falls down in the area where Huelva truly excels: accompanying. Although MORAÍTO is a knowledgeable accompanist of both the *cante* and the *baile*, his accompanying contains one major fault; he finds it difficult to take a back seat to the singer or the dancer, and often commits the ultimate sin of overshadowing them. This makes it difficult for everyone concerned, for a guitarist that is not subordinate to the leading element will detract from the performance as a whole. In the *cante* it is often difficult for the *cantaor* to find an opening until MORAÍTO decides that he is through playing *falsetas*, and when he should fall into the background he far too frequently plays loudly and forcefully. When accompanying Antonio in a solo dance MORAÍTO becomes so complex in his accompaniment that it becomes necessary to follow either him or Antonio; perhaps what he is playing at the time is interesting or beautiful, but it definitely detracts from Antonio's performance. MORAÍTO simply seems by nature to be a soloist, not an accompanist.

In his early forties, MORAÍTO is first guitarist with Antonio's ballet. When not on tour, he can often be found in Pastora Imperio's El Duende.

Younger brother JUAN MORENO, in his late thirties, is less accomplished and dynamic than MANUEL, but nonetheless a knowledgeable and forceful guitarist. I do not believe that he has pretentions of virtuosity, and perhaps because of this is better able to mix subtlety into his playing. He does not seem to possess, however, the genius potential of his brother.

JUAN presently plays second guitar with Antonio's ballet.

Both brothers can be heard in accompanying roles, together with Melchor de Marchena and Antonio Arenas, on London Records' "An Anthology of *Cante Flamenco*".

MARIO ESCUDERO

(c. 1931 —

MARIO ESCUDERO ranks as one of the four or five top guitar technicians in flamenco today. A student of Niño Ricardo, ESCUDERO has surpassed his *maestro* in fingerboard agility, although he falls far short of Ricardo's maturity of expression and creativity. Other than RICARDO, the major modern influence in MARIO's playing is Sabicas; in moments of certain *toques* he is Sabicas personified.

Born in Alicante, ESCUDERO joined the flamenco movement to America some years ago, and has there remained, making his headquarters in Los Angeles. In America, particularly in California, MARIO has acquired a devoted following in whose eyes he is the *capitán general* of flamenco. I shall tell a curious and thought-provoking story about one member of this devout group who came to Spain a while back playing a respectable guitar *a la* MARIO, looked me up, and more or less asked me just what was all this bull about old-time flamenco, *duende*, and such. He obviously did not believe a word of it, but nevertheless wanted to satisfy any doubt in his mind. Together we heard a little Manolo de Huelva, we put on all of Melchor's discs, and then he went south to take in a little of the atmosphere around Sevilla, more particularly Diego del Gastor and a few others. He came back a changed man, stating that he was just beginning to understand flamenco for the first time. His parting words about MARIO: "An excellent guitarist, but born to play classical music." He went on to express his new-found belief, in fact, that compared to the flamenco to which he had been newly introduced, nearly all of the flamencos whom he formerly admired were nothing but frustrated classical guitarists.

MARIO's most famous *toque* is, perhaps, the *granainas*. While writing this I am listening to two of the recorded versions that I have of his *granainas*, one a solo on Esoteric records (the record also contains El Pili, Alberto Vélez, etc.), the other accompanying El Niño de Almadén on AAMCO. MARIO's solo playing shows excellent technique as he races through an interesting arpeggio exercise and tremolo, then further increases speed and leads us, breathless, through some impressive thumb work; towards the end of his solo MARIO finally slows down and begins to express something, which expression is only too quickly snuffed out by a pounding *picado* which gallops us across the finish line. Exhausting! (Incidently, the *granainas,* in most circles, is a relatively profound lament, one of the slower, more serious *toques* of flamenco). On the record accompanying Almadén, MARIO injects a little more soul into his playing, held down by the necessity of staying with the singer. He accompanies well, and the *cante* comes off very nicely.

The obvious conclusion from these examples, and others that could be pointed out, is that MARIO, together with nearly all of the virtuosos, needs someone or something to subject him to some kind of reasonable playing, or his hands simply seem to run away with him.

MARIO, to date, has remained true to his style of flamenco in that he has not, to my knowledge, 1) superimposed three guitars (Sabicas), 2) played with a jazz combo background (Carlos Montoya), 3) cut flamenco impressions of New York, or any other city (J. Serrano), 4) played flamenco with a full orchestral background (Sabicas), 5) played concerts of one-quarter flamenco, three-quarters folk-popular-classical-flamenco (Sabicas, Carlos Montoya), and so forth. It is said, however, that at one time MARIO did experiment with a completely new style of flamenco guitar-playing, which was not accepted and which he quickly dropped.

Perhaps the only thing MARIO, and many another like him, needs is a graduate school refresher course in basic flamenco concepts, given some place deep in Andalusia far from the demands and pressure of modern life. It had better be soon, however, before all of the qualified instructors, and the basic flamenco concepts, die out!

ALBERTO VELEZ

ALBERTO VÉLEZ, not included in "The Art of Flamenco's" leading concert guitarist list through an oversight, is without a doubt one of flamenco's outstanding concert-style guitarists. Born in Huelva of non-gypsy parents, VÉLEZ began his career as a classical guitarist, and only turned seriously to flamenco with his marriage to a flamenco dancer. The VÉLEZ' have formed their own troupe, and spend most of their time on tour outside of Spain.

JUANITO SERRANO

1988 Update: (1936 —

JUANITO SERRANO has risen from a one-time shoeshine boy in Córdoba to one of flamenco's most accomplished virtuosos. Born in Córdoba, JUAN learned the guitar fundamentals from his father, also a guitarist. Within Spain rumors began circulating as far back as 1955 about the promising playing of young JUAN, and soon JUAN set out to Madrid and other points to show what he could do.

He proved to be no farce, and soon established his reputation as one of the fastest guitars on the Peninsula.

This qualified JUAN to participate in the joys of money-money land, and two or three years ago he set out for New York. Although the United States is studded with virtuosos and competition is stiff, JUAN enjoyed one triumph after another, proving himself not only one of the fastest guitars on the Peninsula, but among the fastest in the world. Soon there was talk of Sabicas and JUAN; JUAN and Sabicas.

It is there, however, that the line must be drawn. True, JUAN might possibly prove to be a potential Sabicas, but he still has to pass through various phases before reaching Sabicas' maturity of expression within the concert style (referring, of course, to the serious playing of each). JUAN in his playing is still a rash youth as compared to Sabicas, and needs considerable mellowing and experience.

JUAN is bound to be a monetary success, as he has proven himself ready to cooperate with sundry Madison Avenue gimmicks. Example: his second stateside record featuring Autumn Leaves and other "flamenco impressions of New York". On personal appearances he is also not above such bad taste, and has thereby qualified to join flamenco's exclusive Marzy Doats Club, main offices in New York.

I am sorry to say, in summation, that JUAN SERRANO appears to be just another extremely talented guitarist in danger of being carried by the System, and the times, beyond any flamenco of great worth.

THE YOUNGER SET

It is difficult and risky to single out young guitarists. Their styles tend to change frequently, they lose or gain stature with bewildering rapidity. In view of this, I shall limit myself to discussing three of the most promising.

PACO DEL GASTOR
(c. 1944 —

Who is going to carry on the Morón de la Frontera guitar tradition when Diego del Gastor is gone? Will the tradition, in the past century perpetuated by such guitarists as Paco Lucena, El Niño de Morón, Pepe Naranjo, and presently Diego del Gastor, run itself out in this day of disappearing regionalism?

It will surely seem so to many *aficionados* unless they have been exposed to the playing of one dedicated gypsy youth, twenty-year-old FRANCISCO GÓMEZ AMAYA "PACO DEL GASTOR", nephew and star pupil of Diego del Gastor. PACO is already playing extremely well, with a hard-driving, gypsy style, and advanced technical ability highlighted by one of the fastest thumbs in the business. His *compás* is excellent; he can weave in difficult counter-rhythms with a natural ease with which one must be born.

Diego del Gastor is not the only influence in PACO's playing. Like all young guitarists in Spain, PACO plays many spiny Ricardo creations, and has also enthusiastically embraced the latest fountain of inspiration within Spain, Sabicas phonograph records. In fact, it is almost certain that PACO would sound like just so many other young guitarists except for one big advantage: he has the great good fortune of being the nephew of Diego del Gastor, not just in name, but in spirit and in much of his playing style (although PACO has a tendency to be much flashier than Diego due to the modern influences). Diego is always there to calm PACO down when he returns to Morón from months-long engagements; to say to him, after a dazzling performance on some *toque:* "*Bien,* now let's see if you can put some meaning into that." PACO tries, and being honest, has to admit that he has lost it, that all of his dazzling playing had, in the bottom, been meaningless. But as the days pass in Diego's presence, it comes back, and before long PACO is again a magnificent mixture of the modern and the traditional and, what is more important, he is again playing with *duende*.

PACO's father, a brother of Diego del Gastor, is also a guitarist of some renown known as Francisco "el Mellizo".

EMILIO DE DIEGO

(c. 1944 —

EMILIO DE DIEGO, a young non-gypsy from Madrid, is gifted with an intense style of playing that immediately singles him out from the noise-makers. He knows instinctively what the *toque* should be, and at present is following his instinct beautifully. When accompanying, above all, EMILIO's playing is full of unpretentious *duende*.

EMILIO has the knack of making his playing sound original; not so much in what he plays, but in how he plays it. His playing emphasizes an important point so little understood by aspiring guitarists: that almost any *falseta*, no matter how seemingly mediocre or worn from use, can come alive if it is only played properly. The material of many virtuosos, which rushes by unheeded like the babbling water of streams, *can* be made significant. All it takes is slowing it down, and inserting something of silence, soul, and *cojones*. Easier said than done, to be sure, judging by the trivia that engulfs us.

EMILIO is largely self-taught, having spent only one year with Patena in formal instruction. Just returned to Spain after spending two years with José Greco's troupe, EMILIO has been immediately snapped up as the prized accompanist of the dancer Antonio Gades.

PACO DE ALGECIRAS

1988 Update: (Dec. 21, 1947 —

If the 1962 Jerez flamenco contest accomplished anything it was the introduction to the public of the brothers Pepe (see *cante* section) and PACO DE ALGECIRAS. Both brothers won well-deserved prizes, PACO's the award given to the outstanding guitar *aficionado* of the contest (the contest was divided into professionals and amateurs). Shortly after the contest, far-sighted José Greco contracted the boys, and they are now with the Greco troupe on tour.

PACO's playing was already well-advanced, showing great promise for the future. He accompanied with knowledge and feeling, and his technique was clear and sharp.

PACO's instructor has been his father, an exceptional *aficionado* equally adept at teaching the guitar (PACO), the *cante* (Pepe), and the *baile* (others of the family).

Barring a boyish shift of interests, PACO will definitely be among the leading flamenco guitarists in the decades to come.

VARIOUS

There have been, and are, many other accomplished flamenco guitarists. A biography of each would be cumbersome, and is unnecessary in fulfilling the purpose of this book; those already discussed have played the most historical roles in the development of the flamenco guitar, or have best served to illustrate certain points and trends.

Here space can be allotted, however, for a brief mention of some of the deserving guitarists who have not been discussed to this point.

Fernando de Triana talked well of a *café cantante* guitarist named *el maestro* BAUTISTA, of whom little is known, and of a guitarist popular in the 1920's and 1930's, SALVADOR BALLESTEROS. Around this same period we could mention MANUEL BONET and PATENA PADRE, and today his son, PATENA HIJO.

PEPE EL CALDERERO, non-gypsy, seventies, from Málaga, is an old-style accompanist of great feeling. Pepe often played second guitar to Manolo de Huelva, and thus managed to pick up something of Manolo's *toque*.

SEBASTIÁN NÚÑEZ, non-gypsy, sixties, from Jerez, has been a leading guitarist, and guitar instructor, in the Jerez scene for years. Sebastián was a great friend of Javier Molina, and plays many of Javier's creations, as well as a great deal of old-time accompaniments of the *cante* and *baile* nearly forgotten today.

EL NIÑO DE ALMERÍA, a half-blind gypsy in his fifties, is a little-known guitarist who plays a fine *jondo* guitar. He particularly excels at accompanying. Born in the province of Almería, he is a long-time resident of Málaga.

RAFAEL NOGALES spent some years as Antonio's featured guitarist, among other activities in his many years as a professional, before retiring to Madrid to teach and play local engagements. I last saw Rafael play in a Madrid recital in which he accompanied Pepe de la Matrona, a difficult task due to Pepe's wide knowledge of the *cante* and exacting demands from his accompanist. As they were unrehearsed there were rough spots, but in general Rafael stayed with Pepe fairly well, and played with an emotion I did not suspect he possessed. A non-gypsy, middle-aged, Rafael's *toque* is a combination of modern and old, making much use of his thumb. Among his many students his favorite has been MARIANO DE CÓRDOBA, today one of the better guitarists and instructors in the San Francisco, California area.

PACO AGUILERA, non-gypsy, around fifty, from Barcelona, is a popular accompanist today whose thumb-driven, down-to-earth style of playing affords happy relief from the razzle-dazzle. Singers and dancers prefer him to many others because he does not compete, and because his playing, relatively simple, has a truly *jondo* ring to it. Paco has a son who is a dancer.

ARACELI VARGAS, gypsy, is an extremely knowledgeable accompanist of the *cante*.

EDUARDO DE LA MALENA, named after his famous gypsy aunt, the dancer La Malena, is one of the few *juerga* guitarists of category left in Sevilla, excelling particularly in accompanying. His playing, an interesting mixture of old and modern, has been strongly influenced by Niño Ricardo. In his middle thirties, Eduardo was a featured guitarist for a time with the ballet of Antonio, but found that he prefers to remain closer to Sevilla and his family of twelve. Eduardo lives in Sevilla's traditional flamenco district, La Alameda de Hércules.

PACO DE LA ISLA, non-gypsy, thirties, from the Isla de San Fernando, is a strong accompanist and soloist presently sparking the small *cuadro* in Madrid's La Zambra.

EUGENIO GONZÁLEZ, fifties, has a fine reputation as a guitarist and an instructor. He presently resides in Madrid.

HABICHUELA, non-gypsy, thirties, from Granada, is a sound guitarist, the preferred of the singer Fosforito. He is not related to the old-time Habichuela.

JUAN EL AFRICANO, non-gypsy, thirties, is perhaps Málaga's most advanced virtuoso. Juan's playing is polished but moving, and he is developing into a fine accompanist.

ANTONIO ARENAS, non-gypsy, thirties, from Ceuta, is a respected accompanist in the Madrid flamenco world. He played for an extended period in the Corral de la Morería, is on records accompanying the reciter, Gabriela Ortega, and others.

JUAN MAYA, gypsy, twenties, from Granada, is a highly-accomplished guitarist presently playing in Madrid's Torres Bermejas.

ANDRÉS HEREDIA is a well-considered gypsy accompanist, having been featured to date in two anthologies of the *cantes de Cádiz*, among other records. He has an easy, moving style of playing, beautifully lyrical although at times lacking in force.

MANOLO ROJAS, non-gypsy, twenties, from Sevilla's *barrio de Triana*, is an up-and-coming modern-style flamenco and classical guitarist who will be heard from in the future.

The following guitarists, all of whom play in a similar concert style, play largely outside of Spain: BERNABÉ DE MORÓN, gypsy, forties, from Morón de la Frontera, played for some years in the San Diego — Los Angeles area before moving over to Florida; Barcelona-born *Sarasate,* non-gypsy, thirties, is presently playing, singing, and dancing in the California area; CARLOS RAMOS, non-gypsy, thirties, from the Málaga coast, has played many years in the United States and Canada; MIGUEL GARCÍA spent some years touring the United States with Greco's troupe; ROGELIO REGUERA is presently in the Los Angeles area, as is ADONIS PUERTA; RICARDO BLASCO has spent some years in the United States and England; FERNANDO SIRVENT is New York based; JOAQUÍN GÓMEZ and ANTONIO NAVARRO dominate the flamenco guitar scene in London; and so on and so forth.

ARTS WITHIN THE ART

The three major arts within flamenco are, of course, the song, dance, and guitar. They are not the only ones, however. For instance, there is the *jaleo*, an essential part of flamenco, which consists of hand-clapping (*palmas*), finger-snapping (*pitos*), tongue-clacking, foot punctuations, finger-nail snapping, and timely shouts of encouragement. The *jaleo*, properly done, is truly complex and extremely difficult. Good *jaleadores* are highly-respected and much sought after.

Generally, however, the *jaleadores* are unsung heroes, and rarely achieve lasting fame. One exception to this was a colorful *jaleador* called El Militi.

EL MILITI used to enter a tavern or *venta*, set himself up in a corner with a bottle of wine, and launch into an astounding display of *palmas, pitos,* and tongue-clacks that sounded like a full orchestra. He made his living in this manner, and achieved lasting fame with his difficult art.

I shall now discuss three present-day artists who are proponents of unusual arts within flamenco: Gabriela Ortega, José María Peña, and Arturo Pavón.

GABRIELA ORTEGA

(c. 1919 —

GABRIEL ORTEGA, a credit to the illustrious Ortega family (see biography of Manolo Caracol and Ortega family chart), has reigned for years as flamenco's outstanding reciter of a type of Spanish poetry which deals with the flamenco way of life: the bulls, gypsies, flamenco, Andalusia...

GABRIELA has a flair for reciting that is at once highly dramatic and truly moving. Besides an impressive gift for words, GABRIELA is capable of sparking her reciting with snatches of dances or *cantes*, in which branches of flamenco she is extremely well-grounded. She usually recites to the *compás* of a guitar, and some of her dancing, particularly in the gayer vein, is highly electric.

The last opportunity I had to see GABRIELA was the most impressive. It was at John Fulton Short's Madrid exhibition of bullfight-inspired paintings (Spring 1964), which featured John's excellent pictorical interpretations of the four parts of García Lorca's *"Llanto por Ignacio Sánchez Mejías"* (1). The poems and pictures both dealt beautifully with the tragic bull ring death of Sánchez Mejías, and GABRIELA's reciting before the paintings, to the guitar *compases* of *soleares, siguiriyas, tarantos,* and *peteneras*, made the occasion overwhelmingly impressive. That GABRIELA had been Sánchez Mejías' niece by marriage undoubtedly added to her profound interpretations.

GABRIELA lightened the atmosphere by finishing her performance with a gay poem, to the *compás* of the *alegrías de Cádiz*. If her Sánchez Mejías recitals had been almost oppressively profound, her reciting and dancing in this poem were sparkling and infectious. GABRIELA had us in the palms of her hands, and could do what she wanted with us. How fine flamenco can be when interpreted by the truly inspired!

GABRIELA, gypsy-born in Sevilla, has performed widely, a great deal with her cousin, Manolo Caracol, and often in conjunction with other fine artists, including a recent tour with Antonio Mairena. She has spent several long periods of time outside of Spain, principally in Mexico.

---

(1) John Fulton Short, America's only active *matador de toros*, has also distinguished himself in his portrayals of bull ring topics. His paintings of bulls and bull scenes, done in actual bull's blood (which dries to a beautiful rust color), have particularly impressed both art critics and bullfight *aficionados*. Incidently, John also dances flamenco in an unschooled but promising manner. «Juan,» say impressed Spaniards, «must have Spanish blood in him somewhere!»

Various fine records are available of GABRIELA's reciting to guitar accompaniment, including her excellent renditions of several of García Lorca's "*Romancero Gitano*" poems.

GABRIELA has recently turned authoress, and is presently completing a book dealing with the Ortega family. She is residing in Madrid.

JOSE MARIA PEÑA

(c. 1923 —

José María Peña, the "Poet of the Hands", stands out due to his unusual contribution to flamenco; he is perhaps today's leading exponent of rapping out *compases*, with his fingers, knuckles, fists ,and open palms of his hands, on sturdy wooden tables. This may sound facetious, but must be seriously considered. It is an art at once difficult, moving, and flamenco, stemming from the primitive method of keeping the *compás* when guitars were not available. Other than José María, Vicente Escudero and Carmen Amaya also developed this exciting facet of flamenco into a fine art.

Born in San Fernando (Cádiz) of non-artistic gypsy parents, José María began his flamenco life as a *bailaor*, an art which he still takes very seriously. As a youth he learned the trade of barber, which has proved valuable to him from time to time.

At the age of eighteen José María left Cádiz for the more active artistic life of Barcelona, and there remained many years engaged in various occupations: dancing, giving increasingly polished performances with his hands, and being the owner of a barber shop. In 1959 José María joined the company of Lola Flores, and for the first time his art of the hands was enjoyed by the general public. After a year with Lola Flores, José María returned to Barcelona to open a flamenco tavern, which occupied his time for three years until one fateful day someone suggested that they had been working too hard and needed a vacation. José María promptly sold his tavern for the equivalent of $125 in order to finance the trip, and off they went.

That rash act proved to be a turning point in José María's life. While "vacationing" in Madrid, José María was befriended by the owner of a *tablao*, and was taken in as a featured performer. There he enjoyed great success with the art of his hands, although his commercial possibilities were questionable. Many were the nights when José María simply refused to act because of lack of inspiration, or stalked off stage in a huff because someone in the audience dared to talk during his performance.

It was around that time that José María tapped still another resource. Overnight he became a painter of surrealistic pictures full of gypsy symbolism, which today is his chief occupation.

Perhaps the highlight of José María's artistic life was his performance in the Italian movie "Marvelous Cities of the World", in which he rapped out a *siguiriyas, soleares* and other rhythms to the accompaniment of three guitarists against the background of Granada. An interesting addition to the scene was a *bailaora* shrouded in nothing other than gypsy symbolism. Needless to say, the movie has not been shown in Spain, and chances are that José María will never see the finished product.

ARTURO PAVON

(c. 1932 —

Arturo's is an unusual case, unique in the history of flamenco. A member of the illustrious Pavón family of gypsies — nephew of singers Pastora Pavón "la Niña de los Peines" and Tomás Pavón, son of singer Arturo Pavón and dancer Eloísa Albéniz — Arturo inherited the family talents and temperament, and naturally acquired a vast knowledge of all of flamenco's elements as he grew up. Arturo learned how to sing and dance, but his first love became the guitar, for which he showed great aptitude and promise.

But gradually another musical interest overshadowed all others. Arturo found that he could best express himself through the piano. "A flamenco pianist. *Vaya*, what next?," proclaims the entire flamenco world. Until, that is, they hear Arturo play. For Arturo's playing, when he wishes and is so inspired, is deeply gypsy and flamenco, his *duende* so evident that even flamenco's hardened cynics find themselves uttering *"olé"*.

Many *aficionados* categorically condemn any instrument in flamenco other than the guitar. I must confess that I am also of this opinion. However, we must accept that ARTURO PAVÓN is another of flamenco's great exceptions, a man capable of molding an art to a new medium of expression, for ARTURO is more profoundly flamenco with his piano than are the vast majority of flamenco guitarists.

ARTURO's gypsy piano playing is extremely reminiscent of Melchor de Marchena's gypsy guitar playing — creativeness, spontaneity, now beautifully lyrical, now with uncontained force, now dredging up the black notes of a *siguiriyas* so emotional, so well phrased, so obviously from the heart that it affords the *aficionado* a rare glimpse of true *jondo* flamenco. In ARTURO's case it is not the medium of expression that counts, but the flamenco genius, *duende*, and knowledge that flow from his chosen instrument.

ARTURO is married to Luisa Ortega, a singer of popular Spanish songs, daughter of Manolo Caracol. He can presently be heard in his father-in-law's Los Canasteros, in Madrid, where his playing comes through surprisingly well considering the night club atmosphere of the club.

CONTENTS

1988 UPDATE

MAIN BODY

INTRODUCTION	331
THE PROVINCE OF CADIZ	333
THE PROVINCE OF SEVILLA	359
THE REST OF ANDALUSIA PLUS TWO	382

Provinces of		
	MALAGA	383
	GRANADA	385
	CORDOBA	388
	ALMERIA	391
	MURCIA	391
	JAEN	393
	HUELVA	394
	BADAJOZ	395

THE REST OF SPAIN		396
	MADRID	397
	BARCELONA	402
	MISCELLANEOUS AREAS	404
THE NON-SPANIARD IN FLAMENCO		408
INDEX		410
INDEX OF SPECIAL SUBJECTS		420
GLOSSARY		421

INTRODUCTION

How to go about this update? Twenty five years have passed since I researched the original edition, years of constant change that I must attempt to document. As I see it, this challenge must be met by the inclusion of three basic categories: a whole new generation of flamencos that have sprung up; the artists that were overlooked the first time; and the mourning of the many revered artists, in the obituary sections, who have passed on to the "land of the great juerga." But how to go about it without the book becoming impossibly cumbersome, a hodgepodge of names and facts? In the first edition, history served as a cohesive theme; flamenco's outstanding artists of days past and their impact on their art was more or less known. In this update, however, in many cases it is too early for accurate historical judgements. Too much could turn out to be guesswork about what could prove to be merely passing trends, both in the art and in the artists' approach to it. In lieu of this, it occurs to me that the most cohesive approach may be to discuss each of flamenco's most important geographic localities, listing the outstanding artists from each, past and present, as well as the type of flamenco traditionally practiced there. This should not only serve as a unifying theme, but is intended to help clarify the subject of flamenco in general.

It seems unlikely that an area as small as Andalusia (roughly the size of Maine, or one-eighth that of Texas, or two-thirds that of England) could change very radically from locality to locality, but it definitely does. As we shall see, entire provinces strongly prefer either gypsy or payo-inspired cante, and even within a small particular area the preferred cantes and general feel for flamenco can vary considerably. For instance, along the province of Cádiz' seacoast the flamenco is far more "salty" (tangy, happy, melodious, lilting) than inland, where the flamenco, and the people tend to be more serious (although still considerably more "tangy" than non-Andalusians). No one can sing the cantes de Cádiz like singers from the port of Cádiz or nearby Isla de San Fernando, not even the artists from Jerez, just fifty kilometers to the north of Cádiz port, and much less so singers from truly inland localities; although inland singers may be equal in ability and knowledge, they simply lack that "salty" something. Conversely, singers from Cádiz port generally cannot conjure up the earthiness inherent in most inland cantes. Each locality prefers its own flamenco forms and has developed its own peculiarities.

My plan, thus, is to open with generalizations about each locality I discuss, followed by an obituary section and continuing with today's outstanding artists. It should be understood that many of the artists discussed no longer live in their home towns. Many have moved to where they can better make a living (Madrid, above all), or for some other reason. But one can almost depend on their continuing preference for the flamenco forms of their youth, although too often in a far more stylized and sophisticated manner. A general rule seems to be that the further one strays from his place of formation, above all to more cosmopolitan areas, the more one's art loses in tradition and takes on more national-international aspects. It follows, thus, that traditional flamenco is found in the provincial areas where it was formed, and that the flamenco found in Madrid and Barcelona (for instance) tends to become more worldly and less pure the longer the artists remain there and the more contact they have with fashionable trends. This is true above all with young, impressionable artists, but by no means exclusive to them.

Recent experiences of mine unfortunately testify to the above argument. I have tolerated El Turronero's renditions of la caña and el polo to the accompaniment of a punk rock group and two sexy go-go dancing girls. I have witnessed La Bernarda de Utrera on stage in Madrid sing only cuplés por bulerías. This is truly sacrilege, for La Bernarda is capable of excellent, meaningful cante. I have watched such excellent flamenco dancers as El Güito and Merche Esmeralda merge flamenco with modern dancing to Emilio de Diego's abstract guitar composition (taped) and the equally as abstract singing of a young cantaor. The guitar composition was interesting if overly repetitious, but the dancing was simply dull and might be crossed off as a not-so-dazzling experiment. What was really maddening is that Güito and Merche, two of today's finest flamenco dancers, were each permitted to dance only one authentic flamenco dance during the entire show. More subtly distressing was the recent performance of Enrique de Melchor, son of the late, great Melchor de Marchena. Enrique, in an accompanying role, proceeded to prove to the audience that he is without a doubt one of flamenco's top guitar virtuosos. He was simply bubbling over with technique, pulling off unbelievably difficult passages with apparent ease. In the process, of course, he completely overshadowed the singers he accompanied, which used to be a major sin for accompanists. Oddly enough, if the singers realized what was happening (they must have) they didn't seem to mind, for Enrique is much in demand as an accompanist. Perhaps the singers are getting used to it, for it is a relatively common practice these days. Lastly, there are the many groups who have incorporated a variety of instruments into their pseudo flamenco efforts. The results may be valid as musical expression, but certainly not as flamenco expression.

During the course of this update I dedicate more space to some artists than to others. This does not necessarily mean I consider them superior to artists who may only receive a one-liner or a name mention, but that: 1) their story is of some special significance or interest; 2) there simply is not enough room to expound at length about everyone; 3) I have more access to the lives of some artists than to others; and/or 4) the artist allotted more space does deserve more space.

Through page 329 this book is largely the same as the original edition. The update begins on P. 330. Page numbers in parentheses signify that the artists in question has been referred to in this book on that page. If the reference refers to another of my books, I shall list the name of the book within the parentheses.

# THE PROVINCE OF CADIZ

with studies of the

PORT OF CADIZ 334

and the following towns,
in alphabetical order:

ALGECIRAS 337

BARBATE 340

CHICLANA 340

JEREZ DE LA FRONTERA 340

LA LINEA DE LA CONCEPCION 355

LA ISLA DE SAN FERNANDO 356

PATERNA DE RIVERA 357

PUERTO DE SANTA MARIA 357

PUERTO REAL 357

SAN ROQUE 357

SANLUCAR DE BARRAMEDA 357

PORT OF CADIZ

In the introduction to the dance section in this book (pps. 173-181) two basic conclusions are arrived at: 1) the flamenco dance descended from the religious dance of the Indian Hindus; 2) the port of Cádiz, one of Spain's oldest cities (p.174), was very probably the port of entry for the Indian dancers hired to entertain the city's royalty during the Greek and/or Roman periods. These dancers were called "bayaderas," a word defined by the Espasa-Calpe dictionary as "Female Indian dancers or singers dedicated to intervene in religious functions, or merely to entertain people."

This signifies, thus, that Cádiz province in general, and the port of Cádiz in particular, were very likely where the first seeds of flamenco began their slow germination. This hypothesis is borne out by the fact that by the second half of the 18th century, when flamenco's poorly documented history begins, all the known singers and dancers of gypsy-oriented flamenco (most, if not all, gypsies) hailed from the fifty-kilometer-long strip of land connecting the port of Cádiz to Jerez de la Frontera. From that small focal point the flamencos fanned out, but principally in a northerly direction, drawn by the thriving city of Sevilla and its gypsy quarter of Triana. There sprang up another hotbed of gyspy artistry and creation, which in turn spread its influence to the rest of the province of Sevilla and further onwards.

But back to the port of Cádiz. One of the earliest known singers from the province of Cádiz, and earliest from the port of Cádiz, was EL PLANETA (p.34), followed not very closely, chronologically speaking, by ENRIQUE EL MELLIZO (p.49), FRANCISCO LA PERLA, PAQUIRRI EL GUANTE, ROMERO EL TITO, DIEGO ANTUNEZ (all p.56), ENRIQUE ORTEGA (p.57), CURRO DULCE (p.57), ANDRES EL LORO (p.57), ANTONIA LA LORO (p.57), and so forth.

The dance in Cádiz port has always been as important as the singing. For instance, the port of Cádiz produced flamenco's first five documented male dancers: MIRACIELOS (p.182), born, it is calculated, around 1800; his student, EL RASPAO (p.182); ENRIQUE EL JOROBAO (p.183); and the father-son combination, ANTONIO EL PINTOR and LAMPARILLA (p.183). Some of the first, and greatest, female dancers were also from Cádiz port, including ROSARIO LA HONRA (p.210), JOSEFITA LA PITRACA (p.210), GABRIELA ORTEGA (p.210), and LA MEJORANA (p.211), all important in the development of the female flamenco dance during the café cantante epoch.

Cádiz port also produced three of flamenco's earliest known guitarists: EL MAESTRO PATIÑO (p.266) and his students, PACO EL BARBERO (p.267) and JUAN GANDULLA "HABICHUELA" (p.270). Since those days Cádiz port has produced no guitarists of major impact, with the possible exceptions of MANUEL PEREZ "EL POLLO", a student of Patiño's who was the preferred accompanist of los Mellizo, and JOSE CAPINETTI, the favorite accompanist of Aurelio Sellé for many years.

TRADITIONAL FLAMENCO FORMS FROM CADIZ PORT.

Alegrías, cantiñas, mirabrás, romeras, tangos, tientos, tanguillos, bulerías, soleares, siguiriyas, martinetes, malagueñas del Mellizo.

OBITUARIES. Singers. Cádiz port.
The port of Cádiz has been hit hard in recent years by the deaths of most of its outstanding singers, as follows:

AURELIO SELLE (p.106), generally considered the finest singer Cádiz has produced since Enrique el Mellizo, died blind and frail in 1974 in his beloved Cádiz. The writer José Blas Vega has recorded many of Aurelio's attitudes, opinions, knowledge and activities in his fine book "Conversaciones Flamencas con Aurelio de Cádiz."

PERICON DE CADIZ (p.123), not far behind Aurelio in artistic prestige, will also be remembered for his marvellous imagination and bubbling sense of humor. Both of the latter traits are generously available in the J.L. Ortiz Nuevo book "Las Mil y Una Historias de Pericón de Cádiz" ("The Thousand and One Stories of Pericón de Cádiz). The book is nearly as hilarious as was Pericón in real life, and has the additional virtue of portraying well the flamenco way of life when a flamenco way of life still existed.

Pericón sang in Madrid's La Zambra until its owner died and its doors were closed, around 1968, if my memory serves me. Then he was able to fulfill his lifetime dream, that of going home and spending his days fishing. He did just that, until his death in 1980, but I cannot say if it was as fulfilling as he dreamed, as I lost contact with him after he left Madrid.

MANUEL VARGAS (p.140), the personification of the spirit of Cádiz, was forced to retire from singing due to a throat illness, from which he subsequently died in the late sixties. Manuel, one of this century's great singers of the cantes de Cádiz, made ends meet in his latter years by running a fried fish establishment in the Madrid *barrio de* Vallecas.

ANTONIO EL FLECHA was not included in the first edition of this book only because I did not know of him at that time, for El Flecha was a fine interpreter of the cantes of Cádiz. He earned his livelihood in the Madrid juerga scene, including many memorable nights at our Madrid flamenco club back in 1964-1965. He died in Madrid in January of 1982.

LA PERLA DE CADIZ (p.160), by far the youngest of this fine quintet, is considered Cádiz' foremost female singer of this, and perhaps any, century. Like El Flecha and Pericón, La Perla also frequented our Madrid flamenco club, but I best remember her singing from an all-night session in the Feria de Sevilla back in the early 1960's. Several of us were in one of the gypsy *casetas* with La Fernanda and La Bernarda de Utrera, sipping drinks and talking, when in walked La Perla with some of her friends from Cádiz. The female artists embraced and then launched into a singing session, without guitar, just rapping out the compás on whatever they could, that went on for the rest of the night. The girls were incredible. The key cante was the bulerías, and all three of them sparkled in her own way. La Perla's effortless, natural manner of singing did not disguise her underlying emotion, and she showed herself to be every bit as great in every way as the famous sisters from Utrera.

La Perla was born Antonia Gilibert Vargas into a family of gypsy flamencos, including her mother, a bulerías specialist who made a living selling potatoes in the local market (and was therefore called Rosa la Papera), her uncle Joseíco, bailaor, her cousin Pablito de Cádiz, bailaor, and many others. At the time of her early death (1925-1975) La Perla had become a revered figure in the world of flamenco.

OBITUARIES. Dancers. Cádiz port.

Cadiz port has always had a colorful supply of juerga-style dancers full of artistic hell and good humor, two of the best of whom have died in recent years: LUIS COMPADRE (1902-1968) and EL BRILLANTINA.

PRESENT-DAY ARTISTS. Cádiz port.

CHANO LOBATO (Juan Ramírez Sarabia; b.1927) is generally considered Cádiz port's most eminent representative of the Cante today, and among the top in the overall world of flamenco. For years he has been recognized as the **best** singer for the dance, a speciality that has taken him around the world with the troupes of Antonio, and Manuela Vargas. In recent years he is receiving belated credit for his fine cantes grandes as well, which are showing him to be a very complete singer.

Chano possesses an abundance of the Cádiz wit and charm, and as such is a quite adequate replacement for the previous masters of same, Manolo Vargas and Pericón de Cádiz. He presently lives in Sevilla, is very active in the festival circuit.

BENI DE CADIZ (Beni Rodríguez Rey; b.1930)(P.169) is an interesting study. If he wished he could be one of today's top singers, but he just doesn't seem to give a damn. If Chano Lobato "possesses an abundance of the Cádiz wit and charm," Beni possesses an over-abundance, which seems to take him beyond any attempt at seriousness. He know a great deal of serious cante (he used to imitate Manolo Caracol nearly to perfection) but will not cease his horsing around even in front of an audience paying to hear him sing seriously. Occasionally he did have serious moments in days past, during one of which he won the National Prize for Cante Flamenco, in Córdoba in 1972. Over the years he has traveled extensively, during long periods with the troupes of Lola Flores, and Antonio, among others.

Today Beni seems content in being one of flamenco's top *festeros* and in having a good time. Perhaps some day he will settle down and take flamenco seriously. Until then, have fun, Beni!

AMOS RODRIGUEZ (1927 -), older brother of Beni de Cádiz and grandson, as is Beni, of the famous singer of the past, Niño de la Isla, is a reticent non-professional singer of great knowledge who is capable of singing very well, according to Fernando Quiñones ("De Cádiz y Sus Cantes"), when he wishes. Instead of singing professionally, Amós has become a noted flamencologist, very prominent on the flamenco lecture circuit.

SANTIAGO DONDAY is a blacksmith in Cádiz of the old school. According to Fernando Quiñones, he retains in his cante the pureness of this most flamenco of professions.

JUANITO VILLAR, a robust young man of husky voice and seemingly fiery temperament, inserts a special spark into his cantes de Cádiz. He will rise high in flamenco's hierarchy if he avoids commercialization (he is already dabbling in crowd pleasers).

MANUEL EL FLECHA carries on the singing tradition of his father, the late Antonio el Flecha. Manuel has been singing for many years in the Madrid tablao El Corral de la Morería.

PABLITO DE CADIZ (Pablo Jiménez Pérez, born c. 1908) has long exhibited the *salero* of Cádiz through his inimitable dance. A natural comedian, Pablo made flamenco audiences roar with delight wherever he went, which was nearly everywhere while with such troupes as La Argentinita, Canalejas de Puerto Real, Manolo Caracol, Pastora Imperio, Conchita Piquer, others. Pablito presently lives retired in his native Cádiz.

Dancer CARACOLILLO, a true promise in the dance thirty years ago, married *cuplé* singer Juanita Reina and long ago settled in Sevilla. Today his main activity is teaching in his dance academy in Triana.

ALGECIRAS. Province of Cádiz.

This seaport, located in the shadow of Gibraltar on the eastern edge of Cádiz province, lies on that imaginary boundry between the gypsy-inspired cantes of Cádiz and Jerez to the west, and the Andaluz-inspired cantes of Málaga province to the east. A famous representative of the gypsy cante was JUAN SOTO MONTERO (p.92), descended from the illustrious flamenco family of LOS CANTORALES (p.33)- disciples of flamenco's first documented singer, Tío Luis el de la Juliana, and sharers of juergas with El Fillo and El Planeta. Soto Montero in his day moved to Jerez' Barrio de San Miguel, and there begat the cantaor said to be the greatest of all time, MANUEL SOTO LORETO "MANUEL TORRE." Among the non-gypsies born in Algeciras we can single out EL CHAQUETON, son of the late ANTONIO EL FLECHA, currently a top singer residing in Madrid. Still another flamenco family, the most famous from Algeciras in modern times, has produced three excellent artists, all non-gypsies. They are: RAMON DE ALGECIRAS, PEPE DE ALGECIRAS (p.166), and PACO DE ALGECIRAS (p.321), the latter two of whom have changed their artistic names, since the first edition of this book, to PEPE DE LUCIA and PACO DE LUCIA. Let us discuss them in that order.

RAMON DE ALGECIRAS is a fine guitarist forever destined to live in the shadow of his phenomenal brother, Paco de Lucía. Most of Ramon's artistic activity today consists in playing in Paco's musical group (which varies, but can include three guitars, a flute, bongos, sax, bass, Pepe's voice, a dancer, and whatever else occurs on the spur of the moment; flamenco it is rarely, good music it is occasionally. On the other hand, Paco usually plays two or three moving, technically unbelievable flamenco solos during the program, which I suppose make up for the rest of the mediocrity).

PEPE DE LUCIA suffered a voice change over the years, but still sings well when he wishes. Which, in public at least, is not often, for Pepe is attempting to climb on the Chiquetete *cuplé*-flamenco band wagon in order to make a few quick bucks. When not, he sings in brother Paco's musical group a variety of Moorish sounding cantes that occasionally touch on flamenco. Pepe has also taken up the guitar, and often plays third guitar behind brothers Paco and Ramón.

PACO DE LUCIA, born Francisco Sánchez Gómez in December of 1947, adopted his mother's name for artistic purposes after beginning as Paco de Algeciras. My contact with Paco dates back to 1962, when Paco and Pepe, Los Chiquillos de Algeciras, were the sensations of a flamenco contest in Jerez de la Frontera. Paco's father, a guitarist, had early discovered Paco's enormous natural talent for the guitar and had determined that Paco was to become flamenco's greatest guitarist ever. Thus, Paco's childhood consisted of the guitar and flamenco, flamenco and the guitar, Paco's father teaching him, training him, driving him through countless hours of solo practice, then letting Paco relax by accompanying the Cante and the Baile, including the singing of brother Pepe, the guitar of Ramón, and the dancing of a sister, María (later, Paco was discouraged from accompanying dancers, as his father considered that too much hand strain is involved in that field due to the necessity of playing much stronger in order to be heard over the zapateado, palmas and general jaleo). His diligence and Paco's hard work got results, and by the time of the 1962 Jerez contest Paco, at fourteen, was already extremely accomplished. In lieu of that success the family moved to Madrid, to the big-time competiton of the virtuosos. Paco continued working hard, still under his father's tutelege and watchful eye. His reputation built rapidly, and opportunity soon knocked, in form of an LP with singer Camarón de la Isla, another young flamenco *fenómeno* from the province of Cádiz. Their first record created a sensation for both the artists, and the two youngsters were launched into first rank prominence. Camarón's singing made the traditional cantes sparkle with vitality, while Paco's accompanying was inspired, full of original ideas and controlled virtuosity. Although just out of his teens, Paco already had created his own style of playing, and was recognized overnight as the force to be reckoned with in the world of the flamenco guitar.

But the many years of hard work and little play (his lack of childhood, as Paco puts it) had taken their toll. Paco had done it all at too early an age. He became restless, and began dabbling elsewhere; an early collaboration on a jazz record, a fascination with bossa nova and other musical forms, all of which began creeping into his flamenco, taking him away from tradition and more and more into the world of international music.

Meantime, Paco continued recording, more records with Camarón, then solo records. With his solo LP that included the rumba "Entre Dos Aguas" the seemingly impossible occurred; Paco passed over the line from flamenco hero to national hero, the first time in history this has happened to a Spanish guitarist, flamenco or otherwise. He was recognized in the streets, hounded for his autograph, lionized by society, played standing-room-only concerts in Madrid's Royal Theater, was news throughout the media. Against his wishes he became too big for an accompanying role. In the last festival in which I saw Paco accompany he was attempting to hold back and accompany like the Paco of old, but the public would not hear of it, drowning out the singer with demands for Paco to do something sensational. Finally, to shut them up, Paco was forced to open up with an extraordinary chord progression followed by an incredible picado run, all in countertime. The crowd screamed its approval, the singer was forgotten, Paco was helplessly embarrassed.

It got so bad that Paco even became a political issue. On one occasion Paco innocently made some remark to a reporter that was printed out of context, and Paco was beaten up on the streets of Madrid by a gang of far-right thugs.

After a time it became a bit much for Paco, an introvert by nature, and he began seeking peace and quiet, together with new musical experiences, outside of Spain. As a result of his extended absences the furor died down a bit, and today he lives in comparative tranquility in Madrid.

What is it about Paco's playing that is so different, so remarkable? For one thing, his technique is the best in flamenco. He can execute anything effortlessly (effortlessly is the big word there). Then there is his impeccable sense of rhythm and counter rhythm, and his talent, in his serious solo playing and singer accompanying, of modernizing tradition without overstepping boundaries (the same cannot be said for his playing with his musical group, but then again the music produced by the group does not pretend to be anything like serious flamenco). And, finally, Paco is one of the few virtuosos who can transmit emotion in his playing. Not the vibrant emotion of a Diego del Gastor or a Melchor de Marchena but, nonetheless, emotion, an exceptional feat for a virtuoso. Most virtuosos turn out a series of more or less beautiful notes and phrases that, when analyzed, often say nothing. Paco's playing, on the other hand, does say something. Regardless of the million notes, Paco's playing is deeply flamenco. It is, in a word, meaningful.

Perhaps Paco's only entry into traditional flamenco at present is via the gathering of intimates who will let him play as he wishes. Apparently such gatherings are not infrequent, and the fortunate participants agree one and all that Paco is still exquisite at what is still considered the flamenco guitar's number one art: accompanying the Cante.

What does Paco think about the music he is making around the world today? He states flatly that much of it is not flamenco, and does not pretend to be. He is the first to say that he has been straying from flamenco for a long time. Paco is experimenting, playing with ideas. He seems to want his followers to know that, for Paco respects true flamenco and does not want it to disappear into the mists of universal musicality.

One thing is certain. Paco has had an impact on flamenco not seen since Ramón Montoya in the guitar and Carmen Amaya in the dance. Aficionados already talk of the flamenco guitar before, and after, the arrival of Paco de Lucia. To my way of thinking, this is well and good for Paco, a musical genius. Geniuses must do their thing. The catch comes with the mass of non-genius imitators attempting to emulate Paco in all ways, down to the way of holding the guitar, facial expressions, note for note copying of his records, playing with musical groups, and so forth. But they cannot emulate Paco successfully. Paco was reared on flamenco and is flamenco through and through, even when he is playing jazz, while most of his imitators know about flamenco only what they can glean from his records. They are the ones doing irreparable harm to true flamenco, just as Carmen Amaya's imitators did to the dance.

BARBATE. Province of Cádiz.

Barbate is a picturesque little fishing port on the Atlantic coast. Its best known flamenco representative was the late NIÑO DE BARBATE (p.123). His nephew, also a singer and also called NIÑO DE BARBATE, is presently keeping the family tradition alive.

CHICLANA. Province of Cádiz.

Chiclana is a wine town near Cádiz port, only a few kilometers from the coast. Its most famous present-day artists are the gypsies ORILLO (often called Orillo del Puerto, although he is not from El Puerto), a colorful and imaginative singer-dancer, and his brother RANCAPINO (Pine Uprooter), one of today's most moving young singers. Due to his inspired cante, Rancapino is presently much in demand at Andalusia's flamenco festivals.

JEREZ DE LA FRONTERA. Province of Cár

This famous wine town, just a sea breeze from the Atlantic, has been, is today, and no doubt will continue to be the world's most fertile breeding ground of flamenco. Jerez never ceases to astound as one observes a never-ending parade of excellent and often creative flamencos blossom there with the regularity and prolificacy of vine shoots in a vintage year.

Exaggeration? If anything, understatement. Let's just list a few of the more well-known singers from Jerez' past (nearly all gypsies, significantly enough for those who attempt to downplay the gypsy contribution to flamenco), and it will become readily evident that Jerez played by far the major role in the creation and development of gypsy-inspired flamenco singing. To wit: TIO LUIS EL DE LA JULIANA (p.33), the first singer in flamenco's recorded history, and various others of his epoch (c.1760-1830); MARIA BORRICO (p.37); TIA SARVAORA (p.37); MANUEL MOLINA (p.37); TOMAS EL NITRI (p.44); EL LOCO MATEO (p.48); PACO LA LUZ (p.54); JUAN JUNQUERA (p.56); JUAN EL DE ALONSO (p.56); JUANELO (p.56) and his daughter,

SOLEDAD (p.88); MARIA LA JACA (p.57); SALVAORIYO (p.62); DIEGO EL MARRURRO (p.68); EL CHATO (p.69); EL CARITO (p.70); RITA LA CANTAORA (p.70); JOSE IYANDA (p.75); CARBONERILLO (p.76); ANTONIO CHACON (p.76); LA LOBATA and EL LOLI (p.87); EL PULI (p.87); FRIJONES (p.88); MANUEL TORRE (p.91); EL NIÑO GLORIA (p.100); LA POMPI (p.100); TIO JOSE DE PAULA (p.75); PEPE TORRE (p.102); JOSE CEPERO (p.111); ISABELITA (p.118); JUANITO MOJAMA (p.119); CABEZA (p.119); and many, many more, a selection of which we shall discuss in this section.

And dancers? Jerez produced many of the greatest of the café cantante period, all gypsies who moved to Sevilla and played an important role in converting Sevilla into the capital of the flamenco dance. The most famous were: MARIA LA CHORRUA (p.210); LA MACARRONA (p.212); FERNANDA and JUANA ANTUNEZ (p.217); LA MALENA (p.218); LA SORDITA (p.218); LA GEROMA (p.210); and LA GAMBA (p.216). A little later JUAN EL ESTAMPIO (p.186) and RAMIREZ (p.187), both non-gypsies, were to play important roles in the development of the male flamenco dance.

Past guitar standouts were non-gypsies JAVIER MOLINA (p.271) and PERICO EL DEL LUNAR (p.285), and gypsies CURRITO DE LA GEROMA (p.288) and RAFAEL EL AGUILA (p.311). As can be judged from the long list of present-day guitarists, Jerez has become one of today's most important flamenco guitar centers.

But, someone may counter, isn't flamenco burning itself out in Jerez as it is doing in most of Andalusia? Aren't the kids following the latest trends and watering down their flamenco with rock, jazz, pop, oriental, flutes, bongos, violins, you name it? If my recent experiences in Jerez can serve as criteria, little of this is happening there. At the Jerez spring fair I had the good fortune to witness an entire program of young Jerez flamencos, some twenty or thirty of them, singing, dancing, playing and participating in the general jaleo. They were amazingly accomplished, and more important still, refreshingly innovative in a traditional sense. Definitely I was not watching the products of academies, but rather spontaneous performances of young people weened on flamenco and at ease with their art.

This youthful enthusiasm for pure flamenco is not unusual if one considers that in Jerez flamenco is still at least somewhat a way of life. The ancient practice of street vendors advertising (*pregonando*) their wares through song, a memory in much of Andalusia, still survives in Jerez (barely). In fact, some of the better *pregones* have found their way into certain flamenco forms - notably por bulerías - and various of the *pregoneros* have achieved lasting fame through their *pregones*. Outstanding examples are Juanito Mojama, who as a youth hawked the dried fish after which he was named in the streets of Jerez, and Gabriel Macandé, from Cádiz port, who sang the charms of his caramelos (type of candy) on street corners, attracting aficionados from far afield. Jerez' Anica la Piriñaca considers that her success as a vegetable vendor - after her husband died she had to support herself and a small army of kids - was largely due to her *pregones*.

But by far the most important aspects of flamenco formation and propagation in the Jerez area were its systems of agricultural laborers, the large majority of whom were from the Barrio de Santiago, and its gypsy blacksmiths, mostly from the adjacent Barrio de San Miguel. Let us discuss these facets separately, beginning with the seasonal agricultural laborers.

Barrio de Santiago. Opportunities were sparce in Jerez, and the poor folk had no alternative but to accept seasonal work in the fields for a pittance. This was, and is, true in much of the rest of Andalusia as well, but in the Barrio de Santiago it is somewhat different due to flamenco's ingrained tradition among these people. Entire families from the Barrio would close up their lodging and take to the country for weeks, or months, at a time for a variety of seasonal tasks: cleaning and preparing the fields for planting, then the planting, weeding, pruning, thinning, harvesting of the various crops (wheat, barley, sugar beets, cotton, sherry grapes, olives, several types of beans, etc.). Then start all over again. Tía Anica la Piriñaca recounts that the work days were long - 7 a.m. to 7 p.m., depending on the season - and the day's pay, when she was a girl, was less than one peseta. There was no time for formal schooling; the elders would attempt to teach their children, or grandchildren, to read and write as best they could. Some of the children would apply themselves and learn, many others remained illiterate.

There were redeeming features, I am happy to report. The owners of the farms provided the sleeping space - camping under trees, or part of the barn,sometimes workers' quarters in a wing of the house - and the food, which cosisted largely of huge bean (usually garbanzo) and salted pork stews, lots of freshly baked, whole wheat bread of the old, highly nutritious type, and chicory coffee. Sometimes the employer would provide wine. So although the wages were meager, the expenses were less so and the workers were able to put money aside for rainy days and the few weeks a year there would be no work. So they managed to get by.

One factor beloved by all was the after work gatherings, when earthenware jugs would be filled with wine at the nearest country inn and transported by donkey to the campsite, and where great sessions of song and dance would ensue. These gatherings were the true school of flamenco, where traditional forms were handed down from generation to generation and creativity was very much alive. EVERYONE sang and/or danced (on rare occasions there would be a guitar and perhaps a homemade country flute), some so well that they gained lasting fame. One such gypsy worker in this century was Tío José de Paula, whose creations and *duende* within the siguiriyas the the soleares were such that he has had a permanent influence in these cantes and is a revered figure regardless of the fact that his singing was confined to country gatherings of laborers and the back rooms of ventas. Rainy days did not bring melancholy, for then the juerga would roar on for whatever number of hours or days the rain lasted, more often than not with the owner of the farm and perhaps some of his family actively participating (the word "farm" is misleading, for a farm in much of the world is a relatively small holding run by one family. In Andalusia the "farms" that hire a large number of laborers are usually huge estates, called *cortijos*, and the owners usually prosperous members in high standing in the community).

Anica la Piriñaca remembers those days with joy, as she has told me and as she told José Luis Ortiz Nuevo, who has put it down so beautifully in his book "Anica La Piriñaca: Yo Tenía Mu Güena Estrella." She worked in the fields with her family throughout her childhood, and loved the country, the life style, the rough food they ate, the comradeship, even the work, singing happily away, but above all, the after work gatherings when she listened, learned and particiated, as they all did.

That system, of course, is fast disappearing with the coming of farm machinery. Some laborers are still needed, for tasks machinery cannot achieve; most of the rest are on the dole - unemployment in Andalusia reaches as high as 30%. Nonetheless, the system still hangs on, which is witnessed by the biography of Manuel Palacín further in this section, a young Jerezano in his 30's who learned his cante in the fields not so very long ago.

Barrio de San Miguel. There still remain a few *fraguas* (smithies) in the Barrio de San Miguel, of the dozens that once existed. These were the nucleus of the cante from Jerez proper, mostly operated by gypsies, where the three principal Jerez forms of cante prospered (siguiriyas, soleares, bulerías) as well as the cantes of the *fraguas* (principally the martinetes and the tonás). These folk worked long, grueling hours for barely enough to get by (large families were the norm), singing as they worked, afterwards retiring to one of the nearby *tabancos* (type of tavern with huge barrels from which inexpensive wine was dispensed, to drink there or take out) to pass a few hours in juerga, beating out the compás on wooden tables, or on the bar, and singing and dancing to their heart's content. Although the song forms were the same as those sung by the agricultural workers, the content was somewhat different due to the distinct life styles of the two groups.

The *fraguas* are discussed in more detail later in this section in the biography of Tío Juane, an old-time flamenco and one of the few blacksmiths still leading the traditional flamenco life of the Barrio de San Miguel.

TRADITIONAL FLAMENCO FORMS FROM JEREZ. **Bulerías, soleares, siguiriyas, tonás, martinetes,** deblas, carceleras, la caña, el polo, **tangos, fandangos.**

OBITUARIES. In chronological order (of death).

AGUJETAS VIEJO, not included in the firt edition of this book due to an oversight, was an excellent singer of the cantes grandes of Jerez. He was one of the many blacksmiths from Jerez' most flamenco Barrio de San Miguel. His son, also called Agujetas, is one of Jerez' outstanding singers today.

Singer SERNITA (p.168) died of cancer in Madrid some years ago.

EL JUANATA was a fine singer por bulerías.

EL CHOZA DE JEREZ (p.169, "A Way of Life") took to the grave with him his absolutely unique renditions of bulerías. Although he was born, and returned to die, in Lebrija, he lived most of his live in Jerez and considered himself a Jerezano.

TERREMOTO DE JEREZ (p.165). After the death of Manolo Caracol there was only one singer remaining with such an exaggeratedly exciting combination of tempestuousness and surging emotion: Terremoto de Jerez. The flamenco world was shocked and saddened, therefore, when in the summer of 1981 48-year-old Terremoto died abruptly of a heart attack. Terremoto by now was far too overweight to dance much (although he still did his *desplantes por bulerías* that made you laugh with joy), but was universally acclaimed for his singing. Who is left that can lift you off your seat with the true duende and raucousness of a gypsy cante? There are many who can give one "*pellizcos*" (momentary thrills) with their singing, but none, in my opinion, to the extent that did Manolo Caracol and Terremoto de Jerez. That throne is vacant at present.

TOMAS TORRE, son of Manuel, was an excellent juerga dancer and an encyclopedia of Cante. His good friend Antonio Mairena gleaned much from him about both fields before Tomás passed away, I believe in the late 1970's.

TIO GREGORIO "BORRICO DE JEREZ" (1910-1983) was one of the last of Jerez' great singers of the pure school. Fame was just beginning to reach him upon his death, by then too late, for in his last years both his voice and spirit had broken. I consider his life of special interest, and shall go into it in some detail.

Borrico's father was an agricultural worker, and lived the year around, with his family, in the worker's quarters of a large estate near Jerez. Borrico was born into that life, and began earning wages at a tender age. Formal schooling was out of the question, but Borrico's grandfather did try hard to teach him the fundamentals, forcing Borrico to learn and thus saving him from a lifetime of complete illiteracy.

But what seduced Borrico was the Cante. By the time he was in his teens he had absorbed enough cante to be able to enter the professional flamenco life of the ventas surrounding Jerez. His first day in one of the ventas he was introduced to a señorito who was so delighted with Borrico's seguiriyas, soleares and bulerías that he handed him 500 pesetas. Borrico had never seen so much money. His next effort garnered him another 500 pesetas. In two nights of doing what he enjoyed he had earned 1000 pesetas, his earnings for nearly two full years of work in the country (at that time they were paying seven *reales*, or 1.75 pesetas, a day)! Obviously, Borrico never returned to agriculture, but did he live happily ever after?

Of course not. While earning well Borrico went the way of all old-time flamencos - blew it as quickly as he could. Some went to help his folks, much was spent on booze and women (the ventas in those days were replete with whores for all tastes, most of whom were also flamencas and all of whom were experts at helping Borrico and his cronies spend their earnings). It never occurred to Borrico, nor to any of them, to put aside some money for the bad times. They lived high, then when their voices cracked, or they got sick, or simply faded from the picture due to the public's changing tastes, utter proverty took over. Borrico spent many such periods, and was living in complete misery when he died.

(Many aficionados deplore the flamenco life style as described above. Caballero Bonald, for instance, in his introduction to the book "Tío Gregorio: Borrico de Jerez," considers it "demeaning, and fortunately nearly extinct." He does not consider, however, the alternatives - nearly a year working in the country to earn what was earned in one night of juerga, or work in some other menial job for a pittance. True, some of the hiring señoritos were often obstreperous, condescending, drunk, or all three, but others were good aficionados and gentlemen. There were good juergas and bad, good señoritos and bad. It was not always pleasant, but what job is?

On the other hand, Caballero Bonald and others do recognize that the flamenco of the juerga artists remained far more pure than that of their peers who went the big-time professional route.

Personally, I think that the major negative aspect of the juerga life was that the artists themselves could not handle their affairs a bit better, instead of behaving like never-learning children in a crab apple orchard.)

Borrico learned his cante from pure sources: his uncles Paco la Luz and Juanichi, Antonio Frijones, and his father, Fernando Fernández, all of whom were non-professionals; they did their day's work, then sang afterwards for pleasure, either in the country gatherings or one of the country ventas, or in the *tabancos* scatterd about the flamenco neighborhoods of Jerez.

Why the name Borrico? The nickname was given him, when still a boy, the first time he sang for one of the Domecqs. The gentleman exclaimed "You sing very well, very flamenco, but with a voice like a donkey." The nickname stuck with him all his life, has been passed on to his daughter, singer-dancer María la Burra, and will no doubt stay in the family for generations to come.

For the first 57 years of his life Borrico was unknown outside the venta life, and señorito circle, of Jerez. So unknown that I had heard of him only vaguely, and did not include him in the first edition of this book. In 1967 he sang for the first time in a large public gathering, and created a sensation among knowledgeable aficionados. The record companies were waiting, and Borrico has been included on eight anthologies between 1967 and 1982, the year before his death. He did not, however, go over with the general public; his cante was much too pure and uncompromising. In fact, his singing, voice and *"eco"* remind me greatly of another singer who did not make it with the general public but was revered by aficionados: Juan Talega (this is not unusual, for much of Juan's cante had its origins in Jerez in general, and with Paco La Luz in particular).

For readers of Spanish who wish to read further about Borrico, I highly recommend the book "Tío Gregorio: Borrico de Jerez," by José Luis Ortiz Nuevo (introduction by Caballero Bonald). (Write to: Excmo. Ayuntamiento, Area de Cultura, Jerez de la Frontera, Cádiz.) The book is written in the local jargon, just as Borrico talked, and imparts strongly the atmosphere, flamenco and otherwise, of those days. In addition, it is accompanied by a valuable 45 r.p.m. recording of four of Borrico's cantes.

OBITUARIES. Dancers from Jerez.

PACO LABERINTO (p.194).

PARRILLA DE JEREZ (p.208) was an inspired juerga-style dancer, and in addition knew a great deal of cante. A true Jerez flamenco.

Dancer-singer PEPA LA CHICHARRONA was an unexcelled *festera* of the old school of Jerez who never failed to leave us clamoring for more (p.169, "A Way of Life").

OBITUARIES. Guitarists from Jerez.

RAFAEL EL AGUILA (pps.48,311) was a fine guitarist who put many of Jerez' top guitarists on the right track. His playing and creations were often along the line of those of Diego del Gastor (they never heard each other and met only once, when we dropped in on Rafael during one of our sojourns to Jerez); that is to say, much thumb, profundity, and his playing sprinkled with delightful surprises.

PRESENT-DAY ARTISTS. Jerez.

It is not easy to make a list of present-day flamenco artists from Jerez. One can only list the better known, for Jerez is pregnant with excellent unknown flamencos who perform only for their and their friends' pleasure. Almost invariably, when one scratches the surface of some Jerez flamenco the flamenco will comment something like "If you think I'm good you ought to hear/see my father-mother-uncle-aunt-cousin-brother-sister-grandpa-grandma-son-daughter," one, some, or all. Flamenco runs very deep in Jerez, so much so that any family gathering is likely to be an amazing experience. Thus, as can be deduced from the above, this list of flamencos does not pretend to be complete.

PRESENT-DAY ARTISTS. Singers from Jerez. In chronological order.

TIA ANICA LA PIRIÑACA (1899 -) was another of Jerez' well-kept secrets until the early-1960's. At that time the tireless Antonio Mairena sought her out, fell in love with her absolutely pure cante with its primitive, no frills delivery, and talked her into going to Madrid to record some of her siguiriyas and soleares. Fortunately, Tía Anica went, and her voice is included in the excellent "Antología del Cante Flamenco y Cante Gitano" (Colombia. 3LPs. 31014/16).

Before going on, let us clear up the naming of Anica. You will notice that when young she was called simply Anica, but with age comes respect and the "*Tía*" (Aunt) is tacked onto a woman's name, "*Tío*" (Uncle) onto a man's.

Anica was born in that hotbed of flamenco, El Barrio de Santiago, into a family of agricultural workers. Her father was half gypsy, on his father's side, her mother a non-gypsy, making Anica one-quarter gypsy. However, she was brought up amongst gypsies and always considered herself gypsy, although in truth it did not bother her much either way; apparently there was little racism in the flamenco neighborhoods of Jerez. They were all poor folk struggling through life together, and had no time for such nonsense.

When Anica's family worked in the country, which was most of the year, they closed up their rooms in their "*casa de vecinos*" (a type of two story apartment complex for the poor) and moved onto one of the surrounding farms until the work was finished, often for a period of months at a time. As was customary then, Anica had no formal schooling, and not much informal, for she never learned to as much as sign her name. She remembers that at a very young age she was put to work earning then, in the early years of this century, two and one-half *reales* a day (two-thirds of a peseta). Of course, she earned it but did not keep it; the money went into the family communal fund, for only in that way could the family survive. Store bought toys and all the other luxuries that today we think of as necessities did not exist for these people.

Sound grim to our flaccid ears? Many of the people who lived that life loved it. Why? For one thing, they enjoyed that special tightly-knit relationship of people struggling together. For another, they were brought up in that life, never had had amenities, expected none, and therefore did not miss them. But the major reason was their shared love of flamenco, its life style and poetic philosophy as expressed through the verses of the Cante. Anica says she never stopped singing. She sang while she worked, and she sang in the gatherings after work, when the wine flowed and the entire work force sang and danced well into the night.

Anica's childhood passed pleasantly in this fashion, but things changed radically with marriage. Anica chose one of those insanely jealous gypsy types who barely permit their women to breathe. He made a large enough salary so that Anica no longer had to work, and Anica's home became her jail; she was permitted out just enough to hustle through the necessary chores. He wanted no one to hear her voice, so she could no longer sing, even in family gatherings and celebrations. She was permitted to reproduce, however, and at the time of his sickness and death several years later Anica had seven children to look after. She rather desperately took to selling vegetables and fruit in the streets, quickly rediscovering her voice when she found that her *pregones* (praising her wares through song) multiplied her sales. Often even this approach was not enough, however, and Anica had to receive help from many, above all from a nearby parish priest who often paid her rent when she could not handle it, or supplied some other essential.

When the word got around that Anica was singing again her old flamenco friends came to her rescue. They calculated that she could do far better in the flamenco life of the ventas, and a gypsy family, owners of one of the ventas, took her under their wing, introduced her to the señorito circle, and soon Anica was making more money then she had ever dreamed of, enough, with careful management, to meet the needs of her large family.

The release of the Colombia anthology gave Anica a further boost, for then the uncertain knew for sure Anica was first rate, to have been included in such a prestigious undertaking. She was chosen for the anthology by Antoio Mairena for various reasons, a basic one being because of Anica's intimate knowledge of the cante of two of flamenco's little known but all-time greats: Juaniquín de Lebrija and Tío José de Paula, both agricultural laborers who created their own styles. They were Anica's idols, and she is very eloquent about them. I shall include her remembrances of each here, as well as those of a few other Jerez flamencos not mentioned, or only sparsely mentioned, elsewhere in this book.

Tía Anica's recollections of the gypsy singer Juaniquín clarify the polemic of just where Juaniquín lived and just which cantes he influenced. She clearly remembers visiting Juaniquín when a girl, in company with her father and other aficionados, at his hut on the outskirts of El Cuervo, a little town up the road from Jerez. Now, seeing as how Juaniquín apparently was born in Lebrija and his hut in El Cuervo was just eight kilometers from Lebrija, while Utrera is some fifty kilometers to the north, it seems reasonable he should be called Juaniquín de Lebrija, not de Utrera, as is often done, and that his cante is native of Lebrija, not Utrera.

Tía Anica remembers with gleaming eyes how on rainy days the olive pickers on a *cortijo* near Lebrija would fetch Juaniquín and several *cántaros* full of wine and juerga until the rain stopped and they had to return to work. She recalls that once the rain, and the juerga, lasted a full week.

Juaniquín was old when Anica was quite young, so we can calculate he was born around 1845, perhaps a little earlier (Anica's age is also doubtful. Her identity card states 1899, but that could well be manipulation on her part, as she herself says she is some years older than that). Anica states that Juaniquín was a small man, uneducated as they all were, a worker in the fields, as they all were, and sang better than all the rest in those days when all the rest sang very, very well. Tía Anica talks about Juaniquín's soleares verse that deals with his difficult son that could cause Juaniquín and the entire gathering to shed tears when deep in juerga (Tía Anica recorded this on the Colombia anthololgy; it is quite unusual and beautiful).

Tía Anica's favorite cante is the siguiriyas, and her favorite *siguiriyero* of all was Tío José de Paula. José de Paula's father was a gypsy from Lebrija called Tío Paula el del Lobo (he of the Wolf). The Wolf apparently sang well, as did his father and brothers and uncles and the entire clan (the Paula clan in Lebrija continues to this day, its latest exponent of note being Manuel de Paula, a young singer presently with Mario Maya). Tío José de Paula, however, was born in Jerez' Barrio de Santiago, as his father married a Jerez gypsy girl and moved there. José therefore lived only a few blocks from Anica, and Anica was weened on his cante. Tío José's siguiriyas are short and to the point. He created his own style and sang only his own verses, and in a style that must have been wonderful to experience; no shouting, and at moments in the cante he would half talk the verse, each time differently. In other words, it was not an exhibition of lungs or knowledge, as it nearly always is today, but a true expression of his emotions. As Tío José's gypsy wife had loved then left him , and he never got over it, during the wine-sodden part of a juerga Tío José would sing about her with such emotion the entire gathering would end up weeping.

No wonder Tío José de Paula is remembered as one of the greatest singers of siguiriyas flamenco has known. Other than in private sessions with señoritos, he never worked professionally; he preferred country labor, and after hours singing for his own pleasure and alleviation. Unfortunately, neither did he record, so his cante lives on basically through Tía Anica, and she is the first to say that his cante is inimitable. Many years older than Tía Anica, Tío José died in his house in the Barrio de Santiago's Calle Nueva, where he had lived all his life.

Tía Anica also talked about other flamenco dynasties from Jerez, such as Los Parrilla, known a few years ago for the excellent juerga dancing of Parrilla el Viejo and his brother, Gregorio, and today for a generation of very accomplished guitarists; Los Morao, an entire clan of exciting guitarists; Los Rincones, singers all; and a long etcetera.

Tía Anica is largely retired today, living out her last years in her beloved Barrio de Santiago. However, in recent years the public has had the opportunity to enjoy Tía Anica, together with many other veterans, in delightful juerga-style presentations throughout Andalusia. These mini-tours, organized by J.L. Ortiz Nuevo in conjunction with the Junta de Andalucía, are appropriately called "*Los Ultimos de la Juerga*" (The Last of the Juerga Artists).

TIO JUANE (1920 -) and Family. As we have seen in the introduction to the Jerez section, gypsy Juan Fernández Navarro "Tío Juane" maintains one of the last blacksmithies in the flamenco neighborhood of San Miguel. For that reason alone Tío Juane is of great interest, but besides that he knows and sings, non-professionally, a great deal of cante, he has produced a very flamenco offspring of seven sons, and between them all and Juane's brothers and other relatives, they are a veritable encyclopedia of the flamenco life of Jerez in general and the Barrio de San Miguel in particular.

Tío Juane learned much of his cante from just being around the constant flamenco of his time, although he singles out his mother, a fine singer-dancer who died at age 84, as a particularly pure source, for she knew and learned from such legendary singers as Diego el Marrurro, Antonio Frijones, and many others.

Tío Juane and his brother Enrique enjoy reminiscing about the sessions in the nearby Plazuela de San Miguel, where there existed the "*tabanco de Ignacio*" and where all the gypsies from the neighborhood would unite after work. They talk reverently about Domingo Rubichi, who they claim to be the best singer of bulerías that flamenco has produced, about Agujetas Viejo, father of today's Agujetas, about Pacote and his brother, Alonso, father of today's Paquera, about Bojiga, nephew of Diego el Marrurro, about el Marrurro himself and Manuel Torre, the latter two who lived in the same house on the calle Alma, about Tío José de Paula, from the Barrio de Santiago but also a frequenter of San Miguel, about Juan Jambre and his brother Salvadorillo, and on and on. The speakers, of course, were just children at the time, and used to sneak into a corner, or under the table, in order to listen.

Both agree that Tomas Torre, son of Manuel, was an excellent, very knowledgeable singer and nearly as good dancer, that the cante of El Borrico is based principally on that of Paco la Luz, that Agujetas Viejo was incredible, basing his cantes on those of Joaquín la Cherna and Juan Ramírez, that Agujetas hijo bases one of his siguiriyas on that of a San Miguel gypsy called Farrabú and other of his cantes on those of Manuel Torre, that Juan Mojama was fantastic but that none were as great as Manuel Torre when the moment was right.

How about the dance? Paco Laberinto in a theatrical style and Parrilla el Viejo in his own genial style were considered tops, followed by Gregorio, brother of Parrilla.

The guitar? Javier Molina, Perico el del Lunar and Rafael el Aguila formed the Jerez school. Today's greats, in their opinion, are Paco Cepero, Manuel and Juan Morao, Manuel Parrilla, Pedro Carrasco "El Niño Jero", and several outstanding youngsters, mainly from the families just mentioned, coming on strong.

Recent singers? The late Fernando Terremoto, born in the Barrio de Santiago but whose family hailed from the Barrio de San Miguel, definitely tops the list. It is agreed that he will be very hard to replace, that his sister, María Soleá, overshadowed by Terremoto during his lifetime, today is gaining enormously in prestige, and that the present-day Agujetas possesses a Manuel Torre turbulence of spirit that would make him a serious contender "if only he would come home and settle down with his people" (for them, living the flamenco life in a flamenco atmosphere is a necessity if one hopes to express true flamenco).

And they talk about many, many others ranging from good to great, a labyrinth of Jerez flamencos too numerous to put in proper perspective; such a study would take a book, or series of books.

Perhaps the most well-known of Tío Juane's offspring is NANO DE JEREZ, a very personable young singer-dancer who lately is beginning to sing more and more the cante grande he has inherited.

For more abourt Tío Juane, and others of the old school, you would do well in reading the excellent series "*De La Vieja Escuela,*" by Manuel Herrera Rodas, in the magazine "Sevilla Flamenca." (Subscriptions: José Hurtado, Apartado de Correos 79, 41530 Morón de la Frontera (Sevilla).

MANOLITA DE JEREZ (p.160), one of Jerez' finest singers a generation ago, reportedly became blind and retired from profesional singing. She presently resides in Jerez.

LA PAQUERA (p.168) still rides high.

LA CHIVA, reportedly, continues as described on P.168.

LA SALLAGO (p.168) gained fame and considerable prestige before retiring in her native Jerez. In recent years she has performed with the veteran groups "Los Ultimos de la Juerga," as described at the end of the Anica la Piriñaca section.

MANUEL SOTO "SORDERA" (c.1929 -) another son of the Barrio de Santiago, is one of today's finest singers of the Jerez school of cante.

Sordera is from a long decendency of flamenco greats, including Paco la Luz and his daughters La Serrana and La Sordita, the family of Los Morao, and, more distantly, Manuel Torre (also named Soto, as are a large number of the gypsy flamencos in Jerez). He says the name *sordera* (deafness) hails from his grandfather, Sordo la Luz, who could not hear even the wine train when it passed close to his house in the Barrio de Santiago. Although Sordera does not suffer from the deficiency, deafness apparently did run in the family, for a cousin of his grandfather, the famous dancer La Sordita, was also nearly stone deaf.

Being from the Barrio de Santiago, Sordera learned much of his cante in the neighborhood *tabancos*. He talks about one in particular, "El Sindicato," where many of the old-time flamencos would unite, such as the families of El Borrico and Los Morao, La Peña, Tío José de Paula, Perico el Tito (father of today's Diamante Negro), Luisa la Pompi, el Niño Gloria, many others. Sordera, thus, learned his cante from the purest sources and carries on the pure tradition, despite his extended absences from Jerez, in a most exciting manner; he is among the few professionals on the circuit today who is capable of transmitting the duende he feels, and feel it he does.

Sordera got an early start in semi-professional flamenco life when he traveled from pueblo to pueblo near Jerez singing for whatever he could get (his first fiesta, in 1942, paid ten pesetas). After his military service he moved to Sevilla and sang in the wonderful old tablao El Cortijo del Guajiro, where many of flamenco's great performers got their start (el Farruco, Chocolate, Manuela Vargas, Paco Cepero, to name but a few). Sordera's next stop was Pastora Imperio's El Duende, in Madrid, after which he has sung around the world, frequently in the troupe of Manuela Vargas. Despite his travels and his residing in Madrid, his home town has not forgotten him; Sordera was awarded the National Prize for the Cante in 1984 by the Cátedra de Flamencología, de Jerez.

Sordera left home, but his heart has remained in the Jerez of his youth, in the Barrio de Santiago teeming with flamencos, when the "great thing was to earn *cinco duros* (25 pesetas), then spend half or more on wine listening to the old-timers sing in the *tabancos*. After singing for the señoritos and drinking their quality wine, you went to a *tabanco* with your people and drank common wine for one peseta a bottle, and it tasted glorious."

Sordera's family continues very much in flamenco. All but one of his eight sons sing, the most well-known of whom is VICENTE SOTO. Sordera also has a nephew who is rising rapidly in the world of cante: José Mercé.

Sordera sings pure cante, and rejects those who do not. He says that only too many of today's cantaores take the easy road, sing the easy things, do not deliver themselves to their cante, throw the public crowd-pleasers. "They label such nonsense evolution, when in reality it is prostitution."

¡Viva Sordera!

AGUJETAS DE JEREZ, gypsy son of the late Agujetas Viejo, is at present one of flamenco's most profound singers. His singing closely resembles himself - the dark, turbulent, rebellious, disconsolate sounds of his cante jondo emerge directly from a dark, turbulent, rebellious, disconsolate nature.

Agujetas (Stiffness) has gone where the money is and resides and performs much of the time in the United States, although he does return to Jerez periodically for extended visits. He is considered a great promise in the Cante if only, as Tío Juane puts it, "he would come home and settle down with his own people." In his early forties, I would guess, Agujetas has a son who is develolping as a singer.

MANUEL PALACIN (c.1953 -). The life of non-gypsy Manuel Palacín, from the Jerez Barrio de San Telmo, shows us that the Jerez system of artistic development is still at work (see Introduction to the Jerez section). Manuel's father was a foreman on the Rancho del Calvario, where Manuel lived his first twelve years. He heard much cante during working hours, but absorbed it above all during the after work gatherings of all the workers. By age twelve Manuel possessed an enviable knowledge of the Cante. At that time has family moved back into Jerez, and Manuel was put to work baking bread in the local bread factory. During the next seven years as a *panadero* Manuel continued in flamenco, including a year's guitar study with the fine guitarist, Rafael el Aguila. He did not stay with the guitar, however, for a very basic reason: when he and his group of young friends began peforming at parties and other festive occasions, it was observed that Manuel knew far more cante than the others, but that there were plenty of good guitarists around. So Manuel concentrated on singing, subsequently winning a number of prizes in contests in and around Jerez. His name began circulating, and one day, when twenty years of age, he received a phone call inviting him to perform in the Madrid tablao Torres Bermejas. That very night he took the train to Madrid, and his artistic career was launched. Since then Manuel has traveled far and wide with various troupes, is today singing for the Ballet Nacional de España in its worldwide performances. Manuel presently headquarters in Madrid, as do so many of flamenco's professionals.

JOSE MERCE is one of today's finer young singers from Jerez. Gypsy nephew of Manuel Soto "Sordera", José specializes in, and sings with knowledge and feeling, the basic Jerez cantes: bulerías, soleares and siguiriyas. Presently residing in Madrid, he was winner of the 1986 Córdoba cante contest.

OTHERS. Brothers FERNANDO and LORENZO GALVEZ are known, above all, for their bulerías; GOMEZ DE JEREZ is a non-gypsy presently singing with Antonio Gades' troupe; JESUS EL ALMENDRO concentrates on singing for dancing; DIAMANTE NEGRO is another bulerías specialist presently performing in the tablao circuit in Madrid; ROMERITO DE JEREZ has cut records and achieved considerable fame. Although he sings all the Jerez cantes, his forte is the festive cantes; NIÑO DE LA BERZA is a gypsy bulerías specialist of husky voice and infectious style; SALMONETE is a young non-gypsy of great promise; JUAN MONEO is another little known but excellent singer from Jerez.

PRESENT-DAY DANCERS. Jerez. In alphabetical order.

FERNANDO BELMONTE, son of bullfighter Manuel Belmonte and nephew of the famous matador Juan Belmonte, is a non-gypsy dancer, more bailarín than bailaor, from Jerez who has been featured male dancer in the companies of both Antonio and María Rosa. Belmonte has recently established a dance academy in Jerez, is turning out young dancers in all branches of the dance, including flamenco, of such merit that his youthful groups are contracted to perform in theaters and festivities throughout Spain.

José Vargas Vargas EL MONO (The Monkey) is an extremely innovative gypsy dancer por bulerías, and in adition sings well the Jerez cantes of both dark and light vein.

JUANA LA PIPA (p.169, "A Way of Life") dances on, as strong and witty as ever.

ROSITA DURAN (p.239) presently teaches the dance in Madrid, and occasionally comes out of retirement to dance for some special festivity, usually accompanied by her old Zambra cronies, Rafael Romero and Perico el del Lunar *hijo*. Each time I have seen them they have stolen the show from their younger peers.

SOLERA DE JEREZ specializes in the masculine dance, replete with traje corto. She has been featured in Luisillo's troupe.

PRESENT-DAY ARTISTS. Guitarists from Jerez. In alphabetical order.

CURRO DE JEREZ, son of the late singer Sernita, presently performs in Madrid.

DIEGO CARRASCO has cut some fine records accompanying Tía Anica la Piriñaca.

EL NIÑO JERO (Pedro Carrasco) is a bearded young man with one of the best thumbs, and senses of rhythm, in the business. He is coming on strong today, basically as an accompanist.

GERARDO NUÑEZ (not related to Sebastian) is an excellent guitarist who specialized in accompanying the dance. More recently he has taken up solo playing, with considerable success.

JOSE MARIA MOLERO, a student of Rafael el Aguila, is presently first guitarist with the Ballet Nacional de España, quite a feather in any guitarist's cap.

LOS MORAO. Under this heading we encompass MANUEL MORAO "MORAITO" (p.315), Jerez' most famous present-day guitarist, now living in semi-retirement in Jerez; his younger brother JUAN MORAO "MORAITO CHICO" (p.315), also living in Jerez; and Juan's son, MORAITO CHICO II, an up-and-coming young guitarist.

LOS PARRILLA. Two of the offspring of the late Parrilla de Jerez (Parrilla Viejo) have turned to the guitar. They are: MANUEL PARRILLA

"PARRILLA DE JEREZ", probably Jerez' hottest young gypsy guitarist today, overshadowing his brother, JUAN PARRILLA. Juan's son, however, ten-year-old PARRILLA CHICO, is already proving himself a strong contender for the future Jerez guitar throne.

MANUEL, of the duo "Lole and Manuel" (see the Montoya Family, under Sevilla), although by no means a virtuoso, has a hard-driving, innovative style of playing that can be very appealing.

PACO CEPERO (1942 -), non-gypsy, born in Jerez' Barrio de San Miguel, was still being formed as a guitarist after instruction with the late Rafael el Aguila when I researched for the first edition of this book. During the twenty-five year interval Cepero made enormous progress, acccompanying nearly all of flamenco's outstanding singers (and dancers, but he prefers accompanying singing) until becoming a truly accomplished accompanist, in my mind one of the few great accompanists today. It is not only experience and excellent technique. He possesses those requisites, but so do many others. Very strong additional assets are the fact that Cepero was also a singer (until overly straining his voice to the tune of two throat operations and eventually having to give up singing altogether), with the resultant in-depth knowledge and instinct this gives an accompanist, and his passion for the Cante and for accompanying it. He throws himself into it and becomes one with each singer, rarely overwhelming with virtuosity (have I detected such an occasional tendency lately?), yet by no means taking a back seat; Cepero and the singer are equals in the search for artistic expression. Cepero plays plenty of guitar while accompaning, comprised of passages so tastefully fashioned and so integrated into the cante and the singer's style that the singer cannot help give the best he can. Cepero's playing style is another part of the secret. Like all great accompanists, Cepero is able to create moods through extremely sensitive passages that, when appropriate, build to crescendoing climaxes that delight both the singer and the audience, mixtures of delicacy, drive, excellent compás and know-how that are sensationally emotive and musical.

After years of playing tablaos, ventas and festivals, Cepero was launched as a concert flamenco guitarist, subsequently concertizing with great success in and out of Spain. His followers, including myself, fully expected the concert life to change Cepero, to somehow destroy the bond between singer and guitarist whenever he did return to accompanying. In short, we figured all the fanfare would go to his head and he would either feel superior to the accompanying role, or take over, perhaps at the instigation of the public, and overwhelm the singers with monumental shows of technique, as happens with so many virtuosos. I am happy to report this rarely happens with Cepero. I recently saw him accompany five singers with distinct styles - El Lebrijano, Juanito Villar, La Fernanda, La Bernarda, and El Turronero - and he was impeccable with each of them. Thus, hopefully we will be able to rely on Paco Cepero to set the standard for inspired guitar playing through accompaniment for many years to come.

But there is another side to the coin. The affirmative part of side two is Cepero's enormous gift for song writing. He calculates he has written between 600-800 songs of all types, from pop ballads to rock to pseudo flamenco (songs with an Andalusian ring put to a flamenco compás). He has been very successfull with his songs. to the extent that royalties from them, plus fees derived from being artistic director for the recording groups in the studios, enable him to live very well and presently to consider his first love, flamenco, more a hobby than a worrisome profession. Flamenco for Cepero is no longer a job, but a pleasure in which he can remain fresh and creative, a feeling that comes through when he is performing.

Now the negative side. His pseudo flamenco songs tend to appeal to singers of infirm integrity, for the songs go over big with the uninitiated or even semi-initiated public and the singers are only too eager to garner the name and money this brings them. Thus, in nearly every festival of flamenco one or more of Cepero's songs creeps in among the pure flamenco, to the delight of the ignorant and frivolous and the dismay of the knowledgeable. Cepero's songs, of course, are not the first nor the last to be introduced into flamenco, nor could any but the most envious and/or irrational blame Cepero if flamenco singers choose to sing his songs. The more serious consideration is that many of his detractors believe that Cepero actually has a hand in introducing his songs into flamenco festivals and records. The result of this line of thought, whether accurate or not, is a turning away from Cepero by a segment of the true afición in the belief that he is contributing to the further contamination of an already contaminated flamenco. For them, his considerable contribution to the maintenance of flamenco purity through his guitar gets lost in the shuffle.

Cepero lives with his family in a chalet just outside of Madrid.

PEDRO DEL VALLE (p.287), son of Perico el del Lunar, continues in Madrid, is still the favorite accompanist of the surviving performers of La Zambra's elite small cuadro: Rafael Romero and Rosa Durán. Pedro plays beautifully the style of his father. In my mind he is one of today's most pure and moving accompanists as he is a master at injecting his playing and personality into his accompanying while still remaining in the background; he sets the mood for the singer/dancer by graceful, very flamenco playing and musicality, not by excessive virtuosity.

At last report SEBASTIAN NUÑEZ (p.322) lives on in Jerez, now completely retired from guitar activity.

LA LINEA DE LA CONCEPCION. Province of Cádiz.

This Mediterranean seaport, nearly within hailing distance of Algeciras across the Gibraltar bay, is best known in flamenco circles for a large gypsy family of singers and dancers, the patriarch of whom was a singer called EL MONO. Most of his offspring were nicknamed after men's apparel. The most famous member of the family was the late ANTONIO EL CHAQUETA (p.157), who was finally taken by the throat cancer that was interrupting his singing career at the time of the printing of the first edition of this book (the cause, and seriousness, of the illness were unknown at the time). El Chaqueta is survived by his siter, ADELA, a fine and exciting singer who is, tragically, the only survivor of the cancer that razed the rest of her brothers and sisters. Other than Antonio el Chaqueta, the victims include dancer SALVADOR EL PANTALON (The Trouser), dancer TOMAS EL CHAQUETA (The Jacket), and singer-dancer EL CHALECO (The Vest), as well as a non-artistic sister who early left her husband, singer EL FLECHA DE CADIZ, a widower. Artistic sons from the latter marriaige are EL CHAQUETON (The Large Jacket), one of today's finest and most complete singers, and MANUEL EL FLECHA, another fine singer, both of whom are residing and performing in Madrid.

Another famous singer who spent much of his artistic life in La Linea (although born in Cádiz port) was GABRIEL MACANDE, some of whose colorful exploits and adventures are told on pps. 310-311.

LA ISLA DE SAN FERNANDO. Province of Cádiz.

This Atlantic port can almost be described as the continuation of the city of Cádiz, until recently connected by a streetcar line (*tranvía*) of which several famous cante verses have been written. One would think, therefore, that San Fernando must have contributed to the development of flamenco on a par with Cádiz, but apparently this is not the case. Few historical figures have emerged from La Isla, the most illustrious being the VIEJO DE LA ISLA (p.56). In more recent times La Isla barely kept its own with the fine singing of the late ALVARO DE LA ISLA and EL CHATO DE LA ISLA, the guitar of PACO DE LA ISLA (p.323), and the finger magic of José María Peña EL POETA DE LAS MANOS (p.327).

Today, however, La Isla has exploded into prominence with the young gypsy singer José Monge Cruz CAMARON DE LA ISLA (Little Shrimp from the Isle)(c.1949) considered by many aficionados to be today's most duende-drenched cantaor. Camarón began making ripples during the second half of the 1960's, when the word spread that some kid was singing up a storm down on the coast, with a wide knowledge of the cantes de Cádiz and a high-pitched, gypsy rajo voice that sent chills up spines. Before long Camarón found himself in Madrid cutting records with Paco de Lucía (see "Algeciras" in this section). Since then it has all been uphill for Camarón, and today he is riding on top.

Nonetheless, all is not perfect for Camarón. He often has personal problems that cause him to miss performances, much to the outrage of aficionados who have gone out of their way and paid good money to see him. Artistically, he also causes much debate, above all about his *cuplé*-inspired bulerías, directed at the young public, that can be considered flamenco only because Camarón, with his fantastic voice and style, sings them.

Camarón is a creator, sometimes with success, oftentimes without. Fortunately, he can revert to tradition when he wishes, which seems to be less and less these days. In short, Camarón at present is a polemical figure, an idol for the young, a question mark for many purists puzzling over, or outright rejecting, many of Camarón's offerings to flamenco.

LOS PUERTOS. Province of Cádiz.

This Atlantic coastal area, which consists of Puerto de Santa María and Puerto Real (discussed on pages 66 and 67), was another hotbed of early flamenco, producing such historical figures as DIEGO EL FILLO (p.34), his brother CURRO PABLAS (p.46), and singers MANOLILLO CARRERA, ROMERILLO and CHAQUETON (all pp. 66-67). In modern times flamenco has declined in Los Puertos, which was not helped by the death of CANALEJAS DE PUERTO REAL (p.133) some years ago, nor by the more recent death of ANZONINI DEL PUERTO (pps.206-207; also a prinicipal character in "A Way of Life"). Anzonini's singing and dancing were not suited for the stage, but he was definitely one of the great juerga artists of his time; he filled a small juerga room with his presence, voice, extremely colorful dance and unquestionable duende as few have or will.

Today's outstanding artists from the area, all from Puerto de Santa María, include EL NEGRO DEL PUERTO, an aging non-professional gypsy who prefers the cante jondo and specializes in *romances*, borderline flamenco cantes that speak of historical events; PEPA CAMPOS (p.207), long ago retired from professional dancing; and PANSEQUITO, a young singer who can be excellent, above all por bulerías.

PATERNA DE RIVERA. Province of Cádiz.

EL PERRO DE PATERNA (The Dog of Paterna) is this town's most illustrious singer, with several LPs to his credit.

SAN ROQUE. Province of Cádiz.

Just up the hill from La Linea de la Concepción lies the village of San Roque, home of ANTONIA LA DE SAN ROQUE (p.68) and ROQUE MONTOYA "JARRITO" (p.161).

SANLUCAR DE BARRAMEDA. Province of Cádiz.

This Atlantic seaport, equally as famous for its adjacent manzanilla vineyards as for being the site where the Guadalquivir River meets the Atlantic, has not played an abundant role in flamenco's development (if compared to neighboring Cádiz port or Jerez). Nonetheless, we can cite two native sons of days past, both singers, of considerable impact: TIO JOSE EL DE SANLUCAR (p.57) (also called "EL GRANAINO" for reasons unknown, as he was not from Granada), thought to have been creator, or at least to have had a hand in developing, both the caracoles and the mirabrás; and EL CIEGO DE LA PEÑA (p.56), said to have created his own style of siguiriyas.

In more recent times we might cite the following standouts:

The late ANTONIO SANLUCAR (p.289, also P.173 of "A Way of Life") died in his adopted Sevilla, where he lived most of his life. His brother, ESTEBAN SANLUCAR (p.289) still resides in Buenos Aires.

Non-gypsy guitarist MANOLO SANLUCAR is a young man who has fast risen to the top as a flamenco concertist. As a boy he was well-grounded in traditional flamenco; his father, Isidro, is a flamenco guitarist, and by age thirteen Manolo was already accompanying first-rate singers. It is revealing to follow Sanlúcar's guitar career by listening to his records in chronological order. At the beginning his accompanying of the cante, driving and imaginative, was exciting. Involvement with a rock group followed, then his concertizing, sometimes alone, sometimes with the usual (for today's concertizers) group of extraneous musicians, which might include bongos, flute, violin, piano, and it seems to me I remember a wind instrument on occasion as well. Many of his musical compositions today are quite lovely, although most touch only vaguely on flamenco; they have a flamenco feel to them, but have broken the bonds that differentiate flamenco from other music.

Manolo talks of evolution and keeping up with the times, as do many others that have generally become bored with traditional flamenco. The thing is, in the hands of these moderns flamenco is not-so-stealthily merging with universal musicality and will eventually cease to exist as a separate art form if no tradition is respected.

Sanlúcar presently is helping his hometown become something of a center for flamenco by presiding over the International Course of Flamenco Guitar, held annually in August.

MARQUITA VARGAS (p.168) generally has turned to commercial singing, but can still sing good flamenco when she wishes.

THE PROVINCE OF SEVILLA

with studies of

SEVILLA CAPITAL 360

and the following towns,
in alphabetical order:

ALCALA DE GUADAIRA 373

ARAHAL 375

AZNALCOLLAR 375

LA PUEBLA DE CAZALLA 375

LEBRIJA 376

LOS PALACIOS 378

MAIRENA DEL ALCOR 378

MARCHENA 379

MORON DE LA FRONTERA 379

OSUNA 380

UTRERA 380

SEVILLA CAPITAL

There is no doubt that the provinces of Cádiz and Sevilla, in that order, were the cradles and principal breeding grounds of gypsy-oriented flamenco. The focal point within Sevilla province was Triana, the famous gypsy quarter located just across the river Guadalquivir from the rest of Sevilla capital. Triana was dotted with the blacksmith forges of many of flamenco's earliest known singing greats, such as the gypsies EL PLANETA (p.34), DIEGO EL FILLO (p.34), LOS CAGANCHOS (p.58), JUAN PELAO (p.60), and FRASCO EL COLORAO (p.57), and was also home of the non-gypsy singer and creator RAMON EL OLLERO (p.74) and the gypsy dancer FAICO (p.185), creator of the dance por farruca. The non-gypsy sector of Sevilla capital in those days was far less prolific in producing great flamencos, with the major exceptions of the legendary SILVERIO FRANCONETTI (p.38), and the nearly as legendary ANTONIO EL DE BILBAO (p.184), who added revolutionary techniques to the flamenco dance.

It can be observed that the first-named above, El Planeta and El Fillo, were born in Cádiz province and migrated to Sevilla in the first years of the last century. This is not surprising. What with the River Guadalquivir connecting Sevilla with the Atlantic Ocean, Sevilla was an important port and Andalusia's most thriving city as far back as Roman times, and thus a land of opportunity for those from poorer regions. As for Sevilla's attraction for the flamencos, it was to increase many times over with the arrival of the café cantante era in the middle of the last century. As a multitude of cafés cantantes opened their doors, the influx of flamencos into Sevilla must have been comparable to the California gold rush. It was during this prosperous period, that was to last well into the present century, that Sevilla truly became the flamenco capital of Andalusia, filling up with many of the best artists from the surrounding provinces, but above all with those from Jerez, Los Puertos, and Cádiz port, sources of a seemingly endless flow of excellent flamenco artists. Most of the arriving flamencos settled in Sevilla proper, in the area of the Alameda de Hércules, and earned their living in the juerga life of an adjacent area called "La Europa," that consisted of several streets full of bars with *apartados* (juerga rooms) that vied for the flamenco trade. Many of the newcomers were from Jerez (Manuel Torre, el Niño Gloria, Juanito Mojama, La Macarrona, La Malena, La Sordita, La Gamba, to name but a few), others, such as Manolo de Huelva, were from elsewhere in Andalusia, still others were native Sevillanos (Niña de los Peines, Tomás Pavón, Niño Ricardo, etc.). Between them all they made the Alameda de Hércules area such an important flamenco nucleus that by the turn of this century it surpassed Triana in flamenco importance and became the focal point for flamenco from, say, 1910-1960.

Sevilla particularly became a haven for dancers. There was, after all, a limit to the singers and guitarists that could be absorbed into Sevilla's flamenco life, and much of the overflow moved on. Dancers were another question. Each café cantante hired many dancers, and there was also considerable demand for them in Sevilla's juerga activity, activity that roared unchecked round-the-clock, above all in La Europa, so much so that any reasonably graceful girl with a decent appearance and liberated mind (they were often expected to do more than just dance) could find work. Sevilla became the mecca for flamenco dancers, and still is.

But times change. Sevilla's wide-open juerga life became so infamous in religious circles that considerable pressure was exerted to enact laws closing down all but specially licenced bars and similar establishments at 1 a.m. That effectively killed the juerga scene, for juergas rarely got started until 1 a.m. So, bewildered, the flamencos either went legitimate and worked in organized flamenco (tablaos, theaters, troupes), which could support a small proportion of them, turned to some other activity, or went hungry. Or went north, drawn by a purportedly lucrative situation in - you guessed it - hustling, bustling Madrid, a city that today contains a large flamenco population scattered throughout its urban sprawl of five million inhabitants.

TRADITIONAL FLAMENCO FORMS FROM SEVILLA. The cantes of the smithies (tonás, martinetes, deblas, carceleras), and the Triana styles of the siguiriyas, soleares, bulerías, tangos, caña, polo, fandangos, and, of course, sevillanas.

OBITUARIES. Singers from Sevilla. In chronological order.

The last time I visited PEPE TORRE (p.102)(c.1887-1967), when he was confined to bed not long before his death, I happened to be accompanied by a pretty young aficionada. Pepe quickly shed thirty or forty of his many years and became quite playful, flattering the girl and becoming so animated that he insisted we go down to his favorite bar on his beloved Alameda de Hércules for some wine and song. That was the last time I heard Pepe sing, a *media voz* as he preferred.

Cigar-chomping, wine-swilling PEPE DE LA MATRONA (p.109)(1887-1980) remained a tough old-time juerga flamenco, who could outlast aficionados a fraction of his age, until nearly his ninetieth year. When his marvellous system finally started breaking down, Pepe was miserable. The last time I saw him, on a street of his adopted Madrid neighborhood, Lavapies, Pepe stated downheartedly: "*Coño*, when you can no longer eat what you want, have to give up tobacco and alcohol, forget about sex, and just subsist on medicine, it is time to go." Not long after, he did. Fortunately, Pepe's enormous knowledge and spirit remain with us in his valuable records, and in the pages of his very colorful book "Pepe el de la Matrona: Recuerdos de un Cantaor Sevillano" (memories and anecdotes as told by Pepe to the author of the book, J.L. Ortiz Nuevo).

The grand old gypsy singer LA PERLA DE TRIANA (p.123, also P.172 of "A Way of Life") apparently never did recover from her motor scooter injury as described in A Way of Life. Her intimate friend, ROSALIA DE TRIANA (same references) died in her native Triana in 1974.

Attempts to honor PASTORA PAVON "LA NIÑA DE LOS PEINES" (p.112)(1890-1969) in her last years as guest singer at several flamenco events were generally disappointing due to her increasing senility; she would forget what she was singing and be generally distracted. The honors she so richly deserved mostly arrived too late.

Pastora Pavón's husband, PEPE PINTO (p.129)(c.1903-1971), lasted only a short time after her death. At the time he seemed to be attempting to return to the more pure style of singing of his youth.

Despite his frequent forays into blatant commercialism, no one could deny MANOLO CARACOL'S (p.146) gypsy genius and immense emotion when he felt like singing well. Upon Caracol's death, in February of 1973 (car accident near Madrid) there was only one singer alive who could assume his tempestuous throne: the late Terremoto de Jerez.

José Bermúdez Vega PEPE EL CULATA (p.150) never did achieve the full recognition his fine singing deserved. His younger brother, ENRIQUE EL CULATA (1919-1983), was also a singer of note although never reaching, in my mind, the stature of Pepe. Both brothers spent most of their artistic careers in Madrid.

MANOLO FREGENAL (1911-1986) was a little man with a high voice who sang very well the cantes intermedios. Born in Fregenal de la Sierra, province of Badajoz, Manolo had learned some cantes but harbored little hope of ever becoming a professional when one day at a local fair singing contest one of the guest artists told him he should go to Sevilla and become a cantaor. So the boy, all of twelve years old, walked the 125 kilometers to Sevilla, somehow arranged a contract, and soon was in Madrid performing with such artists as la Niña de los Peines and Niño Ricardo. From there Fregenal worked all over Spain, but settled his residence in Sevilla.

Thus, in the 1960' and 70's, when we had our flamenco operation near Sevilla, we had ample opportunity to enjoy Manolo's exquisite guajiras, colombianas, fandangos, malagueñas, granainas, etc., nearly always accompanied by his good friend, Antonio Sanlúcar.

ANTONIO "EL NIÑO DE LA CALZADA" was one of flamenco's great innovators por fandangos.

EL GORDITO DE TRIANA (p:157) was, in my opinion, flamenco's most moving singer of the fandangos grandes.

OBITUARIES. Dancers from Sevilla. In chronological order.

PASTORA IMPERIO (p.220), flamenco's reigning queen of the dance for so many decades, finally ran out of energy in 1979, at age 89.

LA QUICA (p.227) in her long career very likely trained more famous dancers than anyone else in recent history. She passed away in her adopted Madrid.

FELIPE DE TRIANA (p.207).

ENRIQUE EL COJO (born 1912 in Cáceres, died 1985 in Sevilla) became such an institution in the Sevilla dance scene that he deserves far more than the brief mention I allotted him (p.249) in the first edition. At the time I must confess I did not take Enrique seriously, which was Enrique's usual fate until one observed his dance with an open mind. Enrique was a lame, somewhat misshapen little man who as a teenager decided he wanted to be a dancer. With patience, intelligence and, above all, humor, he endured the initial public ridicule until finally gaining the respect his dance deserved. Then came more than respect - with time Enrique developed into one of Spain's finest flamenco dancers.

Enrique's dance was unusual, to say the least. Through hard work he developed quite good footwork, but that is beside the point in his case. Enrique's forte was an inherent *gracia* in his dance possessed by few. He moved his arms, and upper torso in general, as well as any woman, which is one of the surprises of a style of dance full of unexpected moments and movements that delighted his audiences and solicited spontaneous shouts of ¡olé! Although Enrique did take early lessons - sevillanas and classical with the *maestro* Angel Pericet, flamenco with Frasquillo and La Quica - he danced like no one else. His dance was so unique it is impossible to describe without sounding ludicrous. It had to be seen.

Enrique was also Sevilla's top dance teacher, helping form many of today's top bailaoras (Manuela Vargas and Cristina Hoyos, to name but two), as well as many popular Spanish singers (*cupletistas*) who want to look flamenco while performing (Juanita Reina, Marisol, Paquita Rico, and so forth).

The poet John Lucas sums up Enrique so beautifully in his poem EL COJO (THE LAME) that I shall reproduce it here, by his kind permission.

EL COJO

With awe I watch
a crippled old
ill-favored gypsy
dancing-master
impart his art
unto a bevy
all sound and young
and well-endowed

His style so pure
as to transmute
the ludicrous
into a beauty
not one of them
can reproduce

FARRUQUILLO, son of Antonio el Farruco, was considered a great promise in the dance when killed in a motorcycle accident, in 1974, at a quite tender age.

OBITUARIES. Guitarists from Sevilla. In chronological order.

MANUEL SERRAPI "EL NIÑO RICARDO" (p.298, also P.106 in "A Way of Life"), one of the great developers of the modern flamenco guitar, returned to die in Sevilla after living many years in Madrid. In the first edition I removed five years from his life when I estimated his age; his true life span was 1904-1972. Ricardo's son, MANUEL SERRAPI hijo carried on the family guitar tradition until his premature death, at age forty, in 1983 (of cancer).

PEPE MARTINEZ (p.300) died in his Sevilla home in September of 1985. It seems the elves of time really got ahold of me in Pepe's case, for in the first edition I estimated his year of birth as 1910, when in reality it was 1922. At least I had him living longer......

JOSE CALA "EL POETA," born in Jerez but early taken to Sevilla, where he was formed artistically, was an accompanist much in demand when he was struck by sickness and premature death.

PRESENT-DAY ARTISTS. Singers from Sevilla. In alphabetical order.

ANTONIO CALZONES is a non-professional who has sung on one or two anthologies.

ANTONIO EL SEVILLANO (p.122) continues retired in Sevilla.

ANTONIO EL CHOCOLATE (p.163), gypsy-born in Jerez but formed artistically in Sevilla, is still considered Sevilla's top cantaor of the cante grande.

CHIQUETETE first made a name for himself singing pure cante, winning various singing prizes including that of Mairena del Alcor some years ago, then decided he preferred money and turned to singing the most syrupy brand of highly commercial pop imaginable. He has become rich and a folk hero. Can he still sing pure flamenco? I would guess he couldn't care less.

Gypsy CURRO FERNANDEZ is perhaps Sevilla's most popular singer for dancing. (See "Families" following the guitar section.)

Diego Camacho EL BOQUERON, an accomplished gypsy singer of the cantes gitanos, is much in demand as a singer for dancing.

ENRIQUE OROZCO (1912 -), although born in Olvera (Cadiz), was formed artistically in Sevilla, on the Alameda de Hércules (where else). With his high, melodious voice, Enrique specializes in the cantes intermedios. His fandangos, malagueñas, granainas and tarantas carry a special emotional impact that sets Enrique apart from most singers of his style. After spending many years in Madrid, Enrique has returned to Sevilla and is presently appearing on the tours of "Los Ultimos de la Juerga."

JUANITO VALDERRAMA (p.139) is still a fading favorite of the masses.

LA TOMASA (Tomasa Torres Gutiérrez - born 1925) is daughter of Pepe Torre (pps.102,365) and niece of Manuel Torre. With that background, la Tomasa could not help sing, and sing well and with purity. Born on the Alameda de Hércules, la Tomasa heard and absorbed the cante of the greats of the Alameda in that epoch - her father, uncle Manuel Torre, la Moreno, la Niña de los Peines, Tomás Pavón, Juanito Mojama, el Niño Gloria, el Carbonerillo, many others. When she was a small girl she remembers that both her father and uncle Manuel would sit her on their knees for a spell while in juerga, so she actually experienced that life style at firsthand. She reminisces that her father went daily to La Europa to look for juergas; if he got one, they would eat well that day; if not, often there was no food (there were nine children), or they ate very poorly. Nonetheless, there was a favorite source of free food, which was fishing in the nearby Guadalquivir river, at that time clean and with abundant fish. But when everything else failed Tomasa's stomach found a solution, which was to go to the house of uncle Manuel to see what he could offer, for he usually fared better than Pepe (by that time Manuel was living with María, the woman that followed La Gamba, with whom he had five daughters, at least one of whom, AMPARO, has some fame as a singer). When old enough Tomasa took odd jobs or worked as a maid until marrying a non-gypsy flamenco, Manuel Gregorio Rodríguez PIES DE PLOMO (Leaden Feet). Manuel, of Italian ancestry but born on the Alameda de Hércules, also was born into the flamenco of those days, and began singing at an early age.

Both Pies de Plomo and La Tomasa presently sing in the group "Los Ultimos de la Juerga" (The Last of the Juerga Artists) on its tours through Andalusian towns and villages, a wonderful opportunity for both the veteran artists and the public.

Their son, José Gregorio Soto JOSE EL DE LA TOMASA (1951 -), born on the Alameda de Hércules, today is considered one of flamenco's top singers of cante jondo. His first break was winning the Mairena del Alcor singing contest one year, which brought him contracts and to the attention of the public. He is definitely considered a great promise for the future of pure flamenco.

LOLE MONTOYA. See "Families" following the guitar section.

MANUEL OLIVER hijo (1906 -). In the December 1986 issue of the magazine "Sevilla Flamenca" the flamencologist Manuel Herrera Rodas presents an interview he had with Manuel Oliver, a non-professional singer who has lived his entire life in Triana. In this biography I shall draw basically from that article, for the life of the flamencos of Triana is of utmost importance if we wish to more-or-less understand flamenco's complete picture, and who better than an old-timer like Manuel Oliver to give us the inside information about a Triana most of us had no opportunity to know (my first experiences in Triana date back only to 1956).

First and foremost, Manuel Oliver states that flamenco in Triana was part of everyday life. Aficionados sang while they worked and they sang afterwards in the sessions of friends that might last several hours, all night, or several days. Few of even the best of them became professionals; they were content with their daily occupations and the Triana life style.

Of course, Manuel is talking about a Triana it is difficult to visualize. His father, for example, had a large herd of goats, and Manuel spent much of his youth tending them. His friends included other shepherds, as well as *areneros*, men and youths who made their living hauling sand by donkey train from the river to construction sites. Manuel himself, when not tending goats, helped his father make and bake bricks. In short, a low stress way of life that left ample time, and silence, for singing.

Manuel talks about some of the better singers Triana produced. He says his father claimed that RAMON EL OLLERO (p.74) was the best of them all *por* soleares and also sang excellent siguiriyas, and that his nickname does not signify "pot maker" (as I put in the first edition) but is a misspelling of "*hoyero*" (hole maker), as Ramón used to prepare the holes in the streets to receive the cobblestones. He talks highly about PEPE DE LA MATRONA (p.109), who he says actually was from Sevilla but moved to Triana when young and learned all the Triana cantes. The singers Manuel himself learned the most from were his father, also called MANUEL OLIVER, ENRIQUE VIGIL, Pepe de la Matrona, PACO REYES, EL CARTUJANO, MORALITO, PANCHO, EL MALINO, JOAQUIN CASTILLARES, others. Manuel reminisces about hearing FERNANDO DE TRIANA (p.89) sing, several times and well, after he left Triana and opened his tavern in nearby Camas. Among Manuel's friends of his age group, he singles out ANTONIO and JOAQUIN BALLESTEROS, EMILIO ABADIA, and SORDILLO as fine singers. And then there were the two ANTONIO EL ARENEROS, father and son, DOMINGO EL ALFARERO (ceramics maker), who avoided singing in public but when he opened up he was really something, GARFIAS, a night watchman in the streets who sang as he made the rounds, much to the delight of the neighbors, and who sang *por* serranas better than anyone.

Manuel claims that no racism has existed in Triana during his lifetime, that the *gitanos* and the *payos* respect and like each other. The gypsies had different occupations (blacksmiths, butchers, cattle dealers) and sang the cantes somewhat differently, according to Manuel, with more *rajo* and more *compás* than the payos; the payos sang the cantes de Triana in a sweeter, more lyrical manner.

Manuel talks about LA NIÑA DE LOS PEINES' (p.112) first artistic appearances, when a small girl with her hair loaded down with little colored combs (thus, "The Little Girl of the Combs"). She used to visit her uncle in Triana and at night they would take her to the Casa Ballesteros, where she would sing a few times, above all the tangos de Triana, which Manuel says she sang beautifully, and pocket perhaps two pesetas for her efforts. (We must remember that two pesetas then probably was a laborer's daily wage, if not more.)

Manuel also enjoys the dance and the guitar. In the dance he admired greatly RAMIREZ (de Jerez - P.187), who from the waist up was the best he has seen and used just enough footwork. ANTONIO DE BILBAO (p.184), on the other hand, was "all crashing feet and no *arte*." Today he favors RAFAEL EL NEGRO, husband of Matilde Corral. Of the guitarists, he singles out NIÑO RICARDO (p.298) and MIGUEL BORRULL (p.273), and his friend, MANOLO DE HUELVA (p.278). He recounts that he was fortunate to be with Manolo de Huelva the last time Huelva recorded, in the home of a rich *señora*. Apparently Manolo de Huelva visited her nearly every day, often bringing along one or another singer he could accompany.

Why did Triana lose its flamenco atmosphere? Sr. Herrera Rodas states it was because of the "lack of sensitivity of many administrators," which "provoked an exodus too late now to remedy." What apparently happened was when they decided to urbanize Triana, which is to say make it fit for the upper classes with large blocks of luxury apartment buildings, they sent many of the poorer people, gypsies and payos alike, to suitable housing in the surrounding towns and villages. Whether intended or not, the relocation of these people effectively killed the flamenco atmosphere in Triana around the same time the *"PROHIBIDO EL CANTE"* signs were put up in nearly all bars and other public places throughout Andalusia. It looks to me like a big victory for the "respectable" classes, who have been irritated by that lowdown flamenco life style for some generations now.

NARANJITO DE TRIANA (José Sánchez Bernal - c.1932), Triana-born non-gypsy, began as a guitarist, became quite accomplished, then decided that singing was for him. Since making that decision Naranjito has risen high in the world of cante, above all in the cantes best suited to his high-pitched, clear voice: the non-gypsy cantes intermedios. Naranjito is not lacking in versatility; besides playing and singing well, he is also a luthier, and reputedly a good one.

Susana Amador LA SUSI both sings and dances well, although much of her singing is highly commercial.

TRAGAPANES (Joaquín Rodríguez Lara - 1908) is another veteran from Triana who has seen his share of the flamenco world. Born into a family of bullfighters and flamenco singers, LOS CAGANCHOS (p.58), Tragapanes (The Bread Gobbler) was a bullfighter in his youth, then returned home to sing professionally in the juerga scene of La Europa with the greats of the period, and in Triana with his friends for pleasure (la BELLITA, la CONCEPCION, FERRER, ANTONIO CAMACHO, etc.). His favorite cantes are those from Triana, particularly the martinetes, soleares and siguiriyas.

Tragapanes was a victim of the Triana-destroying relocation plan discussed under "Manuel Oliver," now lives alone in a flat in the town of Torreblanca. Presently he performs with the veteran group "*Los Ultimos de la Juerga*" (Last of the Juerga Artists) in its tours through Andalusia.

PRESENT-DAY ARTISTS. Dancers from Sevilla. In alphabetical order.

ANA MARIA BUENO is building a big name for herself both as dancer and instructor. She has mastered the dance techniques; now aficionados want something more. Too often one hears said about her dance: "Too much head, not enough heart."

ANGELITA VARGAS. See "Families" following the dance section.

The *maestro* ANTONIO (Antonio Ruiz Soler) is living in retirement in his adopted Madrid.

ANTONIO DE TRIANA (p.208). Back in 1966, not long after the first edition of this book had been published, I enjoyed correspondence with the famous dancer Antonio de Triana. One of his letters in particular I consider of great interest to this book, as it is full of insights and data that help clarify the already misty artistic past of the first half of this century. As the letter is in English and extremely well written, I shall print it verbatim. (The text within parentheses was written by Sr. Triana.) <Enclose my observations>.

"I was born in Sevilla (Barrio de la Macarena). Soon after, my father moved our family to Triana. I entered the Academy of Maestro Manuel Otero at eight. He had previously refused to teach male dancers, but one day he caught me peering through a window at the beautiful young Sevillanas, and he invited me to join his class. He appreciated my daring, and thought perhaps I could partner his more advanced pupils. La Quica was by far his best pupil. We became partners and made our debut at the Salón Imperial. Otero taught a basic technique of heelwork and castanets that he himself described as *'Bailes Típicos Andaluces y Clásicos.'* That was all that was demanded of him. There was no cry for flamenco, as the average café dancer of the time earned a mere six pesetas a day. Through Quica, I became acquainted with her *novio* Frasquillo, who instructed me in the rhythms of the Alegrías, Farruca and Zapateado de Cádiz, which were the only flamenco dances considered masculine.

"I was then hired to perform at the Café Novedades to appear with La Malena, La Fernanda (Antúnez), La Sordita, Frasquillo, Malenita, El Tiznao and Javier Molina. I was only nine years old, but they accepted me in their dance and I proceeded to learn and absorb from those wonderful surroundings. Nowadays, I am not moved by the 'Flamencos' I see. They are for the most part imitating an art that defies imitation. It is that undefinable *'gracia'* that I remember and miss the most.

"Unfortunately, the spirit of the Café Flamenco was dying. Before long, the dancers were copying one another and the techniques degenerated into memories.

"It was many years later (1933), at the urging of Sánchez Mejía and Garcia Lorca that Argentinita came out of her semi-retirement and decided to stage the *'El Amor Brujo'* of De Falla. She sent me a telegram in Madrid (where I was appearing in musicals) and I soon joined her and her sister Pilar (López) for rehearsals in Seville. To give the ballet enormous authenticity, they contracted La Malena, La Macarrona and La Fernanda for the scenes in the gipsy caves. The choreography of the ballet itself was achieved through a mingling of ideas and improvisations on the part of Encarna (La Argentinita), Pilar, Rafael Ortega (who was to play the Spectre) and myself (as Carmelo). We had a triumphant opening night in Cádiz, the birthplace of De Falla. We then went on a complete tour of Spain with the Amor Brujo, and we also performed what we called *'Conciertos de Danza.'* This was truly the birth of the *'Ballet Español'*

"Then came the revolution in Spain (1936). The theater had an uncertain future, and many of us migrated to Paris. While in Paris, La Argentinita, Pilar and I renewed our friendship and began rehearsing for our debut at the Salle Pleyel Theater. Manuel Infante was our pianist, and Manolo de Huelva, the guitarist. On the strength of our performance there, Sol Hurok engaged us for an American tour. We traveled through South and North America, and it was the first time that Alegrías, Bulerías, etc., were ever seen in Carnegie Hall. Argentinita was an inspired performer! Our association was one of mutual admiration for many years. But on our second tour with Hurok she became ill, and with much regret Hurok began looking for her replacement.

"(I must now regress to the early 1930's. I was peforming in Madrid when I was approached by the father of a young dancer who was about to make her debut. She danced only flamenco, and her father asked me to teach her some routines that could be performed with the orchestra. I proceeded to teach her my choreography to a Paso-doble written by my brother. She responded admirably. Her father saw us as an ideal team and was intent on joining us. So it was, that at a casino in San Sebastián, Carmen Amaya and I danced together for the first time. Our paths soon separated however, as I had other commitments.)

"Now, I had heard that Carmen was in Mexico City. I recommended her to Mr. Hurok who gave me full authority to sign her for her first American tour. She came to New York with her entourage of eighteen, which included her chauffeur (no car - but a chauffeur). She first performed at the old Beachcomber night club and during the day I was busy giving her and her sisters, Leo and Antonia, instruction in the choreography necessary to fill the two-and-one-half-hours concert program. Their entire gipsy repertoire took only about forty minutes. We had a bombastic tour and we also did the complete 'El Amor Brujo' at the Hollywood Bowl in California, where I unexpectedly assigned Paco Amaya (the guitarist) the role of the Spectre, which he danced with considerable wit and much compás.

"I later settled in California, where I have done the choreography for many films. Frankly, my various business endeavors have not allowed me to travel about as much as before.

"Jerónimo Villarino, a guitarist from Huelva, who toured with me and the Amaya troupe, is a fine instructor and an excellent tocaor for the Baile. He has also settled in the Hollywood area.

"I have always taught, and I have given instruction at one time or another to Conchita Piquer, Charito Leonis, Conchita Leopardo, Reyes Castizo (La Yanqui), Ana María, Luisillo, José Greco, Manolo Vargas, Rafael de Córdoba, Roberto Iglesias. I am teaching now, but only professionals, and select individuals who want to learn the true dance and not the watered down commercial flamenco. I am spending a good part of my time in training my son, Antonio Jr., who in all honesty is a wizard at eight years. I intend to take him to Spain very soon.

"I have no criticism of your book. I agree with many of your impressions, but may I tell you that Antonio de Bilbao, who was my good friend (as I danced with his wife, Julia Verdiales, on several occasions), never taught anyone his technique! He told me once, 'Yo no enseño ni a mi padre.' ('I teach no one, not even my father')." (This statement contests Vicente Escudero's claim on P.190 that he learned the essentials of the dance from Antonio de Bilbao, a counterclaim no doubt accurate, for I have heard from various sources that Antonio de Bilbao considered Escudero 'un chalao' - 'a nut').

CARMEN CARRERA (p.249) rose to considerable prominence before marriage and retirement.

CRISTINA HOYOS, who maestro Enrique el Cojo considered his masterpiece, has long been the dance darkhorse of Sevilla, the behind-the-scenes favorite of many knowledgeable aficionados because of her natural, very flamenco way of dancing. In recent times she blossomed forth as Antonio Gades' dancing partner when he was artistic director of the Ballet Nacional de España, then as the superior female dancer in the three Gades-Carlos Saura movies, "Bodas de Sangre," "Carmen," and "El Amor Brujo." Presently she is still highlighted in Gades' troupe in its worldwide tours.

ENCARNA "LA CONTRAHECHA" (literally "Made Backwards," but also a curious Andaluz way of calling a girl pretty) is an attractive woman who began making a name for herself as a dancer some fifteen years ago, then disappeared from artistic sight.

JUANA LA DEL REVUELO is an inspired juerga-style dancer-singer who steals the show at many of Andalusia's flamenco festivals.

LAS ALBENIZ. ELOISA ALBENIZ (p.99) more and more is turning her teaching responsibilities over to her niece, CARMEN ALBENIZ, an excellent dancer whose career was nipped in the bud years ago by marriage (which was a shame, for Carmen was a natural). However, I am happy to report that today the family does have an active dancing representative, and a good one, in form of Carmen's niece, also called CARMEN ALBENIZ. The youngest Carmen has performed in a touring troupe in America, has been in several movies in dancing roles, and more recently has been a longtime headliner in the Sevilla tablao "Los Gallos."

LOS FARRUCO. ANTONIO EL FARRUCO (p.202, also p.189 in "A Way of Life") has suffered a heart atack and has gotten quite obese over the years. Nevertheless, he still possesses that dancing magic of old when he lets himself go, although not nearly to the extent of his youth. El Farruco was hard struck by the accidental death of his son, El Farruquito, but has fared better with his daughters, PILAR and LA FARRUQUITA, who are building a fine reputation for themselves. Often the three dance as a group.

MANOLI DE SEVILLA. Whatever happened to Manoli de Sevilla? Just two or three years ago we were attending a flamenco function, during San Isidro in Madrid, that featured some pretty formidable dancing. First a dancer, a relative of Carmen Amaya, apparently, who raised forgotten dust from the floor with her steel-driving footwork, but nothing else. Then a well-considered American girl of many years study at Amor de Dios, who also pounded well and was effectively academic. Then a breath of fresh air! Manoli rose from her seat and began dancing por alegrías. Her dance was happy, it was natural (not frowning with concentration in attempting to remember an arrangement), her arms and body were beautifully flowing, she was tasteful, it was everything an alegrías should be. I saw Manoli dance again in the now defunct Café de Silverio. Again she was perfect. I have not seen nor heard about her since. Don't stop dancing, Manoli, wherever you are. Flamenco needs you, and a lot more like you.

MANOLO MARIN retired from active performing some years ago to become one of Sevilla's most popular dance instructors. His academy is located in Triana.

MANUELA CARRASCO exploded out of Sevilla with her fiery dance as a young woman in the late 1960's and became the flamenco dance rage for a number of years. Presently her dance seems to be burning itself out after all those years of intensity; her appearances are fewer and her programs shorter, and her dances seem to have lost some of that spark. Perhaps a more subtle dance from La Carrasco lies in store for us in the future.

MANUELA VARGAS (p.249) has gone on to become a complete and excellent bailaora, probably the Sevilla-produced dancer who has gained the most international acclaim since Rosario and Antonio. After her beginning in Sevilla's "El Cortijo del Guajiro" tablao, back in the late 50's, early 60's, as a very electrifying *rumbera*, Manuela began serious study with Eloisa Albéniz and Enrique el Cojo. Once prepared, she formed her own troupe, with excellent supporting artists, and has toured worldwide. Of late she is dancing more non-flamenco than flamenco, also very tastefully and well.

MARIA ROSA heads one of the few remaining large Spanish dance troupes. Her dancing consists mainly of regional and Spanish classical, with flamenco being a distant, and mediocre, last.

MATILDE CORAL won a dance contest in Córdoba in 1964 which helped launch her to considerable fame and a prominent position in the hierarchy of flamenco dancers. Her very pleasing dance is of the old style, unfortunately watered down by overly long arrangements and sessions of footwork. Presently semi-retired, she teaches in her dance academy in Sevilla.

Matilde's family is also very much in the dance. Her husband, RAFAEL EL NEGRO, is a gypsy bailaor who as a youth gained fame with his spectacular, very acrobatic style of dance, which over the years has mellowed to a more orthodox and mature style. Matilde's brother, EL MIMBRE (The Reed) is very highly considered in the flamenco world. He has been dancing in festivals and with various groups for some years. Lastly, Matilde's sister, PEPA CORAL, is also an accomplished dancer who has a following of her own, although she has always been overshadowed by her more famous older sister.

Non-gypsy beauty MERCHE ESMERALDA rose to fame in the late 1960's with a highly refined dancing style quite classical in nature. After several years of semi-retirement, Merche is making a strong comeback and is dancing better than ever. Although her direction these days is not exclusively flamenco - she also dances modern, Spanish classical, bolero, flamenco abstract - her flamenco is still very much alive, as I witnessed recently when she took time out from a modern dance program to sing and dance a garrotín in which she mimed beautifully the highly feminine bailaoras of the past. During moments free from active dancing, Merche teaches dance in Madrid.

PEPA MONTES is the latest dancing sensation from Sevilla. Everyone who has seen her raves about her, many of whom are aficionados I respect highly. I must, thus, take their word for it, for I have not had the opportunity to see Pepa Montes dance as yet. They are, in fact, so carried away in writing accolades and poetry about her that no one, to my knowledge, has returned to earth to write even a minimal biography about her; in which Sevilla neighborhood she was born, with whom she studied, if with anyone, only that the guitarist RICARDO MIÑO is her husband and accompanies her very well. Pepa is a great hope that awaits us all in the future.

I have lost track of PASTORA LA POSAERA (P.248, also p.172 in "A Way of Life"). May she be doing well.

ROSARIO (p.,237) and ANTONIO roared out of Sevilla fifty-some years ago as "Los Chavalillos de España" and took the dance world by storm. Presently retired from active performing, Rosario teaches dance in her Madrid studios on the calle Ballestas, 6.

TRINI ESPAÑA (p.249) enjoyed many years of glory before slowing down to semi-retirement and teaching in Madrid.

PRESENT-DAY ARTISTS. Guitarists from Sevilla. In alphabetical order.

The years have converted EDUARDO DE LA MALENA (p.323) into Sevilla capital's most noteworthy veteran guitarist. Presently he tours with the group "*Los Ultimos de la Juerga*" ("Last of the Juerga Artists") around Andalusia.

JOSE LUIS POSTIGO is the guitarist most in demand today to accompany in Andalusia's festivals, for both singers and dancers feel comfortable with his style of accompanying. He also teaches in his guitar shop in Sevilla's Barrio de Santa Cruz.

LUIS MARAVILLA (p.307) continues teaching in his Madrid guitar shop on the calle León.

MANOLO BARON played around the world before settling down in the USA. He is married to the fine American flamenco dancer, Carolina de los Reyes.

MANOLO BRENES has long been a favorite accompanist in the Sevilla area.

MANOLO DOMINGUEZ is considered one of today's more accomplished accompanists.

MANOLO FRANCO (1960 -) surged into prominence upon winning Sevilla's "Giraldillo del Toque," in 1984, a guitar contest presided over by very knowledgeable judges, including Paco de Lucía, Manolo Sanlúcar, Mario Escudero, Víctor Monge "Serranito," others of prestige. Since then Manolo is much in demand, above all in Andalusia's festival circuit. He is nephew of Manolo Barón, started out studying the flamenco guitar with Antonio de Osuna.

RICARDO MIÑO is an accomplished accompanist who performs mostly with his wife, dancer Pepa Montes.

RAFAEL RIQUENI (1962 -) startled the flamenco world by wining the 1976 Córdoba flamenco guitar contest when only fourteen, then captured first prizes in Jerez in 1977 and 1981. He has gone on to become one of flamenco's top virtuosos. Riqueni has been strongly influenced by Paco de Lucia, as all of the younger virtuosos are, and is taking Paco's same route into international group music with a flamenco base.

The brothers JOAQUIN and RAMON AMADOR are hard driving, very flamenco guitarists who usually play in family with wife/sister-in-law Manuela Carrasco and another brother who sings, Juan José Amador.

Veteran TRIGUITO (p.309) lives in semi-retirement in Madrid.

Reports have it that VICTOR ROJAS (p.287), brother of the late Pastora Imperio, lives on in his adopted Mexico.

FLAMENCO FAMILIES

As we have seen, flamenco tends to run in families. So what is so unusual about the below listed families? Only that they bill themselves as families, and thus must be considered as such.

FAMILIA MONTOYA. This Moroccon-Spanish family of gypsy artists, permanently settled in Sevilla some years ago, has captured the public's imagination with its flamenco interpretations in which a touch of Moorish culture is often discernable. This is especially true of daughter LOLE, who was born in Melilla and who absorbed enough Arabic before moving to Sevilla that she often sings entire passages of her dreamy bulerías in Arabic and with the Arabic singing style. These arrangements are composed by husband MANUEL, born in Ceuta of a Jerez de la Frontera gypsy family. Besides being a straight-forward, no frills guitarist with imagination, and a singer along the same lines, Manuel is a poet whose images, when sung by Lole and by himself, are quite touching and which comprise a new approach to flamenco that took the youth of Spain by storm, vaulting Lole and Manuel straight to the top. The young couple went on to do a multitude of recordings and recitals on their own, and today rarely perform with the family.

Without them it was thought the family would be lost, but to everyone's surprise it also went on to became a top attraction with the dancing of JUAN MONTOYA (masculine and elegant) and the youngsters CARMELILLA and EL MORITA, and the very flamenco singing of LA NEGRA, ANTONIA, CARMEN MONTOYA and CARMELILLA.

FAMILIA VARGAS. The gypsy family Vargas is comprised of a vey effective husband-wife-teen-age son combination. ANGELITA VARGAS is an accomplished dancer who substitutes gypsy clout for finesse in a very rousing and effective manner. She is definitely one of the more exciting dancers today. Husband EL BIENCASAO (The Well Married) is a very masculine dancer of straight lines and force who one wishes would dance more himself and be less subordinate to his family. Son JOSELITO is a colorful and quite accomplished dancer for his age. He and his father have worked out some duo routines por bulerías that are reasonably impressive.

FAMILIA FERNANDEZ. One has the feeling that the gypsy Fernández family performing group was thrown together as an act in order to jump on the present family bandwagon. With the exception of the singing of CURRO FERNANDEZ, the Fernández family is not of the caliber of the families Montoya and Vargas, although they are improving and becoming more professional by the year.

MISCELLANEOUS ARTISTS FROM SEVILLA.

Reports place the excellent reciter and performer GABRIELA ORTEGA (p.325) in Mexico.

ARTURO PAVON (p.328) presently gives flamenco piano recitals in and out of Spain, and directs his Spanish dance academy in a Madrid suburb.

Flamenco comedy in Sevilla, like in Cádiz and Jerez, has always played an important role. Three of the best flamenco comedians in Sevilla are EL GRAN SIMON, EL GASOLINA, and EL GRINGO.

ALCALA DE GUADAIRA

Out from Sevilla some sixteen kilometers along the Guadaira river lies the hilly town of Alcalá de Guadaira, famous in days of yore for its bread, so good that the demand for it even in Sevilla was great. From the hilltop Roman castle down to the Guadaira river there is quite a lengthy and steep, rock-bound bank into which the poorer element of Alcalá dug and chipped their caves. Among the cave dwellers was a gypsy family that produced some of flamenco's greats of this and the past century, including: JOAQUIN EL DE LA PAULA (1875-1933)(p.99), his brother, AGUSTIN TALEGAS (p.105), Agustín's son, JUAN TALEGAS, and his nephew, MANOLITO EL DE LA MARIA. Other singers of note from Alcalá have been LA ROEZNA, gypsy mother of Juan Barcelona reputed to have been a creator *por* soleares, and two town-dwelling non-gypsies, BERNARDO EL DE LOS LOBITOS and PLATERITO DE ALCALA.

They are all gone now, leaving the flamenco scene in Alcalá rather desolate. In following I shall obituarize those that have died since the first printing of this book.

The last few times JUAN TALEGAS (p.104)(1887-1971) came out to juerga at our Andalusian flamenco center he was popping pills for his heart condition at a frightening pace; we finally had to stop having him for fear that he would not make it through one of the juergas. Juan achieved much overdue recognition from the flamenco world during his last years, a great deal due to the efforts of his good friend, Antonio Mairena. Posthumously, the town where Juan lived much of his life, nearby Dos Hermanas, honored him by naming after him both a street, and its annual flamenco festival.

BERNARDO EL DE LOS LOBITOS (p.116)(1887-1969) spent his last years in Madrid scratching out a bare existence; although one of the most knowledgeable, and best, cantaores of flamenco, he was too old to be an attraction in the tablaos, and the juerga scene that provided his livelihood during most of his life was disappearing. I am happy to report that we were able to remedy that situation for Bernardo when we had our Madrid flamenco center in 1964-65, for he became one of our juerga regulars, much to our delight. Shortly after his death a record was released in homage to Bernardo, featuring his singing to the accompaniment of Luis Maravilla.

MANOLITO DE MARIA (p.129)(c.1904-1966) lived his life to the hilt and finally went down swinging. There was no mellowing, no aging gracefully for Manolito. Oh no, he roared along unchecked until a multitude of ailments landed him in Sevilla's general hospital. There, unless strapped down, Manolito wandered around the ward singing to his fellow patients until his flame snuffed out.

The considerable recognition Manolito achieved arrived posthumously. Due to his bohemian, irresponsible life style very few took Manolito seriously. Only upon his death did the flamenco world realize what it had lost.

PLATERITO DE ALCALA (p.167)(c.1912-1984) sang a wide range of cantes, but was far better in the non-gypsy forms. The cante for which he was best known was the alegrías de Córdoba.

PRESENT-DAY ARTISTS FROM ALCALA. I am afraid they are limited to one, that I know of, who is MANOLO EL POETA (p.139 of "A Way of Life"), gypsy reciter of flamenco verses, and juerga dancer.

ARAHAL

Arahal's one famous native son in flamenco has been PEPE PALANCA (p.122).

AZNALCOLLAR

This little mining town, to the NW of Sevilla capital, has produced three flamencos of note to my knowledge, all non-gypsy: the late PEPE AZNALCOLLLAR (p.122), famed singer of fandangos who created his own style; singer LUIS CABALLERO (1919 -) is a well-known specialist of the cantes intermedios. He also writes very interesting and well-written articles for the magazine "Sevilla Flamenca"; and singer EL CABRERO, the present-day goatsherd of powerful delivery and personality. El Cabrero's past occupation and forceful singing have captured the public's imagination and he is voluminously applauded in Andalusia's festivals.

LA PUEBLA DE CAZALLA

This small town, located on the plains between Morón de la Frontera and Osuna, possesses a fierce afición that produces a preponderance of famous singers well out of proportion to its size. Among them we can list:

LUIS TORRE CADIZ "JOSELERO," who long ago moved to Morón de la Frontera and is thus listed there.

LA NIÑA DE LA PUEBLA (p.139) is a blind singer who enjoyed great commercial success.

Non-gypsy JOSE MENESE (1942 -). I wrote twenty-five years ago that "Menese is the boy to watch." (p.169). Since then Menese's serious cantes, powerful delivery and rajo voice have carried him to the top and have kept him there. With the fall of the Franco regime, Menese revealed a strong leftist leaning and since then sings verses describing the Andalusian masses' hunger and oppression in his ultra-grave soleares, siguiriyas and tangos. There is no doubt that Menese is being accurate, from his humorless, single-minded point of view - oppression and hunger did exist in Andalusia, but so did a lot of very pleasant factors that he chooses to ignore. One wonders if Menese is not overly exploiting the theme, or working towards a political end, or both for, after all, the very oppression he cannot stop singing about has largely disappeared today.

MANUEL GERENA rose to fame singing of the same oppression and hunger as does Menese, but with one major difference: Gerena was doing so even during the Franco regime, and as such found himself in jail more than once. Due to highly placed friends, Gerena was generally just given stern warnings and released; nevertheless, he was risking his neck. Gerena's fearless cante made him a revolutionary symbol, above all to Spain's youth. When Franco's regime began noticeably liberalizing, in the early 1960's, Gerena was permitted to sing at student gatherings and the like and became even more a hero. With the arrival of democracy, however, Gerena's message was no longer appropriate, and he has slipped back into obscurity because, unlike Menese, Gerena is not a great singer; without a gospel to preach, he will not go far in the flamenco world.

DIEGO CLAVEL is another non-gypsy from La Puebla to rise to fame in the last years. As also typifies Menese and Gerena, Clavel is long on seriousness, short on the cantes *graciosos* that so brighten one's existence; neither of the three, for instance, can adequately sing a sparkling bulerías or a happy tango, giving one the idea that life indeed must have been grim around La Puebla de Cazalla. Clavel, however, does not seem too hung up on political issues, as are the other two.

MIGUEL VARGAS (1942 -) is still another well-known, non-gypsy singer from La Puebla, presently living in nearby Paradas. Like the above listed, Vargas sings very well the serious cantes from the area, as well as a wide variety of other cantes.

LEBRIJA

Lebrija has always been one of Andalusia's most flamenco towns. (Why one town is teeming with flamencos and the town alongside not nearly so much is an interesting study.) Way back with DIEGO EL LEBRIJANO (p.56), Lebrija was a flamenco town, remained so in the times of JUANIQUIN (pps.74,348) and the PAULA clan (p.348), and is so today, with several families that keep up the tradition.

Perhaps foremost among them in recent times has been the Peña family, the queenpin of which is María Fernández Granados LA PERRATA. But wait a minute, that sounds like Utrera. Sure enough, La Perrata, sister of Utrera's El Perrate, was born and raised in Utrera and moved to Lebrija when she married a local gypsy butcher, Bernardo Peña. (The wedding was celebrated for months, true gypsy style, with such flamenco dignataries as La Niña de los Peines, Juan Talegas, and Antonio Mairena taking part.) La Perrata says she always sang in juergas with members of her family in Utrera when a little girl, in Lebrija only in family after marriage, in some festivals and for recording companies after her husband died. Meantime, she begot two very flamenco sons, as follows:

JUAN PEÑA EL LEBRIJANO has gone on from "showing great promise in the cante gitano" (p.169) twenty-five years ago to a solid position as one of flamenco's very top singers today. When he is on and feeling traditional (which seems to be less and less these days), El Lebrijano sings all the gypsy cantes, from bulerías and tangos to soleares, siguiriyas and those a palo seco, with authority and duende. When feeling innovative he will toy with the compás and introduce his own touches into the cantes, sometimes with interesting, often with lamentable, results. Lately he is singing *"Cante Andalusí"* in which he alternates singing with an excellent Moorish singer, the Moorish singer taking a Moorish riff, el Lebrijano taking a sort of flamenco riff. The result is less than inspiring. El Lebrijano justifies all this by stating that it is keeping him on top in record sales and in the public's eye. Purists say he is going to hell and are turning off on him. Meantime, el Lebrijano spends much of his time in Madrid socializing and singing in the moneyed crowd.

PEDRO PEÑA. During their children's formative years the Peñas made sure to expose the boys to some good gypsy guitar, in case that was their calling, in form of Diego del Gastor. Diego came to juergas, the boys listened and absorbed, and both brothers took up the guitar. Juan eventually switched to singing, but PEDRO PEÑA kept at it and now plays a very driving, very gypsy guitar that is a pleasure to hear. A school teacher by trade, Pedro also sings quite well, as many of flamenco's best accompanists do. Both Pedro and his mother have moved to a town just outside of Sevilla so as to be closer to his work. I have been told that Pedro has recently accepted an important position in the area of flamenco with the *Junta de Andalucía*.

PEDRO BACAN (Pedro Peña Peña - 1951). This Peña, a cousin of the Peñas above, is a guitarist who is able effectively to combine duende with advanced technique and whose knowledge of, and intrinsic instinct for, accompanying makes him one of flamenco's most sought after accompanists of the Cante. Like his cousin, Pedro Peña, Pedro Bacán also sings, quite extensively and quite well.

Pedro Bacán descended from a long line of flamencos, beginning with his great grandfather, the legendary Fernando Peña Soto "PININI" (p.75), a Lebrija gypsy who married a gypsy woman named Josefa Vargas Torres. That union produced nine very flamenco children, including Inés, mother of La Fernanda and La Bernarda de Utrera, BENITO EL DE PININI, said to have sung beautifully por soleares, LUISA, likewise por siguiriyas, and FERNANDA, another singer of fame and mother of Bastián Bacán, Diego Lagañas, and Fernando Funi, and grandmother of today's Pedro Bacán and Miguel Funi.

Pedro Bacán's uncles, BASTIAN BACAN (1911 -) and DIEGO LAGAÑAS (1916 -) are non-professional cantaores said to sing with such purity they are nearly living legends in flamenco's inner circle. The other brother, Fernando Funi, begot MIGUEL EL FUNI (Miguel Peña Vargas - 1939). Gypsy butcher by trade, Miguel is one of the best of the old-style *festeros* around today. With his white silk scarf and black suit, his inspired and very gypsy dance, and his wide knowledge of the cantes of his area, El Funi is an elegant, artistic and tireless addition to any gathering.

CONCHA VARGAS, another of the Lebrija Peña family, is a fiery and moving dancer who is gaining a fine name for herself.

CURRO MALENA (Francisco Carrasco Carrasco - 1945) is product of another Lebrija family of non-professional flamencos. Upon winning the Mairena del Alcor singing contest Curro achieved a name, and has risen since to his being recognized today as one of flamenco's finest singers of the cante gitano. Of Lebrija's cantaores of the past he remembers most fondly Fernanda la Vieja (grandmother of Pedro Bacán), LA COCHINA (The Pig) and ANTONIA POZO, the latter of whom was a creator within the bulerías who he says inspired Antonio Mairena in some of his bulerías.

MANUEL DE PAULA is the latest member of note of still another dynasty of Lebrija singers, the *Familia* Paula. This family goes way back in time, and includes as its most famous exponent the *jerezano* Tío José de Paula, as well as a multitude of other singers and bullfighters. Today's Manuel de Paula began by winning several singing contests, including that of Mairena del Alcor. In recent years he has been singing in the group of Mario Maya.

LOS PALACIOS

RERRE DE LOS PALACIOS (Eduardo Arahal Gómez - 1920) was a well-known singer during the Marchena-Valderrama era. His considerable merit is that he created his own cante verses, and had his distinct manner of singing the cantes. He lives retired in Dos Hermanas (Sevilla).

MANUEL CARMONA (1905 -) is a veteran guitarist who has made his living in flamenco through juergas in Sevilla's many ventas of old. He states that the greatest influence in his playing has been Niño Ricardo. Presently Manuel is part of the troupe "*Los Ultimos de la Juerga*" ("The Last of the Juerga Artists").

José Sánchez "ITOLY DE LOL PALACIOS" is another young singer whose springboard has been a first prize in the Mairena del Alcor contest of cante. As a result of his prize he has cut a record with Hispavox, accompanied by José Luis Postigo.

MAIRENA DEL ALCOR

The little white town of Mairena del Alcor suffered an irreparable loss on September 5, 1983, with the death of ANTONIO MAIRENA (p.141)(1909-1983). Over the twenty year period between the first edition of this book and his death Mairena continued his efforts on behalf of flamenco and guided it to unheard of levels of dissemination and purity of expression within, of course, the framework of having to present, and sell it to the general public in festivals, theaters and bull rings. That is the catch, for anything presented to the general public eventually must be watered down to its likes and preferences or it will stop attending. So the purity of expression is relative, above all with Mairena no longer here to guide and prod, for he possessed for a time great behind-the-scenes power; at the drop of a word he could help or hinder another artist's career and thus exert considerable pressure to keep things rolling as he wished. Overly commercial artists simply were banned from the pure scene for a number of years, but today are slipping back in, to the delight of a sizable segment of the public.

But the Mairena legacy will not die easily. Five years after his death he is still very much alive in the minds of many aficionados and artists, and it is still important, if nothing else in their subconscious, whether or not Mairena would approve of their cante. Nonetheless, his movement is losing impetus, and before long we shall be reminded of his gigantic contribution to pure flamenco only by the enormity of his recording releases, which in themselves assure us that his dream can never be entirely forgotten.

Flamenco in the town of Mairena del Alcor carries on without Antonio. Family surviving his death are FRANCISCO MAIRENA (p.146, also P.174 in "A Way of Life"), unchangingly excellent in his siguiriyas and soleares, and MANUEL MAIRENA (p.166), who does not seem to be living up to his potential; his cante is erratic, sometimes quite good, sometimes less so.

Among the younger set the clear stand-out is CALIXTO SANCHEZ, a non-gypsy school teacher by profession and knowledgeable singer of great integrity by *afición*. One has to admire his cante while lamenting the fact that it does not get under one's skin.

MARCHENA

In recent years Marchena has lost the two artists who put this white plains town on the flamenco map: MELCHOR DE MARCHENA and PEPE MARCHENA.

MELCHOR (p.304) was one of the truly great and moving accompanists of the Cante. His son, ENRIQUE DE MELCHOR, carries on the family guitar tradition in a technically brilliant, far less sensitive manner. But comparisons with his father aside, Enrique today is definitely one of flamenco's top accompanists and virtuosos.

With the passing of PEPE MARCHENA (p.137), a true idol to flamenco's masses for the past four or five decades, the *cante bonito* suffered perhaps a mortal blow; since his death it is declining rapidly in popularity.

MORON DE LA FRONTERA

Morón has long been one of Andalusia's most flamenco towns. Its cante tradition includes such legendary figures as DIEGO EL FILLO (p.34), who worked in a smithy in Morón for some years, and SILVERIO FRANCONETTI (p.38), who was reared in Morón and steeped himself in the cante of El Fillo (there are still Franconettis living in Morón). Later on singer DIEGO BERMUDEZ "EL TENAZAS" (p.71) was widely acclaimed upon winning Granada's 1922 flamenco contest (apparently El Tenazas was backed for the contest by his friends in Puente Genil, where he was living at the time, and arrived in Granada by train and well dressed, contrary to the more romantic version formerly circulating and printed in this book). Morón also has a strong tradition of guitar, beginning, as far as we know, in the last century with EL NIÑO DE MORON (p.270), a prize disciple of Paco Lucena's, then PEPE NARANJO (p.270) and PEPE MESA. The latter two were the principal inspirations for the fabulous DIEGO DEL GASTOR, Morón's guitar wizard in more recent times (p.293, also the principal character in "A Way of Life"). EL QUINO (p.208) has been Morón's most famous dancer.

Those who have read "A Way of Life" know in detail about how the traditional flamenco scene in Morón was injured in recent years by the death of FERNANDILLO DE MORON in 1970, then dealt a nearly mortal blow by the combination of the death of DIEGO DEL GASTOR (1908-1973) and the changing times. Another nail was driven into the coffin with JOSELERO's death in 1985. Fortunately, artistic elements still remain, most of them directly related to Diego del Gastor. As seems fitting, four of Diego's sisters have helped propagate flamenco in Morón, as follows:

Sister Carmen begot the late FERNANDILLO DE MORON (1937-1970), Morón's finest *festero* of recent years. His sister, LA CHICA, sings in family fiestas, and her son, JESUS, is a guitarist.

Sister Amparo married singer LUIS TORRE CADIZ "JOSELERO" (p.151)(1910-1985), who for years was Morón's purest and best singer. They produced son ANDORRANO (p.151), a singer and excellent and unique juerga dancer, and guitarist DIEGUITO DE MORON, who can sound (and look) very much like his uncle Diego when he can control his urge for speed. A daughter, AMPARO, has danced professionally, but retired years ago due to marriage.

Sister Teresa contributed with two artists: dancer PEPE RIOS (p.209), who presently teaches dance in Sevilla; and AGUSTIN RIOS, an imaginative, moving, potentially excellent guitarist presently residing in San Francisco.

Sister Paca married a fine non-professional gypsy singer. Their offspring include PACO DEL GASTOR (p.320), one of flamenco's accompanists most in demand who plays a mixture of Diego del Gastor and modern , and JUAN DEL GASTOR (a principal character in "A Way of Life") who is staying with a more pure Morón style of playing than his older brother.

Other artists from Morón include guitarist BERNABE DE MORON, presently residing in Madrid after living many years in the USA; singer PEPE PALOMO, a non-professional, non-gypsy aficionado with a good knowledge of the Cante and a huge voice who sings well at the right moment; and guitar aficionado MANOLO MORILLA, always ready to accompany the local singers.

OSUNA

This picturesque town, although always very flamenco, has not produced any great historical figures. Two accomplished present-day singers fromn Osuna, both presently residing in Madrid, are CHIQUITO DE OSUNA and PACO DE OSUNA. An Osuna-born flamenco pianist of repute is JOSE ROMERO, while Osuna's most well-known guitarist is ANTONIO DE OSUNA.

UTRERA

Our earliest flamenco reference to this ancient plains town, called Utricula by the Romans and Gatrera by the Arabs, lies with the gypsy singer LA ANDONDA (p.47), tempestuous wife of the legendary Diego el Fillo. The famous bailaor FRASQUILLO (p.193) was also born in Utrera, but the artist most remembered and revered in Utrera is MERCEDES LA SARNETA (p.54), who moved there from the province of Cádiz in the last century with her singing and guitar playing. The famous soleares of La Sarneta, together with the creations of two singers from Lebrija who spent long periods in Utrera, JUANIQUIN (p.74,348) and PININI (p.78,377), make up the base of the traditional cantes of Utrera.

Today Utrera has several artists of note that carry on the tradition, which include:

The sisters FERNANDA (p.155, also P.20 of "A Way of Life") and BERNARDA (same references), and cousin PEPA DE UTRERA (La Feonga), the latter a semi-professional who sings and dances well as a *festera* when she wishes;

PERRATE DE UTRERA (p.169), a fine gypsy singer, now retired, who possesses Utrera's widest knowledge of the Cante. His son, GASPAR DE UTRERA, is a very eccentric singer capable of exciting singing when it happens;

MANUEL DE LAS ANGUSTIAS is a gypsy non-professional with a preference for the cantes gitanos.

Others include: CURRO DE UTRERA (p.169), Utrera's representative of the *cante bonito* who has lived in Córdoba for many years; BAMBINO, a gypsy singer-dancer of promise who went the full commercial route but who can revert to decent flamenco when he wishes; DIEGO CHAMONA, Bambino's brother, who stayed at home and sings well the cantes of Utrera; DIEGO EL CABRERILLO also specializes in the cantes de Utrera; ENRIQUE MONTOYA (p.139) had a fling at serious flamenco in the USA, but is much more at ease with the commercial fringe stuff, with which he has had notable success; FELIX DE UTRERA, although born in the Canary Islands, is the most accomplished guitarist to have been fashioned in Utrera.

THE REST OF ANDALUSIA
PLUS TWO

PROVINCES OF

MALAGA 383

GRANADA 385

CORDOBA 388

ALMERIA 391

MURCIA 391

JAEN 393

HUELVA 394

BADAJOZ 395

PROVINCE OF MALAGA

If the gypsy-inspired flamenco sprang up and flourished in the provinces of Cádiz and Sevilla, so the province of Málaga was the breeding ground of the non-gypsy segment of flamenco, from where it spread north into the provinces of Granada, Córdoba, and Jaén, east into Almería and Murcia, and west into Huelva and Badajoz. The first manifestation of this nature is believed to have been *los verdiales*, from the mountains rimming Málaga capital. Los verdiales was, and is, a group dance accompanied by singing and various instruments. Perhaps simultaneously, perhaps soon afterwards, a type of verdiales was created for solo singing, called the *bandolás*. Also around that time, it is thought, the primitive fandango, existent throughout Spain in many forms, was flamencoized and became popular in the area. (It was precisely this combination of bandolás and fandangos, or fandangos abandolaos, that made Juan Breva famous and which were mistakenly called malagueñas.) It is believed certain that from these cantes were derived the malagueñas, jaberas (probably the cante of the bean vendors - bean=*haba*=*jaba*) and rondeñas within Málaga province, and the entire breed of flamenco fandangos and their derivitives (tarantas, cartageneras, granaínas, etc.) throughout the rest of Andalusia and adjacent provinces.

But why the lack of gypsy influence in Málaga province? One gets the idea that very few gypsies settled in Málaga, and that those who did were so far removed from the gypsy centers of inspiration and creativity (provinces of Cádiz and Sevilla) that the vibrations did not reach them until progress made the world smaller in this century.

There is a notable exception to this lack of gypsy influence, which is the area around Ronda, the beautiful, remote mountain town in the northwestern corner of Málaga province. Probably due to its closer proximity to both Cádiz and Sevilla provinces, Ronda did become a haven for gypsies and a center for their art. This is verified by Ronda's three most famous singers, all gypsies: ANILLA LA DE RONDA (p.64), whose soleá is still sung thereabouts; EL LOCO MATEO (p.48), who became a great creator within the soleares when living in Jerez later in his life; and TOBALO (p.56), whose version of the polo (there were said to have been over thirty polos at one time) is the only one remembered today. This area also produced the cante serranas, which to my ears is a mountainized version of the gypsy cante siguiriyas, very likely created by the gypsies from the Ronda area.

However, as we have seen, the vast majority of the province of Málaga seems to have had very little gypsy influence whatsoever (with the major exceptions of PIYAYO (p.90) and EL COJO DE MALAGA (p.122)). The most renowned cantaores from this non-gypsy sector were the singers of malagueñas (pps.80-83) LA TRINI, EL PEROTE, EL CANARIO, and LA RUBIA, and of course the most famous of them all, JUAN BREVA (p.50)(1844-1918).

CANTES FROM MALAGA PROVINCE. Verdiales for dancing, verdiales for singing (bandolás), fandangos, jaberas, malagueñas. From the Ronda area: serranas, rondeñas, soleares.

OBITUARIES Málaga province.

EL NIÑO DE LAS MORAS (Juan Ternero Rodríguez - 1889-1970)(p.99) went on to win the National Contest of the Cantes of the Mines (La Union, 1969) before passing on the following year. The Málaga neighborhood of his birth, El Palo, has since erected a statue in his honor. The singer-writer Alfredo Arrebola states that Juan Ternero's nickname "of the Brambleberries" came about due to Juan's *pregones* when he was selling the berries in the streets.

LA ANTEQUERANA's (p.117) fierce spirit finally expired in her adopted Madrid.

LA REPOMPA's promising dance, and song, was nipped in the bud many years ago.

PEPE EL CALDEDRERO (p.322). I was surprised to read in the poetic, quite beauitiful book "Vida de Juan Breva," by Miguel Berjillos (1976), that Pepe el Caldereo, one of my first guitar instructors back in 1956, had been a favorite accompanist of his friend JUAN BREVA during the latter part of Breva's life, when he was eking out a living from singing in juergas in Málaga capital's colmados and ventas. As far as I can remember, Pepe never mentioned this to me.

DIEGO EL PEROTE (Diego Beigveder Morilla, 1884-1980) was another famed singer of malagueñas from the village of Alora. As a youth he sang with all the greats during the latter part of the café cantante period, including Juan Breva, Manuel Torre, etc., and lived long enough to record his knowledge on various records. He created his own style of malagueña.

NIÑO DE VELEZ (José Beltrán Ortega, 1906-1975), from Velez-Málaga, land of Juan Breva, sang the cantes of the region (bandolás, malagueñas) and created his own style of malagueña.

JUAN DE LA LOMA (1912-1983)(p.167) went on to win more honors and to be considered among the great singers of the cantes of Málaga and Levante.

PRESENT-DAY ARTISTS from Málaga province. (All non-gypsies.)

ANTONIO DE CANILLAS, ANGEL DE ALORA, EL NIÑO DE MONTEFRIO (p.167) and MANUEL AVILA all have won contests singing the cantes of Málaga and Levente.

ALFREDO ARREBOLA is a fine young singer of, and tireless researcher and writer about, flamenco. His book "Los Cantes Preflamencos y Flamencos de Málaga" (Universidad de Málaga -1985) is essential reading for those who wish to study the region in depth.

LA CAÑETA is a very *graciosa* singer-dancer who usually performs with her husband, singer José Salazar.

Singer MANOLO LEIVA long ago moved to the Washington, D.C. area of the USA.

Dancer MARIQUILLA was a performer in the Torremolinos tablao El Jaleo for many years, has also toured with her own troupe.

Guitarist JUAN EL AFRICANO (1927 -)(p.324) is presently ailing and in semi-retirement. Although born in La Linea, Juan lived several years in Ceuta (for which reason he is called "El Africano") before beginning his longtime residence in Málaga capital. Juan is half gypsy.

CARLOS RAMOS (p.324) left his native Velez-Málaga many years ago to establish himself as a top flamenco concertist, first in Spain, then in the USA. He has been the featured guitarist for years in the Washington, D.C. restaurant El Bodegón.

Guitarist PACO DE ANTEQUERA has risen to become one of today's better accompanists of both the Cante and the Baile. He performs mostly in Madrid tablaos.

PROVINCE OF GRANADA

Granada has played a strange role in flamenco, for it is on the fringe of flamenco territory. Other than the practitioners of the fandango granadino and its derivitives, the granaina and the media granaina, basically there were only the gypsies of the Sacro Monte, the cave area just outside of Granada capital proper, who practiced flamenco. If it could be called flamenco, for those gypsies had so little contact with the real flamenco world that their attempts were only misconceived approximations (their non-flamenco folklore was of far more interest). Their idea of flamenco was noise and flamboyance; any attempt at subtlety would be drowned out and overwhelmed. What the hell, they had fun, and the tourists, who as a rule knew even less about it than the gypsies, coughed up the *parné* (money). When a youngster of promise did come along the best thing he could do was leave town and learn elsewhere.

Things could only improve, and they did with the coming of the radio and the phonograph. At least singers and guitarists now had something authentic to imitate. Dancers still had to flounder in the dark until recent times, however. Today, with the wide dissemination of flamenco, including television's considerable offerings, there is no excuse not to familiarize oneself with the authentic if one wishes.

In the past, thus, Granada produced few artists of fame. The best of the singers, FRASQUITO YERBAGÜENA, and a few others, are discussed on page 85, while on page 248 I mention Granada's two most famous dancers, both of whom had caves, both now deceased, LA FARAONA and LOLA MEDINA. With the exception of FRANCISCO RODRIGUEZ MURCIANO (p.265), there is a complete lack of famous flamenco guitarists in Granada's past. I am glad to report that void has been remedied in modern times. In fact, Granada capital has become more or less a guitar center, both for playing and for constructing.

CANTES FROM GRANADA PROVINCE. Non-gypsy sector: primitive fandangos granadinos, granaina, media granaina. Sacro Monte gypsies: zambra (their version of the tangos, and also a term used instead of "juerga").

ARTISTS FROM GRANADA. Singers, dancers, guitarists, in that order.

MANUEL C. COBOS "COBITOS" (1896-1986), non-gypsy, although born in Jerez de la Frontera, lived in Granada the last seventy years of his life and is thus listed here. In addition, he dominated the cantes of Granada, and of Levante in general, to perfection. Over his long career he won prizes, including that of La Union, and other honors. In his last years he toured throughout Andalusia with the group "Los Ultimos de la Juerga." ("Last of the Juerga Artists.")

ENRIQUE MORENTE (c.1942 -) is today's most controversial flamenco singer. I remember in Madrid, back in the early sixties, when Enrique was young and freshly arrived from Granada. He sang purely and well, and went from there to become one of flamenco's top singers. Then some years ago something happened. The combination of the new creativity wave and a personal ego trip grabbed Enrique and will not let him go. The new creativity, I believe, was caused by boredom with a flamenco many considered stagnant, and the ego trip by his desire to go down in history a creator, not merely a fine singer. Both motives are understandable, even commendable, IF you have what it takes to change the face of flamenco. At the beginning Enrique's innovations were interesting, and recognizable as creations, good or bad, within traditional flamenco, but with time he roared past the flamenco limits and just kept going.

This trend makes Morente a hero to a hip Madrid group of young aficionados, also bored with traditional flamenco, and a sort of ridiculous figure to most of Andalusia. I suppose it depends on each aficiondo's actual experience, how much he has really _lived_ flamenco, how much his memory bank of experience and his gut feeling is activited by the traditional. Why should youth and/or outsiders care about what is meaningless to them? For them, anything goes, and as long as they are willing to pay for it, we'll have the pseudo creators with us. As generations pass, in fact, they are bound to win, and in time most or all of the traditional will disappear. Except for one saving factor. Flamenco, like most things, moves in cycles, and I am sure that periodically a return to the roots will become fashionable (and profitable).

MARIO MAYA is another controversial figure in flamenco, although in ways quite distinct from Enrique Morente. What is at play here is not Mario's dance - he is extremely accomplished along generally pure lines - but his manner of presenting it. Mario is theatrically-minded and wishes to present his flamenco to a wide audience. In order to do so successfully, he feels he must have some sort of story line that the public can understand and identify with. The plot for most of his representations is the margination and repression of the gypsies. Mario's characters continually struggle against the forces of repression in a most grim manner. Fun, smiles and laughter are all no nos, which of course is nonsense. My many years in Andalusia showed just the opposite: fun, laughter and smiles amongst the gypsies (and non-gypsies) were the norm. As for the margination, the gypsies were fringe people because they wanted to be. Until their fierce tribal rites and pride began disappearing in recent times, the gypsy felt his world was normal and the rest of us were strange and margina He wanted as little as possible to do with the *payo*, resisted intermarriage, intermingling, inter everything for centuries. Mainly due to this, repression was a matter of course. Any minority who is different has always been a prime target in our "civilization." But the repression was by no means, constant, and mostly ineffective as long as the gypsies either settled down and integrated, as the law prescribed, or kept on the move and entirely to themselves, without noticeable chicken or clothesline pilfering from the *payos*. It is now, when they have decided they wish to integrate, that prejudice is hurting them, but by no means in the relentless manner depicted by Mario Maya.

Mario Maya was gypsy-born in Córdoba but early taken to Granada's Sacromonte. At age thirteen he began dancing in Madrid's La Zambra, followed by some years in the Ballet of Pilar López. With Pilar, he states proudly, he learned about theatricality and stylization for the flamenco dance, which he believes to be superior to just plain flamenco dancing. (Perhaps he is right when dancing for audiences completely ignorant of flamenco.) There is no doubt his formula works, for his small troupe is among the most popular both in and out of Spain.

MANOLETE, bearded gypsy brother of guitarist Juan Maya Marote, is one of flamenco's most respected dancers.

JUAN MAYA "MAROTE" (p.324) is an excellent all-round guitarist who has garnered special fame for his dance accompaniment. Marote has toured with many dancers, including Carmen Amaya and La Singla, to name but two, and could have done much more had it not been for his preference of staying home in Granada, where he owned two flamenco-oriented bars, one in downtown Granada, the other in the Sacromonte. Presently, the entire Marote family resides in Madrid. Among them, brother Manolete is a dancer, Marote's son a guitarist.

LOS HABICHUELA. Patriarch TIO JOSE HABICHUELA EL VIEJO (1910-1986) passed on recently, leaving his guitar legacy in the very capable hands of the rest of the Habichuelas. Tío José was poor and had many sons, causing him to take his guitar and become a sort of wandering flamenco minstrel around the Granada capital area. He would play and sing at the surrounding farms and *cortijos* for whatever they would give him - bread, olive oil, whatever he could feed his children. In recent years he, together with his sister, TIA MARIÑA, toured with the troupe "Los Ultimos de la Juerga" ("Last of the Juerga Artistas").

JUAN CARMONA "HABICHUELA" (c.1936 -)(p.323), is without a doubt one of today's most sensitive, moving and knowledgeable accompanists of the Cante. He is not hard to see in person, for he is in constant demand by flamenco's outstanding cantaores. Juan now resides in Madrid, as do his guitar-playing brothers PEPE HABICHUELA, LUIS HABICHUELA, and CARLOS HABICHUELA, all of whom are making big names for themselves, above all PEPE. Juan's son also is said to play well.

ROMAN EL GRANAINO (p.292), at last report, was retired in Madrid.

MANUEL CANO (1926 -), non-gypsy, is an accomplished concert guitarist, and professor of the flamenco guitar at the University of Córdoba, crusading to raise the flamenco guitar to the proper intellectual level(?)

LOS HEREDIA. Of this gypsy family of father, from Granada, mother, from Córdoba, and eleven children, most of them raised in Los Angeles, California, only two are still artists: SARITA, whom we used to see play, sing and dance, and well, in Los Angeles many years ago, and RENE (c.1942),   the youngest of the family, who has become a very well-known guitarist and composer. René toured with Carmen Amaya for four years, then went with José Greco, then with others, until eventually settling down in the Denver, Colorado area, where he resides today.

PROVINCE OF CORDOBA

The province of Córdoba has always been on the outskirts of flamenco creativity, having had to borrow creations from further south and adapt them to its particular personality, a personality far more payo than gypsy-oriented. Thus, the happy-go-lucky alegrías de Cádiz were converted into the slower moving, less infectious alegrías de Córdoba, while such cantes as the soleares and the siguiriyas lost in Córdoba the gypsies' stormy abandonment to misery and became dirge-like philosophical.

To my knowledge, there were only two artists, both from southern Córdoba province, who were exceptions to the mentioned lack of creativity: PACO DE LUCENA (p.268), who expanded the scope of the flamenco guitar some one hundred years ago, and CAYETANO MURIEL "EL NIÑO DE CABRA" (p.98), who is credited with the creation of the fandangos de Lucena. Other famous singers from Córdoba province have been DOLORES LA DE LA HUERTA (p.75), RAFAEL RIVAS (p.75), and LOS ONOFRES.

But that was a long time ago, and when the new flamenco craze swept through Andalusia in the 1950's, Córdoba woke up to the fact that it was seriously lacking in flamenco artists of scope. Afición there was in abundance, however, highly placed amongst the intellectuals of Córdoba capital, who were eager to propagate flamenco through Córdoba-held and organized contests and festivals. The problem was, they could not find even one local representative of sufficient artistic merit and knowledge to represent Córdoba. What shame! But wait a minute, there was that lad from Puente Genil, presently living in Cádiz, said to have an excellent knowledge of the Cante .....

And ANTONIO FERNANDEZ DIAZ "FOSFORITO" (1932 -)(p.162) saved the day, running away with first prizes in all four categories of Córdoba's 1956 Cante contest. Fosforito is the first to explain this phenomenal success. In the contest a singer had to sing well four cantes in each of the four categories. He says it wasn't that he sang better than some of the other contestants, but that he simply knew more cantes and thus garnered more points. Although only twenty-four years old at the time of the contest, through necessity Fosforito had turned professional at age eight and had really been around, including a military stint and some time after in Cádiz, where he learned the cantes of lower Andalusia. In addition, Fosforito has a very curious and intellectual nature, which led him to many cantes other cantaores had no interest in. Another factor that certainly must help him is that he is a quite accomplished guitarist; singers that both sing and play hold a definite advantage.

At any rate, Córdoba's flamenco fathers were delighted and Fosforito became their hero and remains so, as can be deduced by an elegant book published by Córdoba's city hall in 1981 as a silver anniversary tribute to Fosforito's 1956 victory, replete with many photos, entitled "Homage from Córdoba to Fosforito."

Córdoba is not the only province to hold Fosforito in high esteem. Presently there is a movement to award him with the Golden Key of the Cante, now that Antonio Mairena is gone and the Key has no present-day holder. Others say that it is too soon, it would be disrespectful to Mairena's memory, still others that no one can replace Mairena .... Obviously, the issue is far from settled.

Actually, Córdoba's present-day flamenco scene is not at all destitute. There are several artists of quality, other than Fosforito, well deserving of praise. They follow below, in order of singers, dancers, and guitarists.

Well-kept secrets are not unusual in flamenco. In the magazine "Sevilla Flamenca" writer Manuel Herrera Rodas has unearthed another, by name of MARIA LA TALEGONA (María Zamorano Ruíz - 1909). María has interrupted her calling, that of servant, only once, in the sixties, in order to participate in one six year tour of Europe and Spain, in company of such fine artists as Enrique Morente, guitarist Andrés Batista, dancers José and La Susana .... With the earnings of the tour María bought herself the house in Córdoba in which she lives, quite an accomplishment for an illiterate maid.

La Talegona sings cantes like la granaína, tanguillos, the soleá de Córdoba, but her glorious specialty is por saetas, of which she has long been the undisputed queen of Córdoba. Her nickname was handed down from her grandmother, who used to carry two *talegas* (sacks) full of produce through the streets, *pregonando* her wares through song.

During the interview it was made clear that Córdoba always sang the peripheral cantes well, but not the basic ones (in other words, preferred the Andaluz and not the gypsy-inspired cantes). Also, that until recently no one sang with the guitar, and they still prefer the free cantes without compás.

María's nephew, EL TALEGON, seems to defy the above statement, as he is much in demand as a singer for the dance. He resides in Madrid.

DOLORES DE CORDOBA (p.167) carries on in the tablao circuit.

LUIS DE CORDOBA sings the non-gypsy cantes with ease and authority.

BLANCA DEL REY. I first saw dance Blanca del Rey (formerly Blanca de Córdoba) years ago in a Córdoba tablao when she was quite young. She looked promising. A couple of years later I saw her again in Madrid. She looked more promising. Three or four years later she married the fine aficionado, D. Manuel del Rey, owner-director of the Madrid tablao El Corral de la Morería. As is traditional upon marriage in Spain, Blanca retired from public performing, and spent the next ten unhappy years badly missing it. During this time Blanca kept up her dance privately, and both she and her dance matured nicely. But the unhappiness continued, until finally, in 1979, doctors advised Blanca that the only way to overcome the cronic depression that had her in its grip was to return to active performing. Fortunately for herself and for flamenco, she did, for Blanca today is a bubbling woman whose dance is electrifying the flamenco world, a style of dance as steeped in tradition as it is in innovation. Blanca is highly intelligent, and has known how to create intelligently and tastefully within the traditional context.

For instance: normally I am not much on the use of *mantones* (large shawls) other than for brief periods in a flamenco dance. Blanca dances an entire soleá making her *mantón* the center of attention, but with such agility, femininity, effectiveness and grace that the dance is charming. Nevertheless,I thought, so she handles the mantón well. What now? What now was an incredible alegrías that was both traditional and different, a beautiful blend of advanced technique, sensibility and sensuality that was captivating. It was not only excellent choreography and beautifully danced; that is not so terribly unusual. It is that Blanca possesses that something, that spark of artistic genius, if you may, possessed by very few. The next dance, a very earthy tango, rounded out the impression that Blanca is one of the most sensational bailaoras today.

Besides dancing, Blanca has also studied all aspects of flamenco and has become very well versed in the subject, so much so that she fences easily with flamencologists on radio and TV talk shows. She also very effectively explains her numbers before performing them, which is not only interesting, but a fine way in a tablao to get the attention of a distracted public.

JUAN SERRANO (p.318), who first studied guitar with his father, Córdoban Antonio del Lunar, is still one of flamenco's better concert guitarists. In a recent article in "Guitar International" magazine Serrano states that I was wrong, that he did not shine shoes as a boy. Sorry about that, Juan; that's what they were saying back in the fifties. Serrano is presently a Professor of Music at the University of California, at Fresno.

PACO PEÑA's story is unique in the flamenco world in that this accomplished flamenco guitarist, born in 1942, has achieved international fame while remaining almost completely unknown within Spain. Here's how it happened. Paco began playing at an early age, picking up the basics of the guitar from his older brother, accompanying his singing father and dancing sisters (all non-professionals) and involving himself with folklore and flamenco at school. He began playing professionally at age twelve as accompanist for various groups in Spain. At the age of twenty-one one of the groups played London. When Paco saw the enthusiasm of the English for the flamenco guitar he decided the time was right to turn soloist. In 1966 he played his first London solo concert, and was on his way as a concertist. In 1970 he formed a flamenco company, and was on his way as an entrepreneur. In subsequent years he has cut various records, written flamenco sheet music, played TV programs and concerts with John Williams, among others, performed and been acclaimed the world over. He is a good ambassador for flamenco, for his taste is traditional, his touch clean, and he does not overly virtuocisize.

Each July Paco returns to Córdoba (he maintains residences both in London and Córdoba) and directs *Encuentros Flamencos*, which instructs students both foreign and Spanish in the guitar, the dance, singing if they wish, and in general puts them in contact with the flamenco of Córdoba. According to reports, the program is enjoying great success.

MERENGUE DE CORDOBA is an excellent, highly sensitive accompanist with whom singers must be delighted to sing.

MANUEL DE PALMA is more hard driving and earthy than Merengue, and is thus exciting to hear in a different way. Manuel claims he has studied with Diego del Gastor, which could account for his style.

JOSE ANTONIO RODRIGUEZ (1964 -). Everyone who has heard this young *fenómeno* has been overwhelmed. In 1981 he won first prize for the guitar in La Union, in 1982 first prize in Jerez, in 1986 first prize in Córdoba. His imagination, as shown through his compositions, is first rate, his technique perfect, his touch sublime. I have heard him play on the same day as already established, highly heralded flamenco guitar concertists. Technically he plays circles around most of them. He is not generally, however, as flamenco as they, for José Antonio is at the front of a youth movement that converts flamenco into classical. The themes are vaguely flamenco in nature, the compás becomes blurry and unimportant, the earthiness and vibrancy disappear. What remains is ethereal, a music light and delicate, a drawing room music for ladies and gentlemen dressed in their finest. It is beautiful music as far removed from flamenco's roots as it can get and still be called flamenco.

What to think about it? Personally, I enjoy José Antonio's playing on occasion. That is one side of the coin. The other side is, I can only hope the movement does not become all-encompassing, for it would drive one more peg into the heart of an already badly mauled authentic flamenco.

PROVINCES OF

ALMERIA AND MURCIA

These two provinces, Almería on the eastern rim of Andalusia, Murcia just above it but not part of Andalusia, go hand in hand in flamenco, as if the borders separating them did not exist. From this general region evolved the cantes tarantas, tarantos, cartageneras, murcianas, and mineras, as did the principal singers who developed them . The creation of these cantes has been described so perfectly - with humor, nostalgia, sympathy - in an article by María Adela Díaz Párraga in the March 1975 issue of the now defunct "Flamenco" magazine I shall translate and reproduce it here, as follows:

"There has been much talk and writing about cafés cantantes. Nonetheless, an unpardonable oversight, nothing has been said about a place that saw the birth of our *cantes levantinos*, which was The Tavern in the alley of the Huerto del Carmen, in the town of Cartagena. Its owner was ROJO EL ALPARGATERO (p.86) who, in reality, opened it so as to provide a living for his inseparable friend, PERICO EL SOPAS. In 1894, Perico, pure bred gypsy, walked for three months from Sevilla to La Unión (near Cartagena). Luckily, back in those days time was unimportant and hurrying had not been invented. In 1895 The Tavern opened. The length of the alley leading to it was filled with livery stables and coach houses, and in the tavern was its proprietor, who knew of good Cante, for Perico el Sopas had been servant of the great Silverio Franconetti.

"In that setting, lit up, and never better said, by the liquid specialties of the house, created and sang the legendary pillars of the Levantine sound: CHILARES, PACO EL HERRERO, ENRIQUE EL DE LOS VIDALES, el PECHINELA, JUAN EL ALBAÑIL, el PORCELANA ... The strong wine, together with such house specialties as *carajillos* (coffee with anis from Cazalla), *reparos* (brandy with moscatel wine) and *languenas* (aged wine with anis from Cazalla), was enough to raise the dead.

"The tavern walls listened to the humorous discussions between EL PAJARITO, carriage driver by profession, and PEPE EL MORATO, from the town of Vera (Almería). Both men possessed a great facility for improvisation, both in their talk and in their cante.

"There, to the background of horse carriages and strong wine, was born the cante supreme among the *cantes de Levante*, the taranta, fabulous fruit of the marriage between the lament of los tarantos and the *cante de madrugá*. (The same authoress explains this statement in a later article. In 1890 a huge influx of miners, from the provinces of Jaén and Almería, arrived in La Unión, bringing with them the cante tarantos, which she says mixed with a local cante, de madrugá <dawn> in forming the taranta.) There opened her eyes the beautiful cartagenera and the terrible lament of the minera.

"The Tavern of the Callejón del Huerto del Carmen was the crib in which these beautiful cantes were rocked. The death of Rojo el Alpargatero, in 1906, marked the dusk of these cantes and the closing of their place of birth."

As we see on pps. 85-87, these cantes were popularized throughout Spain by a bevy of fine singers, to whom should be added the son of Rojo el Alpargatero ANTONIO GRAU DAUSSET, and EMILIA BENITO LA SATISFECHA. But the home base of the cantes remained La Unión, a lead mining town just above Cartagena on the east coast of the province of Murcia. Today annual flamenco festivals and contests are held there that uncover an unsuspected number of good cantaores singing the cantes of the area, some of whom are miners, some not. Of this group, one singer in particular has gone onto national fame: ANTONIO PIÑANA, as has his guitar playing son who accompanies him, ANTONIO PIÑANA hijo. We might also single out PENCHO CROS, EL PETI, and ANTONIO SUAREZ as three of the finer singers of the cantes de Levante.

By far the most famous guitarist of the area is TOMATITO, who has risen to fame in the last years as the preferred accompanist of Camarón de la Isla. Tomate's impetuous style of abrupt starts and stops and unusual chording and effects fits perfectly with Camarón's modern singing style, but the same cannot be said for his accompaniment of more mature and reposed singers. With them the effect is like a bull in a china shop. Tomatito is one of the few of today's popular flamencos who resists moving to Madrid or Sevilla. He maintains his residence in Almería capital.

PROVINCE OF JAEN

As we have seen under Provincias of Almería and Murcia, the lead miners from the province of Jaén were among those who migrated to the new mines of La Unión in 1890, bringing with them a cante Maria Adela Díaz Párraga calls "tarantos" which, she goes on to say, was coupled with the cante de Madrugá to form the taranta sung in Levante today.

Not all the miners of Jaén province left, however, and their original cante continued to be sung in and around the mines of Linares. This cante, quite similar to its sister cante further east, today is called the *taranta de Linares*. Two of its most famous exponents were CABRERILLO DE LIÑARES and FRUTOS "EL TONTO DE LIÑARES."

Other well-known artists born in Jaén province:

JOSE IYANDA (p.75), born in Linares in the last century but early taken to Jerez de la Frontera, went on to become creator of his own soleá.

RAFAEL ROMERO (p.154), born in Andújar, longtime resident of Madrid, remains one of the few hardline purists of the Cante.

PACO DE VALDEPEÑAS (p.205), born in Linares, taken to Valdepeñas as a boy, longtime resident of Madrid, possesses in-depth knowledge of the mining cantes of Linares, among others, in addition to his fine juerga style dance.

CHARITO LOPEZ, from Jaén capital, enjoys a fine reputation as a singer.

CARMEN LINARES, from Linares, is one of flamenco's most compléte, and exciting, singers. Still young, much will be heard from Carmen in the future. She resides in Madrid.

GABRIEL MORENO (1941 -), from Linares, is perhaps the best young male singer to emerge from Jaén province in some time. He resides in Madrid.

PEDRO SEVILLA is a promising young singer from Jaén presently performing in Madrid's tablao circuit.

ANTONIO PEREZ "PUCHERETE" is a well-known guitarist from the town of Ubeda. His son, PUCHERETE hijo, sings and plays well. Both father and son live in Madrid.

PROVINCE OF HUELVA

The province of Huelva is famous for its wide variety of fandangos. Nearly every town in Huelva province sings some variation of the fandango chico (fandanguillos), of which it is very proud. As fandangos are truly a cante of and for the people, almost everyone in the province sings them, singly, in duos, or in groups. Amongst all these participants there are many fine singers who are more or less taken for granted and do not gain fame outside their immediate localities; fame for the *fandanguero* comes only to the truly exceptional. Two of the exceptional in the past were the creators and outstanding interpreters PEPE PEREZ DE GUZMAN (p.121) and ANTONIO RENGEL (p.121), considered the greatest fandangueros remembered.

Fandangos comprise most, but not all, of Huelva's flamenco. A famous complete singer of the last century, often compared with this century's Niña de los Peines, was DOLORES LA PARRALA (p.62). Her sister, TRINIDAD LA PARRALA (p.63) was also well considered, and even more so Dolores' best disciple, ANTONIO SILVA EL PORTUGUJES (p.63).

More recently other artists from Huelva province have made names for themselves as complete artists. To wit:

The great MANOLO DE HUELVA (1892-1976)(p.278) lived his last years in his home on Sevilla's Alameda de Hércules, scene of so much of his juerga life over a sixty year span. In the first edition I left Manolo when he was about to enter the Madrid tablao La Zambra for a six months stint (p.283). During that period we frequented La Zambra, hoping Manolo would one night open up. He never did, limiting himself to accompanying very well, always in the background. I tried another tack. One night after they had finished at La Zambra I took Manolo and Pericón to our home, where were assembled a group of very interested guitarists. Manolo's eagle eye quickly sized up the situation - all those young people with long, reinforced thumb nails - and commenced to play the same two or three falsetas all night. He played them in the alegrías, in the soleares, in the siguiriyas, in everything, and they were not even amongst his good ones. Were it not that I had heard Manolo more than once when he was fabulous - in Sevilla's La Europa in the fifties - probably I would have put him down as a good accompanist of the Cante of mediocre technique.

Previous to La Zambra, in Madrid's Villa Rosa where Manolo would be waiting for juergas to materialize, occasionally we drank and talked the hours away, which is when he told me about some very good friends of his for whom he was making tapes as an aid to teaching the wife to accompany singing (I think it was). If I am not mistaken those friends must have been the de Zayas, and the *señora* referred to, Virginia de Zayas (who was also very likely the *señora* mentioned in connection with Manolo de Huelva on P. 371). At any rate, the Virginia de Zayas family apparently possesses many tapes of Manolo, which I imagine account for some of the bands on the Manolo de Huelva - Ramón Montoya release (Dial Discos, 54.9318, Concierto de Arte Clásico Flamenco, 1984). This release by no means shows Manolo at his uninhibited best (when his private flask of *aguardiente* was nearly empty and he could just cut loose), but is by far the best of Manolo available on record.

JOSE SALAZAR is a fine singer who specializes in the cantes de Málaga, Granada and Levante. For years he performed in his tablao near Marbella with his dancing-singing wife, La Cañeta de Málaga. I have heard the tablao is no longer open.

EL NIÑO MIGUEL caused considerable splash as a child guitar protégé. He still plays very well, seemingly prefers to stay close to home in Huelva capital, where he gives guitar instruction.

ALBERTO VELEZ (p.318) recently retired from teaching the flamenco guitar in Madrid's Conservatory of Music.

PROVINCE OF BADAJOZ

The province of Badajoz lies just outside of Andalusia, but you would never know it on traveling from Huelva into Badajoz province; the same white villages, forests of cork oak, rugged hills, and pronounced southern accent (not identical, but similar). Badajoz is a land of many gypsies, who have taken the fandangos from Huelva and adapted them to their nature, in the process converting them more into fandangos grandes with a gypsy punch. The other favorite cante of the Badajoz gypsies is their adaptation of the tangos, in Badajoz called "tangos extremeños," or "jaleos extremeños" (*"extremeño,"* from Extremadura, the name given the region comprised of the provinces of Badajoz and Cáceres).

The late PORRINA DE BADAJOZ (1926-1977) (p.158) has been the most famous cantaor from this region. Today's most well-known representative is singer RAMON EL PORTUGUES, a young gypsy with a rajo voice whose singing for dancing carries impact. Ramón performs in the Madrid tablao circuit.

The main non-gypsy contribution from Badajoz has been a family of guitarists, MANOLO DE BADAJOZ (p.284), PEPE DE BADAJOZ (1899-1970)(p.284), and Manolo's son, JUSTO DE BADAJOZ (p.285).

THE REST OF SPAIN

MADRID 397

BARCELONA 402

and

MISCELLANEOUS AREAS 404

MADRID

Madrid? Flamenco? Strange as it may seem, Madrid presently contains, and by far, the largest concentration of flamencos in the world, flamencos from all over Spain who migrate to this city of tablaos, teaching opportunities, frequent flamenco theatrical spectaculars, private flamenco clubs, some juerga life, and abundant afición and tourists to keep it all financed.

This phenomenon is not particularly new. It started during the café cantante period of the last century, when a bevy of cafés opened their doors and needed artists, and carried on through the first half of this century in the theater, as well as in the *ventas* and *colmados* (Los Gabrieles, Las Villas Rosas (there were two of them, one on the Plaza de Santa Ana, in the center of the city, one on the outskirts of the city), La Capitana, Venta de Manzanilla, to name but a few of the most important), where large sums of money exchanged hands and where the artists prospered.

Nonetheless, Madrid was not taken too seriously in the past. Artists would go to work in Madrid, but not often with a mind to permanence; the charms of Andalusia usually lured them back. This changed during the last half century, during which period artists arrived in Madrid with the intention of staying if things went well with them. Today, moving to Madrid (or Sevilla) is a matter of course for the more ambitious artists who are no longer content to scrape by in their home towns, which presented me with the bizarreness of being able to accomplish as much research for this update in Madrid than in all of Andalusia.

Thus, generally speaking it has been only in recent years that flamenco artists have actually been born and/or formed in Madrid, although there have been notable exceptions to this, foremost among them the father of the modern flamenco guitar, RAMON MONTOYA (p.273). Others have been Ramón's two earliest imitators, LUIS YANCE (p.277) and LUIS MOLINA (p.278), singer MERCEDES, LA CHATA DE MADRID (p.89), her brother, dancer-guitarist JOAQUIN EL FEO (p.187), jondo guitarist PATENA PADRE (p.322), and a few others of lesser name.

OBITUARIES. Madrid artists.

Singer ANGELILLO (p.136), of "Opera Flamenca" fame, died in his native Madrid.

CARMEN MORA, wife of flamenco dancer Mario Maya, was among flamenco's top dancers when killed in an automobile accident in Mexico in 1981. Carmen's dance was a mixture of old-fashioned and modern, an interesting and quite exciting combination. She performed, and taught dance, for a number of years in Los Angeles, California.

Guitarist EUGENIO GONZALEZ (p.323) received his guitar formation from Patena Padre and Javier Molina. As was the case with most old-time guitarists, he preferred the dark sounds to excesive technique, which his good friend Vicente Escudero appreciated when he had Eugenio help him work out a danceable version of the siguiriyas in 1940 (apparently, up to that time the siguiriyas had only been sung). Eugenio spent his last years as the guitar expert in the Ramirez guitar shop in Madrid.

PATENA HIJO (p.322) carried on the jondo guitar-playing style of his father.

Guitarist MANUEL BONET (p.322).

Guitarist ARACELI VARGAS (p.323) was an impressive gypsy guitarist along the lines of Patena Padre. His son, ARACELI HIJO, carries on the family tradition.

PRESENT-DAY ARTISTS FROM MADRID. Singers.

PEDRO JIMENEZ "EL PILI" (p.134) lives in retirement in Madrid.

Veteran FELIX MORO learned how to sing by absorbing the cante,in Madrid's flamenco *colmados* and ventas, of such singers as Pepe de la Matrona, Bernardo de los Lobitos, and others.

PRESENT-DAY ARTISTS FROM MADRID. Dancers.

LOS PELAOS (pp.194-196). JUAN and FATI are largely retired today. FAICO is still performing and does some teaching in his Madrid dance studio. ANTONIO and RICARDO (EL VENENO) are very actively dancing around the world, Antonio (Toni) with an accomplished, normally masculine style, Ricardo with a brute force and dancing demeanor that is quite refreshing in this flamenco world of supposedly virile dance where too often it is anything but.

PACO FERNANDEZ was born in Madrid of Andalusian parents from La Carolina (Jaén). As was the case with most Madrid dancers in those days, Paco began his studies with La Quica, in 1946. He learned quickly, and in 1948 was ready for a tour of the USA with the troupe of Mariemma, under the agentry of Sol Hurok. A long period of time followed in which Paco performed principally in America, including another tour with Mariemma, followed by some years with La Cabalgata, a troupe of Spanish newcomers that used to tour the world, and a number of years with José Greco. Paco finally remade Spain his base of operations in 1968, and continued actively performing until about 1973, at which time he settled down to a very busy life of instruction and choreography. Paco concentrates largely on flamenco. The feminine dance is his specialty, the dance of the upper torso his basic concern in his laudable effort to keep dancing females feminine. This approach is much appreciated, judging by the long list of professionals who have studied with him, including Manuela Vargas, Cristina Hoyos, Blanca del Rey, Carmen Mora, Chuni Amaya, Sara Lezana, and so forth.

ANGEL TORRES is another popular dance instructor in Madrid who has an interesting past. Angel began as a flamenco singer, and did not begin to dance until age twenty-four, at which time he studied with Antonio Marin and La Quica. During the years 1957-1962 he danced in the company of Pacita Tomás, then left to form his own group(s).

TOMAS DE MADRID is a respected dance teacher in Madrid who is also active as a performer with his own group.

ROSA MERCED. After years of active performing, Rosa has settled down to become one of Madrid's most popular dance instructors and choreographers. She also give frequent lectures on the subject of dance at universities and other institutions.

ROSA MONTOYA. One really had to have the afición strongly ingrained in the days of Rosa's youth, for Society took a very dim view of flamenco. In Rosa's case she had to go against the wishes of her family, even though her great uncle, the fabulous RAMON MONTOYA, had been a consummate flamenco artist if ever there was one. Ramón died when Rosa was only eight, however, so I suppose whatever opinion he may have had came too early on. At any rate, Rosa prevailed and early began dance instruction with Regla Ortega and La Quica, and by 1958 was dancing in Madrid's La Zambra. From there she went on to other Madrid tablaos, in one of which she met young CIRO and formed a dancing partnership with him that before too long had them on a Sol Hurok tour of the United States (further details in the Ciro biography). Rosa's partnership with Ciro lasted until 1973, at which time Rosa opted for the married life with a San Francisco guitarist, Charles Mullen. (They were married in 1967, but the lure of the artistic world kept Rosa performing another six years.) They settled down in San Francisco, but Rosa by no means gave up flamenco. Today she is San Francisco's most celebrated dance teacher, and she also embarks on periodical tours, mostly along the west coast, with her own troupe. In addition, each September Rosa organizes a sort of Spanish festival in San Francisco that features flamenco as well as Spanish food and wine.

LUISA MARAVILLA (p.243) today limits her artistic life largely to concerts at colleges and universities, in which she explains flamenco in general and her dance in particular. She also gives some dance instruction in Madrid.

SARA LEZANA first caught the public's eye in the theatrical version of "La Historia de Los Tarantos," back in the late 1950's. She danced well and acted convincingly. A few years later she played the female lead in the movie version. She was better in both fields. Since then she has developed into quite an accomplished dancer, well-balanced in all aspects of the flamenco dance, although prone to excessive commercialism.

EDUARDO SERRANO "EL GüITO" (p.209) has long been considered one of Spain's outstanding flamenco dancers. Gypsy-born in Madrid into the family of Los Pelaos, El Güito was in constant contact with flamenco in the family from birth, which he early supplemented with dance classes with the flamenco maestro Antonio Marín. At age fifteen he entered the troupe of Pilar López for a four year stint. In 1969 he received the best dancer of the year award in Paris (Premio de Las Naciones), and in 1970 a similar award in Spain. Since then he has toured widely with his own flamenco group, appeared as guest artist with Manuela Vargas over a long period of time, danced in trio with **Mario Maya** and Carmen Mora, was a featured dancer in Antonio Gades' troupe (and appeared in the Gades-Saura movies), and has been featured in various tablaos.

El Güito dances with great purity and strong masculine lines, and with a highly polished technique that, fortunately, he does not overly stress. His dance is serious, perhaps too Spartan at times, for it is getting rare to see him insert that spark of gypsy temperament that separates a good from a great performance. He is certainly capable of it, as I have witnessed many times por bulerías (which he also sings), soleares and alegrías. It is when the spark ignites that he becomes a truly memorable dancer. He resides in Madrid.

LA TATI began her dancing career full of tempestuous flame and humor, today has matured into one of flamenco's more accomplished dancers. Tati began dancing in neighborhood fiestas at an early age, in one of which she attracted the attention of La Quica. La Quica encouraged her, and soon Tati was hanging around Quica's dance studio absorbing the dances Quica was teaching. The moment arrived when Quica had to leave one of her dance classes and could find no one to take over. Tati, by now nine or ten, confidently told Quica she would oblige. Quica, incredulous, asked Tati to dance some of the more difficult steps, which Tati accomplished with a flourish. From that day on Tati became Quica's substitute teacher and shadow, even sleeping many nights in Quica's studio. At age twelve Quica introduced Tati into the Madrid tablao La Zambra, and Tati has not stopped dancing professionally since, picking up various dance prizes along the way. Today Tati is much in demand in Spain's flamenco festivals and tablaos, and as well is one of Madrid's favorite dance instructors.

MARIA ALBAICIN (p.249) retired for a number of years due to marriage, then returned to the dance a more accomplished dancer than when she retired. She seems to live, and perform, mostly in Mexico.

ESTRELLA MORENO has built a fine reputation for herself as a dancer. She early began studying all facets of Spanish dance, including flamenco, with Paco Reyes. When in her teens she entered Madrid's flamenco tablao circuit, eventually working her way up to headliner. Subsequently, she has performed worldwide as the featured female dancer with the companies of Rafael de Córdoba and Antonio. She is presently active both as performer and teacher in her adopted New York City.

PRESENT-DAY DANCERS RAISED AND FORMED IN MADRID, BORN ELSEWHERE.

ANTONIO GADES (p.204) has not let down in his dance for a moment in the twenty-five years since the first edition of this book. He is, in fact, Spain's number one overall male dancer at present, including a very high placement on the flamenco list. In recent years Gades served as artistic director of the Ballet Nacional de España, stepping down from same to film Carlos Saura's "Bodas de Sangre," "Carmen," and "Amor Brujo," and to take on a variety of performing commitments, including world-wide tours with his own troupe.

MARIA MAGDALENA, born in Medina de Rioseco, province of Valladolid, was early taken to Madrid, where at age nine she began dance instruction; bolero and Spanish classical with Luisa Pericet, flamenco with La Quica. When nineteen she began giving an extended series of dance recitals, both in and out of Spain, the first of which was in Madrid's Teatro de la Comedia in 1954. María retired from active performing at a relatively early age and has since become one of Madrid's most popular dance teachers. Her knowledge and teaching ability are such that at one time she was contracted to teach the entire company of Pilar López. Today she is a *maestra* for the Ballet Nacional de España, as well as a seemingly tireless teacher and choreographer at the Amor de Dios studios.

RAQUEL PEÑA began studying dance in Madrid at age five, later moving to the USA where she met her husband, Madrid guitarist FERNANDO SIRVENT. Raquel has her own troupe, and also dance academy, in the Washington, D.C. area, and has been the featured female dancer, and Fernando featured guitarist, for many years in the Washington restaurant Tío Pepe.

PRESENT-DAY ARTISTS FROM MADRID. Guitarists.

VICENTE GOMEZ, born in Madrid in 1911, is one of the first Spanish guitarists to make a big name for himself outside of Spain. He has played for movies both in and out of Spain (Blood and Sand, Captain from Castile, The Sun Also Rises, etc.), has composed an impressive number of guitar compositions, has owned his own NYC supper club (La Zambra, opened in 1948), and opened (1953) and managed the Academy of the Spanish Arts, in the Los Angeles, California area (he has since sold both ventures).

Gómez is an accomplished guitarist who neither fits into a flamenco nor a classical niche, for which he is widely criticized by both camps. He personally considers his position "flexible," which is true enough - it has brought him a good deal of fame and fortune. If Vicente does not play pure flamenco, he certainly knows it. His father owned a Madrid tavern where many of the old-time flamencos used to hang out before the Spanish civil war, such as guitarists Ramón Montoya, Habichuela, Patena hijo, Estéban Sanlúcar, and Pepe de Badajoz, and dancers El Estampío, El Pelao, and Faico. Young Vicente, therefore, grew up with "real flamenco which," he states, "almost doesn't exist today compared with the old days." He currently teaches guitar in Burbank, California.

GABRIEL RUIZ "GABRIELITO" accompanied most of the famous singers and dancers of his day before settling down in Glendale, California.

VICTOR MONGE "SERRANITO" has long been considered one of flamenco's outstanding guitarists, above all in the concert style. He has been the featured guitar soloist in a variety of tablaos (for some years in the Corral de la Morería, in more recent years in the Café de Chinitas) as well as in national and international flamenco and guitar festivals. In his mid-forties, he plays an elaborate version of traditional flamenco still down-to-earth enough to permit moments of emotional profundity to seep through.

EMILIO DE DIEGO (p.321) has been very active in the guitar and music worlds since I last wrote about him. He has continued his guitar playing with various troupes as first guitarist, but what is bringing him the most fame at present is his talent for musical composition; he has composed music scores for more than a dozen movies and theater productions, the most famous being García Lorca's "*Bodas de Sangre*."

ENRIQUE ESCUDERO, a Madrid resident from early childhood, is one of flamenco's many unsung pillars, an expert and moving accompanist of the Cante.

FELIPE MAYA is an excellent guitarist and accompanist lost in the tablao world. If you were not a frequenter of Madrid's Corral de la Morería you would have no way of knowing his playing, except for the publicity afforded him these days through the promotion of his son, a budding guitarist by name of GERONIMO. At ten Gerónimo is a child protégé and will certainly go on to great things if his determination lasts and he does not burn out.

Other accomplished guitarists from Madrid include AURELIO GARCI, ANASTIO DUQUE, ALEJANDRO MANZANO, GONZALO ORTEGA, JOSE MARIA PARDO and son, CARLOS PARDO, concertist RAFAEL ANDUJAR, and ANTONIO GARCIA ALONSO.

BARCELONA

If flamenco in Madrid seems out of place, flamenco in Barcelona seems absurd. The Catalanes decidedly do not like flamenco, nor flamencos, nor Andalusians; they, in fact, hardly approve of anyone, and are not even very sure about themselves. Why, then, is there flamenco in Barcelona? Andalusian immigrants, of course, who flock to places like Barcelona, Mallorca, and Madrid in search of work. If they prosper, they remain, and a new little community of flamencos may spring up.

Such is the case of Somorrostro, the largely Andalusian neighborhood on the outskirts of Barcelona, birthplace of the incomparable CARMEN AMAYA (p.230), born of gypsy parents who had migrated from Granada's Sacro Monte. The same neighborhood can also boast of LA CHUNGA, the famous gypsy dancer whose bittersweet story I tell on P.245. La Chunga has been a longtime resident of Madrid, presently is featured in the Madrid tablao Café de Chinitas.

Another fine dancer to emerge from the poverty of Somorrostro is ANTONIA LA SINGLA, who first came into public view in the flamenco movie "La Historia de Los Tarantos," in which she played the role of a dancing ingénue from the neighborhood; which is to say, she played herself. La Singla, whose father is a French gypsy nicknamed "El Singla," was born deaf and mute in 1949 and remained that way the first nine or ten years of her life. Nonetheless, she observed the flamenco that surrounded her in the neighborhood - the singers mouths, the guitarists fingers and tapping feet, the occasional dancer - and began imitating at an early age. Her heroine and inspiration was Carmen Amaya, of course, even though Carmen had left the neighborhood long before.

La Singla grew up to become an excellent gypsy-style dancer, sensuous and full of fire, in many ways reminiscent of La Chunga in years past. She has formed many groups and done much touring, Europe and the rest of the world during autumn and spring, summertimes along the Catalán coastal tourist areas. In very recent years she seems to have disappeared from the picture. Hopefully, it is only temporary.

LA CHANA, a woman of explosive footwork but mediocre everything else in her dance, the rage nine or ten years ago, is no longer heard about. A dancer of similar temperament and style, LA TOLEA, is having some success today.

CARMEN CORTES, gypsy-born in Barcelona of Andalusian parents, cousin of the flamenco family of Los Remolinos (see guitarists), danced without studied technique for years before deciding to go the dancer's route. In 1980 she began studies with Ciro in Madrid, and advanced so rapidly that only half a year later Mario Maya asked her to be his dancing partner. Carmen injects fire and sensuality into her dance, as well as nice arms and upper torso, which has carried her high in the hierarchy of dancers.

Guitarist PACO AGUILERA (p.323) died in Barcelona around 1980.

The REMOLINOS are guitarists of some fame. Remolino Father plays a great deal for the flamenco clubs in the Barcelona area. Remolino son was Juanito Valderrama's main guitarist for a number of years.

PESCADILLA is an accomplished guitarist who provides wife Lola Flores with most of her guitar accompaniment. He also sings well por rumbas.

ANDRES BATISTA is no doubt the most accomplished flamenco guitarist to emerge from Cataluña, and among the best in Spain today. He began with eight years of classical guitar (ages 10-18) with Antonio Francisco Serra, then one fateful day heard the late MIGUEL BORRULL hijo (p.273) play and fell in love with flamenco. His family, however, was not in love with the thought of Andrés becoming another "drunken flamenco," and resisted the idea. Andrés persisted, Miguel Borrull talked to his parents, and his father compromised by giving Andrés a three months trial period - if Andrés came home drunk just once, flamenco was out.

Fortunately for flamenco, Andrés stayed sober, and soon began his first professional employment in a tablao called El Brindis (now Los Tarantos). Soon Carmen Amaya heard of him, and arranged for Andrés to perform with her. Young Andrés wondered if they should rehearse something; Carmen scoffed at the suggestion. "If you know how to play and I to dance, why rehearse?" The trial turned out well enough for Carmen to contract Andrés for the last tour of her life, that took them through North and South America during the years 1960-1962.

Andrés was still Carmen's guitarist back in Cataluña when she sickened and died, in 1963. At that time Vicente Escudero contacted Andrés, and they began working together, along with Vicente's well-considered dancing partner, MARIA MARQUEZ. Andrés describes Vicente as having had a very strong personality, full of creativity and ideas, and goes on to say that as Vicente was also a painter, the painting world influenced strongly in his dance - he was more concerned with the plasticity of a dance than such bothers as the compás. But the arms, fingers, postures, carriage had to be just right; if a dancer varied only slightly from Vicente's rules, Vicente crossed him off. At any rate, regardless of his eccentricities Andrés considered Vicente a genius who has done much good for the traditional flamenco dance. Apparently Vicente also scorned rehearsal; you either play the guitar well or you do not.

After Escudero, Andrés accompanied many dancers and singers, among them El Farruco, who told Andrés "Look, you play well, I dance well, why rehearse?" By now Andrés got the picture; in the true flamenco world rehearsing is a dirty word, a hindrance to inspiration and a waste of time.

Backed by his solid formation, Andrés began concertizing and has become one of flamenco's top concertists, with twelve solo LPs to his credit. He is also a prolific composer, with 267 guitar pieces published to date. In addition, he has turned out one of the best flamenco guitar methods, a separate book on accompaniment of both the Cante and Baile, two books of guitar studies, and several more of flamenco solos in both cifra and classical annotation. Somehow he found time to marry lovely flamenco dancer ANA MERCEDES, with whom he often performs in duo.

To top it all off, Andrés is still young (mid-forties). What lies in the future for his boundless energy and talent?

DIEGO CORTES is a young guitarist who won the Jerez de la Frontera annual guitar contest in 1979 and should, it is generally agreed, go on to big things.

MISCELLANEOUS AREAS

A scattering of flamenco artists have come from areas of Spain other than those discussed. A quite illustrious scattering, as you can judge for yourselves. To wit:

Singer JACINTO ALMADEN (1905-1968) (p.133) lived quietly in Madrid his last years.

Singer JUANITO VAREA (1913-1985)(p.153) became one of flamenco's top purists the last two or three decades of his life, for which he received much deserved recognition. He was a longtime resident of Madrid.

Singer CHININ DE TRIANA, from the northern Spanish town of Logroño, is much solicited in USA flamenco circles.

VICENTE ESCUDERO (1895-1980)(p.188) has been flamenco's most polemical dancer. Opinion has placed him in a multitude of categories ranging from genius to ignorant to purist to clown to crazy, and very likely they were all correct at one time or another, and perhaps occasionally all at the same time. The last time I saw Vicente perform, in a Madrid theater in the early 1960's, his dance was stranger than ever - virile as always, but eccentric to the point of ludicrousness. He lived the last years of his life in Barcelona.

PILAR LOPEZ (p.229) continues living in retirement in Madrid.

Valencia-born MARTIN VARGAS dedicated most of his life to active performing before becoming one of Madrid's most popular dance instructors and choreographers. Martín began as a self-taught flamenco and Spanish style singer who punctuated his performances with bits of dance, much as his good friend, Lola Flores, has done. This carried him into a stint with Pastora Imperio, at age fourteen, followed by other troupes, including his own, one of which landed him in Sao Paulo, Brazil. One day in Sao Paulo he participated in a farewell performance in honor of Carmen Amaya, who was moving on with her company. When Carmen saw Martín dance, she had two suggestions for him: that he turn more seriously to the dance, for which he had an abundance of talent; and that he join her troupe as a dancer. Martín took her first suggestion to heart, and at age twenty-eight he began the career of full-fledged dancer. The second suggestion he reluctantly turned down - Carmen's troupe was famous for its cronic economic woes, and Martín decided not to join the ranks of the sporadically paid. Today he laments his decision, practical as it may have been; he feels the experience would have been well worth the financial risk.

The years have proven the wisdom of Carmen's suggestion that Martín should concentate on dancing. Martín's extroverted and basically happy style of dance has carried him far. Besides his own groups, Martín has spent two years with Mariemma, two years as dancing partner of María Rosa, many years with Lola Flores both as featured male dancer and choreographer, ditto the last two years that Pilar López had her company (early 1970's), and many years as *maestro* and first dancer with Madrid's Teatro de la Zarzuela (working with artistic director and chief choreographer Alberto Lorca). In 1980 Martín opened his dance academy in Madrid, which ties him down most of the year. On holidays, however, he reverts to active performing, often as guest artist outside of Spain.

CIRO DIEZHANDINO NIETO "CIRO" was born and raised in a small town in Palencia province. But how can a boy from a village buried in Old Castile have gotten mixed up in, or even heard about, flamenco? Let's take a look.

Ciro's father, it happens, was a flamenco buff with the custom of running off to flamenco happenings at every opportunity, be they in Valladolid, distant Madrid, or even further afield. Father also had a collection of flamenco records featuring such purists as La Niña de los Peines and Manuel Torre, which young Ciro fell in love with. Before long, Ciro was singing and dancing his boyish version of flamenco, and longing to be able to take lessons and really plunge into it. That desire had to wait for several years, however, until Ciro finished high school in Palencia and began the study of law at the University of Valladolid. In Valladolid Ciro did find instructors in flamenco, ballet and regional dance, with whom he studied during his three years stay at the university. At the end of that peiod Ciro could wait no longer; he was dying to go to Madrid and immerse himself completely and full-time in the dance. Father, however, cast a jaundiced eye at the idea of Ciro's leaving college (and respectability) for such an undertaking, and put his foot down hard - no boy of his was going to get mixed up in the lowlife of the profesional flamenco, and that was all there was to it!

Ciro, of course, quit the university and went to Madrid anyway, but without support, monetary or otherwise, from his family. Hard work for sustenance (unloading trucks, whatever) mingled with hunger and hope and countless dance classes; ballet in the Círculo de Bellas Artes, the entire rainbow of Spanish dance with Antonio Marín, La Quica, Albero Lorca, and Héctor Zaraspe. When prepared, Ciro danced in the ballets of Tamayo, Alberto Lorca, and Mariemma, followed by a three year stint with the Ballet of Antonio. During this period he also studied classical ballet with the famous *maestra*, Ana Ivanova.

During all these years flamenco kept gnawing at Ciro. Flamenco interludes in a ballet program were not enough. Ciro wanted flamenco in depth, wanted to live and breathe it. So Ciro began in Madrid's flamenco tablao circuit, and before long met another young dancer, Rosa Montoya (see Madrid section), who Ciro describes as a great bailaora and his best friend. They formed a flamenco duo, and soon found themselves in the United States with a four week contract that stretched into three years performing here and there, including representing Spain at Seattle's world fair and performing in the first international satellite TV transmission. They opened at a tablao in San Francisco, where opportunity truly knocked in the form of Igor Moisseiev, director of the Russian ballet company of his name, who was so impressed with them he arranged for them to audition for the then top artistic agent in the USA, Sol Hurok (who handled Mariemmna, Antonio de Triana, Carmen Amaya, Antonio, Sabicas, etc.). Mr. Hurok liked them and they were on their way on an immediate 94 city tour of the USA. followed by performances throughout the world, culminating several times in packed houses and rave reviews in New York City's Lincoln Center. Upon Mr. Hurok's death they were contracted by Columbia Artists for some years more. This profitable relationship ended only when Rosa married a young American guitarist and settled down. Ciro continued, substituting another fine dancer, Chuni Amaya, as his partner. Following this period Ciro decided to dive head first into another venture: his own tablao flamenco in New Orleans, a city that had captured his fancy while on tour. Plenty of hard work followed, but Ciro found it rewarding and stuck to it for several years before finally deciding it was time to return to Spain. Upon so doing, he settled in Madrid, where he is much in demand as a choreographer and instructor.

Now, if I were reading this I would probably picture Ciro as another general dancer whose flamenco is a watered-down, ballet-type imitation of the real thing. True, his dance is highly technical, but he handles it with such effortless mastery and in such a flamenco manner that it again becomes obvious that the flamenco element comes from within. If the dancer is flamenco, his dance will appear flamenco. If not, forget it.

Will Ciro ever return to active performing? He thinks not. He enjoys choreographing and teaching, and feels he has had enough of performing for this lifetime. However, he is still young, and could easily change his mind in the future. Flamenco aficionados hope so.

CARMEN ALGABA AMAYA "CHUNI" is a fireball whose dance is the closest to that of her aunt, Carmen Amaya, that I have seen, far more so even than that of Carmen Amaya's sisters. This is not surprising, for Chuni was raised on the road with her aunt's touring group, and by age five was already part of the show.

When I state that Chuni was "raised on the road," I am being literal. Chuni's mother, Antonia Amaya, gave birth to her in Brussels when the troupe was on a prolonged tour of Europe in 1948. One tour led to another, and Chuni went right along, loving it all. Consequently, Chuni never went to school, and has had to teach herself all the academic essentials. Shortly after aunt Carmen's death in 1963, Chuni and her family moved to Mexico, and soon Chuni was dancing in Mexico City's "Gitanerías" with dancing partner Antonio de Córdoba, an artistic union that lasted three years. Among Chuni's other artistic highlights were two USA tours with the dancer Ciro (1973 and 1974).

Chuni now has her own small troupe, which includes her Spanish husband, Carlos Gómez "El Tano," a former bullfighter from Huelva province of considerable fame who also happens to sing well for dancing. If you ever get a chance to see Chuni perform, by all means do so. Her diminutive body emits fire, her tiny feet sparks, her whole being artistry and *gracia*. Your best chance will be in Mexico City's "Gitanerías."

GUITARISTS.

When fabulous guitarist SABICAS (p.301) finally returned to Spain after a thirty-some-years absence, he was clamourously received by Spanish aficionados, for through his recordings Sabicas has had a profound influence on the development of the flamenco guitar. Sabicas returns to Spain, both concertizing and relaxing, frequently now, although he maintains his residence in New York City.

Guitar virtuoso MARIO ESCUDERO (p.316), like Sabicas, also has returned triumphantly to Spain, for he too has been influential *en absentia*. But once the fanfare died down, both Mario and Sabicas found their playing has something in common in the modern (young) world of the flamenco guitar: their playing is considered outdated - interesting, technically brilliant, but old-fashioned to a revolutionary youth drifting further and further from traditional flamenco.

Talk about a fast-moving guitar world. Mario has moved from ultra-modern to outdated in twenty-five years. His head must be spinning.

Mario currently resides in Sevilla.

ANTONIO ARENAS (p.324) continues as a favorite accompanist in the Madrid tablao circuit.

THE NON-SPANIARD IN FLAMENCO

The non-Spaniard in flamenco. Out of place? I think not. There have been several non-Spaniards already mentioned in the first edition of this book who have made names for themselves in the theatrical flamenco dance. Others of merit have come along since, as have many accomplished guitarists in the true sense, meaning they have not merely picked off a few solos from records, but have actually immersed themselves in flamenco in Spain, have learned about the Cante and the Baile and how to accompany them and, once reasonably based in those arts, have or have not turned to solo playing.

In addition to the performers, it must be admitted by all aware Spaniards that non-Spaniards are in part responsible for the renewed interest in flamenco; the French publication of flamenco's first anthology in 1952, for instance, when flamenco was more a lost than a live art both in and out of Spain.

Legions of fresh non-Spaniards become staunch aficionados each year. As is natural, many of these aficionados are not content solely with a spectator's role. They energetically begin taking lessons in the flamenco guitar, dance, and even the song, they devour whatever there is of the Written Word, and they mingle in the world of flamenco. Most of these aficionados are able to retain some sort of perspective and flamenco to them remains a pleasureable hobby. Others of us fall hard, and before we know it flamenco has become the major interest in our lives. From this group accomplished artists have emerged, some of whom are professionals in the sense that flamenco provides the major portion of their income.

Spaniards do not quite know what to think of this disconcerting foreign influx into their art. When confronted by an adequate to good performance by a foreigner they immediately insist that he or she is of Spanish ancestry, even if the foreigner himself is unaware of his Spanish blood. It is inconceivable to them that an Anglo, or Oriental, or any non-Spaniard, for that matter, can feel and understand flamenco, regardless of the years he may have spent practicing his adopted art and, more important, living the flamenco life. For this reason, many non-Spanish artists feign Andaluz and/or gypsy mannerisms (at times to a very comical extent), adopt Spanish artistic names, and claim that their mothers, or at least their grandmothers, are Spanish. However, times are changing. Non-Spanish flamenco professionals are everywhere these days, both in and out of Spain, and everyone is getting used to the idea. Most important, many of these artists have achieved considerable mastery of their chosen fields, causing intelligent and open-minded Spaniards to consider what was once unthinkable: that flamenco is not necessarily the unique domain of Andalusians, firstly, and other Spaniards, secondly; that it is after all not caused by some ingredient exclusive to Spanish blood; but rather seems to have more to do with a profound feeling for, and prolonged contact with, flamenco and its life style.

Instead of the word "many" when referring to non-Spaniards who have achieved a certain mastery, I might better have said "several," for in truth not many have reached this plateau in their artistry. Even amongst the few non-Spaniards who have the opportunity to immerse themselves in flamenco and its way of life in Spain for a long period of time, it is rare to find the complete dedication that is required, nor the willingness to sacrifice, perhaps permanently, the amenities and security that steady jobs bring, nor the dogged determination and patience to continue in the face of the condescension of the vast majority of the Spanish artists and aficionados during the many, many years of formation, years that seem never to end.

In the first edition of this book I listed eight pages of non-Spaniards in flamenco. There were not many then, and I probably covered most of them. Today, however, there are enough of them to fill a large volume by themselves, an undertaking awaiting its undertaker.

INDEX

The black numbers indicate the material of most significance about each artist, the lighter numbers mentions of lesser importance.

Abadía, Emilio: 366
Acosta, Jeromo: 208
Acosta, Juan: 122
Africano, Juan el: 324,385
Aguado, Dionisio: 255
Aguarocha, la: 142,185
Agüero, Juan Antonio: 236
Agujetas hijo: 343,349,350,**351-352**
Agujetas Viejo: **343**,349,350,351
Aguila, Paco el: 269
Aguila, Rafael el: 48,311,341,**346**,350, 352,354
Aguilera, Paco: **323**,403
Albaicín, Flora: 249
Albaicín, María: **249**,284,400
Albaicín, Maria del: 284
Albañil, Juan el: 392
Albeniz, Carmen (aunt): 370
Albeniz, Carmen: 370
Albeniz, Eloisa: 99,249,328,370
Alcalá, Platerito de: 167,374
Alfarero, Domingo el: 366
Algeciras, Paco & Pepe: see Lucía
Algeciras, Ramón de: 337,**338**
Almadén, Jacinto: **133-134**,317,404
Almendro, Enrique el: 122,149
Almendro, Jesus el: 352
Almería, Niño de: 322
Alonso de Jerez: 349
Alonso, Juan el de: 54,56,210,288,340
Alora, Angel de: 384
Alpargatero, Rojo el: 86,392
Alvarez de Sotomayor: 164
Amador, Joaquín: 372
Amador, Ramón: 372
Amaya, Antonia: 369.407
Amaya, Carmen: 109,112,178,189,192, 194,199,**230-237**,242,246,248,284, 286,302,304,327,340,368,387,388, **402,403**,405,406,407
Amaya, Chuni: 398,406,**407**
Amaya, Leonor: 237,369
Amaya, Maria: 232
Amaya, Paco: 233,237,369
Amaya Jiménez, Juan: 233
Ana María: 369

Andaluz, Máximo: 85
Andonda, la: 35,36,45,47,380
Andorrano, el: 151,379
Andújar, Rafael: 402
Angelillo: **136-137**,153,299,397
Angustias, Manuel de las: 380
Antequera, Niña de: 139
Antequera, Paco de: 385
Antequera, Tomás de: 139
Antequerana, la: 117-118,384
Antonio: 116,**197-200**,238,249,284, 316,336,367,371.400,406
Antúnez, Diego: 54,56,photo.
Antúnez, Fernanda: 213,**217**,226,341,368
Antúnez, Juana: 213,**217**,341
Anzonini del Puerto: **206-207**,357
Araujo: 313
Arenas, Antonio: 316,324,407
Arenero, Antonio (hijo): 366
Arenero, Antonio (padre): 366
Argentina, la: 191,**224-225**,239
Argentinita, la: 102,125,136,178, 191,197,201,214,217,219,224,**225- 227**,229,277,281,284,337,368
Arrebola, Alfredo: 384
Avila, Manuel: 384
Aznalcollar, Niño de: 122,375
Azpiaza, José: 253
Bacán, Bastián: 377
Bacán, Pedro: 377
Badajoz, Ernesto de: 284,285
Badajoz, Justo de: 284,285,395
Badajoz, Manolo de: 284,285,395
Badajoz, Pepe de: 159,**284-285**,395,401
Badajoz, Porrina de: **158-160**,284,395
Ballesteros, Antonio: 366
Ballesteros, Joaquín: 366
Ballesteros, Salvador: 255,**322**
Bambino: 381
Barbate, Niño de: 123,340
Barbate, Niño de (hijo): 340
Barcelona, Juan: 374
Barbero, Paco el: 266,**267-268**, 271,274,334
Barón, Manolo: 372
Basilico, Padre: 255

410

Batista, Andrés: 389,**403-404**
Bautista, el maestro: 322
Bellita, la: 367
Belmonte, Fernando: 353
Benito Revuelto, Vidal: 253
Bernal, Juan: 33
Berjillos, Miguel: 384
Berza, Niño de la: 352
Biencasao, el: 373
Bienvenida, Antonio: 203
Bilbá, la: 89
Bilbao, Antonio el de: 178,182,183,
    184-185,190,193,278,292,360,366,369
Blasco, Ricardo: 324
Bojiga de Jerez: 349
Bonald, Caballero: 187,216,345
Bonet, Manuel: 322,398
Boquerón, el: 364
Boquilla,el: 206
Borbón, D. Carlos de: 234
Borrás, Tomás: 77
Borrico de Jerez: **344-345**,349,351
Borrico, María: 37,40,340
Borriquera, Consuelo la: 214
Borrull, Miguel: 273
Borrull, Miguel hijo: 273,366,403
Brenes, Manolo: 372
Breva, Juan: 41,42,**50-54**,76,78,80,
    383,384
Brillantina, el: 336
Bueno, Ana María: 367
Burro, María la: 345
Butler, Augusto: 188
Cabalgata, la: 398
Caballero, Luis: 375
Cabeza: **119-120**,341
Cabra, Niño de: 85,98,388
Cabrerillo, Diego el: 381
Cabrero, el: 375
Cachivero, el: 27
Cádiz, Beni de: 169,**336**
Cádiz, Feo de: 208
Cádiz, Joseíco de: 336
Cádiz, Pablito de: 336,**337**
Cádiz, Pericón de: 107,**123-128**,283,
    335,394
Cádiz, Perla de: 28,**160-161,335-336**
Cagancho, Antonio: **58-60**,360
Cagancho, Joaquín: **58-60**,360
Cagancho, Manuel: **58-60**,360.
Calabacino, el: 85
Calderero, Pepe el: 322,384
Calvo, Pilar: 308
Calzada, Niño de la: 362

Calzones, Antonio: 364
Camacho, Antonio: 367
Camacho, Juan: 123
Camarón: see Isla
Campos, Pepa: 205,207,357
Canalejas de Puerto Real:222,337,357
Canario,el: 80,81,**82-83**,383.
Candelas: 139
Cano, Manuel: 388
Cantaora, Rita la: **70-71**,341
Canillas, Antonio de: 384
Cantoral, José: 33,337
Cantoral, Juan: 33,337
Cañeta, la: **384**,395
Cañito, el: 275
Capinetti, José: 334
Capitana, la: 222,397
Caracol, padre: 102,148,149
Caracol,Manolo:28,34,35,57,68,73,115,
    139,145,**146-150**,164,165,194,203,229,
    305,306,326,329,336,337,344,**362**
Caracolillo: 337
Carito, el: 42,49,70,341
Carmona, Manuel: 378
Carrasco, Diego: 353
Carrasco, Manuela: 370
Carrera, Carmen: 249,369
Carrera, Manolillo: 66
Cartujano, el: 366
Caruso: 227
Casado, Curro: 33
Casals, Pablo: 199
Castellón, Diego: 304
Castillares, J.: 366
Cautivo, Tío Luis el: 33
Centeno, Manuel: 85,121
Centeno de Villaverde, Dr.: 96
Cepero,José: 111,233,341
Cepero, Paco: 350,351,**354-355**
Ceuta, Antonio de: 168
Chacón, Antonio: 28,41,42,50,72,73,
    76-80,83,85,91,98,133,134,135,136,
    137,138,150,213,214,271,272,274,
    275,278,286,296,313,314,341
Chalao, el: 119
Chaleco,el: 356
Chamona, Diego: 381
Chana, la: 403
Chaqueta, Adela la: 355
Chaqueta, Antonio el: **157-158**,355
Chaqueta, Tomás el: 356
Chaquetón: 67,357
Chaquetón, el (modern): 337,356
Chata de Madrid, M. la: 89,397

411

Chato de Jerez, el: 69,341
Chelita, la: 303
Cherna, Joaquín la: 93,96,350
Chicharrona, Pepa la: 346
Chiclanita: 75
Chicote, Pedro: 152
Chilares: 392
Chinitas, Café de: 401,402
Chino, el: 232,235
Chiquetete: 364
Chiva, la: 168,350
Chkara, Mohamed: 32
Chocolate, el: **163-164**,166,351,**364**
Chorrúa, María la: 210,219,341
Choza, el: 343
Chunga, la: 195,**245-247**,402,403
Chunguita, la: 247
Ciego, el: 220
Ciro: 399,**405-406**,407
Clavel, Diego: 376
Cobitos: 386
Cochina, la: 377
Cochoca, Pepa la: 36
Cojo, Enrique el: 249,**362-363**,369,370
Colorao, Frasco el: 57,360
Compadre, Luis: 336
Concepción, la: 367
Contrahecha, la: 369
Coral, Matilde: 366,**371**
Coral, Pepa: 371
Córdoba, Antonio de: 407
Córdoba, Dolores de: 167,389
Córdoba, Luis de: 390
Córdoba, Mariano de: 323
Córdoba, Rafael de: 369,400
Cordobés, el: 244
Corro, Tío: 33
Cortés, Carmen: 403
Cortés, Diego: 404
Cortés, Paco: 208
Cros, Pencho: 393
Cruz, Antonio: 168
Cuadrillero: 33
Cuco, Enrique el: 149
Cuéllar, José: 73
Cuenca, Amalio: 73,**273**
Cuenca, la: 216,220
Cuende, el: 60
Cuervo, el: 75
Culata, Enrique el: 362
Culata, Pepe el: **150**,362
Currela, Paco: 208
Curro de Jerez: 353

Dalí, Salvador: 199
De Falla: 72,73,74,368
Diamante Negro: 351,352
Diego, Emilio de: 201,**321**,332,401
Domecq, Alvaro: 313
Domínguez, Manolo: 372
Donday, Santiago: 337
Dios, Juan de: 36
Duende, el: 351
Dulce, Curro: **57**,148,149,334
Duque, Anastasio: 402
Durán, José: 119,240
Durán, Rosita: 119,**239-240**,286,**353**
Encueros, Juan: 36,39,46
Escacena, Niño de: 85,**122**
Escobar, Manolo: 139
Escudero, Enrique: 402
Escudero, Mario: 299,304,305,**316-318**,372,**407**
Escudero, Vicente: 176,178,182,184,186,**188-193**,200,225,232,286,327,369,398,**403-404**
Esmeralda, Merche: 332,**371**
España, Teresa: 215
España, Trini: 249,371
Espinel, Vicente: 255
Estampío, el: 183,**186-187**,197,199,201,220,239,272,341,401
Ezpeleta, Ignacio: **75**,123,148,149,226
Faico (old): **185**,188,360,401
Faico Pelao: 194,**195**,398
Falla, Manuel de: 73,74,221
Fandita, la: 65
Faraona, la: 232,**248**,385
Farina, Rafael 139
Farrabú de Jerez: 350
Farruco, Antonio el: **202-204**,351,363,370,404
Farruco, Pilar: 370
Farruquita: 370
Farruquito: 363,370
Feo, Joaquín el: 187,397
Fernández, Curro: 364.373
Fernández, Familia: 373
Fernández, Fernando: 345
Pernández, Paco: 398
Ferrer: 367
Fillo, Diego el: 28,33,**34-36**,37,38,40,45,46,47,58,69,141,337,357,360,379
Fillol, Alfredo: 206
Flamenca, María la: 248
Flecha, Antonio: **335**,337,356

412

Flecha, Manuel: 362
Flores, Lola: 148,194,203,**240**,272, 327,336,403,405
Fosforito, Antonio: **162-163**,164, 168,324,**388-389**
Fosforito, Francisco: 80,**83-85**,211, 213,286
Franco, Manolo: 372
Franconetti, Silverio: 36,**38-44**,45, 49,57,62,63,69,83,93,98,121,141, 213,360,379,392
Frascola, Perico 56
Frasquillo: **193-194**,199,227,228, 363,368,380
Fregenal, Manuel: 362
Frijones: 79,**88**,119,341,345
Funi, Fernando; 377
Funi, Miguel: 377
Gabrieles, Los: 84,397
Gades, Antonio: **204-205**,229,369,**400**
Gallo, Fernando el: 148,149
Gallo, Joselito el: 148,149,210
Gallo, Rafael el: 148,149,210,222
Gálvez, Fernando: 352
Gálvez, Lorenzo: 352
Gamba, la: 97,**216**,221,341,360
Gandul, Paco el: **58**,83
García, Aurelio: 402
García, Fray Miguel: 255
García, Miguel: 201,324
García Alonso, A.: 402
García de la Mata, Juan: 314
García Lorca, Federico: 43,53,64,73, 113,260,293,305,326,327,340,368
Gardner, Ava: 126
Garfías: 366
Gas, Paquillo el del: 85
Gasolina, el: 373
Gastor, Diego del: 91,92,105,151, 209,244,259,263,270,**293-298**,301, 315,317,320,346,377,**379**
Gastor, Juan del: 380
Gastor, Paco del: 297,**320**,380
Gato, el: 194
Genil, el Niño del: 133
Gerena, Manuel: 375
Geroma, Currito de la: 95,272,**288-289**,293,295,305,341
Geroma, la: **210**,288,341
Glink: 266
Gloria, Niño: 79,**100-102**,119,142, 166,226,340,341,351,360,364
Gómez, Joaquín: 324
Gómez, la: 75

Gómez, Vicente: 401
Gomez de Jerez: 352
González, Antoñito: 267
González, Eugenio: 323,**397-398**
González Climent, Anselmo: 115,119
Gooding, Cynthia: 261
Granaíno, Román el: 292,387
Granaíno, Salvador (father): 292
Granaíno, Salvador (son): 292
Granaíno, Tío José el: **57**,58,123, 126,357
Grau Dosset, A.: 392
Greco, José: 154,160,167,**200-201**, 204,228,229,321,369,388,398
Gringo, el: 373
Guajiro,Cortijo del:164,206,351,370
Guanté, Paquirri el: 49,**56**,334
Güito, el: 209,332,**399-400**
Habichuela, Carlos: 387
Habichuela, Juan Carmona: 323,**387**
Habichuela, Juan Gandulla: **270**,334
Habichuela, Luis: 387
Habichuela, Pepe: 387
Habichuela, Tío José: 387
Heredia, Andrés: 324
Heredia, René: 388
Heredia, Sarita: 388
Heredía Flores, Jesús: 168
Herrero, Fernando el: 98
Herrero, Paco el: 392
Hita, Archpriest of: 256
Honrá, Rosario la: **210**,213,334
Hoyos, Cristina: 363,**369**,398
Huelva, Cojo de: 122
Huelva, Manolo de: 48,73,226,257, 259,260,263,**278-283**,288,289,293, 295,296,301,302,304,305,315,317, 322,360,366,368,**394-395**
Huerta, Dolores de la: 75,388
Huerto del Carmen, Tavern: 392
Hurok, Sol: 368,398,399,406
Iglesias, Roberto: **208**,322,369
Imperio, Pastora: 103,142,191,192, 211,**220-222**,245,287,288,337,**362** 372,405
Infante, Manuel: 368
Isla, Alvaro de la: 356
Isla, Camarón de la: 32,338,**356**,393
Isla, Chato de la: 356
Isla, Paco de la: 323,356
Isla, Viejo de la: 56,336,356
Ivanova, Ana: 406
Iyanda, José: 75,341,393
Jaca, María la: 57,341

Jambre, Juan: 349
Jarrito Montoya: 161-162,307,357
Jerez, Carbonillero de: 76,341,364
Jerez, Chato de: 49,69,340
Jerez,Isabelita de:118-119,240,341
Jerez, Manolita de: 160,201,350
Jerez, Terremoto de: 35,146,165-166,
  343,350,362
Jero, Niño: 350,353
Jesús, Luis: 33
Jimenez, Roberto: 196-197,229
Jorobao, Enrique el: 182,183,292,334
Jorobao, Juan el: 267
José & La Susana: 389
Joselero de Morón: 151-153,375,379
Juanata,el: 343
Juane, Tío: 343,349-350,352
Juanelo: 56,93,340
Juanelo, Soleá la de: 88,341
Juanichi: 345
Juaniquín: 74,155,348,376,380
Juliana, hijo de: 33.
Juliana, Tío Luis el de la: 33,
  34,141,337,340
Junquera, Juan: 56,340
Laberinto, Paco: 194,346,350
Lagañas, Diego: 377
Lamparilla: 183-184,213
Lavado, Pedro: 168
Lebrijano, Diego el: 56,376
Lebrijano,Juan el:32,169,354,376,377
Leiva, Manolo: 384
León, Mercedes: 194,229
Leonís, Charito: 369
Leopardo, Conchita: 369
Levi-Provençal: 255
Lezana, Sara: 398,399
Linares, Cabrerillo de: 393
Linares, Carmen: 393
Linares, Frutos de: 393
Llobet, Miguel: 274,308
Lobata, la: 87,341
Lobato, Chano: 336
Lobitos, Bernardo de los: 112,
  116-117,374,398
Lola, la: 36
Loli, el: 87,341
Loma, Juan de la: 167,384
López, Charito: 393
López, Pilar: 155,196,197,201,203,
  204,208,225,229-230,231,308,368,
  387,399,401,405
Lorca, Alberto: 229,405,406

Loreto, Juana: 250
Loreto, Maleni: 219,241
Loro, Andrés el: 57,334
Loro, Antonia la: 57,334
Los Palacios, Itoly de: 378
Los Palacios, Rerre de: 378
Lucas, John: 363
Lucena, Paco de: 268-270,274,320,
  379,388
Lucía, Paco de: 167,201,321-322,
  337,338-340,356,372
Lucía, Pepe de: 166-167,201,322,
  337,338
Luisillo: 208,369
Lunar, Antonio del: 390
Lunar, Perico el del: 79,110,223,
  239,272,285-287,341,350
Luz, Paco la: 54,62,218,340,345,
  349,351
Luz, Sordo la: 351
Macaca, Miguel Cruz: 66
Macandé: 48,208,310-311,312,341
Macarrón, Juan: 33
Macarrón, Vicente: 33
Macarrona, la: 73,125,210,212-215,
  217,218,219,221,226,273,292,341,368
Madrid, Tomás de: 399
Magdalena, María: 401
Mairena, Antonio: 12,27,28,34,41,49,
  68,75,76,90,100,106,115,121,129,
  134,136,141-146,156,164,166,200,
  244,250,326,344,346,347,376,378,389
Mairena, Francisco: 145,146,378
Mairena, Juan: 145
Mairena, Manuel: 145,166,378
Málaga, Cojo de: 85,122,383
Málaga, Niño de: 151
Malena, Curro: 377
Malena, Eduardo de la: 219,323,371
Malena, la: 125,210,217,218-219,221,
  226,241,292,341,360,368
Malenita: 360
Malino, el: 366
Malvido, Mariquita: 211
Manolete: 387
Manoli de Sevilla: 370
Manuel: 32,354,373
Manzanilla,Manolo: 123
Manzanilla, Venta de: 283,397
Manzano, Alejandro: 402
Mañas, Alfredo: 235
Maravilla, Luis: 112,154,225,277,
  295,305, 307-308,372

Maravilla, Luisa: **243-245**,399
Marchena, Melchor: 34,125,150,165, 259,263,279,288,301,**304-307**,315, 316,317,329,332,379
Marchena, Pepe: 29,113,136,**137-139**,153,159,163,301,314,379
María, Manolito el de la: 100, 129-132,141,155,**374**
María Rosa: 370
Marianas, Niño de las: 111-112,307
Mariemma: 141.398,405,406
Marín, Antonio: 399,406
Marín, Manolo: 370
Marina, Tía: 387
Mariquilla 385
Marisol: 363
Marmolista, Pepe el: 86
Marote, Juan Maya: 324,**387**
Márquez, María: 403
Marrurro, Diego el: **68**,93,119,239, 341,349
Martínez, Pepe: 164,**300-301**,305, 315,343,**363**
Mateo, el Loco: **48-49**,69,70,340,383
Mateo, la Loco: 49
Matrona, Pepe de la: **109-110**,286, 323,**361**,365,366,398
Maya, Felipe: 402
Maya, Gerónimo: 402
Maya, Mario: 209,348,377,**386-387** 397,400,403
Medina, Lola 248,385
Medina, Manuel: 288
Medina, Niño: 122
Mejorana, la: **211-212**,214,221,334
Melchor, Enrique de: 332,379
Meller, Raquel: 232
Mellizo, Antonio el **50**,79,140
Mellizo, Enrique el: **49-50**,56,78,79, 81,96,103,106,115,123,140,272,334
Mellizo, Francisco el: 297,320
Menese, José: 168,**375**
Mercé, José: 351,**352**
Merced, Rosa: 399
Mercedes, Ana: 404
Merengue: 391
Mesa, Pepe: 379
Mezcle, Fernando el: **56**,213
Miguel, Niño: 395
Militi, el: 325
Millet, Paco: 287
Mimbre, el: 371
Miño, Ricardo: 371,372
Miracielos: 182,334

Mojama, Juanito: 79,119,341,350, 360,364
Molero, José María: 353
Molina, Antonio: 139,299
Molina, Javier: 78,143,188,240,268, **271-272**,274,279,280,286,288,293, 299,302,305,315,322,341,350
Molina, Luis: 184,**278**,287,397
Molina, Manuel: 37,69,70,119,340
Molina, Marcelo: 308
Molina, Ricardo: 27,41,49,74,75,88, 106,121,136,143
Molina Fajardo, Eduardo: 265
Moneo, Juan: 352
Mono de Jerez: 353
Mono, el: 355
Montefrío, Niño de: 167,384
Monterito: 267
Montes, Pepa: 371,372
Montoya, Carlos: 232,**289-292**,318
Montoya, Enrique: 139,381
Montoya, Familia: 372-373
Montoya, Juan: 373
Montoya, Lole: 32,372-373
Montoya, Rosa: **399**,406
Montoya,Ramón:73,80,222,262,272, **273-277**,278,280,286,290,293,298, 302,308,313,340,395,397,399,401
Moralito: 366
Moraíto Chico II: 354
Morao, el: 315
Morao, Familia: 351
Morao, Juan: 301,**315-316**,349,350, 353,354
Morao, Manuel: 146,272,301,**315**, 349,350,353,354,
Mora, Carmen: **397**,398,400
Moras, Niño de las: 99,**384**
Morato, Pepe el: 392
Morena, la: 119,364
Morena, María la: 75
Moreno, Antonio: 273,299
Moreno, Estrella: 400
Moreno, Gabriel: 394
Morente, Enrique: 32,**386**,389
Morería, Corral de la: 337,401
Morilla, Manolo: 380
Moro, Félix: 398
Morón, Bernabé de: 324,380
Morón, Chica de: 379
Morón, Dieguito de: 379
Morón, Fernandillo de: 379
Morón, Jesús de: 379
Morón, Niño de: 270,320,379

415

Morsilla, Enrique Hermosilla: 50, 79,128,140
Nano de Jerez: 350
Naranjo, Pepe: 105, **270**, 296, 320, 379
Navarro, Antonio: 324
Negra, la: 373
Negro, Rafael el: 366.371
Negro del Puerto, el: 357
Niña de los Peines: see Pavón, P.
Nitri, Tomás el: 36.37.38.**44-45**, 48,49,69,141,340
Nogales, Rafael: 323
Novedades, Café: 368
Núñez, Gerardo: 353
Núñez, Sebastián: 240,**322**,355
Núñez de Prado: 46,47,62,65,70,71
Oliver, Manuel (padre): 366
Oliver, Manuel (hijo): 365-366
Ollero, Ramón el: 74,360,365
Onofres, Los: 388
Ordóñez, Antonio: 244
Orillo: 340
Orozco, Enrique: 123,364
Ortega, Carlota: 148,149
Ortega, Carola: 149
Ortega, Enrique El Gordo: **57**,148, 149,272,334
Ortega, Enrique: 149
Ortega, Gabriela (dancer): 148,149, 210,334
Ortega, Gabriela (reciter):148,149, **325-327**,373
Ortega, Gonzalo: 402
Ortega, José El Aguila: 149
Ortega, José La Morala: 149
Ortega, Loli: 149
Ortega, Lolita: 149
Ortega, Luisa: 149,329
Ortega, Manuel: 149,208
Ortega, Manolo: see Caracol
Ortega, Manuela: 149
Ortega, Paquiro: 149
Ortega, Rafael: 149,**208**,368
Ortega, Regla: 148,149,192,**238**,399
Ortega, Rita (earlier): 149
Ortega, Rita: 148,149,**248**
Ortega, Rosario: 149
Ortega family chart: 149
Otero, Maestro: 367
Ortiz Nuevo, J.L.: 342,345,349
Osuna, Antonio de: 380
Osuna, Chiquito de: 380
Pablas, Curro: 36,**46**,357

Pacote de Jerez: 349
Pajarito, el: 392
Palacín, Manuel: 343,**352**
Palanca, Pepe: 122,375
Palma, Manuel de: 391
Palomo, Pepe: 380
Pamplinas, Manolo: 208
Pancho: 366
Pansequito: 357
Pantalón, Salvador el: 356
Pantoja, María: 240
Papelista, Tomás el: 75
Papera, Rosa la: 336
Paquera, la: 168,349,350
Pardo, Carlos: 402
Pardo, José María: 402
Parrala, Dolores la: **62-64**,98,114 121,394
Parrala, Trinidad: 63,394
Parrilla, Gregorio: 349,350
Parrilla, Juan: 354
Parrilla, Manuel: 350,353-354
Parrilla Viejo: 208,**346**,349,350
Parrilla Chico: 354
Patena, hijo: 320,322,398,401
Patena, padre: 322,397
Paterna, el Perro de: 357
Patiño, Maestro: **266**,267,271,334
Paula el del Lobo: 348
Paula, Joaquín de la: 79,96,**99**, 103,130,142,374
Paula, la: 248
Paula, Manuel de: 348,**377**
Paula, Tío José de: 54,75,119,341 342,**348**,349,351
Pavlova: 227
Pavón, Arturo: 79,**99**,114,328
Pavón, Arturo (hijo): 99,114,149, 325,**328**,373
Pavón, Pastora (Niña de los Peines): 49,62,72,73,76,79,85,97,99,105,**112-114**,115,142,150,157,161,232,272, 280,286,299,305,328,360,**361**,364, 366,376,405
Pavón, Tomás: 28,50,79,99,114,**115-116**,141,144,150,161,162,232,280, 299,328,360,364
Pechinela, el: 392
Pelao, Antonio: 194,**196**,398
Pelao, Faico: 194,**195-196**,398
Pelao, Fati: 194,**195**,398
Pelao, Juan (dancer): 194-195,398
Pelao, Juan (singer): **60-61**,360

416

Pelao, Ricardo: 194,**196**,398
Pelao, Sebastián: 194,235,401
Pemán, José María: 109
Pena hijo: 85,122
Peña, Bernardo: 376
Peña, Ciego de la: 56,357
Peña, José María: 325,**327**,356
Peña, la: 351
Peña, Paco: 390-391
Peña, Pedro: 376-377
Peña, Raquel: 401
Peñaranda, Conchilla la: 86
Pérez, Antonio: 211,**266-267**
Pérez, Antonio (hijo) 211,267
Pérez, Antonio (grandson): 267
Pérez, Carmelita: 211
Pérez, Manolo: 211
Pérez, Manuel "El Pollo": 334
Pérez de Guzman, Pepe: 121,394
Pericet, Angel: 363
Pericet, Luisa: 401
Perla, Francisco la: 121,334
Perosanz, Jesús: 122
Perote, Diego el: 384
Perote, el: 80,**81-82**,211,383
Perrata, la: 376
Pescadilla: 241,403
Picasso, Pablo: 199
Pies de Plomo: 365
Pili, el: **134-135**,317,398
Pinini: 75,**377**
Pinini, Benito el de: 377
Pinini, Fernanda la de: 377
Pinini, Luisa la de: 377
Pinto, Pepe: 114,**129**,139,361
Pintor, Antonio el: 183,213,334
Piña, Perico: 36
Piñana, Antonio: 393
Piñana hijo: 393
Pipa, Juana la: 353
Piquer, Conchita: 125,194,195,208,
   214,218,219,337,369
Piriñaca,la:122,341,342,**346-349**.353
Pitraca, Josefita la: 210,214,334
Piyayo, el: **90-91**,383
Planeta, el: **34**,35,144,148;149,334,
   337,360
Plata, Juan de la: 74,160,186,214
Poeta, el: 364
Poeta, Manolo el: 374
Pompi, la: **100-102**,119,341,351
Porcelana, el: 392
Portugués,A.S. el: 98,121,394
Portugués,Ramón el: 395

Posaera, la: 248,371
Postigo, José Luis: 372
Pozo, Antonia: 377
Pozo, Manuel: 267
Pregones: 341,347
Pucherete: 394
Pucherete hijo: 394
Puebla, Niña de la: 139,375
Puerta, Adonis: 324
Puli, el: 87-88,341 ·
Quica, la: 187,193,201,211,
   227-229,248,260,**362**,363,
   367,398,399,400,401,406
Quino, el: 152,**208**,379
Quiñones, Fernando: 337
Ramírez: 184,**187-188**,341,366
Ramírez, Juan: 350
Ramirito: see Ramírez
Ramos, Carlos: 324,**385**
Rancapino, el: 340
Raspao, el: 182-183,334
Realito, Maestro: 199,238
Reguera, Rogelio: 324
Reina, Juanita: 363
Remolinos, Familia: 403
Rengel, Antonio: 121,394
Repompa, la: 384
Revuelo, Juana la del: 369
Rey, Blanca del: **390**,398
Rey, Manuel del: 390
Reyes, Hermanos: 169
Reyes, Julio de los: 288
Reyes, Miguel de los: 139
Reyes, Paco (dancer): 400
Reyes, Paco (singer): 366
Ricardo, Niño: 272,**298-300**,301,
   302,314,316,323,**363**,366,378
Rico, Paquita: 363
Rincones, Familia: 349
Riopa, Mario: 206
Rios, Agustín: 380
Ríos, Pepe: 209,380
Ríos, Tomás: 230
Riqueni, Rafael: 372
Rivas, Rafael: 75,388
Robles, Pepe: 267
Rodríguez, Amos: 336-337
Rodríguez, José Antonio: 391
Rodríguez Murciano,F.: 265-266,385
Rodríguez, Salud: 186,**219-220**
Roezna, la: 374
Rojas, Carmen: 249
Rojas, Manolo: 324
Rojas, Víctor: 211,**287**,372

417

Romerillo: 67
Romerito de Jerez: 352
Romero, Fernanda: 248
Romero, José: 380
Romero, Rafael: 154,201,393
Ronda, Anilla la de: 64-65,383
Rosa, Manolillo la: 194
Rosario: 199,237-238,284,314,371
Roosevelt, Franklin Delano: 234
Rubia, la: 80,82-83,383
Rucichi, Domingo: 349
Rueda, Luis de: 33
Ruiz, Gabriel: 401
Sabicas: 236,237,261,281,289,293,
  301-304,316,318,319,320,406,**407**
Sacromonte: 385,402
Salazar, José: 384,**395**
Salinas, Carmen: 73
Sallago, la: 168,**350**
Salmonete: 352
Salvadorillo: 349
Salvaoriyo: 54,**62**,341
San Roque, Antonia de: 68,357
Sánchez, Calixto: 378
Sánchez Mejías, I.:149,226,326,368
Sandita, Juana la: 36
Sanlúcar, Antonio: **289**,358
Sanlúcar, Estéban:125,**289**,295,358,401
Sanlúcar, Isidro: 358
Sanlúcar, Manolo: **358**.372
San Miguel, Barrio de: 343
Santiago, Barrio de: 342
Sarasate: 324
Sarneta, Mercedes la: 49,**54-56**,57,
  155,380
Sarvaora, Tía: 37,340
Satisfecha, la: 392
Saura, Carlos: 400
Segovia, Andrés: 73,199
Sellé, Aurelio: 35,50,103,**106-108**,
  123,140,157,160,222,275,334,**335**
Sernita: 168,343,353
Serrana, la: 54,351
Serranito, Víctor Monge: 372,**401**
Serrano, Juan: 302,**318-319**,390
Sevilla, Pedro: 394
Sevillano, Antonio el: 122,364
Shiva, Lord: 261
Short, John Fulton: 326
Simón, el Gran: 373
Singla, el: 402
Singla, la: 387,**402-403**
Sirvent, Fernando: 324,401

Sol, Antonio: 268,293
Soleá, María: 350
Soler, José: 73
Solera de Jerez: 353
Somorrostro, Barrio de: 402
Sopas, Perico el: 392
Sordillo: 366
Sordera: **350-351**,352
Sordita, la: 54,125,217,**218**,226,
  341,351,360,368
Soto, Vicente: 351
Suárez, Antonio: 393
Susi, la: 367
Talegas, Agustín: 100,105,374
Talegas, Juan: 34,45,68,91,**104-106**,
  115,129,142,144,146,156,164,244,
  250,295,296,345,**374**,376
Talegón, el: 389
Talegona, María la: 389
Tamayo: 406
Tano, el: 407
Tarantos, Historia de los: 204,
  232,236.237
Tarrega, Francisco: 274
Tarriba, Oscar: 196,287
Tati, la: 400
Tatiana: 250
Tejeringuero, el: 86
Tena, Lucerito: 241-242
Tenazas, el: 71-73,379
Terremoto de Jerez: 35,**165-166**,
  343,350,362
Tito, Perico el: 351
Tito, Romero el: 57334
Tiznao, el: 75,368
Tobalo: 56,383
Tomás, Pacita: 399
Tomasa, José de la: 365
Tomasa, la: 364-365
Tomatito: 393
Toronjos, Hermanos: 168
Torre, Amparo (granddaughter): 365
Torre, Juan Soto (father): 92,337
Torre, Juan (grandson): 97
Torre, Manuel (son): 28,48,49,50,72,
  73,79,**91-97**,103,105,112,113,115,
  139,141,142,144,146,150,156,203,
  214,216, 222,232,272,273,279,280,
  286,292,299,305,312,313,**337**,341,
  344,349,350,351,360,364,365,384,405
Torre, Pepe (son): 34,50,93,94,
  102-104,105,222,280,288,295,341,
  364,**361**,365

418

Torre, Tomás (grandson): 97, 208, 344, 349,
Torre, Tomás (grandnephew): 104.
Torres, Angel: 398-399
Torres Bermejas: 206, 222, 352
Tragapanes: 367
Triana, Antonio de: 208, 228, 367-369, 406
Triana, Antonio de (hijo): 369
Triana, Chinín de: 404
Triana, Felipe de: 205, 207. 362
Triana, Fernando de: 27, 42, 56, 60, 63, 75, 83, 89, 91, 119, 193, 206, 210, 211, 214, 218, 225, 227, 239, 267, 271, 286, 288, 289, 322, 341, 366
Triana, Gitanillo de: 222
Triana, Gordito de: 157, 362
Triana, Luisa de: 208, 228
Triana, Naranjito de: 367
Triana, Perla de: 123, 361
Triana, Plight of: 366
Triana, Rosalía de: 123, 361
Triguito: 309-314, 372
Trini, la: 80-81, 383
Troni, el: 76
Tuerto, el: 75
Tumba, Juan el: 207
Turronero, el: 332, 354
Utrera, Bernarda de: 155-157, 244, 332, 354, 380
Utrera, Curro de: 169, 381
Utrera, Félix de: 381
Utrera, Fernanda de: 145, 155-157, 244, 354, 380
Utrera, Gaspar de: 169, 380
Utrera, Pepa de (La Feonga): 157, 380
Utrera, Perrate de: 169, 376, 380
Valdepeñas, Antonio de: 206
Valdepeñas, Paco de: 205-206, 393
Valderrama, Juanito: 29, 113, 136, 139-140, 299, 364

Valencia, Pepe: 154-155, 308
Valencia, Pepe (Sevilla): 150
Valle, Pedro del: 239, 287, 355
Vallejo, Manuel: 85, 120, 296
Varea, Juanito: 139, 153, 404
Vargas, Angelita: 373
Vargas, Araceli: 201, 323, 398
Vargas, Araceli (hijo): 398, 402
Vargas, Concha: 377
Vargas, Familia: 373
Vargas, Joselito: 373
Vargas, Juan de: 33
Vargas, Manolo: 107, 196-197, 229, 369
Vargas, Manolo Martín: 149
Vargas, Manuel: 140-141, 335
Vargas, Manuela: 336, 351, 363, 370, 398
Vargas, Mariquita: 28, 146, 168, 358
Vargas, Martín: 405
Vargas, Miguel: 376
Vega, Alejandro: 208, 229
Vega, José Blas: 80, 335
Vélez, Alberto: 317, 318, 395
Vélez, Niño de: 384
Verdiales, Julio: 369
Vidales, Enrique: 392
Vigil, Enrique: 369
Villa Rosa: 222, 283, 395, 397
Villar, Juanito: 337, 354
Villarino, Gerónimo: 369
Viruta, Antonio: 208
Yance, Luis: 225, 277-278, 397
Yanqui, la: 369
Yerbagüena: 73, 85, 293, 385
Zambra, la: 126, 140, 150, 153, 154, 228, 239, 240, 283, 309, 314, 335, 353, 355, 394, 400
Zaraspe, Héctor: 406
Zayas, Virginia de: 395
Ziryab: 255, 256
Zuloaga, Ignacio: 73

419

INDEX OF SPECIAL SUBJECTS

Andalusí music: 32
Anti-flamenco movement of '98: 42-43
Antonio Mairena's Drive for Purity: 12, 378
Ballet Flamenco: 223, 368
Big Spenders, or Live Today, Tomorrow May Never Arrive: 53, 80, 97, 344-345
Cafés Cantantes and *Tablaos*: 52
Cantes de Levante: 85, 391-392
Creation in the *Cante*: 12, 25, 32, 356, 376, 386
Difference in *Cante* between *Gitanos* and *Payos*: 366
Drugs and Liquor: 12
Fads: 30, 32
Families in Flamenco: 100-101, 337, 346, 355, 372-373 (and many more)
Famous Flamenco Neighborhoods:
    Alameda de Hercules (Sevilla): 143, 360, 364, 365
    La Europa (Sevilla): 360, 364, 365
    Sacromonte (Granada): 233, 385
    San Miguel (Jerez): 342, 343, 349
    Santa María (Cádiz): 127-128, 226
    Santiago (Jerez): 127, 165, 341, 342, 346, 347, 351
    Somorrostro (Barcelona): 232, 233, 402
    Triana (Sevilla): 127, 360, 365, 366
Flamenco in the Country: 342, 344, 347, 348
Flamenco of *Los Tabancos* (Jerez): 343, 345, 349, 351
Flamenco of the Blacksmiths: 343, 349, 360,
Flamenco Pop Songs: 354-355
Golden Key of the *Cante*: 45, 120, 143, 389
Granada's Flamenco Contest of 1922: 71-73
Guitar: Accompanying and Solo: 262-265, 267
Guitar: Overdosing on Evolution: 339-340, 358, 391, 407
Gypsies in Flamenco: Creators or Imitators? 175-177, 281-282, 340
Indian Dancing and Flamenco: 173-176
Juerga Dancing in Commercial Settings: 125, 205, 226
Juerga Artists' Life Style: 344, 345, 351
Last of the Juerga Artists: 349, 364, 365, 367, 371, 378, 386, 387
Manuel de Falla's Flamenco Dreams: 73-74
Opera Flamenca: 135
Over-popularization of Flamenco and the Long Range Effects: 51-52
Pepe Marchena Initiates Flamenco Prosperity: 314
Physical and/or Mental Deficiencies in Flamenco: 183, 218, 310-311, 362
Racism: 346-347, 366, 386-387
Rehearsals Scorned by Supreme Flamencos: 228, 403, 404
Religious Dancing: 174, 177
Respectable-Class Triumphs Over Flamenco: 361, 366
Respectable-Class Losses to Flamenco: 399, 403, 405-406
Revolutionary Cante: 375
Singing a *Media Voz*: 104, 361
Spontaneity Down the Drain: 179-181
Street Selling through Song (*Pregones*): 341, 347, 384, 389
Traditional Jerez System of Artistic Formation: 341-343
Triana's Flamenco Plight: 366
Vocal Types: 27

GLOSSARY

afición — enthusiasm.
aficionado — fan, enthusiast.
afillá — see Vocal Types, p. 27.
aguardiente — dry **anís**, a fiery, licorice-flavored alcoholic drink.
alegría — gaiety.
amigotes — friends, oftentimes through convenience.
andaluz, -ces — Andalusian, -s.
antiguo — ancient, old.
arpegio — arpeggio.

bailaor, -a — male, female dancer.
bailar — to dance.
bailarín, -a, -es, -as — classical dancer, -s.
baile — dance, dancing.
barrio — neighborhood.
bata de cola — flamenco dancing dress with a train, formerly used as common street wear.
bonito — pretty; when used in «cante bonito», it denotes a pretty, not very flamenco type of singing.

cachondeo — hell-raising.
café — coffee, coffee house-bar.
café cantante — nineteenth century café-bar with flamenco entertainment.
caló — the language of the Spanish gypsies, consisting of **romaní** (the pure gypsy language) and Spanish.
cantaor, -a — male, female flamenco singer.
cante — singing, song.
casino — club.
cazalla — **aguardiente** from Cazalla de la Sierra.
cejilla — capo.
chau,chau — in English pronounced «chow, chow»; Spanish nonsense symbols which denote the unintelligible sounds of foreign languages.
chavalillos — youngsters, kids.
chico — light, small, not serious.
ciego — blind.
cojo — lame, crippled.

cojones — a term, literally meaning testicles, which is used in flamenco to denote force and manliness.
colmao — flamenco tavern.
compás — rhythmic beat.
concurso — contest.
coño — an intimate part of a woman's body; the term, however, is widely used in Spanish as an exclamation of surprise or enthusiasm.
copita — little shot, glassful.
copla — verse of a **cante**.
cordobés — from Córdoba.
corto — short, simple.
cuadrilla — bullfighter's aides.
cuadro — flamenco group.
cuna — birthplace, cradle, center.

de — of, from.
duende — deep, trance-like emotion. (See p. 424).

fácil — easy, see Vocal Types, p. 27.
falseta — a melody played on the flamenco guitar, also called **variación** (variation).
falsete — falsetto, see Vocal Types, p. 27.
fandanguero — singer of **fandangos**.
fenómeno — phenomenon, a real wonder.
fiesta — party.
flamencólogo — flamencologist; flamenco theorist, scholar, and writer.
frachute — humorous way of referring to the French language.

gaditano, -a — native of Cádiz.
gallina — hen, chicken-hearted.
gazpacho — a type of vegetable salad (without lettuce) in liquid form, typical of Andalusia. Morón de la Frontera's «Gazpacho» is a flamenco festival, based on Utrera's «Potaje», at which **gazpacho** is served. Celebrated annually around the first of September.
genio — genius.
gitanerías — originally a term signifying «gypsy neighborhoods», presently expanded to mean «gypsy doings, carryings-on».
gitano, -a — gypsy.
golpe — blow, knock.
gracia — natural wit and charm, colorful way of being.
grande — long, grand, complex, serious.
guitarra — guitar.

hijo, -a — son, daughter

intermedio — intermediate.

jaleador, -a — one who specializes in the **jaleo**.
jaleo — see p. 325.
jondo — also written «**hondo**»; deep, profound.
juerga — big bash, flamenco style.

kithara — zither.

Levante — eastern, southeastern coast of Spain.

llave de oro — golden key.

macho — stud; an optional ending to a **cante** involving a change of pace and mood.
maestro — master, teacher.
malagueñero — singer of **malagueñas**.
mantón de Manila — shawl, originally imported from Manila.
manzanilla — dry, white wine from Sanlúcar de Barrameda.
me hice un taco — I got mixed up.

natural — natural, see Vocal Types, p. 27.
novia — sweetheart.

obra — work.
ojú, ozú — **Jesús,** Jesus.

padre — father.
palmas — hand-clapping.
pañolillo de Manila — mantón de Manila.
patria — home country.
payo — non-gypsy.
pena — sadness, grief.
peña — club.
picado — two-fingered runs on the guitar.
picador de toros — horseman who pics bull.
pitos — finger-snapping.
por — by, of, for.
propio — own.
puro — pure.

que — what.
¡qué pena! — what a shame!
¡qué vida aquélla! — what a life that was!

rajo — hoarseness.
rasgueado — often pronounced «rasgueo»; a basic flamenco guitar playing technique, consisting, generally, of striking the strings with four or five fingers of the right hand consecutively, which produces a rolling, drumming effect.
redonda — round, see Vocal Types, p. 27.

salero — **gracia** - wit, charm.
sello — stamp.
señorito — upper-class Spaniard, sometimes used in a derogatory sense.
sereno — night watchman/policeman.
siguiriyero — singer of **siguiriyas**.
sin — without.
simpático — charming.

tablao — present-day flamenco establishment, so-called because the platform on which the artists perform is called a «tablao».
tercio — verse of a **cante**.
tinto — red wine.
tío, -a — uncle, aunt; also used in slang to signify guy, doll.
tocaor — flamenco guitarist.
tocar — to play (an instrument).
toque — guitar playing, that which is played.

torero — bullfighter.
traje corto — male dancing costume.

¡vaya! — exclamation of surprise, enthusiasm.
venta — country inn.
vergüenza — shame.
vicio — vice.
viejo — old.
vino — wine.
voz — voice.

zapateado — footwork, also a flamenco dance consisting entirely of footwork.
zarzuela — Spanish operetta.

1988 UPDATE - GLOSSARY

apartados - separate rooms in bars utilized for juergas.
barrio - neighborhood.
cántaro - earthenware jug.
casa de vecinos - literally, "house of neighbors," an old-style apartment complex for the poor built around a large courtyard used for communal cooking, washing and toilet facilities.
cortijo - large farming estate.
cuplé - Andalusian pop songs, often quite dramatic in nature; interpreters of these songs are called *cupletistas*.
de la escuela vieja - from the old school.
duende - profound emotion, which manifests itself differently in different artists, from quiet trance-like to the wild craziness of the possessed. In most artists it never appears. It is the wide chasm that separates the great from the merely good.
eco - echo; personal sound when singing.
familia - family.
fragua - smithy.
Junta de Andalucía - a governing group in Andalusia.
pregones - songs sung by street vendors to attract buyers.
Prohibido el Cante - Singing Prohibited (see P. 366).
rumbera - female dancer of rumbas.
tabancos - Jerez taverns with a large supply of wine in huge barrels where wine can be consumed or taken out, where much of Jerez' juerga flamenco used to take place.
talega - sack.
Yo tenía muy güena estrella - A very good star guided me.

Printed in Great Britain
by Amazon